THE ECOLOGY OF HERBAL MEDICINE

THE ECOLOGY OF
Herbal
Medicine

*A Guide to Plants and Living Landscapes
of the American Southwest*

DARA SAVILLE

University of New Mexico Press / Albuquerque

ISBN 978-0-8263-6217-9 (paper)
ISBN 978-0-8263-6218-6 (e-book)

Library of Congress Cataloging-in-Publication data is on file
with the Library of Congress

COVER PHOTOGRAPHS BY the author
DESIGNED BY Mindy Basinger Hill
COMPOSED IN Parkinson Electra Pro and Copihue
MAPS BY Mindy Basinger Hill based on references created by Akashia Allen

DEDICATED TO *Jerry Lee Williams,*

THE CATALYST FOR MY DEEPLY ROOTED LOVE

OF SOUTHWESTERN LANDSCAPES

Contents

xi   Foreword   *Jesse Wolf Hardin*

xvii   Preface

xxi   Acknowledgments

PART ONE   KNOWING THE LAND

3   *Chapter One*   Ecological Herbalism

13   *Chapter Two*   Medicinal Plant Landscapes of the Southwest

40   *Chapter Three*   Reconnecting with Living Landscapes

50   *Chapter Four*   Rooted in Relationships with the Land and Plants

PART TWO   KNOWING THE PLANTS

67   *Chapter Five*   The Importance of Weeds, Commoners, and Wild-Spirited Gardens

75   *Chapter Six*   Materia Medica

MEDICINAL PLANTS OF THE SOUTHWEST

75   *Achillea millefolium* (Asteraceae)   YARROW / PLUMAJILLO

81   *Anemopsis californica* (Saururaceae) YERBA MANSA / YERBA DEL MANZO

84   *Angelica grayi,* A. *archangelica,* A. spp. (Apiaceae)   ANGELICA

88   *Arnica cordifolia,* A. spp. (Asteraceae)   ARNICA

91   *Artemisia tridentata,* A. *filifolia,* A. *frigida,* A. *ludoviciana,* A. spp. (Asteraceae)   SAGE

96   *Ceanothus fendleri,* C. *greggii,* C. spp. (Rhamnaceae)   RED ROOT

99   *Datura wrightii,* D. spp. (Solanaceae) DATURA / JIMSONWEED / TOLOACHE

102   *Fouquieria splendens* (Fouquieriaceae)   OCOTILLO

105 *Galium aparine* (Rubiaceae) CLEAVERS

107 *Glycyrrhiza lepidota* (Fabaceae) LICORICE / AMOLILLO

112 *Grindelia squarrosa, G.* spp. (Asteraceae)
GRINDELIA / GUMWEED / YERBA DEL BUEY

115 *Gutierrezia sarothrae, G.* spp. (Asteraceae)
SNAKEWEED / ESCOBA DE LA VIBORA

117 *Hypericum scouleri, H. perforatum, H.* spp. (Hypericaceae,
Clusiaceae, Guttiferae) ST. JOHN'S WORT

122 *Juniperus monosperma, J.* spp. (Cupressaceae) JUNIPER / SABINA

126 *Larrea tridentata* (Zygophyllaceae)
CREOSOTE / CHAPARRAL / HEDIONDILLA / GOBERNADORA

128 *Ligusticum porteri, L.* spp. (Apiaceae) OSHÁ / CHUCHUPATE / BEAR ROOT

132 *Mahonia repens, M.* spp. (Berberidaceae)
OREGON GRAPE / CREEPING BARBERRY

136 *Marrubium vulgare* (Lamiaceae) HOREHOUND / MARRUBIO

138 *Monarda fistulosa* (Lamiaceae) BEE BALM / OREGANO DE LA SIERRA

141 *Opuntia* spp. (Cactaceae) PRICKLY PEAR / NOPAL

146 *Pedicularis* spp. (Orobancaceae) PEDICULARIS / BETONY / LOUSEWORT

152 *Pinus edulis, P. ponderosa, P.* spp. (Pinaceae)
PIÑON PINE / PONDEROSA PINE / AND OTHERS

155 *Populus deltoides wislizenii, Populus* spp. (Salicaceae)
COTTONWOOD / ALAMO

157 *Potentilla hippiana, P. pulcherrima, P.* spp. (Rosaceae)
POTENTILLA / CINQUEFOIL / TORMENTIL

161 *Prosopis glandulosa torreyana, Prosopis* spp. (Fabaceae) MESQUITE

164 *Rosa woodsii, R.* spp. (Rosaceae) ROSE / ROSA DE CASTILLA

170 *Rudbeckia laciniata* (Asteraceae) CUTLEAF CONEFLOWER

172 *Scutellaria lateriflora, S.* spp. (Lamiaceae) SKULLCAP

174 *Solidago canadensis, S.* spp. (Asteraceae) GOLDENROD

177 *Sphaeralcea angustifolia, S. coccinea, S.* spp. (Malvaceae)
GLOBEMALLOW / YERBA DE LA NEGRITA

180 *Trifolium pratense* (Fabaceae) RED CLOVER

182   *Usnea* spp. (Parmeliaceae)   USNEA / OLD MAN'S BEARD

186   *Verbena hastata, V. macdougalii, V.* spp. (Verbenaceae)
      VERVAIN /VERBENA

189   *Viola canadensis, V. odorata, V.* spp. (Violaceae)   VIOLET

192   *Yucca* spp. (Agavaceae)   YUCCA / AMOLE

INVASIVE TREES

199   *Ailanthus altissima* (Simaroubaceae)   TREE OF HEAVEN

201   *Elaeagnus angustifolia* (Elaeagnaceae)   RUSSIAN OLIVE

203   *Tamarix* spp. (Tamaricaceae)   SALT CEDAR / TAMARISK

205   *Ulmus pumila* (Ulmaceae)   SIBERIAN ELM

207   Bibliography

275   Index

Foreword

Like people everywhere, herbalists live and practice in a time of planetary stress, at the edge of intense challenges, at the crux of possibilities informed by the land, by the plants themselves—and by books such as this one that remind us to go out and listen, suggesting ways to look and perceive and providing encouragements to feel. Herein is a combination southwestern herbal, manual for conservation and restorative action, and song of love. It inspires us to learn the medicines of many of this region's signature healing plants while acting as agents of healing ourselves. It brings to our attention the immense joys of nature, connection, and service in the face of all that might be arrayed against us.

THE SITUATION

Humankind has forever depended upon the living land for its own existence and sustenance, and paid a high price for disrupting or overtaxing the ecosystems we have always relied upon. We created mythologies and religions to honor inspirited nature and taboos to prevent its despoilment. But as human civilizations and technologies have advanced, so too have the existential affronts that these make possible—mortal threats not only to ourselves, our food crops, and the soil they grow from but to all life forms. Exponentially increasing human population and development, induced climate change, toxic insecticides and herbicides, the destruction of natural habitat, the introduction of invasive species, and genetic manipulation are just a few of the compounding means for this self-destructive course—made possible first and foremost by a shifting of cultural values and focus, and a dangerous and disorienting estrangement.

Both effective herbal healing and our species' ultimate survival depend upon a literal and symbolic return to the roots, a cultural reset, and a deep personal refamiliarization with the plants and our purpose, with whole ecosystems as well as those specific herbs we grow and gather. A substantive and vital belonging. Strangers no more.

THE PRACTITIONER

Herbalism is literally "natural healing," predicated upon the energetics, patterns, and effects of medicinal plants. It is informed and equipped by the natural world and by natural processes, and obviously cannot be practiced without either the herbs themselves or the ground they sprout from. By virtue of their practice, the herbalist sees the connection between conserving or propagating herbs and the protecting and nurturing of the land, between the healing of the human body and the healing of the earth. While we might deny the fact or choose less controversial/triggering terminology to describe it, there can be no meaningful and lasting medicinal plant tradition apart from what we here call ecological herbalism: botanical treatments that both contribute to and depend upon a recovering world.

As herbalists, we need to know about human constitutions and conditions, constituents and actions, and different kinds of preparations, from tinctures and teas to decoctions and topical creams—even the rudiments of psychology and intakes, and practicalities like business and taxes. But as always, one of the things we need most is an accurate, comprehensive understanding of those herbs and trees that we work with.

THE PLANTS

My home is a remote and utterly inconvenient wilderness paradise in the San Francisco Mountains in the Gila bioregion of southwestern New Mexico, seven river crossings from pavement and hundreds of miles from opportunities for incomes and social pleasures. What makes this river-laced canyon a paradise in my estimation is its tribe of green beings and uncompromised creatures, feeding and frolicking, trying to avoid predation and deal with climatic changes in their instinctual, relational ways, unimpaired by civilized aims and controls. I arrived seeking sanctuary for my aberrational self, soon finding a biological sanctuary that I was in place to create—learning how to study, commit to, pledge to, and guard it, helping to restore the health and vitality of what is uncontestedly a rare and precious riparian treasure. A decade of livestock exclusion, removal of invasives, and the replanting of native species resulted in a vibrant willow, cottonwood, and alder forest along the river named after Saint Francis, which then became evidence in a federal court case in support of a thirty-mile-long protective riparian restoration zone that now protects far more than our private property inholding.

Study and observation of the ecosystem from season to season was essential to the successful establishment of the Anima Botanical Sanctuary, finding out what helps or hurts the various natural components and their patterns of interaction. This requires knowing what plants and animals are native, which species are introduced, which species resided in a place prior to human presence or our personal arrival. As herbalists, it also means learning which plants have medicinal benefits for people, their properties, uses, and contraindications. And in all cases, it means figuring out what we can do to contribute to their health in turn.

Fundamental to this book are its excellent plant profiles, describing their places and purposes in their environs, as well as their places and purposes in the herbalist's apothecary. In the book's second part are concise, detailed portraits of some of the most emblematic and most medically significant southwestern species, from angelica to ocotillo and yarrow. While it draws from author Dara Saville's intimate familiarity with the three primary landscapes of her adopted region, her modeling, precepts, and insights apply to any and all bioregions and ecosystems, regardless of where one lives on this planet. By understanding how native species thrive and interact—their needs, advantages, challenges, and vulnerabilities—in one environment, we can more easily recognize such patterns and dynamics in other areas and other different conditions.

THE WRITER

Plants and land speak to us, though not in words but through their beings, examples, and responses to what they interact with. It is thus fortunate that throughout recorded time, there have been people insightful and comprehendible enough to speak for them, as rational agents, determined champions, and wild celebrants intoxicated with their presence, energy, healing effects, and breath-stopping beauty.

When I first met Dara Saville, her gifts, herbal skills, and dedication to share them appeared powerful and pronounced. I at once felt deeply allied, something that only increased upon finding out that she was actively heading a project to protect and perpetuate the native yerba mansa struggling in the river-edge bosque alongside this state's Rio Grande. Her brilliance and knowledge proved grounded in direct, hands-on action, sprouting and transplanting, watering and supporting patches of this healing plant where it had once been extirpated. She has since become an integral part of our plant healer mission, teaching at our annual events and writing a column for *Plant Healer Quarterly* called "Of Wilderness and Gardens." I foresaw and agitated for her authoring her first book and am honored to now pen this foreword to it. You will, I imagine, feel as equipped and as moved as I do after partaking of her plant-hearted words in these poignant pages.

Dara is one of the most insightful, studied, and evocative heroes of natural healing and healing nature, and this book is surely destined to be one of its revealing lights.

THE COMMUNITY

For tens of years I have dedicated myself to speaking, creating annual events, and writing and publishing plant healer books about the essentiality and inseparability of ecological, mental, and bodily health. I have attempted to illuminate the lessons provided by nature and by wilderness to explore human quandaries around healing, identity, purposes, roles, culture, expression, and satisfaction. In the course of such weavings, I have affirmed by experience and revelations, and been alerted to and surprised by, the depth and extent of patterning and phenomena. I have witnessed the coming together of herbalists and conservationists, scientist and mystics, astute students and self-empowered kitchen sink medicine makers, sharing a childlike sense of wonder and a lifetime commitment to what they study, practice, and love. Perhaps more than anything else, I have been impressed by the attractions to and cohesion of a proactive, interconnected "family." Ecologists use terms like *biotic community* and *plant community* to refer to complex interdependent systems, to plants, animals, and microorganisms that recognize, communicate with, and somehow help sustain one another. And I understand that the intimate and accessible folk herbalism that I, my partner, and allies have helped foster and further is itself a diverse, contiguous, adaptive, reciprocating healing community, united by a love for plants and a shared desire to assist and to revel!

THE MEDICINE

As much as we collectively affect land and ecosystems, so too are we in part a product of the regions, landforms, weather, and biotic communities that we exist within, sculpted and infused, tempered and teased by a particular place. Its influence penetrates and permeates, even in the most metropolitan of cities, marking our origins or branding us with the traits and tastes, spirit and feel of an adopted home. Our "sense of place" contributes to the character and momentum of our creations and accomplishments, our pleasures, and the tireless work to help with a crucial return to health. At best, it infuses our potions, lends us its balm, supports our mending, excites our efforts, and awakens our callings and dreams.

I feel strongly that what the land and the plants are saying to us, and through us, is this: We are needed. We have medicine to make. And when it comes to living processes such as earth and healing, that medicine must without a doubt be us.

Jesse Wolf Hardin

CODIRECTOR, PLANT HEALER PUBLICATIONS AND EVENTS

PLANTHEALER.ORG

Preface

Rounding the mountain road that winds down from Albuquerque's Sandia Crest, an astounding view of the valley emerges from a break in the trees. From the passenger seat, one can see the contours of the earth, the textured landforms rising from the desert valley, and the patterns of human use of the land. The intense light of the desert sun washes almost all color away, creating a soft palette of muted earth tones undulating across the surface. The narrative of this place is on full display. Memories of field trips exploring the landscapes of the Southwest with University of New Mexico geography professor Jerry Williams begin to fill my head. Hiking the endless canyons of slickrock country, climbing volcanic mesas along the Rio Grande Rift, touring railroads and mining towns in the high mountains, driving the dirt roads of the desert grasslands, and visiting old homesteads of the eastern plains, we revisited the layers of the land and people that make up this region. Lost in this ancient and enduring story of place, I am suddenly jolted back into reality as the driver, my herb teacher Bert Norgorden, jumps on the breaks, swerves to the right, and skids onto the gravelly shoulder of the road. He slams the truck into park, jumps out, and starts walking briskly up the road without a single word. Stunned and not sure what to do, I submit to curiosity and decide to follow him up the road. When I catch up, I see him standing over a small roadside yarrow plant that is as many shades of pink as the high desert sunset. Since most yarrow plants have white flowers, this is a sweet surprise. For Bert, however, I immediately see that this is so much more. Silently observing, I witness a genuinely loving smile unfurl across his face. He crouches down and stares into the plant with a sparkle in his eye—the kind of sparkle that appears almost magically when a ray of sunlight meets a ripple of water in a trickling mountain stream. In this moment he is drawn into another world. Entranced by the spirit of the plant, his posture relaxes, an expression of pure contentedness appears on his face, and gratitude radiates from his heart. The transformation seems total, as if he really is in another place, where peace and fulfillment are all that exist. In this moment I too am changed. I understand for the first time that such an experience is possible, that deep relationships with plants can bring about altered states of consciousness that have the potency to change our perspective and even clarify the very meaning of life. All the years of rooting into the land with Jerry and now this culminating moment with Bert and yarrow set me forth on

FIGURE 1 Pink yarrow (*Achillea millefolium*).
Photo by author.

a path of discovery to my own relationship with plants and ultimately to a new way of being that is shaped by the living landscape itself. This book is the result of that journey into botanical relationships and allowing myself to be remade by the will of the land.

The circumstances of our current era demand an herbal and ecological manual written for nature lovers and plant practitioners with a focus on the interconnectivity of people, plants, and the land. This book proposes an evolution in our philosophy and approach to herbal practice and an understanding of the land that highlights the ecological interactions of plants, awakens our empathic experience with the entire living landscape, and promotes a better understanding of the dynamic biological and cultural worlds in which we live. As we move through a twenty-first century characterized by globalization, climate change, intensified land and water use, and humanity's increasing disconnect with the rest of the living world, this book serves as a reminder about the importance of our connection with place, provides a pathway to understanding the medicinal properties of plants through ecological relationships, and offers inspiration for working with plants in a way that restores our union with the land. In our struggle to adapt to new environmental realities, an interdisciplinary approach to herbalism and other naturalist studies is important to understanding our current problems and protecting the biological and cultural inheritance of future generations.

Through the chapters in part 1 of this book, I present different aspects of developing and experiencing relationships with the rest of the natural world. Chapter 1 introduces the concept of ecological herbalism, an approach to working with plants that is based on their interactions with other elements of the natural environment, including us. The chapter outlines why this approach is not only relevant but also necessary in the rapidly changing modern world. Chapter 2 tells the stories of three classic landscapes of the American Southwest and how characteristic medicinal plants are responding to environmental changes unfolding in these places. These stories help us share the experience of wild medicine plants and understand them more deeply. Chapter 3 discusses the need for a new paradigm in understanding human relationships with the land and how to go about creating that within ourselves and on a societal level. It outlines specific practices for making this transformation and the importance of empathy that transcends humanity in this process. Chapter 4 describes three examples of personal relationships I have developed with some of my favorite places and plants. These stories are intended both to illustrate how appreciation for plants and love of the land can change our lives in profound ways and to serve as inspiration for anyone seeking a deeper connection with the network of life.

In part 2 of this book, I describe numerous plants and how to work with them for health and well-being. Chapter 5 is a brief discussion on the importance of long-term sustainable practice and the role that weeds, other common local plants, and cultivated garden herbs can play in enhancing our herbal experience and protecting wild plant populations now and in the future. Chapter 6 is the materia medica, providing an in-depth look at thirty-nine medicinal plants that feature prominently in landscapes and herbal traditions of the Southwest. This selection includes archetypal medicinal plants of the American West as well as naturalized herbs that build a cultural and biological continuum with the Old World. The final section covers a short selection of common invasive medicinal trees and includes a discussion on integrating these species into our apothecaries.

The purpose of this book is multifaceted. The information included in part 1 is intended to encourage awareness and conversation about our changing world and what it means for the plants and places we love. I hope the personal stories will help guide people into meaningful relationships with the land and plants for a better quality of life and will inspire us all to work toward more balanced and sustainable use of the land. The plant profiles in part 2 are designed to increase our understanding of plants' relationships with their environment and with us. These monographs offer a way of getting to know each plant individually and to make personalized connections with those herbs we feel most drawn to. Through plants, we may also become more deeply attuned with the places they grow. It is my hope that this book will provide information, tools, and inspiration for knowledgeable, mindful, intuitive, and passionate engagement with the land and plants through herbal practice and general lifestyle.

Although the days of explorative field trips and herbal apprenticeship with formative teachers are behind me, the legacy of those people, places, and experiences has laid the foundation for a worldview that is based on the interactions of all components of the living landscape. Looking out across the land, I see layers of the biological and cultural worlds that weave themselves together, making a place I call home and inviting me to find my role within it. While hiking in the wilds or standing in my garden, I can conjure again the alterative experience of deep connectivity with plants and the land, returning to that place where the reciprocal exchange of life occurs. In this way, I am drawn into a world where the land becomes my teacher, plants share their life experiences, and I grow and evolve in tandem with the rest of the living world. It is in this moment of joined reality that a clear and simple picture emerges: our union with the natural world nourishes and restores our own wellness, fosters our individual and collective resiliency, and opens the door to limitless possibilities. This place of shared being is where our own vitality is rejuvenated and serves as a fountain of inspiration for actions derived from gratitude and a sincere love of life—all life.

Acknowledgments

This book came about through the generous teachings, inspirations, and assistance of many people through the years. I am deeply grateful for the foundational perspective provided by Jerry Williams, who showed me the curiosities of many forgotten landscapes and taught me about the importance of connection to place. Mary Lou Singleton filled me with passion and empowerment through herbs and provided a critical foothold into the world of plant medicine. Through apprenticeship with Bert Norgorden I came to understand the practical complexities of working with plants and people as well as the potency of beauty in the botanical world. Jesse Wolf Hardin provided sustained encouragement (and accountability) to keep writing and developing my ideas, and kindly wrote the foreword for this book. To the many plants and places described in the following pages that have freely offered their unending wisdom, inspiration, and friendship: my heart is eternally full of gratitude for your life-altering gifts. This book was written on the historic floodplain of the Rio Grande, the homeland of Pueblo people, who have stewarded the land throughout the generations.

In producing this book, numerous people provided critical support and much appreciated encouragement. First and foremost, thanks to the continuous and all-encompassing support of Jason Buckles, who enabled my time to work on this project, became the initial reader and editor of every piece of writing that led to this book, and encouraged me in every way. Akashia Allen kindly served as cartographer for this publication, taking the time to make professional custom maps that are central to a discussion of place. Thanks to Kelly Kindscher, who provided many thoughtful suggestions for improving this work; to Gary Paul Nabhan for his suggestions and encouragement in botanical storytelling; and to Asha Canalos, who provided important contextual insights. I am appreciative of the species clarification and general support provided by Jim McGrath, George Miller, and others from the Albuquerque Native Plant Society. I would also like to acknowledge the support of University of New Mexico Press and Sonia Dickey, James Ayers, Mindy Basinger Hill, and Peg Goldstein, who made this publication possible. Daniel Ryerson of the us Forest Service, Craig Allen of the us Geological Survey, John Peterson of the us Army Corps of Engineers, and Jillian Hartke of the Albuquerque Museum Photo Archives all provided essential landscape photos and related insights. My gratitude also goes out to my family and friends, who served as informal advisers, especially my two sons, who tolerated my absence when I was writing, hiking, and researching. Lastly, thanks to El Camino Restaurant and Lounge and Jack White for setting the scene.

PART ONE

Knowing the Land

Ecological Herbalism

Recent times have brought a plethora of media stories, political speeches, and scientific research heralding a new era of environmental changes unfolding both globally and locally. These changes, in tandem with the pressures of human population growth, including land conversion and intensified water use, often result in habitat loss and ecosystem degradation for native plants. In many areas, people are witnessing the decline or disappearance of native plants from local areas while nonnative invasive species become more prominent. A 2018 summary released by the International Union for the Conservation of Nature and Natural Resources stated that in the United States, 43 plant species are now listed as extinct or extinct in the wild and another 510 species range from critically endangered to vulnerable, with a sample of only 2,147 species assessed. According to the us Fish and Wildlife Service, 946 plant species are categorized as critically endangered or threatened, and more species are likely to be added to these and similar assessments as research and evaluation processes continue. As citizens of the land, we have an imperative to understand what is unfolding in the landscapes around us. Awareness of landscape dynamics not only helps us become more deeply connected to our local wilds but also offers new insights about the way plants work as medicines. When we are able to see what is taking place within plants' habitats, we put together the pieces of their past and can begin to imagine their future. Observing the reciprocal interactions between native plants and their environments illuminates both the changing ecological conditions in our local area and the intelligence of the plants.

Ecological herbalism is a way of understanding where we live and learning about the plants around us. It is an interdisciplinary approach to herbal practice that includes learning about the natural processes unfolding in wild areas and how plants interact with each other and their environment. By embracing an ecological herbalism perspective, we gain insights about how plant communities are changing and develop newfound clarity about the herbal actions of plants in the land and as remedies for people. When we understand the landscape around us and see it as a living system, it affects the way we view the natural world and how we practice as herbalists. We can read changes in

FIGURE 2
Pedicularis
gathered and
fresh-tinctured in
a high-elevation
meadow. Photo
by author.

the land, recognize the value of healthy native plant communities, and allow that wisdom to guide our relationships with the land and plants. In the face of what often feels like overwhelming environmental devastation, ecological herbalism gives us a framework for understanding ongoing changes, seeing how these changes impact medicinal plants, and showing us what we can learn from the interaction of plants and their habitats. It is also a way for us to better know ourselves and begin to take actions that bring us into harmonious relations with our world.

A NECESSARY APPROACH IN A CHANGING WORLD

An ecological approach is an important component of a sustainable herbal practice in the twenty-first century and beyond. Many of us are poorly acquainted with the landscapes that surround us every day. Looking beyond the boundaries of our urban environment or hiking through familiar places, we may not be aware of the natural and cultural history of the land, what changes have already taken place, and what the future is likely to hold. If we desire to harvest plants from the wild or otherwise enjoy being present in our local natural areas, we have a responsibility to acquire knowledge and understanding about the places we frequent and love. While earth systems have always been dynamic and in a state of constant evolution, the modern era has come to be characterized by rapidly unfolding changes, with human activity implicated as the primary player influencing these systems. This new era, unofficially referred to as the Anthropocene, is defined by a number of characteristics affecting terrestrial plant communities. These include rising carbon dioxide in the atmosphere, increased levels of nitrogen in soils, the spread of invasive species, changes in disturbance patterns such as natural fires and floods, the creation of new anthropogenic habitats (farms and cities), and the significant alteration of relict habitats (Franklin 2016).

Worldwide, these characteristics may put an estimated one-third of all existing plants at risk for extinction (Corlett 2016). A recent assessment, *The State of the World's Plants* (RBG Kew 2016), listed 391,000 known species with an estimated 21 percent (about 50,000) at risk for extinction, but numbers could be even higher if additional factors are considered. For example, Pimm and Raven (2017) estimate that an additional seventy thousand species may be unknown to science—likely rare plants with a high extinction risk—and that extinctions could be occurring without any documentation (Corlett 2016). Also, as Cronk (2016) pointed out, extinction counts tally only actual extinctions and do not consider the potentially large number of plant species undergoing functional extinction, which may extend the actual extinction timeline by many decades as small isolated remnant populations continue to live out a possibly long life span while being unable to successfully reproduce or as the existing soil seed bank continues to sprout new individuals whose required habitat no longer exists. Additionally, recent research reports that, globally, plant extinctions have accelerated since the 1750s, surpassing 570 known species and reaching a rate determined to be approximately five hundred times higher than would be expected by natural forces alone (Humphreys et al. 2019). Another study suggests that worldwide, from 1900 to 2015, the number of plant species doomed to extinction rose by 60 percent and that climate change could surpass land use as the primary cause of extinction (Di Marco et al. 2019). Although some studies propose lower global extinction rates (1.26 extinctions per year since 1990 from Le Roux et al. 2019; less than 0.1 percent from Velland et al. 2017) or increased species richness for cooler regions of the world in the coming decades (e.g., Suggitt et al. 2019; Thomas 2013; Venevskaia et al. 2013), they do not take into account impending slow-motion functional extinctions or other important factors that are likely to negatively affect plant diversity in the longer run.

Many wild areas are in ecological flux, and while the future can never be certain, research suggests that dramatic changes are unfolding before our eyes. On the global scale, many assessments and predictions are dire: 58 percent of terrestrial habitats already crossing below the "safe" threshold of 10 percent loss of total biodiversity (Newbold et al. 2016), a 75 percent loss of all biotic species in three hundred years (Barnosky et al. 2011), and more than 50 percent of European plants likely to be threatened by 2080 (Thuiller 2005). The biological impacts of historic and current land use patterns, including grazing, agriculture, energy development, urbanization, logging, fire suppression, water diversion, and other economic land uses, are serious concerns for ecosystem functioning and plant diversity. These human activities contribute to habitat loss, fragmentation, and degradation; overexploitation; pollution; climate change; and the spread of invasive species, all of which are expected to continue or accelerate in the coming years. Already humans have transformed three-quarters of natural habitats into anthromes (anthropogenic biomes), and the process of change within these altered plant communities is still unfolding (Ellis 2012). This realization not only calls for a change in paradigm regarding the view of humans in nature but also acts as a catalyst for a flurry of research and debates about what changes are unfolding, the timeline for those changes, and what should be done about it. The additional changes that are undoubtedly coming will vary from region to region and affect different species in various ways. For the American West specifically, climate change predictions include prolonged drought and major shifts in vegetative communities and the medicinal plants they support.

Understanding the changes unfolding right now is one of the ways we can anticipate more immediate plant community responses to our legacy of land use and those related to the predicted climate changes of the coming centuries. In the American West, we have already seen severe alteration of riparian plant communities and large-scale transformation of grasslands. The conversion of mountain forests has also begun. Floodplains have been reduced to small areas that are often devoid of wetland habitats and dominated by nonnative plants. Grassland communities may be invaded by newly advancing drought-tolerant shrubs; scrubland and montane plants are likely to expand; and subalpine, alpine, and tundra plants are expected to decline (Rehfeldt et al. 2006). Western forests will likely transform as the effects of fire suppression and climate change converge, resulting in large-scale tree die-offs and the inability to reestablish due to sustained drought (Franklin et al. 2016; Redmond et al. 2013; Williams et al. 2013). While many studies in different regions of the West have been conducted with similar results (e.g., Breshears et al. 2005; CIRMOUNT 2006), recent surveys by the US Forest Service (June 2016) in California found that the state had lost 66 million trees since 2010, with an additional 36 million lost during 2016 alone (USFS November 2016). Millions more hectares of forest will likely die as drought and rising temperatures continue (Asner et al. 2016). As much as 47 percent

FIGURE 3 Extensive loss of piñon, ponderosa pine, and Douglas fir trees in the 2011 Las Conchas Fire, Jemez Mountains of New Mexico. Photo by Craig D. Allen, *USGS*.

of future western landscapes may become entirely different, without any currently recognizable plant communities (Rehfeldt 2006). No matter how we look at it, the shifting of plant communities is likely to be extensive.

What does all this mean for our medicinal plants? This question is an open and evolving subject as we continue to understand more clearly the effects of current land use patterns and climate change on botanical communities. As previously discussed, global plant diversity is likely to decline overall as large-scale conversion of land continues to take place, but the mysteries about global patterns of plant diversity exceed what we currently understand. One of the major aspects of uncertainty is the role that invasive species will play in plant diversity over the long term. (See the materia medica on invasive trees.) Total eradication or restoration to preexisting ecological conditions is not possible; these plants are here to stay as a part of our newly evolving natural systems (Head et al. 2015). While it is true that an estimated five thousand nonnative plants reside in the United States with most causing little disturbance to ecosystem functioning, these species have only recently arrived and have likely not yet spread to the extent of their possible ranges (Kerns and

Guo 2012). In fact, it is very likely that invasive plants will continue to expand beyond their current distributions because economic land use patterns and climate change conditions, including higher temperatures, increased disturbances such as fires, elevated levels of atmospheric carbon dioxide, increased soil nitrogen levels, and other anthropogenic stressors, are expected to favor the invaders (Evans 2014; Kerns and Guo 2012).

Many questions regarding the long-term balance between natives and nonnatives remain, however, including uncertainty about natural factors that could curb invasive plants, such as the possible migration of insects and pathogens that have limited the influence of these plants in their native ranges (Evans 2014). Invasive plant species have long been viewed as disrupters of ecosystems (e.g., DiTomaso 2017; Elton 1958; Evans 2014; Kerns and Guo 2012; Pimm and Gilpin 1989; Westbrooks 1998) and also more recently as the saviors and rehabilitators of transformed and degraded lands (e.g., Pearce 2015; Scott 2010). In some cases, nonnative plants outcompete native plants, altering water availability, shading out smaller native species, changing soil chemistry, and accelerating the shifting of other ecosystem functions already put into place by humans (Evans 2014). In other cases, native plants continue to thrive alongside the newly introduced species and a new plant community with increased biodiversity emerges (Suggitt et al. 2019; Velland et al. 2013; Venevskaia et al. 2013), at least in the short term. In yet other areas, native plants (see creosote discussion in chapter 2) will act as invasive species, steadily expanding into new territories and shifting biotic balances as land disturbances continue and temperatures rise, facilitating their advances (Evans 2014). The differences in the roles of invasive plants are likely due in large part to the degree of alteration to the ecosystem caused by development, agriculture, grazing, and water diversions, which may or may not allow native plants to effectively reproduce and grow to maturity. With many uncertainties and wide-ranging variability in environmental changes, we have much to learn about how plants will adapt, migrate, or otherwise respond to this rapidly shifting world.

FIGURE 4 Invasive nonnative kochia (*Bassia scoparia*) covering the understory along the middle Rio Grande. Photo by author.

Many of us continue to struggle with the idea of seeing local plant communities remade by unsustainable land use decisions, large-scale disturbances such as wildfires, or newly introduced species that change the character of our favorite wild or semiwild places. Many scientists have argued that, as part of adapting to present and future conditions, new paradigms regarding emerging landscapes and the role of humans in nature must be accepted (e.g., Ellis and Ramankutty 2008; Head et al. 2015), a notion that has long been embraced and advanced by indigenous people (e.g., Kimmerer 2011, 2013). While concerns about invasive species are legitimate, the total rejection of new species in familiar landscapes is irrational in the modern world and may inhibit our ability to engage in effective debate and decision-making about how to handle the changes unfolding in the natural world. Furthermore, instead of viewing our role as one of disrupting natural processes, we must come to see ourselves as an integral aspect of those processes. We are part of the living landscape. Human influence should become part of our modern understanding of how ecosystems function. Our attitude toward invasive plants is a perpetual reminder of this inner struggle to adapt to changing environmental

circumstances. Ecological herbalism provides a pathway for us to make sense of our changing world, find our place within it, and develop a new approach for engagement with the land and plants.

The medicinal plants discussed in this book are primary characters in the modern wild landscapes of the American Southwest. There are many more than could be covered in one book, but collectively, these plants portray a new botanical reality in a globalized world. Some are native plants, having lived in balance with this land for eons. Some are migrants from long ago; they crossed over the Bering Land Bridge, arrived by way of northbound migrating birds, or arrived through other means. Others developed relationships with people and traveled into new territories more recently as medicinal or otherwise valuable companions. Some need to be protected while others might need to be controlled. Together they weave the ecological tapestry of our modern medicinal plant landscapes, our herbal apothecaries, and our new botanical configuration. These ever-evolving plant communities of the current era are often characterized by the comingling of native plants and recent arrivals, all of which are responding

FIGURE 5 Engaging the land: planting cottonwood (*Populus deltoides wislizenii*) poles. Photo by author.

in their own ways to shifting environmental conditions. As we learn more about how these plants interact with the land, with each other, and with human activity, we develop a clearer understanding of what makes healthy living landscapes and how we can begin to foster them with deliberate intentions. Ethical and respectful wildcrafting, cultivating gardens, working with the most common plants of our bioregion, speaking out on behalf of plants, working to restore threatened plants or critical habitats, and advocating for more sustainable land and water use are just some of the ways we can shape native medicinal plant landscapes wherever we live.

Renewed landscapes and redesigned plant communities are part of our future. Let us shake off the fatigue of disheartening environmental news and come to a place of informed and passionate action. We must get to know the land, come to understand it, fall in love with it, and allow ourselves to be shaped by it. It is time to begin walking the land as if we were part of it, not to take anything but ready to simply give and receive what is shared. Our connection to plants may serve as a conduit to an individual and societal change in consciousness that brings us closer to realizing our beneficial role in the ecological world. It is my hope that this book will serve as a pathway and inspiration for readers to come into relationship with the land and plants so that we can better understand how to interact with the natural world in a mutually beneficial manner. Our presence is already felt throughout every landscape. Let us begin to engage the land with mindful, attentive, and deliberate awareness rather than allowing our worst inclinations to haphazardly resonate. In doing so, we will create a new kind of ecological mosaic—one that is robust, diverse, resilient, and crafted by knowledgeable minds and empathetic hearts. The new ecological reality will be a reconjuring of our own wildness in what seems like a post-wild world.

In manifesting this new ecological mosaic, we must find our way to a shared vision for what natural landscapes can be and what our role within them will look like. An interdisciplinary approach marked by cooperation, dialogue, sharing of knowledge, and personal experience is more important than ever. Working together, we can create the kind of world in which we wish to live. Never before has it been so important to allow our intellect and passion to work in tandem to conjure a viable, beautiful, vibrant vision for the future. With that perspective in mind, we can foster healthy native plant

FIGURE 6
"Heal" graffiti on jetty jacks in the middle Rio Grande bosque. Photo by author.

FIGURE 7
A mountain
trail beckons us
onward. Photo
by author.

communities in new and interesting configurations suited to anticipated environmental conditions while embracing a novel regional plant composition. Landscapes resonating with life and diversity can be part of our future, and we are the ones to make it happen. We must follow the lead of plants, begin to accelerate our own adaptations, and amplify our own responses to a changing environment. If, in fact, we have become the primary players in ecosystem functions, affecting plant communities in a multitude of ways, let us conceive and bring about vitality-filled living landscapes of a new kind that manifest our vision for land and culture. It is our prerogative to become healers of the land, protectors of plants, invigorators of life—not just our own lives but all life.

The practice of ecological herbalism ultimately brings us into thoughtful and heartfelt relationship with the natural world by helping us develop the requisite knowledge and emotional connection to the land and plants that will serve as our guiding force as we move into the future. These connections are vital to navigating change in a way that builds resiliency and vitality rather than diminishing it. To shed light on the kinds of environmental changes discussed here and to illuminate the role of ecological herbalism in understanding plants in our fluctuating world, chapter 2 examines three examples of how specific keystone medicinal plant species are responding to the changes in their ecosystems and how their responses uncover or confirm aspects of their medicinal actions.

Medicinal Plant Landscapes of the Southwest

The American Southwest is a vast region with widely diverse landscapes and a variety of unique habitat types that create a rich biological heritage. This area includes numerous different deserts, mountain ranges, coastal areas, riparian corridors, grasslands, woodlands, and shrublands that collectively host thousands of plant species. Changing environmental conditions and their effects on plant communities are apparent. Our awareness of these changes can profoundly affect the way we perceive our relationship with the land and influence the way we work with plants. When we take the time to understand the reciprocal relationships between plants and the land or plants and other plants, we fall even more deeply in love with the complex beauty of life and wilderness. Through this process, we may also see herbal medicine in a new light as we integrate what we learn from new newly acquired knowledge and through our direct experience in awe-inspiring places. Many people never consider the idea that plants are capable of telling us stories about themselves and the land. Part of our role as active participants in the natural world is to help others hear those stories. This chapter includes three examples that illustrate how landscapes of the Southwest are changing, how primary medicinal plants are responding, and what we can learn from these processes.

THE DESERT BASIN Creosote (*Larrea tridentata*) and the Arid Grasslands

Standing on a rocky outcrop above the open plains of southern New Mexico's high desert grasslands, the senses are guided into the landscape, bringing the rest of me along for the journey. The visible heat and pervasive aroma penetrate, envelop, and draw me into the land of creosote. It is a place decorated by dryland shrubs, endless open blue skies, unrelenting sun, and the remains of Piro Pueblo communities that merged themselves with the land and the spirits of the plants and animals that sustained them. Long-term ecological studies reveal what the petroglyphs of the area suggest: this place was once dominated by a community of grasses, which provided expanses of rich forage

top to bottom

FIGURE 8
High-elevation
mountain meadow.
Photo by author.

FIGURE 9
Desert basin.
Photo by author.

FIGURE 10
Volcanic mountain.
Photo by author.

for the array of animals whose images are etched into stone mesas. Rabbit tracks and ungulate hooves were pecked into the rocky surfaces like a trail of footprints leading to small, shallow, water-filled *tinajas*, perhaps drawing the animals into the lives of the people by the life-sustaining offering. Individual creosote plants now hold their ground as far as the eye can see. The general lack of forage and scarcity of animals are now part of the character of the land. The antiquity of the landscape resides not just in the enduring pottery sherds and red ocher paintings of the people who made their homes here long before but also in the plants themselves. Creosote plants can be quite ancient beings, with the oldest known clone community carbon dated at 11,700 years old (Vasek 1980). Even plants considered to be young by that standard have been around long enough to keep the stories of this place. I sit and wait to hear their whispers.

Creosote is an evergreen woody shrub with a wide geographic range and is one of the most abundant medicinal plants found in the Desert Basin and Range. Its small yellow flowers bloom in the spring and later turn into fuzzy white seeds carried by the wind. Shiny leaves, a rich green color in times of adequate moisture, grow in clusters at the end of woody branches and exude an aromatic resinous coating that cools the plant by reflecting the desert sun (Dodson 2012). *Larrea tridentata* has a long and successful history of advancing its range, having relatively recently (mid-Pleistocene and late Pliocene) migrated long-distance from ancestral populations of *L. divericata* in South America (Laport et al. 2012). Accepting of nearly all desert soil types, it occupies a wide range of habitats, stretching from southern Utah and Nevada southward and covering much of Mexico from Baja to West Texas. While found in all the southwestern deserts, creosote is an indicator

left to right

FIGURE 11
Middle-elevation mountain forest.
Photo by author.

FIGURE 12
Shrubland.
Photo by author.

FIGURE 13
Volcanic mesa.
Photo by author.

Medicinal Plant
Landscapes
of the
Southwest

top to bottom

FIGURE 14
Mountain foothills.
Photo by author.

FIGURE 15
Mountain stream.
Photo by author.

MAP 1 *Major Habitat Types of the American Southwest*

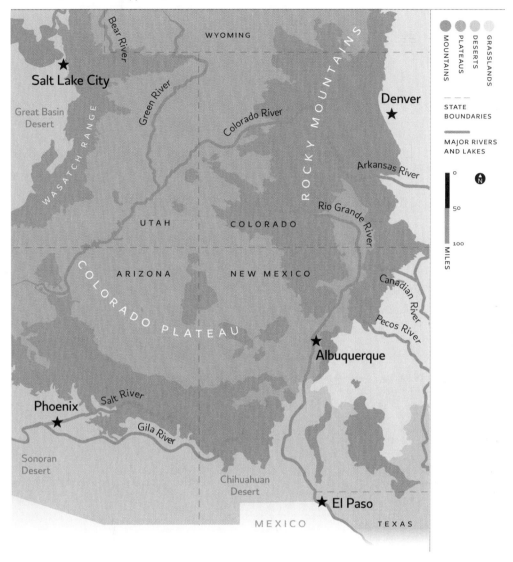

plant for the Chihuahuan Desert and may be limited in range primarily due to prolonged (six consecutive days) freezing temperatures and excessive soil moisture (Dalton 1961). It continues to extend its range, making a foothold in areas of bare desert soil, usurping available water, and using its allelopathic powers to impair competing plants and change desert plant communities in the Chihuahuan Desert and across the Southwest. Frequently described as a worthless forage plant or a noxious weed rather than a native shrub, creosote has been studied most often from an economic perspective due to its expansion into grazing lands.

Creosote finds a welcoming home in the lowlands of the Desert Basin and

Medicinal Plant
Landscapes
of the
Southwest

17

MAP 2 *Physiographic Regions of New Mexico*

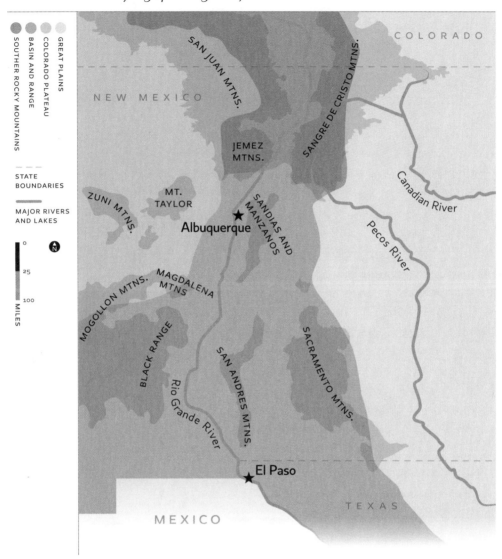

Range. This physiographic region is a repeating pattern of mountain ranges with expansive hot and dry deserts in between. It stretches from Nevada and southern California across much of Arizona and into the southern portion of New Mexico, where it meets the southern Great Plains. The Chihuahuan Desert, spreading across northern Mexico and southern New Mexico, is a part of this region and includes vast expanses of creosote. Recorded stories of this landscape, which includes the Jornada Basin of New Mexico, go back to the early Spanish explorers heading into this remote territory. Their documents include few remarks about the vegetation, so we rely more on

FIGURE 16
Creosote (*Larrea tridentata*).
Photo by author.

information provided by us military expeditions, explorations, and surveys from the early part of the nineteenth century to understand what the plant community was like. On his way from Santa Fe to Chihuahua in 1807, us military officer and explorer Zebulon Pike described the area as a "large flat prairie" (Gardner 1951:381). Twenty-two years later, in 1829, writing of what would become the state of New Mexico, explorer and naturalist Josiah Gregg said that the "high prairies of Northern Mexico … are mostly covered with different species of a highly nutritious grass called grama" (381). In the late 1840s botanist Friedrich Wislizenus listed mesquite (*Prosopis glandulosa torreyana*) as the most common woody plant in the area, and surveyor W. H. Emory described black grama (*Bouteloua eriopoda*) as being in great abundance (Gardner 1951). us military officers Philip St. George Cooke, William Marcy, and John Pope, who traveled separately through southern New Mexico around that time, all substantiated Emory's view by describing the area as having "luxuriant" grama grasses of several different species (Gardner 1951:382). A military officer and surveyor named Edward Fitzgerald Beale, who came through the region in 1857, went even further, saying there were "hundreds and hundreds of thousands of acres, containing the greatest abundance of the finest grass in the world" (382). Not one of these travelers made a mention of creosote in his descriptions of the landscape. The first to do so was the botanist Charles Christopher Parry, who listed the shrubs of the area during a boundary survey in 1859 (Gardner 1951).

Every landscape is in a constant state of change throughout every stage of its natural history. In the case of the Chihuahuan Desert, these changes appear to have accelerated since the arrival of colonists and imported grazing animals. Scientific research investigating the transformation of New Mexico's Jornada Basin and other western grasslands from diverse vegetative communities into biologically reduced desert scrublands, frequently dominated by near monocultures of creosote, is plentiful. This process is often described as "brush encroachment" because, along with creosote, come other native shrubs, such as mesquite (*Prosopis* spp.), that were present in the local environment for thousands of years but in much lower densities (Van Auken 2000). Grazing of livestock is universally cited as the primary factor behind this process as it creates conditions that impair the reproduction of native grasses and annual species while favoring the spread of woody shrubs such as creosote as well as nonnative species (e.g., Fleischner 1994; Whitfield and Anderson 1938; York and Dick-Peddie 1969). Livestock grazing is ubiquitous across the American West, with 70 percent of land (229 million acres of federal public land) subjected to this type of use (Council for Agricultural Science and Technology 1974; Glaser et al. 2015). This has resulted in profound and pervasive effects, such as changes to vegetative communities through reduction of species richness and declines in the density and biomass of individual species; interference in ecosystem functions, including the destruction of cryptobiotic crusts that fix nitrogen, increase organic matter and phosphorus, stabilize soil, increase water filtration, and provide germination locations for seeds; and alteration of ecosystem structure by affecting soil composition and water availability, leading to erosion, soil compaction, reduced water filtration, and desertification (Fleischner 1994).

While all the southwestern deserts have been impacted by grazing, the Chihuahuan Desert has changed most significantly (Smith et al. 1997). According to one study of the Chihuahuan Desert, creosote becomes two times more prevalent in areas that are grazed by livestock, while locations protected from stock demonstrate a 50 percent higher grass cover and a 35 percent higher total biomass (Mata-Gonzalez 2007). In 1951 a botanist named J. L. Gardner completed his detailed investigations of creosote's influence over the land. During his plant transects, he observed something unique about creosote: the higher the percentage of creosote coverage in any area, the less grass coverage there was. Gardner specifically noted the co-occurrence of grasses with tarbush (*Flourensia cernua*) and mesquite

FIGURE 17 Biotic soil crust in the Chihuahuan Desert. Photo by author.

(*Prosopis* spp.), the latter having a very localized grass suppression effect through the formation of a small dune around its base. Gardner also reported that creosote was by far the most dominant plant, constituting a solid majority of the total shrub population and having established itself on nearly all the surveyed areas. With regard to grasses, Gardner noted that of the twenty-one species present in the ecosystem, only four (fluffgrass, or *Dasyochloa pulchella* syn. *Tridens pulchellus*; burrograss, or *Scleropogon brevifolius*; bush muhly, or *Muhlenbergia porteri*; and black grama, or *Bouteloua eriopoda*) were present at a significant number of surveyed areas and that they averaged a mere 0.36 percent of coverage. A more recent study that tracked vegetation changes in the Jornada Basin over a span of 140 years gave additional details about this transformation (Gibbens et al. 2005). Starting data from 1858 showed that 54 percent and 86 percent of the two study areas had no presence of creosote at all (Gibbens 2005). In contrast, by 1998 creosote had become dominant on 20 percent and 59 percent of those areas, with mesquite also making dramatic gains (Gibbens 2005). Likewise, black grama, which had been dominant or subdominant on nearly half of the area in 1916, held that status on only 1.2 percent of land by 1998 (Gibbens 2005). Creosote's propensity for spreading in grazed lands has been documented in other areas too. A study in the Santa Rita Experimental Range in Arizona recorded the expansion of creosote beginning in 1905, when it covered 950 acres (Humphrey and Mehrhoff 1958). By 1934 it covered nearly twelve thousand acres, and by 1954 creosote had expanded to cover seventy-three times the original acreage of fifty years prior (Humphrey and Mehrhoff 1958). These results support Gardner's observations regarding creosote's ability to change the landscape relatively rapidly and profoundly.

In addition to grazing, there are other contributing factors in this landscape transformation. Creosote is known to contain allelopathic chemicals, including phenols, condensed tannins, and nordihydroguaiaretic acid (NDGA), which inhibit the growth of nearby roots, even those of other creosote plants (Hyder et al. 2002; Mahall et al. 1991). This activity creates low root density in the soil and maximum water availability for each creosote plant. The chemical NDGA has been shown to be phytotoxic, significantly reducing the seedling root growth of numerous grasses and herbaceous plant species; it may even kill creosote's own seedlings (Elakovich and Stevens 1985; McAuliffe 1988). Creosote is known to establish itself on areas with no perennial plant cover and then change the soil to impair soil stability and electrical conductivity while reducing calcium and nitrate, making it more difficult for annuals to grow (Whitford et al. 2001). Furthermore, the warming of the

FIGURE 18 Creosote (*Larrea tridentata*) growing with grasses, forbs, and other shrubs in an ecological study area. Photo by author.

FIGURE 19 Creosote (*Larrea tridentata*) on overgrazed land with a lot of bare ground and few other plant species (only snakeweed [*Gutierrezia sarothrae*] and yucca [*Yucca* spp.]). Photo by author.

climate and periodic droughts have undoubtedly favored the advancement of shrubs, which have both deep and shallow roots, enabling them to better withstand hot and dry times. Desert annuals, including grasses, have less tolerance for water and heat extremes (Smith et al. 1997). They revert to seed dormancy during the most stressful times of the year but must undertake a rapid growth cycle to build an entire plant structure and reproduce each year. This renders them more vulnerable when resources are lacking or environmental conditions become undesirable. Nutritive native grass seeds are also a primary food source for many rodents and other animals of the desert, which reduces grass reproductive capabilities as seeds are harvested and eaten (Van Auken 2000). The initial reduction in grasses then furthers momentum in favor of creosote and other shrubs. As biodiversity is reduced, there is less competition for resources. The loss of grasses also reduces the fuel load present in the environment and results in the near elimination of wildfires that would help slow the spread of woody plants (Van Auken 2000). The continuing advancement of creosote's range and density also creates unstable surface conditions that result in the loss of topsoil, a resource that is critical to many desert grasses (Buffington et al. 1965). While it is likely that creosote, mesquite, and other desert shrubs would have made advances into new territories simply through changing environmental conditions, there is no doubt that grazing has hastened and intensified this process. Restoring Chihuahuan Desert grasslands is no small task, and some scientists question if it is possible at all (Van Auken 2000). If the ecological scales tip too far out of balance, the naturally occurring topsoil will no longer provide the habitat requirements and the existing wild seed stock may become too sparse to regenerate biodiversity. A continuing pattern of extensive livestock grazing, warming temperatures, reduced rainfall, and rodents and rabbits eating the remaining grass seeds further complicates the problem.

Filling a niche created by decades of unbalanced land use, creosote is spreading into new territory, usurping available resources, overtaking the ecology, shifting the biotic balances, and creating a new reality on its own terms. It is a resilient and transformative plant once it gets a foothold. This ecological trait is also expressed as an herbal remedy and has made creosote an important medicinal plant used by many cultural groups. (This plant is discussed in detail in the materia medica section.) Its unusual role as a native encroaching plant distinguishes it from many others in discussions about changing plant communities. Its sheer "brute force" sets it apart as an herbal medicine, often relegating it to topical applications or the most stubborn of infections or inflammatory conditions. Its power is so strong that driving home with the wafting aroma of freshly harvested creosote in my enclosed backseat sometimes overwhelms me. Creosote's landscape interactions reflect its character and its workings as medicine. It takes over disturbed environments, making critical resources unavailable to other living organisms and otherwise disrupting their habitat, which are traits that contribute to its broad antimicrobial actions in herbal medicines. The aromatic chemicals that protect the plant and move energy through the landscape also purify and decongest the body, breaking up stagnancy and invigorating the system. These characteristics, which cleanse and stimulate body functions, ultimately reduce inflammation in the body and produce similar effects environmentally as creosote transforms exhausted and overworked land. Its stubborn and relentless nature also supports what recent scientific research is suggesting with regard to its potential in cancer treatments. If, in a geologically short period of time, it can remake the harsh and unforgiving environments of the major deserts of the North American continent, forming monotypic stands thousands of square kilometers, imagine what it can do in the human body's ecosystem.

Walking along one of my favorite trails in the Sandia Mountains, I arrive in a spot that I have been visiting for two decades. It is a place I have returned to so many times for so many reasons. At first I came for the comforting respite this place provided. Three thousand feet above the valley floor, the cool air, the trickling waters in the mountain stream, and a multitude of plants nourished me and seemed to replenish what urban life drained away. Conifers dominated the slopes, creating shaded habitat, rich with pine needle mulch that gave rise to pedicularis (*Pedicularis centranthera*), valerian (*Valeriana arizonica*), corydalis (*Corydalis aurea*), Oregon grape (*Mahonia repens*), bearcorn (*Conopholis alpina* var. *mexicana*), clematis (*Clematis columbiana*), and so many others. The little canyon was also home to a small mountain stream running with snowmelt from above. Along the cool waters grew cutleaf coneflower (*Rudbeckia laciniata*), wild strawberries (*Fragaria vesca*), bedstraw (*Galium boreale*), brook mint (*Mentha arvensis*), horsetail (*Equisetum arvense*), veronica (*Veronica americana*), and others. Among this colorful group of companions was a riotous and fragrant patch of bee balm (*Monarda fistulosa*), blooming vigorously and often covered in foraging butterflies. This large bee balm cluster had several other sister groups along the stream, all growing with similar vitality. Change inevitably unfolds around us and within us, however, and one summer I came back to find that this place had changed dramatically from the prior year. Bark beetles had been infesting the trees, and most of the canyon slopes were now covered in dead brown skeletal remains reaching toward the sky. Along the stream, the Forest Service had cut all the dead trees down, and the trail was lined with stacks of coarse firewood and sawdust. It felt apocalyptic. Without the shade of the wooded slopes, the streamside plants now had to endure the stress of baking in the sun most of the day. Over the years, less water has been coming down the stream, and now it often runs dry during the hottest months. Many of those plants have retreated to other areas of the mountain in search of shade and moisture. Along the stream bank, dramatic changes have unfolded: strawberries and cutleaf coneflower are scarce and that once glorious stand of purple bee balm blossoms has become an isolated remnant. Opportunistic nonnative species such as sweet clover (*Melilotus officinalis*), alfalfa (*Medicago sativa*), and yellow dock (*Rumex crispus*) are claiming their places in the new conditions. Witnessing such a rapid and dramatic transformation unfolding in a familiar and beloved place had a profound impact on me. It fed a growing realization that over a relatively short period of time, the entire character of a place can become something vastly different from what a person once knew. Seeing the twenty-year evolution of this one bee balm stand and its habitat was a catalyst for cultivating my own understanding about landscape dynamics and fueled my quest to understand how the land and its plant communities are changing all around me.

FIGURE 20
Bee balm
(*Monarda fistulosa*)
with foraging
butterflies.
Photo by author.

Bee balm makes its home in pine and mixed conifer forests of middle to upper elevations in the West. It especially likes to be near watercourses, even those that are intermittent, as long as there is enough sand or gravel to act as effective mulch. *Monarda fistulosa* has a large geographical range encompassing most of the United States and Canada, while *M. fistulosa* var. *menthifolia* is associated with the mountain West and northern plains. As a member of the mint family (Lamiaceae), it has the expected botanical characteristics, including square stems and opposite leaves, and is also quite aromatic. Bee balm plays an important role ecologically as its nectar- and pollen-rich flowers remain open for up to two thousand hours continuously, providing an important and reliable foraging source for bees, butterflies, and hummingbirds (Anderson 2003; Cruden et al. 1984). There are sixteen to eighteen species of *Monarda* across North America, with numerous subspecies

FIGURE 21 *left* Bee balm (*Monarda fistulosa*)
stand (center) amid a diversity of streamside plants.
Photo by Jason Buckles.

FIGURE 22 *below* Post–bark beetle infestation.
Photo by author.

and variations. The American West is home to about five species, including
M. citriodora, *M. pectinata*, *M. punctata*, *M. fistulosa* (var. *menthifolia*), and
M. humilis, the latter proposed by Prather and Keith (2003) to be a distinct
species endemic to New Mexico. Taxonomical debates continue among botanists, who have differing ideas about what constitutes a separate species
and exactly how members of this variable genus should be classified (e.g.,
Fernald 1901, 1944; Fosberg and Artz 1953; Graham 1829; McClintock and
Epling 1942; Meehan 1892; Prather et al. 2002). Differences between some
of the proposed or accepted species appear to be so slight that they could be
considered a single species with variations (McClintock and Epling 1942).
Furthermore, hybridizing among closely related species such as *M. fistulosa*
and *M. lindheimeri* further complicates taxonomical agreement (Prather et al.
2002). Despite the varied morphological differences among all the *Monarda*

species, Prather et al. note that there is little molecular diversification among these plants, which suggests a common ancestry for them all.

While the granite and limestone rock formations placidly maintain their towering stance above the valleys and mesas below, the plants that make up the western mountain habitats are on the move. That once riotous bee balm patch holding its ground in the bark beetle–infested pine forest is not an isolated or unusual occurrence in the Southwest in recent years. In fact, forest ecosystems are undergoing massive changes around the world and large-scale tree die-offs are considered to be one of the most obvious effects of climate change (Hicke et al. 2013). According to a report from the USDA, "There is a consensus that the direct and indirect effects of climate change on forest dynamics may be profound. Climate change will affect the geographical distribution of vegetation types, ecosystem processes such as primary production, and the distribution and abundance of individual species of trees and other plants" (Kliejunas et al. 2009:3). Along with this statement came a projection for increased frequency, duration, and intensity of forest disturbances such as fire, drought, nonnative species proliferation, insect infestation, and pathogens, which may be of a magnitude to enact an irreversible cascade of changes in the ecosystems (Kliejunas et al. 2009). Recent events have shown this to be accurate. Massive forest die-offs have recently occurred throughout the West due to a combination of climate change factors and fire suppression policies. These have created unusually dense forests that are especially vulnerable to disturbances (CIRMOUNT 2006). California lost an estimated 27 million trees during 2012–2015, with 10.6 million hectares of forest (up to 888 million large trees) experiencing significant canopy water loss (Asner et al. 2016). The same study revealed massive areas of progressive canopy water stress extending from growing populations of dead trees, suggesting that millions more hectares of forest will likely die as drought and rising temperatures continue (Asner et al. 2016). Between 2000 and 2004, the Colorado Plateau also lost 1.5 million hectares of piñon (*Pinus edulis*) and 1.0 million hectares of ponderosa pine (*Pinus ponderosa*) as a response to environmental triggers (CIRMOUNT 2006).

You may wonder why this current drought is so deadly to forests compared to the long-term cycles of drought that have been part of the Southwest's natural history for millennia. According to many climate scientists and botanists, current and future droughts will be driven by rising temperatures rather than decreasing precipitation (e.g., Breshears et al. 2005; Gutzler and Robbins 2011; Williams et al. 2013). In one example, in 2002–2003, a 12,000-square-kilometer area of New Mexico experienced a 90 percent loss of piñon accompanied

FIGURE 23 Aerial photograph of ponderosa pine (*Pinus ponderosa*) mortality caused by bark beetle activity in the Pinos Altos Mountains, Gila National Forest. Several species of bark beetles were identified in this area, including *Ips*, roundheaded, and western pine beetles. Photo by Daniel Ryerson, USDA Forest Service, Southwestern Region.

FIGURE 24 Massive forest die-off of piñon pines (*Pinus edulis*) showing the progression from 2002 to 2004 in the Los Alamos area of New Mexico. This type of event is projected to occur more frequently in the Southwest. Photo by Craig D. Allen, USGS.

by unusually high temperatures and bark beetle infestation (Breshears et al. 2005). Bark beetle populations are known to surge with warmer temperatures, and slight increases in drought stress can result in exponential beetle outbreaks, with devastating consequences in areas where fire suppression policies have created dense canopies (Williams et al. 2013). In contrast to previous recorded droughts, in which fatalities were limited to drier areas and older trees, mortality in recent droughts includes the higher and wetter areas of the range and trees of all ages (Breshears et al. 2005). The large-scale canopy loss also resulted in a 50 percent reduction in native understory species, including blue grama grass (*Boutelua gracilis*), which provides an important food source for wildlife (Breshears et al. 2005). Dramatic ecological changes like this are expected to unfold most prominently in semiarid transitional zones, such as the Sandia Mountains, where many species are already at the extent of their ranges (Allen and Breshears 1998).

The exact mechanism of drought-induced tree mortality is not always known. Rising temperatures bring a triad of mortal threats for trees in southwestern forests: bark beetle infestations, the physiological processes of hydraulic failure, and carbon starvation (Dickman et al. 2014). Bark beetles (*Dendroctonus* and *Ips*) are attracted to stressed trees, feed on the cambium layer, and disrupt both the flow of photosynthesized sugars downward from the leaves through the phloem and the movement of water and nutrients upward from the roots via the xylem (Meddens et al. 2015). Meanwhile, drought-stressed trees also face the delicate balance between retaining moisture and photosynthesizing. When temperatures increase, a plant may close the stomata to decrease transpired water loss, but this also results in decreased ability to photosynthesize. If the plant remains in this state for too long, it risks starvation as carbon stores (sugar and starch) are used up. Alternately, if the plant opens the stomata to photosynthesize, it risks hydraulic failure, or the breakdown of the xylem as a result of dry soils and transpired water loss (Dickman et al. 2014). Trees such as junipers (*Juniperus monosperma* and others), which have an increased ability to store carbohydrates, have a better chance of surviving predicted climate change patterns compared to piñons and ponderosa pines (*Pinus edulis* and *P. ponderosa*), which cannot sustain long periods of zero carbon assimilation (Dickman et al. 2014; McDowell et al. 2013). One study showed that piñons began dying after one year of drought with a high occurrence of bark beetles in dead trees, while junipers began to show partial canopy loss after three years of continued drought (Gaylord et al. 2013).

With all projections pointing to higher temperatures across the Southwest, more changes for bee balm's forest habitat seem inevitable. There is a general consensus regarding what conditions will be like, with the timeline for reaching those predictions being the main point of discussion. Climate scientist David Gutzler (2007, 2011) has reported projections for temperatures increasing about 8°F over the next century, with precipitation patterns continuing within historical ranges. Gutzler also projected no winter snowpack south of Santa Fe and all snowmelt runoff occurring one month earlier by the end of the century. Recent research by Williams et al. (2013) used tree ring data and living trees to compare forest drought stress indexes (FDSI) in the Southwest from AD 1000 to 2007. They found that previous large-scale die-offs have occurred, including a mega-drought from 1572 to 1587, as suggested by the scarcity of conifers older than four hundred years. To paint a picture of future forest changes, Williams noted that between 1000 and 2007, the FDSI of the mega-drought was exceeded in only 4.8 percent of years. But the study predicts that between 2000 and 2100, 59 percent of years will exceed the mega-drought FDSI, and up to 80 percent in the latter half of the century. With unrelenting heat and the progressive large-scale loss of required parent trees, regeneration of forests, which historically has taken place during cooler, wetter years, may not occur (Redmond et al. 2013; Williams et al. 2013). This process ultimately leads to the transformation of pine forests into shrublands and grasslands (Williams et al. 2013), with another study projecting that half of the evergreen forest in western North America will become shrubland or grassland by the end of the twenty-first century (Jiang et al. 2013). What all this means for bee balm and other forest plants of the desert mountain ranges remains to be seen. Just as the Pleistocene montane and subalpine coniferous forests that covered nearly all of New Mexico eighteen thousand years ago (Dick-Peddie 1993) have retreated to the middle- and upper-elevation mountains today, further upward migration is likely in the future. As the snowline creeps up the mountain in coming years, the pine forests and all the companion understory plants are likely to follow. They may become plants of higher elevations until they have reached the top with nowhere else to go.

Bee balm and its medicine help us understand the story of the changing coniferous forests of the West and the migrating plants of these ecosystems. Its medicine is a reflection of this movement in the biological world and connects our bodies to that of the forests. Encouraging movement in the landscape and in our bodily functions, bee balm's aromatic oils disperse stagnation, stimulate the activity of biological systems, and encourage the circulation of energy within the body or ecosystem to create a beneficial health cascade. Eye-catching and enduring flowers promote the migration of pollinators through the landscape, building vitality in the land, animals, and other plants while also providing a potent remedy for people. Its warming action stimulates biological functions while also dispelling heat to cool inflammation. Bee balm moves the vitality of the forest, invigorates the health of the body, and knows how to soothe inflammatory responses in the land and in ourselves. (A detailed account of this plant appears in the materia medica.) Furthermore, this plant lures us into awareness about an evolving world and the new environmental conditions unfolding around us, ultimately evoking a sense of movement or advancement for humanity's relationship with the natural world. Understanding this plant's story is an invitation to begin the process of emotional acceptance within ourselves and to take meaningful action in our lives that will facilitate the process of healing for the wild places around us. Embracing this story is an opportunity for us to grow in harmony with these plant communities and become a more integral part of the wilderness by acknowledging that we a part of this interconnected system of life. We must decide for ourselves what those changes are for us as herbalists and as members of the planetary ecosystem.

During our lifetimes, most of us will likely experience the dramatic ecological change of a beloved wilderness area and witness the geographical range of plants shift as forests move to higher elevations and latitudes and new plant communities of the shrublands and grasslands migrate. Exactly what this means for bee balm and other forest understory plants is a story that is still being written. Our natural and primary reactions to such profound environmental changes are most often deeply emotional ones. While sorting through our denial and feelings of loss, it is important to remember that our beliefs and actions now are influencing what the future will bring. In presenting bee balm's story, I hope to inspire others to learn more about this plant and the landscape dynamics where we live, to meet these changes with rational minds, and to begin to accept and discuss the evolving circumstances around us. This will enable us to take meaningful steps, including advocating for policy changes and adapting our herbal practices and individual actions for a more sustainable future in the world we will inhabit.

THE RIPARIAN FLOODPLAIN

Yerba Mansa (*Anemopsis californica*) and the Bosque

Yellow confetti of the forest flutters through the air as deciduous trees shed their golden autumn leaves. Red speckles the understory as thicket creeper sprawls across the ground and climbs tree trunks. With crisp blue skies overhead and the striking Sandia Mountains dominating the background, I enter the Rio Grande bosque seeking my old friend yerba mansa (*Anemopsis californica*). The bosque is a unique riparian ecosystem consisting of a mosaic of habitat types, including woodlands dominated by cottonwood stands (*Populus deltoides wislizenii*) and coyote willow thickets (*Salix exigua*) connected to the ancient river running through them. In the Southwest, the two largest watersheds and associated bosque habitats are the Colorado River and the Rio Grande. Although riparian corridors cover a mere 1 percent of the land in the western United States (Montgomery 1996), they are of vital importance to all life in the region. Rivers are the lifeblood of western bioregions, facilitating the movement of energy and nutrients through the landscape while recharging critical groundwater supplies. In addition to providing water, food, and cover for wildlife, riparian areas also establish migration corridors and connectivity between habitats. Furthermore, riparian vegetation improves water quality by filtering excess nutrients, sediments, and contaminants from surface flows and shallow groundwater. Riparian plants also shade streams contributing to aquatic habitat and reduce downstream flooding by dissipating energy and allowing more time for the absorption of water through the soil. Rivers and their associated floodplains typically have a much greater degree of biodiversity than upland areas, but a long list of threats to our rivers endangers native medicinal plants residing along their banks and imperils everything else they provide.

The Colorado River originates in Rocky Mountain National Park and passes through eleven national parks and monuments, seven states, and two countries, draining 8.5 percent of the continental United States along the way (Cohn 2001). The Colorado Compact was signed in 1922 and secured water allotments for seven us states. Unfortunately, the agreement was based on years of unusually high precipitation. Consequently, it established a permanent water deficit and doomed the Colorado's reservoirs to lower than anticipated storage levels. During the river's 1,450-mile journey, the waters of this system pass through ten major dams and more than eighty diversions and sit impounded in the two largest reservoirs in the nation at Lake Mead and Lake Powell. The Colorado River provides drinking water for 30 million people in cities across the region, including Las Vegas, Phoenix, Los Angeles, Mexicali, and Tijuana (Cohn 2001). Every drop of water belongs to someone, and following a 1944 treaty, the United States is obligated to deliver 1.5 million acre-feet of water annually across the border to Mexico. According to the nonprofit organization American Rivers, the Colorado River drives a $1.4 trillion economy that includes recreational activities, agriculture, industry,

FIGURE 25 Development and habitat loss along the Colorado River. Photo by author.

and residential uses. Once known as the Grande River, the Colorado has become a string of storage pools and now sadly peters out into nothing more than dry sand several miles short of its estuary in the Sea of Cortez. The Bureau of Reclamation estimates that as a result of this exploitation, only six thousand acres of riparian habitat remain from what may have been four hundred thousand acres before dams (Cohn 2001). These remaining acres have seen a dramatic reduction in native cottonwoods (*Populus*) and willows (*Salix*) and are now largely dominated by nonnative species such as salt cedar (*Tamarix*), with reduced biodiversity and declining fish and bird habitat. The lower Colorado was once the most extensive wetlands in the Southwest but now contains only scattered relics, with large expanses of dry barren lands in between (Stromberg 2001).

The Rio Grande has a similar story. Throughout most of its history, the Rio Grande bosque has been a system of wetlands, oxbow lakes, sandbars, and woodlands that migrated with the wild and changing meander of the river. Seasonal flooding cleared debris and enriched the soil. Cottonwoods and coyote willows germinated and thrived in the periodic floods and high water table. Although the valley has a long history of occupation dating back to Paleo-Indian times, it was not until the 1800s that humans began to have a significant impact on the ecology. With the growing numbers of Anglo migrants in the valley came large-scale agriculture, irrigation systems, livestock grazing, and logging. These activities, in turn, created soil erosion, a large sediment load in the river, and increased flooding. To control flooding, a series of major interventions ensued. The twentieth century was marked by the construction of major dams, including Elephant Butte in 1916, Jemez Canyon in 1953, Abiquiú in 1963, Galisteo in 1970, and Cochiti in 1973, along with hundreds of miles of irrigation canals. Additional engineering projects included the draining of wetlands and the installation of jetty jacks. These intensive controls on the ecosystem, along with increasing urbanization, have resulted in a 60 percent replacement of the entire Rio Grande system with agriculture and urban development, river flows decreasing to one-sixth of their historic levels, a significant reduction in channels and wetlands, the invasion of many nonnative species, increased wildfires, and a dramatic decline in the reproduction of the native keystone species: the cottonwoods and willows (USACE 2003).

Today we find our riparian habitats and their associated plant communities facing uncertain times. Along the Rio Grande, the population of mature cottonwoods, born in the last great flood, in 1941, is nearing the end of its natural life, with few young trees to become elders of the forest (Crawford et al. 1996). Invasive tree species such as Russian olive (*Elaeagnus angustifolia*), salt cedar (*Tamarix chinensis*), honey locust (*Gleditsia triacanthos*), mulberry (*Morus alba*), tree of heaven (*Ailanthus altissima*), and Siberian elm (*Ulmus pumila*) have the advantage in the absence of flooding and are expected to replace the two-million-year-old cottonwood forest by the end of the century if water management practices remain unaltered (Crawford et al. 1996). Other weedy nonnatives, such as kochia (*Bassia scoparia*), tumbleweed (*Salsola tragus*), alfalfa (*Medicago sativa*), and sweet clover (*Melilotus* spp.), cover large areas. Reduced water levels threaten native plants and create a high fire danger. The riparian zones across the Southwest have transformed from what the early botanists and immigrants described, and desert bosque environments have become some of the most endangered ecosystems anywhere (Brinson et al. 1981; Crawford et al. 1996). Since this threatened landscape is a central part of the cultural identity of many communities as well as habitat for endangered animals, efforts are under way to improve native species habitat, increase surface water flows, and recharge the water table. The protection the silvery minnow receives under the Endangered Species Act was an important catalyst for restoration efforts now under way. In recent years, various federal agencies have undertaken revitalization

FIGURE 26 Aerial view of Albuquerque looking south, with the Barelas Bridge (Bridge Boulevard) crossing the Rio Grande, circa 1915. Note the river meanders, large sandbars in the river course, undeveloped floodplain habitat, and the mosaic of vegetation types, including cottonwood tree canopy alternating with open areas. Compare with Figure 27. Albuquerque Museum, gift of Margaret R. Herter, PA1994.014.002.

FIGURE 27 Aerial view of Albuquerque looking south, with the Barelas Bridge (Bridge Boulevard) crossing the Rio Grande, 2019. Note the loss of meanders, the reduction in sandbars, the extensively developed floodplain, thick cottonwood forest all along the riverbank, and the narrowing of the river channel. Compare with Figure 26. Google Earth view.

FIGURE 28.
Jetty jacks origi-
nally designed to
trap debris and
control flood-
waters along the
Rio Grande.
Photo by author.

projects, as have local organizations involved in advocating for the health of the Rio Grande. The balance between meeting the water needs of the thirsty Southwest and allowing enough water to remain in the wilderness for plants, animals, and the earth itself is always delicate and fraught with conflicting views. Current climate change predictions include the Rio Grande Basin having up to 14 percent less water in the system by the 2030s and as much as 29 percent less water by the 2080s (Gutlzler 2013). As populations across the American West grow, the demand for water diversion will increase and the resources available to our riparian native plants across the region will likely decline unless we make ecosystem conservation a priority.

As we attempt to restore the balance of the bosque, I drive to a favorite place outside the protected urban woodlands of Rio Grande Valley State Park, where the riparian wilds are still home to a healthy population of native plants. I walk the trails in and out of forest and open spaces, along sandy beaches, through willow thickets, and under jetty jacks—all this in search of the ancient and enduring spirit of yerba mansa. However, the water diversion practices in the bosque have impacted this plant (Saville 2020). A lover of wetlands, moist soils, thick leaf litter mulch, and the shade of cottonwood trees, it suffers from the reduction of the water table, lack of flooding, and nonnative species overtaking the understory. Nevertheless, large stands of yerba mansa still exist in some areas. Late October is the perfect time to harvest the aromatic roots of this most honored herb of the cottonwood forests. With the seasonal song of migrating sandhill cranes in the afternoon sky and the potent scent of the roots rising from the earth, the meditation of medicine gathering begins. Crouched on the forest floor near the occupied web of a black and yellow garden spider, I am reminded to enter into this landscape and the wild harvesting process with respect for and awareness of the life around me. I clear away several inches of forest mulch, mainly cottonwood leaves in varying states of decay, and begin to see individual yerba mansa plants within the dense stand. With my hands in the earth, my work is reminiscent of a paleontological excavation as I carefully expose the horizontal rhizomes and vertical roots reaching downward for moisture. Clearing away the thick silty clay enshrouding the rhizomes is a time-consuming process, with great rewards as the entirety of the treasured roots emerges. Entwined among thick cottonwood roots, yerba mansa rhizomes embody the interconnection of all beings within this forest and all life everywhere, as one root leads to another and the forest floor recyclers, the bugs of the bosque, scurry away from my intrusion. The penetrating aroma of yerba mansa envelops me and makes us one as our vitality intermingles in the intimacy of the moment. Digging deeper, the continuum of thick rhizomes and entangled roots reveals new layers in the depths of life of this place that I love. To protect the remaining wild stands, this sacred act has become a ceremonial one, whereby I honor the wild spirit of yerba mansa in mindfully taking a meager harvest to combine with semiwild roots obtained from the margins of organic alfalfa farms along the bosque.

Yerba mansa is a plant of extraordinary beauty as well as an invaluable herb in the medicine cabinet. It creates large dense stands through both seeding and spreading its "lizard tails," or stolons, which root at each node.

FIGURE 29 *left* Large stand of yerba mansa (*Anemopsis californica*). Photo by author.

FIGURE 30 *above* Freshly harvested yerba mansa (*Anemopsis californica*) root. Photo by author.

Its white petal-like bracts reflect a haunting iridescent glow in the desert sunset. Yerba mansa's elegance is unique among desert plants and has been a force holding my heart to this land for many years. As the plants move through their growing season, red splashes begin to appear on their leaves, bracts, and roots. By autumn, most of the plants are entirely deep, earthly crimson, with some sheltered patches holding onto green leaves. Yerba mansa's transformation occurs in tandem with the entire riparian forest as fall colors emerge everywhere, revealing the seasonal beauty of New Mexico's desert valley and exposing views of the Sandia Mountains backdrop.

FIGURE 31 Autumn yerba mansa (*Anemopsis californica*) meets a saltgrass (*Distichlis spicata*) meadow and cottonwood (*Populus deltoides wislizenii*) forest. Photo by author.

Yerba mansa exemplifies how much we can learn about plants as medicines by cultivating an understanding of them ecologically. (A full account of yerba mansa appears in the materia medica.) Observing this plant in the wild, its favored habitat conditions, and its interconnections with other elements of the landscape illuminates its personality and provides implications for its functions in the bodily ecosystem. In its wild habitats yerba mansa enhances the wet boggy earth by absorbing and distributing water and adding antimicrobial and purifying elements to the damp and slow-moving ecosystem. In the Rio Grande bosque, yerba mansa's rhizomes and roots spread through thick, nearly impenetrable, claylike soil, altering and energizing the earth, pioneering foundational changes so that others can gain their own foothold for growth. Once a colony is established, it alters the soil chemistry and organisms, creating an environment more favorable to the growth of other plants by acidifying and aerating the soil. It functions similarly inside the ecosystems of our bodies by regulating the flow of waters, encouraging the movement of stagnant fluids, moving toxins, and inhibiting harmful pathogens while warming and stimulating sluggish functions in the body. Just as yerba mansa contributes to foundational soil conditions where it grows, it also has the ability to tone and tighten the mucous membranes, improving baseline health and safeguarding against microbial imbalances. These characteristics ultimately stimulate, cleanse, disinfect, and strengthen the system, thereby reducing inflammatory responses in the environment and in our bodies. With these attributes that invigorate the overall health of an organism or ecosystem, yerba mansa is of great importance medicinally and ecologically. Yerba mansa's ability to spread into new areas, compete with established thickets of coyote willow or native grasses, and imbed itself into the terrain, slowly transforming and vitalizing it, hints at its potential workings in cancer treatments.

Wild landscapes and the plants that reside there have stories to tell. They may be ancient tales of oceans rising and receding, or of relatively recent raging rivers remaking a valley by force. They may even hint at water hidden underground. Plants may tell us about the changing earth, help us integrate new kinds of knowledge about the world, and ultimately show us new things about ourselves. Ecological medicinal plant stories can help us understand the connection between wild medicinal plants, the land, and ourselves as the same adaptations and phytochemistry that help them thrive in their environments also heal the land and people. Additionally, these stories give clues to the history, present, and possible future of the plants we love every day. They illuminate the personalities, strengths, and vulnerabilities of the plants we use as food and medicine, and help us work with them more effectively and more respectfully. As we become more aware of these workings in the natural world around us, we become more deeply connected to the system of interactions between people, plants, and the land. We become ecological herbalists.

CHAPTER THREE

Reconnecting with Living Landscapes

In the preceding chapter we explored examples of dynamic landscapes, key medicinal plants, and the interactions taking place between them. Let us not forget that we are important parts of these landscapes and their ecological functioning. The way we view these places and interact with them has consequences for us and the rest of the natural world. When we walk through the wilds, the extent of our knowledge and the depth of our passion affect the way we experience and feel about that place. Our perception shapes who we are, forms our guiding principles, and motivates our actions. Who will value the land if they do not understand it, appreciate it, or recognize their interconnectedness with it? Those who see themselves as part of a living landscape, sharing vital forces and ancient memories with soil, landforms, water, plants, and animals, know the intimacy of relationship with land and embrace a way of being that respects all components in the network of life. As herbalists, botanical observers, or naturalists, our bond with plants may be what moves us into connection with the land. The privilege of that relationship comes with an opportunity to advance our practice beyond the realm of everyday herbalism or wildflower identification, deepening our connectivity with the larger ecological system and showing others the path. As environmental imbalances grow, local plant communities change, and our practical considerations shift, we may feel a growing sense of urgency to embrace new approaches in our work and individual actions. Part of this evolution must include accepting an expanded role of advocating for the entire living landscape, home of medicinal plants and cradle of our own existence.

As a living entity, the land has always been dynamic, ever shifting and readjusting according to its own intuition and environmental conditions. From arid grasslands to the mountains and river valleys, the habitats of many medicinal plants in the American West are changing. These changes are occurring at a more rapid rate and in more dramatic ways than ever before. People alive today are experiencing, in some cases, a total remaking of the landscapes around them as devastating wildfires, widespread floods, large-scale tree die-offs, and other disasters converge with decades of land and water use that depletes the vitality and recuperative energy of the land. As discussed in the previous chapter, many of us have witnessed the transformation of familiar places and the remaking of plant communities we have known and loved, seeing them redesigned by the forces of widespread cattle grazing on marginal lands, heat-driven drought, overconsumed and mismanaged waterways, the grinding expansion of nonnative species into new areas, and other anthropogenic factors. The 2018 National Climate Assessment reported that in the Southwest, the amount of land burned by wildfires had doubled since 1984, tree death in mid-elevation coniferous forests had doubled since 1955, and water storage in Lake Mead and Lake Powell had been reduced to the lowest levels since the reservoirs were first filled (USGCRP 2018).

Clearly a change in paradigm is needed for us to more effectively confront such large-scale and potentially life-altering issues, to reawaken our sense of connectivity to the land, and ultimately to protect the integrity of the web of life. A solid foundation and inspiration for our continuing advancement toward that goal can be found within the enduring philosophies of indigenous groups, who have long understood the elements of nature as kin, as well as in the subsequent writings of environmental theorists. Alexander von Humboldt, whose work in the early 1800s influenced many other environmental writers, including Emerson, Thoreau, and Muir, was perhaps the first to formally discuss nature as an interconnected web of life including humans. Humboldt's ideas were shaped, in part, by observing the catastrophic effects that colonization had on the land and culture of Native inhabitants and by witnessing the disconnection of people from the land. Building upon this concept of interrelations, Aldo Leopold's (1970 [1949]) land ethic redefined the extent of our community to include the entire landscape; that is, it encompasses not only ourselves but also flora, fauna, soils, waters, the land, and all life that emanates from it. The land is seen as a dynamic system of flowing energy linking all forms of life. It is capable of slow evolutionary adaptations to maintain its vitality but is also subject to the rapid and shocking alterations imposed by humanity, resulting in ecological imbalances such as those previously described. Leopold called these imbalances "releases of biotic capital" (1970 [1949]:255), which ultimately lead to unintended and wide-reaching consequences for the environment, a reality with which humanity is now coming to terms. As the specter of climate change looms, Leopold's call for people to take responsibility for the health of the land—treating it with care as a living entity, protecting its ability to adjust and renew itself in response to changes—is paramount. This viewpoint further changes the ecological role of each human, from that of subjugator of nature to that of a "plain member or citizen of it" (240) and entails respect for the community itself and for its individual components. This ethic also implies an obligation to interact with the land in a way that goes beyond selfish motivations and instead considers the best interests of the entire system. Leopold noted, however, that "no important change in ethics was ever accomplished without an internal change in our emphasis, loyalties, affections, and convictions" (246). How then do we go about creating this internal change that will expand our community consciousness to include our interconnection with the living landscape as a whole?

Leopold hinted at an answer when he wrote, "It seems inconceivable to me that an ethical relationship to the land can exist without love, respect, and admiration for the land, and a high regard for its value ... in the philosophical sense" (1970 [1949]:261). He further suggested that the remedy is moving past an economic view of the land and incorporating use patterns that also preserve the health, ecological functionality, and beauty of the land. While this is a step in the right direction, it does not address the need to stir the minds and hearts of people in a manner that will produce the kind of deeply rooted change in consciousness that Leopold described as necessary for an authentic land ethic to take hold. The social evolution of this ethic must continue to advance toward one that moves individuals en masse in a profound way. The opportunity to undergo our own personal transformation and to assist others in making this change is always available to us and may be simpler and more accessible than we think.

There are, of course, innumerable pathways to regaining our connection to the land. For some, this will entail a process of the mind: studying, learning, and investigating whatever can be known through observation and scientific endeavors. This unending process of acquiring knowledge forms critical threads in our tapestry of understanding the living landscape and provides the necessary foundation for improving the health and resiliency of the biotic system. Intellectual inquiry also facilitates the kind of intimacy that moves us to revere the land deeply as we begin to understand the complexities of our world and to soak up the beauty and wonder inherent in its existence. It is our responsibility as citizens of the land to obtain some level of familiarity with these threads of knowledge and to share what we know as much as possible. For others, reconnecting with the land is an undertaking led primarily by the emotional heart. Immersing ourselves in the exquisite physical forms and vital interactions of the living landscape and allowing ourselves to be moved by its sheer beauty, we find another path to that transformation. This is a process of

FIGURE 32 Alpine meadow in the San Juan Mountains of Colorado. Photo by author.

present-moment sensory immersion. It is proclaimed by the aromatic particles of silvery sagebrush that usher us into oneness with the flowing energy of the land; annunciated by the desert light steadily creeping across the canyon wall, revealing a fluid palette of ever-changing colors hidden in the story of rocks; whispered by the droplets of river water softly caressing plant roots with the gift of life as they relentlessly move on toward a distant destination. By enveloping ourselves in the sensual interactions of life and allowing new realizations or visions to rise up from the landscape and flow through us, we form additional threads that further expand and fortify the tapestry of our understanding. By weaving our lives with any of these threads, the internal change that Leopold sought to expand community consciousness is within reach.

If filling our minds with knowledge and flooding our hearts with passion underlie the societal change required to advance a sincere land ethic, what tools can we provide people to facilitate and motivate their individual transformations? How can we lead ourselves and others back into deep relationship with the land? Walking across a high alpine meadow filled with blooming wildflowers, you might experience the cacophonous din of diverse and vibrant life forms interacting with one another. You may feel the reverberations of boundless vitality penetrate you, luring you into oneness with the meadow underfoot and the overarching sky. Experiences such as this can be had anytime and anywhere through the processes of "unselfing" (Murdoch,

2014 [1970]) and "interbeing" (Nhat Hanh 2001, 2002). These practices of engaging life beyond the boundaries of the individualized self evoke a state of mindfulness and embodied sensory awareness that opens our capacity for reconnecting with our natural surroundings. Embracing this approach deepens our place-based wisdom, redirects our energy back into a reciprocal exchange with life, creates a foundation for solving current environmental issues, and illuminates our true nature, inviting us into a limitless world beyond our wildest dreams.

Looking outside ourselves to realize our interconnections with the world around us is nothing new. Trees have been doing it for eons and bacteria for even longer. Life does not grow in a vacuum, and living beings exist because of the community to which they belong. That is to say, trees, humans, and other life forms have both endogenous and exogenous sources of knowledge and assistance that help them to survive and thrive despite the difficulties and challenges that present themselves. As Haskell (2017) described, the ponderosa pine (*Pinus ponderosa*) survives in locations with hot dry summers through a combination of internal wisdom and mechanisms, with help from an external complex of soil organisms, including mycelia. When afternoon showers are absent and its own water-saving strategies are not enough, the tree is nevertheless able to obtain moisture through its own deep and spreading root structure, augmented by a vast network of fungi that, using electrical charges, draws water from the depths upward through the mycelium and into the tree roots. The ponderosa pine also sustains itself through a relationship with fire. Before fire suppression policies and modern forces of climate change, forest fires tended to occur much more frequently, regularly consuming fuel in smaller amounts and clearing the understory but causing little harm to tree canopies. This fire pattern aided the ponderosa, whose thick bark and high branches protected it while the forest floor was cleared to prevent overcrowding. Thus the ponderosa makes itself stronger and more successful through external relationships and interconnectedness with other living systems.

Like the ponderosa pine, people have also been thriving for millions of years, in part due to a multitude of relationships with other organisms and vital processes. Our ability to use tools, our advancing intellect, and many other endogenous assets have no doubt helped us to evolve into the widespread species we are today, but we could not have made it on our own. Our interconnection with plants provides critical resources for our survival, nourishing our bodies with vitamins, minerals, sugars, and refreshed oxygen. Nothing illustrates more clearly the profound impact of the interrelations between

FIGURE 33 Ponderosa pine (*Pinus ponderosa*). Photo by author.

humans and plants than the process of respiration. In a deeply intimate exchange, the reciprocal giving and receiving of life force among species through the flow of oxygen and carbon dioxide forms a profound bond. What memories or ancient truths may be imprinted upon these gaseous molecules flowing freely between plants and people may never be proven but can certainly be known through a oneness that transcends species. It is these essential exogenous relationships and interactions that provide an access point for reconnecting to life and land as well as a foundation for unselfing and interbeing.

How can we come to such a place of mutual understanding between our egocentric selves and the rest of the living world? Cutting through the layers of self, eventually coming out the other side, and rediscovering our connection with all beings and life systems is a multifaceted process of letting go of what gets in the way. Most of us spend our days engaged in distractions, limited by coping mechanisms and developing defenses to life's difficulties. This process ultimately moves us away from that eternal connection to life and hinders our ability to connect with other vital entities and places. As an English speaker, I am keenly aware that language can be a barrier to recognizing the value of life outside ourselves. Except for humans (and perhaps our pets), we refer to life as "it," implying the lifelessness of the rest of the world and our separateness from it. Researching and learning deeply about what interests us most is one aspect of pursuing a relationship with our environment, as it brings us an understanding of what a place is and how it functions. Furthermore, moving past our minds, allowing our hearts to take the lead, and letting our senses loose to perceive beauty in the world around us puts us back on the path to reconnection. You do not have to be in an alpine wildflower meadow to do this. A yerba mansa (*Anemopsis californica*) plant in the backyard garden fills the air with its pleasing pungent aroma, steeping my lungs in the plant's vitality and drawing me in for a closer look. Entranced

FIGURE 34 Yerba mansa (*Anemopsis californica*) flower. Photo by author.

by the radiant glow of the gleaming white flowers, I discover an otherworldly range of colors, containing all the hues of the universe. In this moment, I am yerba mansa, and the rest of the world dissolves. Perceiving beauty and wonder in the world brings us out of ourselves and allows us to rejoin the larger biological network, becoming less individuals and more part of an interconnected system. It sets us free to imagine how a tree experiences its surroundings or to contemplate what it feels like for a river to move freely toward its delta. Novelist and philosopher Iris Murdoch (2014 [1970]) referred to this as a process of unselfing, or transcending your individuality or even your own species to become part of the entire community of life. Murdoch describes a moment of seeing a kestrel in flight. Immersed in its pure beauty, she forgets about what worries her. Nothing exists except the kestrel, and when it flies away, she has gained a new perspective. The experience of unselfing allows us to embrace an herbal practice based on interconnection not only with plants but also with entire ecosystems or places. When we are in tune with and engaged in sustained mindful observation and deliberate interaction with our surroundings, we begin to acknowledge that we are a natural part of ecosystem functions (for better or for worse) and we can discern when those systems are out of balance. This allows us to share in the wisdom of the land as we deepen our relationship with the wilds and develop new understanding about how plants work as medicines. This gift also bestows upon us the responsibility to transform our egocentric perspective into an ecocentric one in which we act in ways that nurture the health of plants and the systems that support them through respectful interactions and working toward more sustainable environmental policies. Ultimately the process of unselfing invites us into ascension beyond ourselves, where our relationships are formed and our insights are gained through profound connections to the network of life.

Interbeing is similar to unselfing in that it moves us outside of ourselves as individuals and into the collective consciousness of life. This idea is based upon the notion that there is no birth or death—that birth is simply the continuation of something that has always existed in some form and that death is a transformation of that thing into something else. Buddhist monk and peace activist Thich Nhat Hanh (2001, 2002) provided many examples of this, including an ocean wave. A wave is born of the collective ocean water, rises, crests, crashes, and returns to the ocean water only to be reborn again and again. He furthered this notion by describing a wave as interbeing with the ocean, clouds, rain, earth's atmosphere, the moon, and beyond. Since we are also made of water, this example includes us too. Likewise, when we pick an edible fruit or wildflower and eat it, we are interbeing with that plant, the soil, pollinating critters, oxygen, rain, clouds, sunshine, and the entire cosmos that is interconnected with and played a part in the fruit's or flower's existence. We may be able to see our own interconnection with plants, but if we take that further and extend it to all living systems, our interbeing is infinite and possibilities are limitless. We not only see ourselves as part of nature, but we can see the interconnectedness of everything, including our own actions. This understanding allows us to look into a sunflower, see the seed, and realize that we are looking into eternity. Seeds hold the essence of innumerable generations of sunflowers, all born from the sun's enduring cosmic energy, just as the atoms inside our own bodies are. As noted by astronomer Carl Sagan (2000 [1980]), "The beauty of a living thing is not the atoms that go into it but the way those atoms are put together. The cosmos is also within us. We're made of star stuff. We are a way for the cosmos to know itself." When we apply this kind of thinking to our herbal practice, we can easily slip out of ourselves and into the ecosystems and lands around us and see infinite possibilities for wisdom, harmony, and fulfillment in our wild nature and the limitlessness of life. We can share our being with that of the plants we love, the river that nourishes life, or the land that sustains us all. As Thich Nhat Hahn reminded us, we can become solid like the mountain or fresh like an opening blossom. We can embody the qualities of the river, unyielding, relentlessly moving toward its goal, employing patient softness to wear down even the hardest of obstacles. Through interbeing we return to the source of life for a clearer understanding of plants, places, ecosystems, and ourselves.

Through this practice of unselfing or interbeing we can move beyond the individualized self by reconnecting with the universal wild nature within us, thereby recognizing that we are inseparable from the rest of the natural world. This reconnecting fosters deep relationships with rivers, mountains, canyons, forests, and wildflower meadows while allowing us to see ourselves as part of those ecosystems. Leaving behind the notion that we are somehow separate from life systems, the disrupters or tarnishers of wildness, we can begin to see our actions, including the

FIGURE 35 Sunflower.
Photo by author.

damming of flowing steams and the logging of forests, as acts derived from wildness. If we accept that the massive eruptions of prehistoric volcanoes and their accompanying large-scale remaking of the landscape, including extinctions, are natural events, then so too is the paving of cities around the world invented and undertaken by primate minds and hands. The difference is that we can actively decide to make changes in the way we live our lives. With this understanding we are open to value the heavily altered riparian corridor as much as the remote national park lands, and we can begin the difficult job of evaluating and reconsidering our role in these places. As Thich Nhat Hanh (2015) succinctly stated in a speech before the United Nations, "Only when we've fallen back in love with the earth will our actions spring from reverence and the insight of our interconnectedness." Through this paradigm of recognizing our full integration with wildness and our natural place within ecosystem functions we can not only deepen our relationship with place and medicinal plants but also make more insightful decisions about how to mitigate or solve the environmental problems our modern way of living has created.

All meaningful relationships must be reciprocal, involving a mutually sustaining exchange of give and take. How long can a largely one-sided relationship endure? That is modern humanity's great question. To reconnect with place, we must rediscover the reciprocal flow between life, land, and self. We can begin by learning as much as possible, falling in love with life (not limited to our own lives), and realizing that we can turn the subsequent gifts of that process into actions that revitalize land, plants, water, animals, and therefore ourselves. Moving beyond the idea that we are distinct from or elevated above the rest of life and reentering the ancient reality in which plants existed and began acquiring wisdom long before humans allows us to learn and grow in harmony with the places in which we live. It affords the opportunity to create a mutually beneficial relationship with place and all life, which facilitates becoming rooted in your locale, regardless of where you grew up or where your ancestors originated. As noted by plant ecologist and Potawatomi Nation member Robin Wall Kimmerer, "Reciprocal restoration [of land and culture] has the potential to occur within mainstream society by engaging people with the land, renewing the human-place connection, and enabling people to reclaim their responsibility for sustaining the land that sustains them" (2011:271–72). Unselfing and interbeing ultimately facilitate the transformation of humanity's role in the world; we become a healing force for the land rather than subjugating it as a commodity.

These practices, available to us in any moment, will refocus our values, encourage actions that consider the well-being of the entire biotic community, and elevate our interconnectedness with the living landscape. Furthermore, when we embrace this way of being, we open ourselves to the experience of developing "ecosystem empathy." In my view, this term indicates a state of being in which a person is attuned to the flow of energy through a landscape and feels the movement of life and vitality within the land. In this state, a person may feel physically or emotionally unwell when the ecological system is out of balance. As members of the ecological community, we may experience varying degrees of empathy. While few of us can claim to hear a datura blossom opening in the

FIGURE 36 Datura (*Datura wrightii*) flower. Photo by author.

darkness of night, it is not a far reach for most of us to stand with our bare feet in a cool mountain stream and feel the revitalization that the water brings to all it touches. The more time we spend in the places we love, the more aware we become of the forces of life emanating from the land and what role we are playing within the dynamic system. Through the experience of ecosystem empathy, we can see clearly that environmental degradation contributes to our own suffering and that caring for the land is nurturing ourselves. Given the simultaneous rise in chronic inflammatory illness and decline in environmental health, it could be that many of us are experiencing a form of ecosystem empathy without being overtly aware of it. Whatever our level and experience of empathy, it brings us closer to that fundamental societal shift, the expansion of community consciousness required for meaningful changes in policy, land use, and individual action to occur.

Today, fiercely passionate love, loyalty, and dedication to the living landscape are required more than ever. As herbalists or simply as citizens, it is part of our calling to rejoin this system of life fully and completely. We must rediscover our oneness with the whole biotic community and acknowledge the continuum of experience that binds us to plants, landforms, water, animals, and all other elements of the vital world. Such a sincere and transformative reconnection will inevitably compel us to live in ways that contribute to the healing and strengthening of the land and all emanating life, including our own. In this way, we become honored assistants and guardians of the wild plants we love as well as caretakers of the soil, rivers, rocks, pollinators, atmosphere, sun, and clouds that support them. To do so is both fulfilling an obligation to the web of life and indulging in the overwhelming vitality that feeds us the necessities of life, including inspiration and joy.

CHAPTER FOUR

Rooted in Relationships with the Land and Plants

Once we have a pathway to a united and integrated experience with the land and plants, we can explore the kinds of relationships that develop from it. These relationships can manifest in innumerable and highly personalized ways, illuminating aspects of ourselves as well as the character of the plants and landscapes we know best. Each landscape and each plant species has its own unique personality and way of reaching us to solicit our attention, build relationships, and maintain our commitment. Depending on our own communication preferences and openness, we may enter into connection through a multitude of means, including receptivity through dreamtime, meditations, contemplations, research, heartfelt emotions, creative processes, or other avenues. Our individualized ways of being will inevitably result in bonds that are unique, revealing facets of ourselves and the living entities to which we relate. When you are rooted in relationships with the land and plants, you become aware of the union of your being with the entire biological world and see your entangled and interdependent well-being. Plants and the land can serve as facilitators of deep transformations, and it is within this state of consciousness that the best medicine is made and the most vibrant and awakened life is lived. Following are three short stories from the middle Rio Grande Valley that illuminate the kinds of relationships that can be forged between the living landscape and ourselves.

ENCHANTED BY JUNIPER
(*Juniperus monosperma*) AND THE SCRUBLANDS

Multilayered sunsets, panoramic lightning storms, and cool raindrops under warm sunny skies are all reasons to fall in love with the Southwest, but it is the dusty, rusty red mesas dotted with deep green aromatic shrubs in the piñon juniper woodlands that capture my imagination. It is the rocky, bubbly, black basalt mesa speckled with silvery sand sage (*Artemisia filifolia*), the golden snakeweed (*Gutierrezia sarothrae*), and the sporadic juniper of the desert mesa that make me feel at home. In this world of sensory immersion, we are invited to explore more than our minds can ever tell us. The dramatic color contrasts between the soil and vegetation and sky are visually striking. The stimulating effect of the aromatic shrubs wafts throughout the land, moving vital energy across the landscape, merging our thoughts and feelings with the echoes of all that has ever been in this place. The sensation of still warm air against the skin, instantly replaced by a chilly and shadowy breeze as dark clouds move across the sky, brings a new state of awareness. All these experiences bring us into the present moment, where all things are possible. We find ourselves in a world reverberating with the boundless energy of the living land and its vivacious companions, diplomats from all the kingdoms of life.

The first juniper to become a personal figure in my life is located in the desert scrublands at the edge of a large volcanic mesa in a wide canyon created by the curvaceous edge of a once-fluid lava flow. The singular large juniper is a reliable old friend, providing the only shady respite in my regular hike across this hot and exposed landscape. Stepping into its shade is immediate relief from the relentless sun and visible heat of the desert canyon. A sense of recuperation and relaxation comes over me every time I sit in the sand under its branches. Each visit leaves a touch of gratitude behind to linger in the woody soul of the juniper and filter into the heart of the ancient basalt landscape. This land was formed as the earth's crust pulled apart, creating a long rift between the Colorado Plateau and the Great Plains. Here rivers converged, bringing with them the sand and gravel sediments from nearby mountains and mesas to create the Santa Fe Formation. Sometime between

CHART 1 *Albuquerque Elevation Profile / West to East*

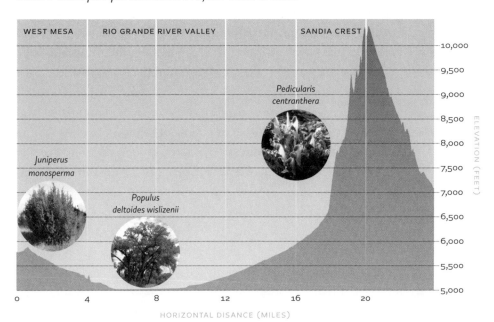

FIGURE 37
Juniper (*Juniperus monosperma*).
Photo by author.

160,000 and 200,000 years ago, fissures formed in the thin crust of the rift zone, allowing magma to rise to the surface and ooze eastward toward the valley overlaying these sediments (Kelley and Kudo 1978). As the lava cooled and solidified, it formed the volcanic cones, numerous vents, the basalt mesa, and the winding rugged escarpment of Albuquerque's West Mesa. These gentle eruptions occurred in at least eight distinct flows, leaving behind a variety of volcanic iterations, including the five cinder and spatter cones that define Albuquerque's western skyline, the dramatic boulder fields with high and steep slopes at the south end, and the relatively gentle sloping basaltic escarpment at the northern end. Flows from these fissure eruptions created a volcanic field that covers twenty-three square miles today but was once likely much larger, before the eastern edge was eroded by the waters of the Rio Grande (Kelley and Kudo 1978). Dotted throughout the landscape are numerous archaeological remains, from all known periods of occupation and spanning at least twelve thousand years of human history.

Walking across the top of this rocky mesa, the whole world seems to come into focus: this vast open stretch of land at the edge of the canyon-filled Colorado Plateau, gritty volcanic cinder cones, meandering canyons created by the cooled edges of the lava that once seeped from these cones and vents, a flowing cottonwood-lined river valley below, foothills rising in the distance,

FIGURE 38 *opposite* Albuquerque's West Mesa escarpment (basalt) with sage (*Artemisia filifolia*), snakeweed (*Gutierrezia sarothrae*), and broom dalea (*Psorothamnus scoparius*). Photo by author.

and towering peaks of the fault-block uplift mountains that line the opposite side of the middle Rio Grande Valley. Beyond view lie the treeless expanses of the Great Plains, the rugged *bajadas* of the Chihuahuan Desert, the high peaks of the southern Rocky Mountains, and a continuum of the grandeur witnessed from this vantage point. At the center of all of this is a place where earth's innermost self is on display, a landscape that reveals its deepest workings and its machinations that create the land anew. The edge of this volcanic escarpment is home to more than twenty-five thousand petroglyphs, pecked into the blackened desert varnish that covers the rocks, formed of the cooled liquid life force that once roiled inside earth with such passion that it spilled beyond its confines. These rocks are now potentiated by images that not only signify the continuum of generations but also represent the union of people and the land. The volcanic vents are conduits for the very breath of earth, evoking the most intimate exchange of life force, a place where memories so ancient come to light that we have no words for such truths. We can only feel them in our deepest primordial tissue and know instinctively that they are real, immediate, and entire. How could a place so abrasive to the touch, so arduous to hike across, so persistent and inflexible, so uncompromising and enduring be so willing to welcome me, embrace me, and shape me according to its own image, characterized by passionate fires churning below the surface, spilling out to remake the localized world within its reach?

Despite these potent experiences, many years passed before I came to realize my relationship with juniper. One spring day I was filled with thoughts of this plant, as if it were calling me relentlessly. I headed out to the foothills, collected some fresh branches, and made juniper oil. The intimacy of covering my body in juniper's tacky resin and powerful scent creates an intense closeness that lures us into deep relationship. The effect is immediate and comprehensive, a transformation of the physical, emotional, and mental states. The potent aromatic particles move awareness into the physical body, bringing me into a state of physical awakening, conjuring the duality of stimulation accompanied by desire and relaxation coupled with fulfillment. Enveloped in the enchanting scent of juniper, the musculature relaxes; the flow of energy opens; emotions, thoughts, movement, and creativity become fluid. Juniper is protective, offering refuge and comfort when one feels exposed or vulnerable. Just as it softens the harshness of a desert environment with nurturing shade for more delicate herbaceous members of the plant community, it envelops me in sensual loving energy so that I may thrive and reach my full potential as any supportive life partner would do. In the shelter of juniper I can relax my defenses and accept the invitation of protected vulnerability. Juniper's persistent and ever-present courtship is exemplified by its own nature; its ability to withstand drought and hard times characterizes its reliable presence in my life and reminds me that I can count on this unwavering relationship. With such a show of enduring loyalty, I know I have been safeguarded, shielded, protected all these years since I met that

FIGURE 40
West Mesa volcanoes with snakeweed (*Gutierrezia sarothrae*) and the Sandia Mountains. Photo by author.

lone juniper on the edge of the volcanic mesa. Juniper has slowly enchanted me and actively courted me with offerings to rival those of any other suitor.

MENTORED BY THE MOUNTAIN
AND PEDICULARIS *(Pedicularis centranthera)*

Standing on a rocky outcrop near the crest overlooking the sprawling city of modern Albuquerque, I am aware that I have left one world and entered another. Nearly eleven thousand feet above sea level, I am well removed from life on the hot valley floor. Cool thin air enters my lungs and misty clouds enshroud the mountain face below while clear blue sunny skies expand above. Hints of citrus hang in the air as towering conifers draped in the lacy effects of green-gray usnea lichen call from the forest behind me. The rocky cliffs below host an array of usual and peculiar plants that found a foothold on the edge of life and now overlook the myriad worlds that converge in central New Mexico. Here, in this crossroads, all things come together in an alchemical fashion, within the land and myself. From this peak one can see the interconnection of all places as the mountain becomes foothills that transition to uplands that merge with the floodplain that abuts the volcanic mesa and on and on beyond the horizon. I become everything all at once, and the possibilities seem infinite. All the while, my feet are firmly planted on rocks that hold the secrets of ancient seas and the immortalized remains of life before earth ever dreamed of humans. The connection between seemingly distant worlds is nevertheless present way up here, as indicated by the ancient sea creatures fossilized in the Permian limestone outcrops that formed hundreds

FIGURE 41
View of
Albuquerque from
Sandia Crest.
Photo by author.

of millions of years ago. Just like the petroglyph boulders on the West Mesa, which I see across the valley, these rocks connect us to the past, present, and future. This living limestone was formed during a time when sea life dominated the planet, and now it crowns an arid desert mountain and makes a home for the queen of the Sandias, coral bells (*Huechera pulchella*). This rare endemic plant grows only in these limestone outcrops on two adjacent mountain ranges. Its presence is just one reason this place is so special. From this vantage point, one can take in a dramatic landscape with a continuous human history of varying cultures dating back to the earliest of times: nomadic Paleo-Indian hunters visiting nearby caves and playas, Pueblo farmers from all directions coalescing along the fertile lands of the Rio Grande floodplain, Great Plains traders and raiders passing through, Hispanic migrants coming up the valley from Mexico, and Anglo settlers traversing the continent from the east. It is also a place where flora from the surrounding bioregions converges to create a truly distinctive environment.

FIGURE 42   Coral bells (*Huechera pulchella*). Photo by author.

Rising above the desert valley, the Sandia range and its sister range to the south, the Manzanos, are at once typical of landforms across the Desert Basin and Range system and yet are entirely unique in this world. Like all other mountains in the Southwest, the rising elevations provide varied habitats for large numbers of plant species, including pedicularis species that evolved in isolated cooler and wetter locations with expansive dry basins between them. Unlike any of the other mountains in the area, however, the Sandias are located at the juncture of several completely distinct physiographic regions of the continent, including the Rocky Mountains to the north, the Great Plains to the east, and the Colorado Plateau to the north and west, with the Desert Basin and Range continuing to the south and west (see Map 2). Together these two mountain ranges extend sixty miles along the eastern flank of the Rio Grande Valley and include the thirty-eight-thousand-acre Sandia Mountain Wilderness and the thirty-seven-thousand-acre Manzano Mountain Wilderness. Formed 25 million years ago as uplifted fault-block mountains along the Rio Grande Rift, these mountains are distinct from the neighboring Rockies in their origin and history. The steep slope of the western face exposes Precambrian granite, 1.45 billion years old, and the 10,687-foot Sandia Peak is capped with the previously mentioned Pennsylvanian limestone and sea fossils dating from 300 million years ago. A bimodal precipitation regime with late summer rains and winter snow produces nearly twenty-three inches of annual precipitation near the crest (Sivinski 2007). Diurnal temperature differences of thirty degrees, great temperature ranges between sun and shade, high-velocity spring windstorms, more than 320 sunny or partly sunny days per year, and summer deluges with high levels of moisture runoff all add up to unique growing conditions (Watson 1912). The combined influences of these vastly different neighboring ecosystems and local environmental influences create a distinctive plant community in the Sandia and Manzano Mountains that is unlike any other. Although the Rocky Mountain plant communities to the north have the greatest influence, representatives from all the nearby physiographic regions contribute to the Sandia and Manzano flora, with numerous species meeting the edge of their geographical ranges in these mountains (Sivinski 2007). The Sandias and Manzanos are home to one-quarter of all flora in the state, providing habitat for numerous species with limited ranges, including several endemic to New Mexico, such as *Scrophularia montana* (figwort) and the strikingly beautiful *Heuchera pulchella* (coral bells), found only in the Sandia and Manzano Mountains (Sivinski 2007).

This landscape highlighting earth's ancient history, the merging of distinct bioregions, and the coming together of unique plant communities is an awe-inspiring place. The exposed silvery limestone caprock intimates a life of reinventing oneself, slowly and patiently evolving from a living community of organisms thriving underneath the depths of ancient ocean waters to become vital energy frozen in time and lifted up through dry air to kiss the cloudless desert sky. These creatures and sediments transformed into living stone illustrate on the geological time scale how we come to play new and different roles as we move through our own lives, becoming what we are destined to be. My union with Sandia's limestone peak is a process of my own becoming, one in which I reinvent myself as new influences enter my life and I embrace the forces of change that drive my own evolution. The merging of diverse bioregions and plant communities, including the presence of *Pedicularis centranthera* in this harmonious chorus of voices, serves as a model for fostering culturally diverse yet unified and cohesive communities in modern civilization and offers lessons in how I can help promote this where I live.

FIGURE 43 Pedicularis (*Pedicularis centranthera*). Photo by author.

The many species of pedicularis are the coordinators

of their biological communities. On the physical plane, they are hemiparasitic plants that reach out through root structures called haustoria to make connections with other plants in their environment. Through this underground networking, pedicularis takes resources from the strongest, most dominant members and reallocates them to benefit the entire biotic community (Schneider and Stermitz 1990). In doing so, it attracts more pollinators, increases the flowering and fruiting of less common species of plants, and enhances the overall biodiversity of the area (Hedberg et al. 2005; Laverty 1992). Pedicularis demonstrates the assets and benefits of a skilled community coordinator that brings the best out of everyone and helps to create a network of life that is stronger, more productive, and more resilient. *Pedicularis centranthera* is a small member of this genus that dons white flowers with spectacular magenta tips and small fern-like leaves. This species prefers the semiarid lower-elevation pine and oak forests in the Sandia Mountains and is usually seen growing in undisturbed areas with pine needle mulch. Capitalizing on early spring moisture from snow cover and melting runoff, it is one of the first plants to flower in this ecosystem every year. It is further adapted to these warmer, drier elevations with its ability to shed its aboveground parts, retreat back into its roots, and disappear during the hottest months of summer. *P. centranthera* models the strategy of retreating periodically to rest and restore oneself to be ready when the seasonal burst begins anew. Like other members of the genus, its muscle relaxant properties open the gateway to the self, soften resistance and rigidity in the body, and unblock the corridors of vital energy that feed and nourish our thoughts and creativity, all deepening its revitalizing effects. Pedicularis lures the seeker into wild and undisturbed landscapes of the mountains and within the self, where the portals are wide open. Under this plant's influence, the teachings of the mountain mentor are clear: we are encouraged to join the underground world of intricate interactions, become leaders in community coordination, engage in periodic self-restoration, and contribute to the synergistic blossoming that resides in both the land and ourselves.

NURTURED BY COTTONWOOD (*Populus deltoides wislizenii*) AND THE RIPARIAN CORRIDOR

The slowly moving muddy waters of the river push onward, diverging around the sandbar and regrouping on the other side. Like the aromatic shrubs of the West Mesa in the distance, the water's rhythms gently carry the vital force of the land through time and space. The same collective waters course through my own body in a similar manner, delivering oxygen, nutrients, and eternities of recycled earthly wisdom to the depths of my cellular structure. Lost in such thoughts, I am brought back to the outer world by the distant sounds of high-flying sandhill cranes, whose moving bodies reflect silvery light like sequins in the mid-afternoon sky. Here the sky has its own layers of landscape, as pure white cottony clouds drift across the background, migrating and resident birds pass by overhead, heart-shaped leaves dance from the arching branches of elder cottonwood trees in the foreground, and brilliant blue damselflies and silent mosquitoes swirl nearby. Knocking back my last sip of water, I find my thoughts drawn right back to the riverbank where life is sustained, including the life of the cottonwood, which nurtures much of the floodplain's livelihood. The Rio Grande bosque stands at the heart of the natural and cultural worlds of New Mexico. Despite more than a century of use that has significantly altered native plant communities (see chapter 2), it remains a critical natural habitat running through the center of urbanized areas and offers a much needed and easily accessible respite from daily life. The remnants of wildness that persist are home to cottonwood forests, saltgrass (*Distichlis spicata*) meadows, scattered fields of yerba mansa, and other treasures. In the modern world, where the influence of humanity reaches even the most remote areas, the bosque is a cherished place where one can remember our wild selves and feel the pulse of the land. Immersing myself in the rhythms of the flowing water, the migrations of birds overhead, and the cycles of familiar plants, I rediscover my home in the world along the banks of one of the West's great rivers. The Rio Grande is the third-longest river in the continental United States, with headwaters in the San Juan Mountains of southwestern Colorado. It runs south through New Mexico, along the borderlands between Texas and Mexico, and east to the Gulf of Mexico near Brownsville, Texas. This river flows through the Rio Grande Rift, a valley created 25 million years ago as earth's crust thinned and pulled apart. This process created a gap that was forty miles wide, several miles deep, and flanked by fault-block uplift mountain ranges to the east and volcanic features to the west. More than a million years ago, the flow of the Rio Grande entered the valley, bringing life-giving waters and sediments to reshape the terrain. Over time there evolved a unique ecosystem, with rich biodiversity derived from a variety of adjacent bioregions.

The riparian corridor is a place where life-sustaining elements move through the land, sometimes as scouring floodwaters that dramatically renew the environment, other times as a slow and deliberate nourishing act. This ebb and flow, with changing intentions and effects, is a defining characteristic of any healthy river and floodplain, including the Rio Grande. Here the

FIGURE 44
Rio Grande
with West Mesa
volcanoes in
background.
Photo by author.

desert bosque was once an oasis of plant diversity born from these oscillations and nurtured by the flow of water through the landscape. Carrying oxygen, nutrients, dynamic movement, and the ancient memories held within the land, it delivered the sustenance of life to all in its free-flowing days. Just as the river's wide meanders gather essential elements and bring new influences from multiple sources to reinvigorate life processes, I embrace the divergent paths available to me, sometimes creating new channels for exploration to collect knowledge, creativity, and motivation, delivering that back to the community in an alchemical fashion of reconfigured beauty and inspiration. I adopt the character of the river itself—relentlessly moving toward its destination, wearing down obstacles with gentle persistence or flowing around them with ease when appropriate, revitalizing and refreshing everything it touches—and I too move through life with ease, malleability, and determination, all the while offering the components I have gathered for others to grow and thrive as I have. Each single drop of water in a collective we call a river has individual memories of all the surfaces it has met, all the transformations it has made from vapor to water to ice, and all the bodies it has inhabited, and it integrates the combined wisdom of these ancient and enduring experiences. Our oneness with rivers allows us to share this collective memory, and this richness of life experience becomes our own. Communion with the river invites us to visualize and manifest our own free-flowing vitality, a paradoxical combination of opposing forces, both creative and destructive; ebbing and flowing as needed, sometimes lingering, absorbing, and contemplating while other times moving rapidly and recklessly through a stretch of

life as conditions permit or demand. This river coursing through the dry and unforgiving desert is the lifeblood of the land just as our empathic experience is the sustenance of interconnectivity within the biological system linking the entire network of life.

Walking through the understory of the Rio Grande bosque, the reaching branches of cottonwood trees wind through the clear blue sky overhead against a backdrop of migrating sandhill cranes, whose song now invokes a slow dance between the heavens and earth. The rough and furrowed bark, the tremendous trunks,

FIGURE 46. Cottonwood tree (*Populus deltoides wislizenii*) bud with resin. Photo by author.

and the curvaceous arms of the elders create a dramatic texture and graceful physical form that adds new layers of richness to the mosaic of sensory experiences of this place. The twisting, elegant branches seem to cut through the air the way roots move through the soil and water trickles across a sandy riverside beach, reminding us of the simple repeating and familiar patterns that define life. The desert light sparkling against the resinous leaf bud seems to reflect infinite truths gathered by the sun from distant places beyond the human imagination. This resin embodies the character of cottonwood as its medicine eases inflammation, discomfort, and pain. These interconnections draw me deeper into the domain of cottonwood, where the nurturing influence of this tree sustains life in the floodplain and has even come to characterize the culture of the people who live here. The mothering nature of cottonwood is reinforced as a fluttering leaf twirls through the air on its way to the forest floor with an effect as soft and caressing as a loving caretaker's touch, reassuring our deepest cellular structure that everything is as it should be. This message is comforting in a place suffering from extensive water diversions and other ecosystem alterations that impair the health and well-being of many native plants living here. As the nurturing influence of the cottonwood forest wanes along the banks of the Rio Grande, I am inspired to continue the loving work of facilitating life in this riparian corridor. We are drawn into the realm of the cottonwood just as we are drawn into the warm embrace of a loving grandmother to receive that which sustains our hearts and to honor the legacy of the matriarchs. The cottonwood is a model of maternal nurturance for all of us to emulate, showing us how to foster the next generation of life in our communities and in the land, inviting us to offer freely of ourselves so that others may grow and thrive, which benefits us all.

FIGURE 45 *opposite* Cottonwood tree (*Populus deltoides wislizenii*). Photo by author.

All of these relationships with plants and place are rooted in the philosophy of ecological herbalism and share the commonality of removing barriers between ourselves and the rest of the vital world. Plants and landscapes have the power to connect us with the past, present, and future and can teach us more than we might have ever expected. Our union with plants and the living land can enchant us, mentor us, nurture us, and so much more. Spending time in wild places, sitting with plants we love, we ultimately open ourselves up to the experience of selflessness, allowing that pattern to imprint itself within us. When we have rediscovered our connection with the living landscape, the boundaries between ourselves and the rest of the biological world dissolve and we gain access to the eternal wisdom that permeates every living being, including mesas, mountains, rivers, and ourselves. Ecological herbalism can take us there.

PART TWO

Knowing the Plants

CHAPTER FIVE

The Importance of Weeds, Commoners, and Wild-Spirited Gardens

Sustainability is under discussion in every area of our lives these days, and the practice of herbalism is no exception. It might be easy to think that herbalism is inherently sustainable. After all, we are using plants for health and wellness. But the growing popularity of natural forms of medicine, when added to expanding human populations and habitat destruction, is putting stress on wild plant populations. It is our responsibility to be aware of this trend, to understand how local plants may be affected, and to incorporate sustainable practices into our own herbal endeavors. One way to do this is to deepen our connections with the most common of plants—those we find living side by side with us in our everyday lives. Another is to create wild-spirited gardens to cultivate our most loved medicinal plants.

WORKING WITH WEEDS

Some of those pesky, weedy plants growing in your yard, garden, and wildlands actually make good medicine. Using these widely available, abundant, and potent plants saves you time and money, and they make effective medicine and help take the pressure off wild populations of less common plants. I particularly enjoy using weeds in my remedies because of their tenacious and persistent nature and their ability to adapt to wide-ranging conditions, thriving in even the most inhospitable of environments. I like imbuing my food and medicinal formulas with these plant personalities because we all need a little more resilience and adaptability at times. If we're looking for herbs to help us achieve success against the odds, we will find that medicine in ordinary weeds.

Our most common weeds are so successful that they are ubiquitous across much of the country. Dandelion (*Taraxacum officinale*) and clovers (*Trifolium* spp.) are familiar to most people, but plants considered to be weeds vary by region. For example, burdock (*Arctium lappa*), St. John's wort (*Hypericum*

FIGURE 47
Mallow (*Malva neglecta*). Photo by author.

perforatum), mullein (*Verbascum thapsus*), self-heal (*Prunella vulgaris*), nettles (*Urtica dioica*), and dock (*Rumex crispus*) are all useful herbs that are considered to be weeds in some areas. Local medicinal weeds commonly seen in the Southwest include dandelion, plantain (*Plantago major*), storksbill (*Erodium cicutarium*), purslane (*Portulaca oleracea*), shepherd's purse (*Capsella bursa-pastoris*), sweet clover (*Melilotus* spp.), mallow (*Malva neglecta*), and wild lettuce (*Lactuca serriola*). Collecting a basketful of these weedy herbs will provide you a wide variety of valuable and effective medicine.

COMMUNING WITH COMMONERS

When you walk near the edges of town or in the wildlands around your home, you will see the familiar faces of common plants in your bioregion. These are the plants that are best suited to your local environment and are therefore the most abundant in wild populations. Invite these commoners into your life and get to know them. Making these plants the foundational herbs in your practice allows plants with smaller populations to simply exist, to be there as teachers, or to be harvested in limited quantities for specific uses. Seek relationships with plants that are most adaptable and tolerant of a wide range of habitat conditions and those that accept our human propensity to disturb the earth. Some herbs, like mullein (*Verbascum thapsus*), are willing to pioneer the recovery of the most distressed areas, including those devastated by forest fires and the massive earthmoving that comes with road building and development. As more of our plant populations come under pressure, I turn to those plants that will be there for us now and in the future, the commoners.

Of course, the common plants vary from region to region too. I have seen the cleared hillsides of northern Appalachia submit to the reign of goldenrod (*Solidago* spp.) and have seen impenetrable fields of nettles (*Urtica*) in the North Woods. In the Southwest, it is common to see vibrant fields dotted with yarrow (*Achillea millefolium*), large stands of globemallow (*Sphaeralcea* spp.), vast expanses of sagebrush (*Artemisia tridentata*), overgrazed plains with snakeweed (*Gutierrezia sarothrae*) and prickly pear (*Opuntia* spp.), endless deserts dominated by creosote (*Larrea tridentata*), and woodlands rich with piñon pine (*Pinus edulis*) and juniper (*Juniperus monosperma*). Harvesting these abundant plants provides us with the makings of a rich and

wide-reaching apothecary. These herbs, along with my
other favorite commoners, help form the foundation of
my high desert herbal practice.

Weeds and common plants hold an esteemed place
in all bioregional herbal traditions. Bioregional herbalism
keeps at its heart the plants found in the surrounding environment. It makes us look beyond our textbooks to see the
teachers waiting for us in the suburban yards, urban parks,
and wildlands beyond. Seeking relationships with local
plants fosters a deep and powerful connection to our regional landscapes,
allowing us to become more acutely aware of the interbeing of plants, people,
and the land. Herbalism quickly crosses over from practical to spiritual when
you feel the life force of your food and medicine and its interconnection
with you and everything else in the living world. When I look to the future, I
see herbalists deepening relationships with weeds and other common local
plants, looking to herbal allies that will adapt to changing local environmental
conditions and those that thrive in the disturbed soils of earth's modern era.
In practicing herbalism with local plants that offer themselves so freely to us
and that harmonize with us in our increasingly urban lifestyles, we will find
the best medicine. We will find the beauty of bioregional herbal practice:
sustainable and affordable medicine that connects us to our local landscape,
protects vulnerable plant populations for the future, and returns us to our
place in the natural world. In practicing this way, we will find our wild selves
in harmony with our reliable old friends, the weeds and the commoners.

WILD-SPIRITED GARDENING

A sustainable herbal practice must include the cultivation of popular and
widely used herbs. Growing favorite medicinal plants in backyard gardens not
only provides a convenient and cost-effective source of fresh organic ingredients for remedies, but it also creates an opportunity to engage in a reciprocal
relationship of mutual care with the plants we love most. We can observe
plants in all their stages of growth, see how pollinators and other animals
interact with them, and gain insights about their behaviors and personalities.
All this results in a deepening of our relationship with plants and new realizations about their medicinal workings. Furthermore, most gardeners will agree
that maintaining a garden is enjoyable and relaxing, and it fosters a sense of
well-being. By gardening, we also invite a little bit of the beauty and wisdom
of our nearby wildlands into our everyday urban lives.

FIGURE 49
Wild-spirited
urban medicine
garden. Photo
by author.

Growing an urban medicine garden is like creating a dynamic and living artwork that integrates us with other elements of the biological world. We become part of its beauty, and by embracing what we learn from our wilderness experiences, we also incorporate the enduring vitality of the land into the creative process. In our gardens we can re-create some aspects of the wilderness we love by doing several things.

First, think about the health of the soil and amend it appropriately. You may need to add organic matter such as compost or horse manure. You will also want to consider the existing underground community of living organisms, including mycorrhiza. Urban soils often contain native mycelia, which we do not want to disturb through unnecessary or excessive tilling, fertilizing, or fungicide applications. Studies suggest that healthy mycelia bring numerous health benefits to medicinal plants, including protection against disease, increased biomass, and greater production of medicinal phytochemicals (Kapoor et al. 2007; Zeng et al. 2012; Zubek et al. 2012). Endophytic fungi residing within plant tissues bring similar benefits and have been shown in numerous studies to produce the same compounds as their hosts (or those that are similar), thereby potentiating the medicinal usefulness of plants (e.g., Venieraki et al. 2017).

Second, choose a selection of favorite native medicinal plants and possibly some desired garden herbs from other regions that are suited to your local climate. While native plants generally are our best medicines and provide the most suitable habitat for local birds and pollinators, many useful European and Asian medicinal plants grow well in western gardens and expand the potential of our apothecaries.

Third, observe wild habitat conditions for your desired native plants and re-create them, or chose locations in your garden that meet those needs. For example, you might build a shade ramada and grow a clematis vine over it to re-create a dappled light effect for higher-elevation forest understory plants. Or you might plant your favorite desert shrubs along a hot, south-facing wall to give them the most winter warmth.

Fourth, observe what plants grow together in the wild and plant them side by side in your garden. You may notice brook mint (*Mentha arvensis*), cutleaf coneflower (*Rudbeckia laciniata*), and horsetail (*Equisetum arvense*) growing together along mountain streams, or you might have observed globemallow (*Sphaeralcea* spp.), Dakota vervain (*Glandularia bipinnatifida*), and grindelia (*Grindelia squarrosa*) sharing space in the dry foothills.

Fifth, allow your gardening practices to be influenced by the wild habits of plants. Gardens are often limited in space, with many plants growing in close proximity. You will likely have to do some weeding and pushing back

TABLE 1 *Medicinal Plants for Southwest Gardens*

Alum root	Huechera spp.	Milk thistle	Silybum marianum
Angelica	Angelica archangelica, A. spp.	Milkweed	Asclepias speciosa, A. spp.
Anise hyssop	Agastache foeniculum	Mint	Mentha spp.
Apache plume	Fallugia paradoxa	Motherwort	Leonurus cardiaca
Arnica	Arnica chamissonis	Mullein	Verbascum thapsus, V. olympicum, V. spp.
Bee balm	Monarda fistulosa		
Betony	Stachys officinalis	Nettles	Urtica dioica
Blackberry	Rubus spp.	Onion	Allium cepa
Calendula	Calendula officinalis	Oregano	Origanum vulgare
California poppy	Eschscholzia californica	Oregon grape	Mahonia repens, M. aquifolium, M. spp.
Catnip	Nepeta cataria		
Chamomile	Matricaria recutita (M. chamomilla)	Oriental poppy	Papaver spp.
Chaste tree	Vitex agnus-castus	Passionflower	Passiflora incarnata, P. spp.
Chocolate flower	Berlandiera lyrata	Penstemon	Penstemon spp.
Cinquefoil	Potentilla spp.	Piñon	Pinus edulis
Cleavers	Galium aparine	Plantain	Plantago major
Clematis	Clematis ligusticifolia	Pleurisy root	Asclepias tuberosa
Comfrey	Symphytum officinale	Potato	Solanum tuberosum
Cota	Thelesperma megapotamicum	Prickly pear	Opuntia spp.
Cutleaf coneflower	Rudbeckia laciniata	Pulsatilla	Pulsatilla vulgaris, P. patens
Dandelion	Taraxacum officinale	Purslane	Portulaca oleracea
Datura	Datura wrightii	Pussytoes	Antennaria parvifolia
Dill	Anethum graveolens	Raspberry	Rubus spp.
Echinacea	Echinacea purpurea, E. pallida, E. paradoxa, E. spp.	Red clover	Trifolium pratense
		Rose	Rosa spp.
Elder	Sambucus nigra	Rosemary	Rosmarinus officinalis
Elecampane	Inula helenium	Sage	Artemisia spp.
Evening primrose	Oenothera spp.	Sage	Salvia officinalis
Fennel	Foeniculum vulgare	Scarlet beeblossom	Oenothera suffrutescens (Gaura coccinea)
Feverfew	Tanacetum parthenium		
Garlic	Allium sativum	Self heal	Prunella vulgaris
Geranium	Geranium richardsonii, G. spp.	Skullcap	Scutellaria lateriflora
Globemallow	Sphaeralcea coccinea, S. spp.	St. John's Wort	Hypericum perforatum
Goldenrod	Solidago canadensis, S. spp.	Snakeweed	Gutierrezia sarothrae
Grindelia	Grindelia squarrosa, G. spp.	Strawberry	Fragaria spp.
Hawthorn	Crataegus spp.	Thyme	Thymus vulgaris
Hops	Humulus lupulus	Valerian	Valeriana officinalis
Horehound	Marrubium vulgare	Vervain	Verbena macdougalii, V. spp.
Joint fir/Mormon tea	Ephedra torreyana		
Lavender	Lavandula spp.	Vinca	Vinca major
Lemonbalm	Melissa officinalis	Violet	Viola spp.
Licorice	Glycyrrhiza lepidota, G. spp.	Wild cherry	Prunus virginiana
Licorice mint/ giant hyssop	Agastache rupestris	Wild lettuce	Lactuca serriola
		Yarrow	Achillea millefolium
Cardinal flower	Lobelia cardinalis	Yerba mansa	Anemopsis californica
Meadowsweet	Filipendula ulmaria	Yucca	Yucca spp.

against the most assertive personalities, but allow plants to complete their reproductive life cycles, practice only necessary interventions, and permit plants to migrate to new locations around the garden according to their own will. Plants will find their preferred locations, and we can soak up the wild spirit of the living land around us. For many, this will be a lesson in letting go, watching things unfold, avoiding the temptation to try to control nature, and most importantly reconsidering our place in the wild landscape.

Working with plants from the wild mountains, deserts, canyons, and river valleys will always be part of herbalism, but you can feel an equally potent bond with your backyard botanicals. As you might already know, planting a medicinal herb garden has rewards well beyond the harvest. The deepest and most profound medicine comes from time spent together. The reciprocal relationship one develops with plants creates a cycle of symbiotic caring and nurturing as we are reminded of the interconnection between all beings. As the growing season progresses, plants evolve into new stages of development, and more wild-spirited revelations connect us to the larger landscape beyond. We feel the warmth of the afternoon sun in the golden spires of Greek mullein (*Verbascum olympicum*). We smell the rich legacy of our local herbal heritage in bee balm's (*Monarda fistulosa*) leaves. We hear the heartbeat of all wild animals in the wings of the hummingbirds hovering over autumn sage (*Salvia gregii*). We transcend time and place, hypnotized by passionflowers (*Passiflora incarnata*). We see the divine colors of the high desert sunset in yerba mansa petals. We sit contentedly in our peaceful gardens and stare endlessly into the heart of life. In my garden, I am completely enraptured by the physical beauty of the scene and enveloped by the ancient wisdom of plants. What better medicine is there anywhere? Anyone can create a healing garden that will connect you with the beauty and intelligence of wilderness. In fact, it is our imperative to do so not only for our own sake but also for the benefit of wildlands in a changing world.

TABLE 2 *Solvency Rates for Dry Herb Tinctures*

Achillea millefolium, yarrow	Flowers and leaves or whole plant 50–60%
Anemopsis californica, yerba mansa	Roots 70% plus 10% glycerin
Angelica spp., angelica	Roots 50–65%, seed 65–75%
Arnica spp., arnica	Flowers and leaves 50% or whole plant 60%
Artemisia spp., sage	Leaves tinctured fresh in 190-proof alcohol or dry leaves 60–75%
Ceanothus spp., red root	Root 50%
Datura spp., datura	Flowers, leaves, seeds (topical only) 50%
Fouquieria splendens, ocotillo	Bark 70%
Galium aparine, cleavers	Herb or whole plant 50%
Glycyrrhiza spp., licorice	Roots decocted and preserved with 25% alcohol
Grindelia spp., gumweed	Flowers tinctured fresh in 190-proof alcohol or dry flowers 70%
Gutierrezia sarothrae, snakeweed	Leaves and flowers 60–70% (topical)
Hypericum spp., St. John's wort	Buds, flowers, leaves tinctured fresh in 190-proof alcohol
Juniperus spp., juniper	Leaves or berries separately 75%
Larrea tridentata, creosote	Leaves 75%
Ligusticum porteri, oshá	Roots 70%
Mahonia spp., Oregon grape	Roots 50%
Marrubium vulgare, horehound	Leaves 50–60%
Monarda fistulosa, bee balm	Flowers, leaves tinctured fresh in 190-proof alcohol
Opuntia spp., prickly pear	Juice preserved with 25% alcohol
Pedicularis spp., betony	Flowers and leaves tinctured fresh in 190-proof alcohol
Pinus spp., piñon, ponderosa	Not commonly prepared as a tincture
Populus deltoides wislizenii, cottonwood	Buds 75%
Potentilla spp., cinquefoil	Leaves and flowers or whole plant 50%
Prosopis glandulosa torreyana, mesquite	Not commonly prepared as a tincture
Rosa woodsii, rose	Buds, flowers 50%; commonly made with brandy
Rudbeckia laciniata, cutleaf coneflower	Flowers, leaves, roots 50–60%
Scutellaria lateriflora, skullcap	Flowers, leaves tinctured fresh in 190-proof alcohol or dry herb 50%
Solidago spp., goldenrod	Flowers and leaves 50%
Sphaeralcea spp., globemallow	Leaves, flowers, roots prepared as cold infusion and preserved with 25% alcohol
Trifolium pratense, red clover	Flowers 50%
Usnea spp., usnea	Tinctured fresh in 190-proof alcohol; double extraction recommended
Verbena spp., vervain	Flowers and leaves 50–60%
Viola spp., violet	Leaves and flowers 50%
Yucca spp., yucca	Roots 50%

CHAPTER SIX

Materia Medica

Medicinal Plants of the Southwest

The medicinal plants covered in this book were selected based on their importance, both ecologically and culturally, to the landscapes of the Southwest, and plant profiles highlight the intersection of ecological, mythological, historical, and modern scientific understanding of these species. Some are native plants that are characteristic of their preferred habitats and also have played a prominent role in the herbal practices of the people who have lived in those areas. Others are nonnative plants that have naturalized from the Old World or are closely related native species whose herbal traditions bridge the biological and cultural continuum of continents. A few medicinal plants discussed here have been the subjects of particularly extensive scientific research or clinical trials, and I include separate research summaries for some of them. Specific methods and techniques of herbal remedy production are detailed in many other herbals and are not repeated here, but a table of preferred tincture solvency rates for each plant is included. The book's last section, "Invasive Trees," is a small selection of medicinal trees native to Asia or Europe that have become widespread in the American West. These trees illuminate important aspects of the relationship between people and the land in the modern era, and offer an abundant source of medicinal remedies that will help define the future of herbal practice as plant communities continue to change in the coming decades and centuries.

Achillea millefolium (Asteraceae)

YARROW / PLUMAJILLO

Native across northern continents and common in most us counties outside the southern states, yarrow has achieved legendary status as a primary medicinal plant by being commonly available to a wide range of cultural groups, spanning large geographical distances, and having broad healing applications for numerous body systems. Yarrow's botanical name, *Achillea millefolium*,

FIGURE 50 Yarrow flowers
(*Achillea millefolium*). Photo by author.

originates with the mythical warrior Achilles and its leaves of thousands of dissections. Yarrow is a member of varied plant communities in wide-ranging ecosystems, including coniferous forests, desert scrub, grasslands, and prairies. It prefers open dry habitats and is a pioneer species of disturbed areas, where it can be an indicator of overgrazed lands and often replaces more valuable forage plants. Differences between the American variety and its European counterpart are possibly due to variations in climate experiences of the plants on two continents or to phytochemical differences, particularly the general lack of azulene in Old World populations. As with many other plants, research suggests that environmental factors may impact the production and quality of medicinal compounds, with some terpenes being absent in higher-altitude populations and numerous other compounds shown to be greatly affected by growing conditions (Giorgi et al. 2005). As we learn more about ecology and medicinal compounds produced by plants and endophytic organisms, the clearer it becomes that these chemicals are produced by plants for optimal health and survival in their localized habitats. They also serve as botanical remedies uniquely adapted to local human populations sharing similar environmental conditions.

Yarrow has a long-standing relationship with people and features strongly in ceremony, lore, and healing practices. Found at a sixty-five-thousand-year-old Neanderthal grave in Iraq (Leroi-Gourhan 1975; Solecki 1975), yarrow is one of the world's oldest known herbal remedies. Its roots in the modern cultural traditions of Europe begin in the ancient world with the siege of Troy in the thirteenth century BCE. Following the advice of his famed teacher, the great healer and centaur Chiron, the warrior Achilles is said to have treated the wounds of his ally Telemachus using yarrow (Richardson 2017). Its historical medicinal context is further substantiated by being among plant remedies found aboard a sunken Roman ship dated between 140 and 20 BCE (Applequist and Moerman 2011). Yarrow's medicinal properties were later recorded by Pliny the Elder and Dioscorides in the first century CE. Along with St. John's wort (*Hypericum perforatum*) and vervain (*Verbena* spp.), yarrow was a primary herb of protection against evil spirits during the Middle Ages and was strung up in garlands and hung in doorways on Saint John's Eve (Richardson 2017). It was also placed under the pillow to bring about love premonitions. In China, the plant stalks were cast in *I Ching* divination practices.

As a medicinal herb, yarrow's uses are extensive. This plant's leaves, flowers, and roots are known to have wide-ranging medicinal actions and can be prepared as tea, tincture, infused oil, liniment, or poultice. Famed as a styptic herb, yarrow has a history of use in wound healing primarily but also in treatments for the circulatory, respiratory, and digestive systems. Yarrow's use in first aid and traumatic injury treatments is legendary but commonly misunderstood. Yarrow is skilled at stopping excessive bleeding and reducing bruising, but it does so as an herb capable of balancing the flow of blood, regulating blood thickness, and adjusting the blood vessel walls through neurovascular control (Wood 2009). These qualities, combined with its diaphoretic abilities, allow yarrow to conserve or augment the flow of blood to the surface and thus be both heating and cooling as it adjusts the release of energy through the blood vessels and pores. Yarrow contains both achilleine and coumarin, two chemicals known for the contrasting forces of slowing and encouraging blood flow. Such herbs that are capable of creating opposing effects in the body are among our most useful because they restore balance to body systems that are out of alignment. In addition to its cardiovascular effects, yarrow's wound healing is potentiated by its antimicrobial, anti-inflammatory, vulnerary, and analgesic properties. Clearly beneficial to the cardiovascular system, yarrow is also useful for treating varicose veins, high or low blood pressure, and clotting disorders. In the treatment of colds and coughs, yarrow's astringent and diaphoretic properties cut mucus and redistribute excessive wetness to decongest while also helping regulate fevers by mitigating chills and releasing heat through the skin. Furthermore, yarrow reduces inflammation that may be present in the sinus, lungs, or throat. As a bitter, drying, and astringent herb, yarrow is useful for stimulating all digestive processes, thereby reducing symptoms of indigestion and aiding the reabsorption of fluids in the small intestine to ease diarrhea. Yarrow also protects gastric mucosa and serves as an antispasmodic for the digestive smooth muscles. Rounding out the panacea-like role of yarrow in herbal practice, it is also used in different forms as a urinary antiseptic and diuretic, a hair rinse to slow balding, a toothache remedy, a mouthwash for sore gums, a regulator for heavy or scant menses, a remedy for arthritic inflammation, and a treatment for melancholy in northern regions. Although it is generally considered safe, some users report contact dermatitis.

Documented Native American relationships with yarrow are widespread, with at least seventy-six groups describing its usefulness (Moerman 1998) and with an extraordinary number of applications reported. The most common uses are related to respiratory ailments, including tuberculosis, cold, cough, sore throat, and fever (Bank 1953; Black 1880; Chandler et al. 1979; Chesnut

1902; Curtin 1957; Densmore 1918; Fleisher 1980; Fowler 1989; Gill 1983; Grinnell 1972; Gunther 1973; Hamel and Chiltoskey 1975; Hart 1981, 1992; Hellson 1974; Herrick 1977; Leighton 1985; Mahar 1953; Merriam 1966; Ray 1932; Rousseau 1945a, 1947; Smith 1923, 1929, 1932; Speck 1917; Steward 1933; Train et al. 1941; Turner 1973; Turner and Bell 1971, 1973; Turner et al. 1980, 1983, 1990; Wallis 1922; Wyman and Harris 1951), and a wide variety of skin conditions, including venomous bites, eczema, chapped skin, pimples, burns, and bleeding wounds (Boas 1966; Bocek 1984; Densmore 1928, 1932; Fowler et al. 1980; Gunther 1973; Hart 1992; Hellson 1974; Kelly 1932; Kraft 1990; Merriam 1966; Palmer 1975; Percy 1952; Schenck and Gifford 1952; Smith 1923, 1929, 1932; Steedman 1928; Stevenson 1915; Steward 1933; Train et al. 1941; Turner 1973; Turner and Bell 1973; Turner et al. 1990; Zigmond 1981). Yarrow was also commonly prepared for sprains, swellings, and rheumatic pain (Barrett and Gifford, 1933; Carrier Linguistic Committee 1973; Chamberlin 1911; Chandler et al.; Chesnut 1902; Gunther 1973; Hart 1992; Hellson 1974; Herrick 1995; Kelly 1932; Mahar 1953; Mechling 1959; Smith 1929; Train et al. 1941; Turner et al. 1980, 1983, 1990; Wallis 1922); used as snuff, tea, steam, or poultice for headaches (Chamberlin 1911; Chesnut 1902; Densmore 1928; Herrick 1995; Leighton 1985; Raymond 1945; Steward 1933; Train et al. 1941; Turner et al. 1980; Wallis 1922; Wyman and Harris 1951); and employed for the treatment of diarrhea, nausea, gas, and other digestive complaints (Bank 1953; Bocek 1984; Chesnut 1902; Gunther 1973; Hamel and Chiltoskey 1975; Hart 1981; Herrick 1995; Merriam 1966; Murphey 1990 [1959]; Rousseau 1945a; Train et al. 1941; Turner et al. 1983, 1990). Topical preparations were also widely made for toothaches (Bocek 1984; Carrier Linguistic Committee 1973; Kelly

1932; Leighton 1985; Mahar 1953; Romero 1954; Swanton 1928; Turner and Bell 1971; Turner et al. 1980, 1990) and eyewashes (Baker 1981; Chesnut 1902; Gunther 1973; Kelly 1932; Perry 1952; Steedman 1928; Teit 1928; Train et al. 1941; Wyman and Harris 1951). Adding to this long list of uses are treatments for breast abscesses (Turner 1973), sunstroke (Herrick 1995), worms (Herrick 1995), heart problems (Hart 1981), and convulsions (Herrick 1995). Yarrow has been used as a childbirth facilitator for pain relief, speedy delivery, and expelling the placenta (Fleisher 1980; Gill 1983; Gunther 1973; Hellson 1974;

FIGURE 51. Yarrow plant (*Achillea millefolium*). Photo by author.

Tantaquidgeon 1928, 1972) and for reviving an unconscious person (Smith 1933). Yarrow has also been used to treat venereal disease (Herrick 1995; Train et al. 1941); diuresis and bladder or kidney problems (Fowler 1989; Hellson 1974; Tantaquidgeon 1928, 1942, 1972; Turner et al. 1990); nosebleeds, heavy menses, and hemorrhage (Bank 1951; Hamel and Chiltoskey 1975; Hart 1981); and liver disorders (Tantaquidgeon 1928, 1942, 1972). It has been used as a general stimulating tonic and blood purifier (Elmore 1944; Gill 1983; Gunther 1973; Herrick 1995; Palmer 1975; Train et al. 1941); as a floral perfume (Hart 1992); and as protection against evil spirits (Smith 1933). Some practitioners inserted a yarrow leaf tip into the skin and burned the plant matter down to the skin surface (Dunbar 1880). I have found oil infused with yarrow to be an indispensable remedy in the high desert, where dried-out nasal passages often lead to nosebleeds. A careful swipe of this oil inside the nostrils tones the blood vessels and astringes excess blood, and the oil moistens and lubricates sensitive dry tissues. Astringing, antiseptic, and anti-inflammatory, yarrow tea also makes a useful face wash for acne and can be combined with other herbs for this purpose. In the wild, yarrow's aromatic qualities are apparent especially in meadows, where it is abundant; the pleasant scent arises from under your feet, creating an enchanting and mood-altering experience. Easy to grow, drought tolerant, and resilient, it is a welcome herb in western gardens.

RESEARCH SUMMARY With such widespread distribution and cross-cultural importance, *Achillea millefolium* and other *Achillea* species have been the subject of fairly extensive research. Much of this has been summarized in reviews by Applequist and Moerman (2011), Saeidnia et al. (2011), and Sayed and Bano (2018). Although few phytochemical studies have been done on the American variety, yarrow is known to contain a large number of active compounds, including flavonoids, phenolic acids including salicylic acid, coumarins, terpenoids, and sterols (Saeidnia et al. 2011; Si et al. 2006), with numerous chemotypes within the species. Since yarrow is renowned for its role in wound healing, much research has focused on its styptic, anti-inflammatory, analgesic, and antimicrobial actions. Studies have confirmed *Achillea* species to be potent healers (Hemmati et al. 2002; Pirbalouti et al. 2010) with styptic qualities (Sellerberg and Glasl 2000). A number of compounds found in yarrow are known to reduce inflammation, and studies have shown yarrow's efficacy to be similar to or greater than that of common anti-inflammatory pain-relieving pharmaceuticals (Choudhary et al. 2007; Maswadeh et al. 2006). Studies have also shown it to have analgesic effects (Gherase et al.

2002; Noureddini et al. 2008; Pires et al. 2009). *Achillea* species are known to be broadly antimicrobial, with activity against bacteria and fungi, including strep, salmonella, *H. pylori*, candida, and others (Candan et al. 2003; Maggi et al. 2009; Mahady et al. 2005; Ozlem et al. 2006; Stojanović et al. 2005; Unlü et al. 2002). One study showed that yarrow increased the efficacy of numerous antibiotic drugs against drug-resistant strains of *E. coli* (Darwish and Aburjai et al. 2010). Another suggested antimalarial activity (Murnigsih et al. 2005).

Yarrow is often regarded as a panacea, and although no cure-alls exist, research does validate many more additional uses for this herb, including antioxidant activity, digestive benefits, anticancer potential, and antidiabetic and hepatoprotective actions. Studies have demonstrated at least fifteen *Achillea* species as having antioxidant and free radical scavenging activity (Candan et al. 2003; Konalioglu and Karamenderes 2005), inhibiting protein oxidation (Ardestani and Yazdanparast 2007), protecting against oxidative stress (Tuberosoa et al. 2009), and showing cytoprotective activity (Giorgi et al. 2009). For digestive health, Yarrow protects mucosa and heals ulcers, even exceeding the efficacy of prescribed medications (Cavalcanti et al. 2006; Hatsuko Baggio et al. 2008). Although the mechanisms of its gastroprotective properties are not certain, they may involve reducing stomach acidity (Cristiana et al. 2002) or antioxidant actions (Potrich et al. 2010). *Achillea* species are also antispasmodic (Babaei et al. 2007; Lemmens-Gruber et al. 2006; Karamenderes and Apaydin 2003; Yaeesh et al. 2006). They act as a smooth muscle relaxant (Moradi et al. 2013) in the digestive system and against *H. pylori* (Mahady et al. 2005), a bacterial pathogen that can lead to ulcers. Anticancer research suggests some inhibitory activity against liver cancer cell lines (Lin et al. 2002), and isolated sesquiterpenoids from yarrow appear to be active against leukemia cells (Tozyo et al. 1994). Another study found that phytochemicals isolated from *Achillea* species had significant cytotoxicity against cervical cancer, leukemia, and melanoma (Trifunovic et al. 2006). Furthermore, Yarrow has shown itself to be hypoglycemic (Yazdanparast et al. 2007,) increasing insulin and reducing glucose levels (Zolghadri et al. 2014). *Achillea* species are also hepatoprotective (Yaeesh et al. 2006), choleretic (Benedek et al. 2006), estrogenic (Innocenti et al. 2007), and mosquito repellant (Tunon et al. 1994). They may also reduce fertility by decreasing sperm count (Nasrin et al. 2010).

Anemopsis californica (Saururaceae)

YERBA MANSA / YERBA DEL MANZO

The uniqueness of yerba mansa is obvious at first glance. Once known as *Houttuynia californica*, it is one of only six plants in the family Saururaceae and the only plant in the genus *Anemopsis*. Its beauty is particularly striking in the evening as its white petal-like bracts capture the changing moods of the landscape, subtly reflecting the shifting hues of the setting sunlight. Yerba mansa's growing habit is to create large dense stands formed through both seeding and spreading its "lizard tails," or stolons, which root at each node. Yerba mansa is considered a paleoherb—a species thought to exist very early in the evolution of flowering plants, near the time when monocots and dicots diverged from each other in the early Cretaceous period (Carlquist et al. 1995). As a wetland obligate plant throughout most of its range, it resides in moist soils near seeps, springs, and riversides, and thrives with thick leaf litter mulch and the shade of cottonwood trees. A detailed discussion of yerba mansa's habitat, ecological interactions, and conservation issues is included in chapter 2. As with any herb, there are important additional considerations for harvesting. Like other wetland plants, yerba mansa is known to absorb arsenic (Del-Toro-Sanchez et al. 2013) and heavy metals (Karpiscak et al. 2001) from its environment, which raises concerns about water and soil quality at any harvesting site. United Plant Savers list yerba mansa as an "at risk" species, a status that should demand increased cultivation for herbal remedy production. Yerba mansa can be easily cultivated under appropriate conditions (Kleitz et al. 2003; Martin and Steiner 2007), but the practice has yet to become widespread and most herbal products on the market are produced from wildcrafted sources. Although cultivated yerba mansa plants and their wild counterparts appear to have identical phytochemical profiles (Medina et al. 2005), research suggests that there may be differences in medicinal activity based on the presence (or lack) of endophytic root organisms in wild versus cultivated plants (Bussey et al. 2015).

FIGURE 52
Yerba mansa
flower (*Anemopsis
californica*).
Photo by author.

Yerba mansa has a long history of use in the Southwest, was widely revered, and was considered a panacea by local practitioners (Munk 1913; Timbrook 1987; Webster 1909). Native American uses documented from the Cahuilla, Costanoan, Diegueño, Isleta, Kawaiisu, Keres, Mahuna, Paiute, Pima, Papago, and Shoshone people

Materia
Medica

81

include treatment of colds, cough, itchy throat, and lung infections (Bean and Saubel 1972; Curtin 1984 [1949]; Train et al. 1941; Voegelin 1938; Zigmond 1981); wounds and burns (Bocek 1984; Curtin 1984 [1949]; Jones 1931; Romero 1954; Swank 1932; Train et al. 1941; Zigmond 1981); digestive upsets, stomach ulcers, constipation, menstrual cramps, and muscular pain (Bocek 1984; Curtin 1984 [1949]; Steward 1933; Train et al. 1941); and gonorrhea and syphilis (Curtin 1984 [1949]; Steward 1933; Train et al. 1941). It has been used as a blood tonic and support during convalescence (Jones 1931) and as an emetic (Castetter and Underhill 1935; Russell 1908). Traditional Mexican and Hispanic uses are similar but also include oral health care; treatments for arthritis, dysentery, colic, sinus infections, and hemorrhoids; and tonifying the mucous membranes (Curtin 1965; Moore 1990; Munk 1913). Yerba mansa was widely described in early eclectic medicine journals. In 1876, Dr. W. H. George of Inyo County, California, was one of the first physicians to extol the virtues of yerba mansa. He sent the first botanical sample to John Uri Lloyd of Lloyd Brothers Pharmacists, Inc., who later marketed it as a specific medicine (George 1877; Lloyd 1880; Webster 1909). George and another physician, Dr. Edward Palmer (1978), described its prominent role in the long-standing folk medicine practices of Native American and Mexican people of southern California and Sonora, Mexico, describing its usefulness in treatments for bowel complaints, malarial fevers, coughs and lung ailments, sore throats, and gonorrhea, and as a stimulant for the mucous membranes. Dr. J. A. Munk, a physician from Los Angeles, also recognized yerba mansa's stimulating effects on the mucous membranes and its effectiveness in treating nasal catarrh, rhinitis, and sore throats. He further reported that his yerba mansa nasal spray caused copious nasal secretions that moved mucous and relieved congestion (Munk 1909, 1913). In 1909 Munk revealed his nasal spray recipe: fill a two-ounce tincture bottle with five to thirty drops of yerba mansa tincture, one dram of glycerin, and the rest water. Physician John Fearn (1909) described other common turn-of-the-last-century uses of yerba mansa, including treatments for tuberculosis, weak mucous membranes, gonorrhea, dysentery or diarrhea with blood and mucus, typhoid, bruises, and syphilitic sores. *King's American Dispensatory* (Felter and Lloyd 1898) provided one of the earliest detailed entries for yerba mansa, but by the middle of the twentieth century, the pharmaceutical industry was beginning to undermine mainstream botanical medicine and yerba mansa's use gradually retreated back to traditional herbal practices in Native American, Mexican, and Hispanic communities.

Today yerba mansa is considered to be an essential remedy in most southwestern herbalists' apothecaries. Yerba mansa contains numerous active constituents, including elemicin, methyleugenol, thymol, piperitone, sesa-min, and asarinin, all contributing to its many useful herbal actions within the body (Acharya and Chaubal 1968; Bussey et al. 2014; Tutupalli and Chaubal 1971). In New Mexico, research has indicated the presence of three distinct chemotypes: high in elemicin, high in methyleugenol, and high in piperitone and thymol (Medina-Holguin et al. 2008). Although traditional uses include a wide range of applications, this herb has a particular affinity for the digestive, respiratory, and urinary systems and is indicated for any physical or spiritual condition that is benefited by alterative action and increased fluidity in the mind, body, or spirit. An example of the latter is yerba mansa's use in New Mexico as a death salve, intended to ease the body and facilitate the passage of the spirit into new territory. As an anti-inflammatory yerba mansa helps the body excrete uric acid through stimulated diuresis and can provide ef-fective support for arthritis and other rheumatic complaints for those who are not adversely affected by its drying qualities in longer-term use. Yerba mansa's antimicrobial workings are supported by research that confirms its activity against *Staphylococcus aureus*, *Streptococcus pneumoniae*, and *Geo-trichim candidum* (Medina et al. 2005) as well as five species of mycobacte-rium known to cause skin, pulmonary, and lymphatic infections (Bussey et al. 2014). Research also suggests that extracts of yerba mansa (all plant parts, but especially the roots) inhibit the growth and migration of certain types of cancer, including breast cancer and colon cancer cell lines (Daniels et al. 2006; Kaminski et al. 2010; Van Slambrouck et al. 2007). Among yerba man-sa's most powerful attributes are its abilities to tone and tighten the mucous membranes, similar to goldenseal (*Hydrastis canadensis*), and the manner in which it moves the waters and energy of the body. In accordance with its ecological interactions as described in chapter 2, yerba mansa functions similarly inside our bodies by regu-lating the flow of waters, encourag-ing the movement of stagnant fluids, moving toxins, and inhibiting harmful pathogens while warming and stimu-lating other sluggish functions in the body. With this combination of char-acteristics that revitalize the health of an organism or ecosystem, yerba mansa is an herb with a wide array of applications, including treatment

FIGURE 53. Yerba mansa leaves (*Anemopsis californica*). Photo by author.

of chronic inflammatory conditions, digestive disorders, skin issues, urinary infections, mucus-producing colds and sore throats, sinus infections, hemorrhoids, and fungal infections.

There are numerous ways to prepare yerba mansa as a remedy. Extracting best in alcohol and water, yerba mansa is most commonly prepared as a tea or tincture but can also be made into infused oil, salve, hydrosol, powder, liniment, poultice, or nasal spray, or it can be simply chewed. Although leaves and flowers can be used, roots are the most potent part for most medicinal preparations. The decocted roots impart their scent and a rich earthy flavor to water, creating an immediate medicinal action through the release of aromatic vapors. This tea is rather strong and medicinal tasting, but a little goes a long way. I have routinely seen a single dose of a few ounces of tea expel thick mucus in respiratory infections, resulting in symptomatic relief and rapid improvement in the condition. Tincture is best prepared using freshly dried root and 60 percent to 75 percent alcohol, along with 10 percent glycerin to avoid precipitants from settling. I consider yerba mansa tincture an essential and irreplaceable component of formulas for urinary tract infections and sinus infections, and I include it in almost all acute antimicrobial formulas. Caution is recommended with longer-term use due to yerba mansa's drying effects. I have noticed that overuse often results in dry nasal passages and a feeling of insufficient secretions in general. Infused oil, salves, and creams can be prepared by using leaves or applying small amounts of alcohol to the roots to initiate extraction prior to macerating in oil (Cech 2000; Moore 1993). Ground roots are also an excellent addition to herbal healing clays for wounds and to body powders for diaper rash, athlete's foot, and the like. Leaves are perfect for poulticing skin inflammations, and flower stalks retain a strong anesthetic property, even well into winter. Liniments and throat sprays also make use of yerba mansa's anesthetic properties to treat bodily aches and pains, sore throats, and coughs.

Angelica grayi, A. archangelica, A. spp. (Apiaceae)

ANGELICA

Angelica is an edible and medicinal herb long held in high esteem among the northern cultures of Europe and also finds a valued place in American herbal traditions. In the Old World, it was once considered a remedy for all ailments and served as a protective charm against witchery and evil spells. Its unique aroma made this plant a coveted perfumery herb and inspired poets in Lapland (Richardson 2017). Legend has it that the archangel Michael revealed

FIGURE 54 Angelica plant (*Angelica grayi*). Photo by author.

angelica to a monk during a dream as a protective and curative remedy for the plague, leading to its species name and the seventeenth-century practice of chewing its seeds (Grieve 1971 [1931]). Angelica has been used as a flavoring for breads, cakes, desserts, jams, fish, fresh vegetables, and a number of liquors, including chartreuse, vermouth, wine, and gin. Approximately eighteen species of angelica are native to the western United States. Angelica is easy to cultivate in the western garden and attracts a variety of insects. It is also a beautiful and mysterious plant that, in its vegetative phase, is frequently obscured by the lush greenery of companion plants. When blooming, however, its orb-like blossoms stand out like a miniature model of a strange and distant solar system.

Medicinally, angelica has accumulated a long list of applications over the centuries, with its leaves, roots, seeds, and stalks being harvested and prepared. Remedies have taken the form of candied stems and roots, chewed seeds, powdered roots applied topically, tea, tinctures, body adornments, smoke, distillates, and liquors. The plant has been used to treat digestive, respiratory, circulatory, and female reproductive issues. Nicolas Culpeper, the seventeenth-century English herbalist, and John Parkinson, the herbalist to King James I and royal botanist to Charles I, relied on angelica as an antidote to poisons and pestilence (Richardson 2017). As a digestive remedy, angelica serves as a general stimulating tonic and a carminative herb, calming indigestion, colic, stomachaches, and constipation. Herbalist Matthew Wood (2008) described angelica as "bear medicine," increasing appetite and digestive efficiency while providing nutrition for undernourished people (or recently hibernating bears, who seek this plant upon awakening in the spring). As one of

FIGURE 55 Angelica leaf (*Angelica grayi*). Photo by author.

the warming aromatic bitters, angelica is suited for folks who need more digestive fire without the cooling effects of most other digestive tonics. In the respiratory system, angelica dries and warms the lungs, brings increased blood flow and oxygenation, provides relief for shortness of breath, dries wet conditions, and calms spasms that lead to excess coughing. Wood astutely notes that angelica roots have pockets of air and grow in damp locations, having a unique ability to bring air to wet places in the landscape and in our bodies. Warming and stimulating the body's circulation, angelica benefits all organs, including liver, brain, and uterine functioning. It helps heal liver disease; eases vertigo, nervousness, and fatigue; increases mental clarity; relieves menstrual cramping; regulates blood flow; and aids in labor and birth. Angelica has been employed as a diuretic and urinary antiseptic as well as a treatment for a myriad of other conditions, including toothaches, gout, rheumatism, and sciatica. It helps in healing old wounds, smoking cessation, relieving depression, stimulating imagination and creativity, and increasing lymphatic flow to reduce swelling and inflammation.

American herbalists use local species particularly for digestive, respiratory, and women's reproductive applications. Numerous Native American groups have used local angelica species similarly, with additional uses as a food vegetable or seasoning (Ager and Ager 1980; Anderson 1939; Bank 1951; Chesnut 1902; Compton 1993; Gill 1983; Goodrich and Lawson 1983; Heller 1953; Merriam 1966; Palmer 1975; Porsild 1953; Powers 1874; Schenck and Gifford 1952; Turner 1973; Wilson 1978) and a treatment for arthritis and headaches (Boas 1966; Bocek 1984; Chesnut 1902; Goodrich and Lawson 1983; Hamel and Chiltoskey 1975; Hellson 1974; Robbins et al. 1916; Sapir and Spier 1943; Swanton 1928; Tantaquidgeon 1942, 1972), malnutrition (Hellson 1974), respiratory infections, colds (Bank 1951; Barrett and Gifford 1933; Chandler et al. 1979; Chesnut 1902; Fowler 1989; Goodrich and Lawson 1983; Hamel and Chiltoskey 1975; Hellson 1974; Herrick 1977; Mechling 1959; Sapir and Spier 1943; Train et al. 1941), fever (Chesnut 1902; Hamel and Chiltoskey 1975),

FIGURE 56 Angelica plant (*Angelica archangelica*). Photo by author.

and sore throat (Bank 1951; Chandler et al. 1979; Goodrich and Lawson 1983; Hamel and Chiltoskey 1975; Mechling 1959; Train et al. 1941). It has been used for menses regulation (Goodrich and Lawson 1983; Hamel and Chiltoskey 1975); to treat venereal disease (Steward 1933; Train et al. 1941), topical wounds, and swellings (Bocek 1984; Goodrich and Lawson 1983; Hellson 1974; Smith 1923; Steward 1933; Train et al.); in ceremonial rites (Hellson 1974); as a good luck charm (Chesnut 1902; Hellson 1974; Turner and Bell 1971); as love medicine (Merriam 1966); for purification (Herrick 1977; Oswalt 1957); for relief from malaise (Smith 1973);

FIGURE 57 Angelica flowers (*Angelica archangelica*). Photo by author.

and as protection against snakes and evil spirits (Barrett and Gifford 1933; Chesnut 1902; Herrick 1977). Although many herbalists consider the North American, European, and Asian species to be very similar, they should not be confused with the remedy known as dong-quai, which is made from dried and cured Angelica roots and has unique properties. It should also be noted that the fresh root of the eastern American species A. *atropurpurea* is said to be poisonous prior to drying (Bhat et al. 2011; Wood, 2008).

Recent scientific research conducted on A. *archangelica* and a variety of Asian species has confirmed many traditional uses and built upon them. Studies have identified numerous medicinal constituents, including an array of volatile oils and furanocoumarins, as well as a resin called angelicin (Bhat et al. 2011). Angelica essential oil has been shown to be antimicrobial against a number of bacterial strains, including staph, strep, *E. coli*, and others, as well as antifungal against species of *Aspergillus*, *Trichophyon*, and *Candida* (Fraternale et al. 2014; Irshad et al. 2011: Roh and Shin 2014). It is also insecticidal, deterring mosquito bites and being toxic to larvae (Champakaew et al. 2015; Chung et al. 2012; Tabanca et al. 2014). Cardiovascular applications are supported by studies that show potent anticoagulant and antiplatelet activity attributed to flavonoids (Mira et al. 2015) and an ability to reduce plaque buildup, lower blood pressure, and provide antioxidant and anti-inflammatory activity, helping limit the damage of strokes and improve neurological deficit scores (Wu and Hsieh 2011). Angelica species have also illuminated a potential use in cancer prevention and treatments, with a fruit tincture acting antiproliferatively on a human pancreatic cancer cell line (Sigurdsson et al.

2004), a leaf extract demonstrating antitumor activity in breast cancer cells (Sigurdsson et al. 2005b), and a fruit essential oil showing cytotoxic effects in human pancreatic cancer cells (Sigurdsson et al. 2005a). Additionally, angelica was part of a ten Chinese herb formula that showed potential for the prevention and treatment of prostate cancer (Jiang et al. 2006). Other studies have shown angelica to improve the rate of wound healing in diabetic patients (Zhang et al. 2017), but it may be contraindicated for people with diabetes because it might cause an increase of sugar in the urine (Bhat et al. 2011). Furthermore, angelica has been shown to be anxiolytic (Chandra et al. 2016; Chen et al. 2004), antiseizure (Luszcki et al. 2009; Pathak et al. 2010), bronchorelaxant (Sharma et al. 2017), anti-inflammatory (Li et al. 2016; Wang et al. 2016; Zhang et al. 2015; Zhong et al. 2016), antioxidant (Irshad et al. 2011; Li et al. 2007; Lin et al. 2009: Prakash et al. 2015; Roh et al. 2014; Wei and Shibamoto 2007), hepatoprotective (Elgohary et al. 2009; Yeh et al. 2003), antimutagenic (Salikhova et al. 1993), and antiulcerative. It is cytoprotective on gastric ulcers by reducing acid secretions and increasing mucin production (Khayyal et al. 2001).

Arnica cordifolia, A. spp. (Asteraceae)

ARNICA

At least twenty arnica species are native to the American West, with A. *cordifolia* and A. *chamissonis* among the most widespread. A. *cordifolia* can be a dominant groundcover in forested mountain areas and is an important food source for mule deer, elks, and other animals. In the Southwest, I most commonly see A. *cordifolia* growing along the margins of forested areas where they meet mountain meadows, and I have been able to coax A. *chamissonis* to grow in moist shady corners of my desert valley garden at five thousand feet. Arnica species are known to respond positively to disturbance events such as forest thinning (Austin 1982), logging (Geier-Hayes 1989), fires (Stickney 1993), grazing, and mowing (Ellenberger 1999; Myklestad and Saetersdal 2004) by resprouting rhizomes and the mass flowering that occurs one to two years after disturbance. As we see with many plants, location often affects phytochemistry, and studies have shown that the antioxidant phenolic content of the European native A. *montana* is altered by altitude, with phenols decreasing at lower elevations (Spitaler et al. 2008) and possibly affected by temperature (Albert et al. 2009). Often growing in poor soils of mountain environments, A. *montana* is also known to have symbiotic relationships with mycorrhizal and endophytic fungi that produce antibacterial and antifungal secondary metabolites (Wardecki et al. 2015), contributing to its survival and also potentiating its medicinal actions in herbal remedies. Although there are numerous arnica species with wide ranges in the American West, the European endemic A. *montana* is endangered due to agriculture practices that change the soil composition of meadows through the use of fertilizers (Michler et al. 2005), as well as overharvesting, land conversion, and high-density cattle grazing (Kathe 2006). Wild populations have been severely impacted in many countries and are protected in some places (Kathe 2006). Cultivation of A. *montana* is undertaken, and one study shows no difference in the composition of essential oils be

FIGURE 58. Arnica flowers (*Arnica chamissonis*). Photo by author.

tween wild and cultivated plants (Sava Sand 2015), but the growing process entails some difficulty and results in high prices.

Arnica is a beloved herbal remedy wherever it grows. Turner et al. (1980) described an interesting Okanagan-Colville tribal use as a love medicine, which was prepared by mixing the roots with a robin's heart and tongue and ocher paint to form a dry powder. This mixture was then applied to the face while the seeker was standing in water, facing east, and reciting certain words along with the desired person's name. In modern herbal practice, flowers are primarily used, but leaves and roots can also be gathered and prepared as tincture, infused oil, salve, or liniment. Arnica is one of our best remedies for sprains, bruises, arthritis, sore muscles, and deep-tissue injuries that benefit from warmth. I commonly prepare topical arnica remedies in conjunction with other herbs, including juniper (*Juniperus* spp.) and pedicularis (*Pedicularis* spp.) for muscular pain or tension, St. John's wort (*Hypericum* spp.) for neural injuries, cayenne (*Capsicum annuum*) for arthritis, and cottonwood (*Populus* spp.) for general aches and pains or older deep body wounds. For acute injuries, Arnica has its best effects when used as soon as possible after the trauma and is also greatly beneficial to chronic or old injuries with dull aching pains. Arnica is not advised for broken skin as it can cause irritation. It is widely relegated to topical use due to its potential toxicity and propensity for upsetting the stomach (Grieve 1971 [1931]; Hoffman 2003). An entry from the *Dispensatory of the United States* (Remington et al. 1918:11) described arnica as "producing symptoms of violent toxic gastro-enteris, with nervous disturbance, reduction or increase in pulse rate, and collapse". Nevertheless, some herbalists use very small doses internally, and famed Southwest herbalist Michael Moore (2003) specifically indicated five to fifteen drops added

FIGURE 59 Arnica stand (*Arnica cordifolia*). Photo by author.

to other tinctures to activate macrophage activity and to stimulate immune function in the treatment of infections. Moore additionally noted arnica's stimulating and vasodilating effects on the cardiovascular system, directing the flow of blood to help heal injuries. Although generally considered safe for topical use, arnica's helenalin is known to cause contact dermatitis in some people, with a significant number of cases reported in the literature (Aberer 2007; Hausen 1980). One last word of caution: Take care not to confuse the arnica species discussed here with other herbs that share this common name, such as camphorweed (*Heterotheca* spp.), also known as Mexican arnica.

Most scientific research has been done on *A. montana* and has focused primarily on its anti-inflammatory, pain relieving, and antioxidant actions. Phytochemical analysis reveals sesquiterpene lactones, including helenalin, phenolic acids, and flavonoids. Clinical trials testing its effectiveness in osteoarthritis treatments support arnica's most common use for inflammatory pain. One trial showed significant improvements in pain and stiffness of the knee (Knuesel et al. 2002), and another demonstrated equal effectiveness in reducing pain and increasing mobility in the hands when compared to ibuprofen (Widrig et al. 2007). Another study investigating the anti-inflammatory mechanism showed that helenalin inhibits transcription factor NF-kB (a protein involved in many cellular processes, including immune and inflammatory responses), differing from commonly used salicylic acid–containing pain relievers (Lyss et al. 2009). Research has also demonstrated strong antioxidant activity, with moderate ability to inhibit acetylcholinesterase (an enzyme found in muscles and nerves that affects nerve impulses in the parasympathetic nervous system) (Dimitrova and Balabanova 2012), and cytoprotective effects against oxidative damage (Craciunescu et al. 2012), suggesting a useful role in neurodegenerative disease, skin conditions, and other ailments benefited by antioxidants. Furthermore, arnica shows antibacterial and antifungal activity (Stanciuc et al. 2011) and is effective against a range of periodontal bacteria (Lauk et al. 2003).

Artemisia tridentata, A. filifolia, A. frigida,
A. ludoviciana, A. spp. (Asteraceae)

SAGE

Artemisia species (sage) have been culture-influencing plants across continents, shaping the lives of people in both the Old World and the New. A widespread genus with a large number of species, *Artemisia* has been associated with mythological lore, supernatural activity, spiritual beliefs and practices, absinthe-inspired counterculture, and healing practices across time and space. There are many *Artemisia* species in the American West, including nonnatives such as A. *absinthum,* but also as many as forty-three native species, some having limited ranges while others (for example, A. *ludoviciana,* A. *dracunculus,* A. *frigida,* A. *tridentata,* and in the Southwest A. *filifolia*) are widely distributed. Although there is considerable overlap, with most species having similar uses, commentary here focuses on these more common varieties. Many of these species are found in a wide range of habitat types, including desert shrub, forest, woodland, prairie, grassland, and even alpine environments, and serve as important forage for pronghorn and other ungulates, small mammals, birds, and insects. Some sages are also useful for revegetation projects, as they have varying qualities of resprouting after fires, a willingness to colonize disturbed areas, rapid growth and spreading habits, and soil stabilization capabilities. *Artemisia tridentata,* in particular, is one of the most widespread shrubs in the American West and includes several subspecies that are important habitat and nutritive forage for sage grouse and numerous other animals. It is also valuable for range restoration. It is associated with mycorrhiza from the genus *Glomus* and may be dependent on that relationship, making it difficult to reestablish after severe burns or mycorrhiza-damaging infestations of cheatgrass (*Bromus tectorum*).

The lore of sage takes us back to ancient Greece, when the goddess Artemis gave this plant to the famed herbalist centaur Chiron for use in his medical teaching and practice. Sage, also known as wormwood, shapes biblical stories as a plant that rose up from ground in Eden that was touched by the serpent and became associated with disaster and sadness (Richardson 2017). Another Christian story tells of a star named Wormwood that fell from the sky into waters and springs, contaminating them with bitterness that sickened and killed those who drank it (Richardson 2017). Wormwood also became a literary symbol for the bitterness of words in Shakespeare's *Hamlet*. But this herb also has positive associations, including a use in love potions and divinations, increasing psychic powers, protecting against evil spirits and disease, and bringing good luck (Richardson 2017). It has also been used as an antidote to

FIGURE 60 Sagebrush (*Artemisia tridentata*). Photo by author.

deadly poisons, including hemlock, mushrooms, and sea dragon bites; as a vitality-promoting nervine and digestive tonic; and in various libations such as beer, wine, absinthe, and vermouth (Grieve 1971 [1931]).

An herb of potent medicinal actions, sage has a long history of use. Described by Pliny and Dioscorides in the first century CE, this herb was famed for its digestive actions, but is widely useful for a variety of conditions. Leaves and flowering tops are harvested and prepared as an alcohol extraction in the form of tincture or liniment, or as a dried powder, infused oil, poultice, steam treatment, or tea for both internal and topical applications. Nicolas Culpeper (2018 [1653]) wrote that sage clears excesses of the choleric temperament and prescribed it as a whole-body tonic. Herbalist Matthew Wood (2008) indicated sage for those with sluggish vital forces and people who are overwhelmed by the stressors of life. As a bitter digestive tonic, sage stimulates secretions and peristaltic action; increases liver and gall bladder functions; reduces heartburn, gas, cramping, and other symptoms of indigestion; and revitalizes those suffering from low appetite or otherwise poor digestion. Sage also helps clear the body of stagnancy and toxins through diuretic action that also moves urinary gravel and reduces edema. These stimulating and detoxifying actions in the digestive and urinary systems may be the driving force behind sage's anti-inflammatory and pain-relieving effects, making it a useful treatment for musculoskeletal pain, arthritis, gout, and physical trauma resulting in bruising, sprains, broken bones, or damaged connective tissue. Sage is also a well-known vermifuge, antiparasitic, and antifungal capable of ridding the body of worms (especially pinworms and roundworms), repelling moths and other insects, and clearing athlete's foot, scabies, and lice. Furthermore, sage's antiseptic and anti-inflammatory properties are useful for treating wounds, bites, and stings, making oral health care mouthwashes, creating antimalarial medicines (*A. annua*), and treating jaundice. The herbal legacy of sage is most certainly shaped by its use in making absinthe, a potent liquor that is considered to be a nervine, mental restorative, and vermifuge. For many years, absinthe remained within the confines of herbal medicine but eventually crept into social culture and became an intoxicating beverage of poets, writers, artists, and the elite. The subject of much controversy, absinthe has been banned in many countries and heavily regulated in others but has remained a beverage of legend and intrigue throughout much of Europe and beyond.

Additional layers in sage's story are woven in the New World, where long-standing traditions from different continents merged. Wide-ranging Native American groups prepared a large number of local *Artemisia* species as a decoction, poultice, smoke, or bath for numerous medicinal purposes, especially aromatic stimulation and purification. Only uses documented for southwestern species and tribes, including the Cahuilla, Tewa, Mahuna, Costanoan, Havasupai, Navajo, Zuni, Hopi, Kawaiisu, Miwok, Paiute, Shoshoni, Isleta, Keres, Haulapai, Jemez, Gosiute, and Diegueño, are summarized here. Sage's dispersive action made it a commonly used treatment for

left to right

FIGURE 61
Sagebrush leaves (*Artemisia tridentata*). Photo by author.

FIGURE 62
Louisiana sage (*Artemisia ludoviciana*). Photo by author.

FIGURE 63
Fringed sage (*Artemisia frigida*). Photo by author.

colds, coughs, asthma, and respiratory ailments (Bean and Saubel 1972; Bocek 1984; Chamberlin 1911; Fowler 1989; Hinton 1975; Kelly 1932; Mahar 1953; Robbins et al. 1916; Stevenson 1915; Steward 1933; Train et al. 1941; Vestal 1952; Watahomigie 1982; Weber and Seaman 1985; Zigmond 1981); diaphoresis and fever (Chamberlin 1911; Fowler 1989; Murphey 1990 [1959]; Nickerson 1966; Robbins et al. 1916; Stevenson 1915; Steward 1933; Swank 1932; Train et al. 1941; Vestal 1952; Weber and Seaman 1985); indigestion and cathartic action (Barrows [1900] 1967; Bocek 1984; Colton 1974; Cook 1930; Jones 1931; Murphey 1990 [1959]; Robbins et al. 1916; Steward 1933; Train et al. 1941; Watahomigie 1982; Weber and Seaman 1985; Whiting 1939; Wyman and Harris 1951); and painful conditions including arthritis, toothache, earache, and headache (Barrett and Gifford 1933; Bocek 1984; Chamberlin 1911; Elmore 1944; Swank 1932; Train et al. 1941; Vestal 1952; Watahomigie 1982; Zigmond 1981). Artemisia was also prepared for soft-tissue injuries and ailments including eczema, boils, snakebites, rashes, wounds (Bocek 1984; Colton 1974; Elmore 1944; Mahar 1953; Steward 1933; Train et al. 1941; Vestal 1952; Weber and Seaman 1985; Wyman and Harris 1951), and venereal disease (Steward 1933; Train et al. 1941). It was used as an eyewash (Train et al. 1941) and for scalp infections and hair growth (Mahar 1953; Zigmond 1981). Additionally, it was used for stimulating menses, facilitating childbirth, postpartum healing, easing menopause, and other gynecological applications (Bean and Saubel 1972; Gifford 1967; Romero 1954; Train et al. 1941; Zigmond 1981) and for treating urinary issues (Bocek 1984; Murphey 1990 [1959]; Train et al. 1941). In the magical realm, sage was a protector against evil and ghosts (Barrett and Gifford 1933) and featured in numerous purifying rituals and other ceremonies (Bean and Saubel 1972; Colton 1974; Mahar 1953; Vestal 1952; Wyman and Harris 1951).

Modern herbal traditions in the Southwest have maintained many of these uses with a focus on movement of stagnancy, especially in the respiratory and digestive systems. In high desert regions of the West, with cold dry winters, herbs that support the lungs are of great importance. Aromatic constituents including camphor make sage an effective clearing and decongesting remedy for colds, flu, coughs, asthma, bronchitis, sinus infections, and other respiratory ailments and diseases. Diaphoretic action also helps release the heat of accompanying fevers. Sage is known to stimulate uterine circulation, bringing healthy blood flow to the pelvic region in cases of scant or clotty menstrual flow and cramping. As a digestive remedy, Moore (2003) distinguished the *Artemisia* species that lack thujone, including *A. filifolia*, as these have differing effects. Whereas most species are considered stimulating digestive tonics that increase secretions in a cold and sluggish

FIGURE 64 *left*
Sand sage (*Artemisia filifolia*). Photo by author.

FIGURE 65 *below*
Sand sage leaves (*Artemisia filifolia*). Photo by author.

system, the thujone-lacking species are used instead to calm excessive secretions caused by gastric heat and inflammation. Thujone is also the reason for reported safety concerns with *Artemisia* species. The essential oil may expose people to high doses of this compound and should be used with caution. Dried herbal preparations, however, have much lower amounts of this chemical and when used appropriately should not be a cause for concern (Hoffman 2003). Although sage is quite potent

as an internal remedy, topical uses make this herb more accessible for many people. I make an alcohol-based spritz for environmental purification or for household cleaning. This same preparation with some glycerin added can be used topically for self-purification and bodily pain relief. Building on all these medicinal actions, sage has transformative powers that can be experienced only through knowing this plant in wild places. The species I know from the high desert grow in expansive dramatic landscapes, where vulnerability and exposure are woven into the relationship we make with this plant. As one passes through sagebrush flats, the aromatic particles on the wind perform their sensuous dance, moving the energy of the land around us and through us, transforming our state of being by shifting our awareness into the present moment through sensory immersion. In the American West, the magic of *Artemisia* is always at hand.

Scientific research adds more depth to our understanding of *Artemisia* in healing practices and highlights its potential role in the prevention and treatment of infectious diseases. Studies have identified numerous constituents, including alkaloids, amino acids, flavonoids, phenols, quinines, tannins, and terpenoids, contributing to its antimicrobial activity against numerous gram-positive and gram-negative bacterial strains and diverse fungal strains (Ahameethunisa and Hopper 2010; Bilia et al. 2014) as well as potential use in mycobacterial tuberculosis treatments (Gemechu et al. 2013). Abad et al. (2012) provided a detailed summary of a variety of *Artemisia* species, their active constituents, and antipathogenic activity but did not include specimens from the United States. *Artemisia* has also shown insecticidal (Liu et al. 2010) and anthelmintic activity (Akkari et al. 2014), including against ticks (Godara et al. 2014). This plant is perhaps best known in the medical world for its artemisinin, a highly prized chemical that is extracted from A. *annua* and used to make drugs that have become increasingly important in treating drug-resistant forms of malaria (O'Neill 2004). One artemisinin study observed rapid resolution of clinical malarial symptoms and cure rates of 74 percent, compared to 91 percent for drug therapy with quinine but with higher rates of recurrence (Mueller et al. 2004). *Artemisia* also exhibits antiproliferative actions against human breast carcinomas in both estrogenic-responsive and -unresponsive cell lines (Shafi et al. 2012) and cytotoxic activity against human colon cancer cells (Khalilli et al. 2017). Additional studies show that *Artemisia* is highly antioxidant (Ahameethunisa and Hopper 2012; Djeridane et al. 2007) and antidiabetic, and it lowers cholesterol by significantly reducing blood glucose, triglycerides, and other biochemical markers (Ghazanfar et al. 2014).

Ceanothus fendleri, C. greggii, C. spp. (Rhamnaceae)

RED ROOT

Ceanothus fendleri and *C. greggii* (red root) range across the Southwest and frequent dry open areas of middle-elevation mountains, desert shrublands, and woodlands. Red root may be a dominant plant in some areas and is an important foraging source for browsing wildlife such as deer, elks, and bighorn sheep, as well as small mammals, birds, and insects. It is also a valuable shrub for restoring disturbed areas as it readily transplants, fixes nitrogen in the soil, and stabilizes a variety of soil types. *C. velutinus* is more widely distributed in the Mountain West and prefers open rocky areas and semi-shaded coniferous forests. It is a pioneer species that is known to increase after logging and in the years following fires (Francis 2004) and is also valued for revegetation projects as it is willing to spread quickly on disturbed land. *Ceanothus* readily cross-hybridizes, sometimes complicating species-specific identification. *C. americanus*, which is widespread in the eastern part of the United States,

FIGURE 66
Red root shrub
(*Ceanothus
fendleri*). Photo
by author.

is commonly called New Jersey tea since it was used as a tea substitute during
the Revolutionary War.

Red root is not as widely described as many other herbs included in this
volume, but it is nonetheless a valuable addition to the apothecary. Tea or
tincture are prepared from the roots, and leaves can be gathered for a beverage tea. One of my favorite remedies for the lymphatic system, red root
encourages healthy flow of fluids throughout the system and into the inter-
stitial spaces for deep movement of vital forces. I consider it an indispensable
remedy for swollen tonsils, sore throats, and inflamed lymph nodes, and it
is useful for other areas of the body experiencing stagnancy. As described
by Moore (2003), red root's tonic action is derived from its effects on the
blood: it helps separate stacked red blood cells that may clump together as
a result of infections, inflammatory responses,
or other imbalances. These aggregated blood
cells are problematic because they reduce the
flow of blood throughout the body as the cap-
illaries refuse their entry. By unstacking these
cells, red root increases the flow of blood and
lymph, improves the circulation of nutrients
and oxygen throughout the body, expedites
the elimination of waste, and improves immune
functioning. In this way, red root is a useful herb
to add to formulas when an illness reaches a
plateau in healing since it can help reinvigorate

FIGURE 67
Red root flowers
(*Ceanothus fendleri*).
Photo
by author.

the immunological response and provide momentum in recovery. Matthew Wood (2009) explained red root's medicinal value by evoking the Doctrine of Signatures, describing the harvested root as curvaceous with nitrogen-fixing nodules that shrink upon drying. This reflects its ability to encourage water absorption in the intestines and to reduce swollen tonsils or inflamed glands. Although it's not generally associated with any side effects, Wood noted that some people experienced irritation of the tongue and taste buds, and Cech (2000) contraindicated it for people taking the anticoagulant drug warfarin or those with spleen inflammation.

Ethnobotanical documentation and modern research augment our understanding of the ways in which red root can be used medicinally. Many indigenous groups have reported uses, including as a wash for injured legs and feet (Swanton 1928; Taylor 1940) and a tea for constipation, diarrhea, and other digestive complaints (Gilmore 1933; Hamel and Chiltoskey 1975; Herrick 1977; Smith, 1928; Turner et al. 1990). Indigenous people also used it for weight loss (Turner et al. 1990), healing broken limbs (Turner et al. 1990), encouraging menses (Herrick 1977), and treating colds, coughs, and lung hemorrhages (Bushnell 1909; Densmore 1928, 1932; Herrick 1977; Merriam 1966; Palmer 1975; Taylor 1940). It also treated fevers (Merriam 1966), venereal disease (Herrick 1977; Steedman 1928), hemorrhage, broken bones, rheumatic pains (Perry 1952; Steedman 1928), sore mouth, and toothaches. Red root was used as a blood tonic (Herrick 1977) and as a powdered poultice applied to a variety of soft-tissue injuries, including burns and wounds (Hedges 1986, Herrick 1977; Swank 1932; Turner et al. 1980). It served as an emetic (Wyman and Harris 1951) and treated snakebites (Smith 1928), nervousness (Elmore 1944), eczema (Turner et al. 1980), and "curious ailments" (Murphey 1990 [1959]). An ethnobotanical study in Mexico reported that a *C. coeruleus* whole-plant preparation was made for the treatment of diarrhea and wounds (del Carmen Juarez-Vazquez et al. 2013). Although little scientific research has been done on *Ceanothus* species, studies suggest promising applications through antimicrobial and antioxidant activity. A number of terpenes, flavonoids, alkaloids, and other compounds have been identified from *C. americanus* and *C. greggii* (Klein and Rapoport 1967; Li et al. 1997; Lucero et al. 2010; Warnhoff et al. 1965). One study showed that *C. americanus* extract containing ceanothic acid and ceanothetric acid was antibacterial against pathogenic oral microbes (Li et al. 1997). Another demonstrated that *C. coeruleus* extract was antimicrobial against staph and candida as well as potently antioxidant (Salazar-Aranda et al. 2011). The authors of the latter study noted that among all seventeen plants tested, *Ceanothus* showed the strongest antioxidant and strongest antimicrobial activity and suggested that a synergistic effect may exist between antioxidants and other bioactive compounds in plants.

Datura wrightii, D. spp. (Solanaceae)

DATURA / JIMSONWEED / TOLOACHE

There are few plants with more allure than the hypnotic and foreboding datura. Its large white tubular blossoms open at night, reflecting the moonlight for a dramatic show of botanical grandeur. Prehistoric and historic usage of the plant highlights its duality: it is found at ancestral Pueblo archaeological sites dating back centuries, but modern Rio Grande Pueblos have no reported uses for the plant and often describe it with both attraction and fear (Dunmire and Tierney 1995; Yarnell 1965). Although there are twenty species worldwide, most occur in the American Southwest and Mexico and favor dry areas with natural or human disturbance, such as foothill drainages or urban areas up to seven thousand feet. While it is believed that all datura species originated in the New World, there is evidence from ancient texts for a pre-Columbian migration of *D. metel* to the Old World (Geeta and Gharaibeh 2007). Ethnobotanists theorize that datura and its ceremonial usages may have been brought to the Southwest from Mexico and that datura's noncontiguous distribution and its association with sacred sites may be explained by its relationship to prehistoric cultures (Dunmire and Tierney 1997; Yarnell 1965). Further supporting this theory is the local common name toloache, derived from the Aztec *toloatzin*. A powerful and poisonous plant, datura beckons both pollinators and herbalists with its offers of intoxication and transformation. Hawk moths, lured by the scent of night-blooming flowers, descend into the depths of the tubular blossom in search of nectar. With wings beating against the corolla, they dust themselves with pollen and often fall to the ground or fly away erratically, in search of their next intoxicating flower (Dodson 2012; Grant 1983).

Likewise, humans have a long history of seeking pain-relieving or other transformative experiences with datura. The first recorded medicinal uses come from an ancient Babylonian tablet and include references to datura's poisonous, sedating, and aphrodisiac qualities (Dodson 2012). As a highly toxic plant, datura teaches us caution and respect for the powers of

FIGURE 68
Datura flower
(*Datura wrightii*).
Photo by author.

the plant world. Furthermore, alkaloid proportions can vary between plants (Moore 2003), making the plant unpredictable (Bean and Saubel 1972), increasing the danger of misuse, and highlighting the importance of relationship with this plant. I have personally witnessed a rash develop from brushing bare skin against its leaves, and Dunmire and Tierney (1997) noted that simply smelling a flower can make some nauseous or sedate children into drugged sleep. Consuming twenty seeds can be fatal (Dunmire and Tierney 1997), and ethnobotanists Bean and Saubel (1972) reported accidental deaths among the Cahuilla. Disturbing stories from people who have consumed the plant are common. One such tale comes from Jamestown, Virginia, where soldiers boiled and ate spring shoots (likely *D. stramonium*), with hallucinations and foolishness ensuing for eleven days before they returned to normal, with no memory of the events (Beverley 2013 [1722]). Ethnobotanist Matilda Coxe Stevenson (1915) related details of datura intoxification and listed licorice (*Glycyrrhiza lepidota*) root decoction as an antidote; Vestal (1952) reported that the Navajo drank a cold winterfat (*Krascheninnikovia lanata*) infusion for overdose. Clearly, datura should not be consumed internally and is reserved for topical use. As a topical remedy, datura leaves and flowers are among our best analgesics and are prepared as a bath, poultice, infused oil, or liniment. These can be helpful for wounds, headaches, cramps, achy muscles, sports injuries, arthritis, hemorrhoids, and hot, inflamed skin conditions. I find datura especially helpful when there is an emotional or psychological component to a person's pain, as this plant can be deeply transformative beyond the physical realm. For this purpose, I prepare a salve with datura and other analgesic herbs appropriate for the specific condition, such as cottonwood (*Populus deltoides wislizenii*), snakeweed (*Gutierrezia sarothrae*), goldenrod (*Solidago* spp.), or creosote (*Larrea tridentata*). Datura, mullein (*Verbascum thapsus*), and sage (*Salvia officinalis*) smoke is also valuable as an emergency medicine for asthma constriction and severe allergic reactions as it relaxes bronchial spasms and reduces excess secretions (Bean and Saubel 1972; Moore 2003). I have made this blend with added red clover (*Trifolium pratense*) blossoms and observed its ability to quickly avert the onset of an allergy-induced asthma attack. Side effects of misuse include dry mouth, blurred vision, acute confusion, fever, rapid heart rate, inflamed skin, dilated pupils, urinary retention, hallucinations, headache, irregular pulse, convulsions, coma, or death (Monira and Munan 2012).

Native American relationships with this plant vary, with some groups using the plant medicinally, others using it ceremonially, and some avoiding or fearing it. The uses and preparations of datura were recorded by early ethnographers across the Southwest, and clay vessels resembling datura seedpods have been found at many archaeological sites across the Southwest and Mexico, dating back thirteen hundred years or more in New Mexico and Arizona (Huckell and Toll 2004). Reported uses are consistent with what has already been described and include additional ceremonial and medicinal knowledge, the details of which are largely unknown outside the respective cultural groups. Ethnobotanists Bean and Saubel (1972:60) referred to datura

FIGURE 69
Datura seed
capsules (*Datura
wrightii*). Photo
by author.

as "one of the most universally used hallucinogenic and medicinal plants known to man." Bean and Saubel reported that the Cahuilla smoked dried leaves to transcend worlds, have visions, encounter spirits, transform into other animals, diagnose illness, alleviate pain, increase stamina, enhance mental perception, give hunters increased power and connectivity to animals, or to "pursue a falling star to recapture a lost soul and return it to its owner" (61). Many other tribes have used datura in similar ways. The Paiute ate seeds while gambling to guess the opponent's hand or to invite visitations with the dead (Steward 1933). The Zuni used it to see ghosts, empower rain priests to bring water, and enable victims to identify perpetrators in their dreams (Stevenson 1915). The Hopi used it to cure meanness (Whiting 1939) and to induce visions for diagnosis (Colton 1974). Datura has a strong association with Pueblo ruins—seeds have been found at numerous settlement sites dating from the 1100s to Spanish colonial times—but little documented use from modern Pueblo people (Dunmire and Tierney 1995; Yarnell 1965). Looking beyond the American Southwest, Safford (1922) noted datura's remarkable consistency of use in ceremony, magic, and medicine among diverse and geographically remote cultures of both the Old and New Worlds.

Scientific research on datura's applications in herbal medicine have been fairly extensive for the Old World *D. metel*, which features prominently in Ayurvedic traditions along with *D. stramonium* (Kadam et al. 2018; Monira and Munan 2012; Parveen et al. 2016). Toxic alkaloids identified for *D. metel* include atropine, hyoscamine, and scopolamine (Shaik 2012) along with compounds such as saponins, tannins, steroids, flavonoids, phenols, and glycosides with numerous medicinal actions (Monira and Munan 2012; Parveen et al. 2016). Alkaloids from smoking a *Datura stromonium* cigarette were shown to be an effective asthma treatment, with anticholinergic and bronchodilating action (Charpin et al. 1979). Studies suggest that *D. stramonium* combined with herbs such as skullcap (*Scutellaria lateriflora*) may reduce seizures

FIGURE 70 Datura (*Datura wrightii*). Photo by author.

(Peredery 2004) and also act as a hypoglycemic treatment, effectively lowering blood glucose levels (Murthy et al. 2004). Other research has shown datura to be antibacterial against gram-positive and gram-negative organisms, including staph, pneumonia, and *Vibreo* strains (Akharaiyi 2011; Eftekhar et al. 2005; Shagal et al. 2012; Sharma et al. 2009), as well as antifungal against numerous species, including candida (Dabur et al. 2004; Khan and Nasreen 2010; Mdee et al. 2009; Sharma 2002). Datura is also a proven anti-inflammatory (Sonika et al. 2010), shown to be as effective for the treatment of gouty arthritis as standard drugs (Umamaheswari 2007). Additionally, datura is antioxidant (Akharaiyi 2011) and anticancer, showing antiproliferative activity against a human colorectal carcinoma cell line (Ma et al. 2006) and cytotoxicity against lung, gastric, and leukemia cell lines (Pan et al. 2007).

Fouquieria splendens (Fouquieriaceae)

OCOTILLO

Ocotillo is a unique plant of lower-elevation deserts across the Southwest, commonly found in rocky soils on south-facing slopes and bajadas. Its name is likely derived from the Nahuatl word *ocotl*, meaning "torch" or "pinewood." Ocotillo is highly adapted to its desert environs; its shallow roots quickly absorb any available moisture. It also produces tiny leaves after rains and may drop them in times of drought, relying on its waterproof and photosynthetic bark instead (Mooney and Strain 1964). Ocotillo's striking scarlet blossoms appear in harmony with migrating hummingbirds, a mutually critical synchronicity held in the genes of the plant that benefits both species and provides important habitat for the endangered Lucifer hummingbird. This relationship is further explained by a study showing that ocotillo plants dug up and replanted farther north and farther south still bloomed in time with their original locations (Waser 1979). In addition to pollination by migrating hummingbirds, ocotillo relies on the solo carpenter bee for reproduction. Although common throughout much of its range, it is limited to the Mojave, Sonoran, and Chihuahuan Deserts in the United States and adjacent desert states of Mexico. Ocotillo's ability to spread may be limited by its lack of tolerance for cold nights, its unwillingness to germinate in disturbed soils, and the rarity of resprouting after fire. Wild harvest of plants for use in landscaping and fence-building is a potential threat worthy of mention. According to the Borderlands Research Institute, nearly one hundred thousand wild-harvested desert plants, 67 percent of those being ocotillo, were removed from areas of West Texas between 1998 and 2001. Ocotillo is a protected native plant in Arizona but not elsewhere.

Use of ocotillo in herbal practice has been primarily related to stimulating the movement of fluids in the body to invigorate overall health and treat certain conditions affected by stagnancy. Remedies are most commonly made with bark and are prepared as a tincture or tea. Flowers are also harvested for tea, infused honey, and elixirs. As with other prickly or spiny desert plants, harvesting from healthy and abundant populations should be undertaken with mindful and respectful care. Using tree pruners, clip a single branch near the base. Using hand pruners, remove the thorns. Next take a hammer and smash the branch repeatedly along the entire length to release the bark from the heartwood. Remove the bark and with the hand pruners chop it into small pieces for tincturing along with some thorns, if desired. Mature plants can be up to two hundred years old and may be the keepers of stories unknown by smaller plants in their vicinity. Mildly expectorating and sedating, as well as decongesting to lymphatic tissue, ocotillo is beneficial for treating spasmodic coughing, swollen tonsils, and sore throats. Its antimicrobial and anti-inflammatory actions also make it a useful powder for wound care. Ocotillo's most notable traits are related to its decongesting action on the lymphatic system, with a clear affinity for the pelvic region, and therefore it finds its way into formulas for bladder infections, prostatitis, cysts, benign tumors, hemorrhoids, constipation, delayed menstruation, and poor digestion of fats and oils (Moore 1989, 1990). Ocotillo helps clear these conditions by

stimulating blood and lymph flow and improving extracellular fluid movement (Kane 2011). Due to it liver-stimulating effects and increasing intestinal absorption, ocotillo might alter the way pharmaceuticals are processed by the body. Native people made use of ocotillo throughout its range. The Mahuna prepared it as a blood tonic and purifier (Romero 1954). The Cahuilla made a beverage tea from flowers and a flour produced from ground seeds (Bean and Saubel 1972). The Papago harvested flower nectar, hardened it, and prepared it as a rock candy–like specialty food (Castetter and Underhill 1935). Krochmal et al. (1954) noted that the Apache prepared it as a soak to relieve tiredness and fatigue and applied powdered roots to reduce painful swellings.

Although the first scientific analysis of ocotillo bark was published in the *Journal of American Pharmacy* by Helen Abbott in 1885, research since then has been scant. A small set of studies has identified numerous anthocyanins (flavonoids with antioxidant effects) (Dominguez et al. 1972; Scogin 1977; Wollenweber and Yatskievych 2014), an array of iridoid glucosides (Jensen and Nielsen 1982), and other chemical compounds (Bate-Smith 1964). Very little medicinal research has been conducted on ocotillo plant extracts, but some studies have examined ocotillol, a triterpene originally isolated from *Fouquieria splendens* (Warnhoff and Halls 1965) but also found in the popular medicinal plant ginseng (*Panax* spp.). Studies on synthesized ocotillo or extracts derived from other species have shown this compound to have neuroprotective, anti-inflammatory, antibacterial, and antitumor activity (Liu et al. 2017). Since these studies have been conducted on plants other than ocotillo, they will not be explored here. A study conducted on ocotillo leaf extracts showed antibacterial activity against staph and *E. coli* (Menchaca et al. 2013). These initial findings suggest ocotillo's potential in a wide array of medicinal applications, including treatment of infectious disease, cancer, skin conditions, wounds, chronic inflammatory conditions, and degenerative neurological diseases.

Galium aparine (Rubiaceae)

CLEAVERS

Cleavers can be found growing across most of the United States in an extensive list of habitat types, including coniferous forests, meadows, deciduous woodlands, and disturbed areas. The species is highly adaptable and can be weedy in nature, assisting its proliferation and migration by grabbing onto other plants and animals with its hooked bristles. The species name *aparine* is likely derived from the Greek word *aparo*, meaning "to seize," in reference to its ability to cling onto animal fur and human clothing. This trait, along with its square stems and whorled leaves, make the species easy to identify. Although still the subject of debate, cleavers are generally regarded as native to both the Old World and the New, likely arriving in North America stuck in the fur of animals that migrated across the Bering Strait (DeFelice 2002). Cleavers provide forage for numerous insects and have long been part of human culture. They are juiced or eaten as a spring green, their seeds are roasted and used as a coffee substitute, and they also feature in herbal remedies. Cleavers are easy to cultivate and a willing occupier of the weed niche in any garden. Just throw some seeds down in a moist area and wait.

Ranging across a wide swath of the world, cleavers are a part of many herbal traditions. Indigenous groups in Nepal use juice from the plant for

FIGURE 73. Tiny cleavers flowers (*Galium aparine*).
Photo by author.

wound care (Malla and Chhetri 2012). Groups in the Indian Himalaya region made whole-plant preparations for eyewashes and wound care (Bhat et al. 2013). In Jordan, people consumed aerial parts for kidney stones and other urinary disorders (Al-Quran 2014). Also in India, people made whole-plant preparations for diuresis and detoxification (Kumari et al. 2013). Numerous Native American groups across the United States have also reported uses for cleavers, with the most common related to its diuretic action and beneficial effects on the kidneys and bladder (Campbell 1951; Chandler et al. 1979; Herrick 1977; Holmes 1884; Smith 1923, 1928, 1932). Other documented uses include as a laxative (Hamel and Chiltoskey 1975), emetic (Smith 1928; Vestal 1952), diaphoretic (Campbell 1951), and treatment for rheumatism (Bocek 1984; Powers 1874), coughs and asthma constriction (Hamel and Chiltoskey 1975), poison ivy (Herrick 1977), wounds (Bocek), skin diseases and inflammations (Gilmore 1933; Smith 1932), gonorrhea (Chandler et al. 1979; Speck 1917), spitting blood (Chandler et al. 1979), and hair loss (Gill 1983; Gunther 1973; Turner et al. 1983).

In modern herbal traditions, cleavers are known not only as a remedy for urinary problems and skin conditions but also as a mover of stagnant lymph. Aerial parts are either juiced or prepared as a tea or tincture. In the urinary system, cleavers are diuretic and employed for inflammation and gravel or stones. Cleavers are also a tonic for skin conditions, including eczema and psoriasis, as well as burns, bites, stings, wounds, and swellings. Hoffmann (2003) described their usefulness for treating chronic dry skin conditions as well as cysts, tumors, and ulcers though lymphatic stimulation and anti-inflammatory and astringent actions. Additionally, they are considered to be a purifier for the blood, a general alterative, and a treatment for colds (Grieve 1971 [1931]). As they are abundant in my garden and considered one of the best tonics for the lymphatic system (Hoffmann 2003), I use cleavers extensively as a cooling and stimulating remedy for earaches and swollen tonsils and other glands. Herbalist Matthew Wood (2008) cited cleavers' blood-thinning coumarins as helpful for infiltrating and breaking down fibrous tissues and calcifications in the muscles, lymph glands, or kidneys. Wood also indicated cleavers for inflammation or oversensitivity in the nerve endings.

Recent scientific research has been largely focused on antimicrobial and anticancer applications. Al-Snafi (2018a) provided a summary of research

FIGURE 74.
Cleavers (*Galium
aparine*). Photo
by author.

pertaining to cleavers' phytochemical analysis and pharmacological uses. *Galium aparine* contains a number of constituents, including phenols, tannins, alkaloids, anthraquinones, coumarins, iridoids, asperuloside, alkanes, flavonoids, and saponins (Abbas et al. 2012; Aslanturk et al. 2017; Jian et al. 2010; Mocan et al. 2016). Studies have shown it to be antibacterial and antifungal, having inhibitory effects against staph, bacillus, candida, and others (Goryacha et al. 2014; Vasilevna et al. 2016). Cleavers have also exhibited a high degree of antioxidant activity and free radical scavenging (Aslanturk et al. 2017; Bokhari et al. 2013; Neelam and Zu 2012; Vlase et al. 2014) as well as curative effects on liver toxicity when combined with the Asian plants Indian barberry (*Berberis lycium*) and crab's claw (*Pistacia integerrima*) (Khan et al. 2008). Furthermore, studies on extracts of *Galium aparine* show cytotoxicity against human breast cancer, colon cancer, and peripheral lymphocytes (Aslanturk et al. 2017; Bokhari et al. 2013) and antiproliferative activity against leukemia (Shi et al. 2016).

Glycyrrhiza lepidota (Fabaceae)

LICORICE / AMOLILLO

American licorice is widely distributed across much of the United States, primarily in moist prairie, grassland, or riparian areas of the plains and western states. It is well adapted to disturbed soil and often grows along ditches and

Materia
Medica

roadsides, and in altered riparian environments. Licorice can form colonies through spreading rhizomes and serves as forage for numerous animals, including deer, elks, pronghorn, birds, and small mammals. The genus name *Glycyrrhiza*, meaning "sweet root," is derived from Greek, and the well-researched Old World species *G. glabra* is about fifty to sixty times sweeter than sugar. This quality has made licorice a valuable flavoring for herbal remedies and foods, in addition to its many medicinal uses. The historical herbal traditions surrounding American licorice are not nearly as well documented as those pertaining to *G. glabra*, whose uses are recorded in ancient texts such as the Code of Hammurabi of ancient Babylonia, dating back nearly four thousand years, and the herbal writings of Hippocrates and Dioscorides.

Glycyrrhiza lepidota has a history of medicinal use in the American West, and other species have been used similarly around the world. The large spreading rhizomes and deep growing taproots are collected for tea or tincture and used for a wide variety of ailments, including chronic inflammation, liver disease, respiratory illness, and digestive issues. For tincturing, I prepare a double-strength decoction and add 25 percent alcohol as a preservative. Licorice leaves and roots have been used by Native people including the Bannock, Blackfoot, Cheyenne, Dakota, Isleta, Keres, Lakota, Navajo, Paiute, Pawnee, and Zuni for treating the flu (Rogers 1980), sore throat (Hart 1992; Murphey 1990 [1959]; Nickerson 1966; Swank 1932), cough (Hellson 1974), fever (Gilmore 1991 [1919]; Hart 1992; White 1945), earaches (Gilmore 1913a, 1991 [1919]; Hart 1992), chest pain (Hellson 1974), upset stomach, and

FIGURE 75
Licorice leaves and burrs (*Gly-cyrrhiza lepidota*). Photo by author.

diarrhea (Hart 1981, 1992). It has been used as a laxative (Vestal 1952), and its roots are chewed to relieve toothache or for a general cooling effect (Camazine and Bye 1980; Gilmore 1991 [1919]; Hart 1992). Licorice has been applied topically to swellings (Hellson 1974), and its shoots and roots are eaten as food (Grinnell 1972; Hart 1992). Kindscher (1987, 1992) reported variation in the flavor of licorice roots described by early ethnographers and explorers, ranging from sweet to bitter, suggesting that different soils or other

environmental conditions could be responsible. Curtin (1965) described licorice's use among Hispanic communities of the Southwest for postpartum care, restoring the uterus, and acting as an emmenagogue. Anti-inflammatory activity similar to cortisone makes licorice useful for autoimmune conditions, including allergies and asthma. I often include licorice in formulas for various forms of chronic inflammation. Its hepatoprotective qualities have resulted in a long history of use in chronic liver disease, such as hepatitis and cirrhosis. Licorice has beneficial effects on the respiratory system by inhibiting viral infections, loosening mucus, and reducing bronchial inflammation. In the digestive system, licorice can help strengthen the mucosa to protect against ulcers and also directs more fluids into the feces, acting as a stool softener and easing constipation. Its steroid-like actions can also stimulate estrogen and adrenocorticosteroid activity and positively affect menstrual imbalances and many other bodily functions. Licorice also acts as an effective synergist for herbal formulas, potentiating the effects of other herbs. As little as 10 percent in an herbal formula brings out the best of other plants. Due to licorice's ability to cause sodium and water retention along with the excretion of potassium, it is associated with side effects, including hypertension, edema, and potassium depletion. Its use is therefore contraindicated for people with high blood pressure or edema. A form of deglycyrrhized licorice (DGL) has been developed to provide licorice's benefits while minimizing such risks (Dastagir and Rizvi 2016).

RESEARCH SUMMARY Despite a history of medicinal use, very little research has been conducted on *G. lepidota*. Phytochemical analysis has identified an assortment of specific bioactive compounds, including antimicrobial bibenzyl, glabranin, pinocembrin, and glepidotin A, B, and C (Gollapudi et al. 1989; Mitscher et al. 1983). A more recent study revealed an antiviral compound, diprenylated bibenzyl, which showed moderate inhibition of

HIV-infected white blood cells (Manfredi et al. 2001). Conversely, a significant body of research exists on the Old World species G. *glabra*, which is commonly sold in the herbal market and warrants attention here. Research has isolated a large number of compounds, including steroids, flavonoids, saponins, glycosides, and terpenoids, with glycyrrhizin generally considered to be a primary medicinal constituent (Chopra et al. 2013; Varsha et al. 2013). Many review articles summarizing G. *glabra*'s phytochemical breakdown and pharmacological uses have been published (e.g., Kaur et al. 2013; Parvaiz et al. 2014; Sharma and Agrawal 2013; Zadeh and Kor 2013).

Research on licorice has involved numerous potential therapeutic applications, including use as an antioxidant, immune modulator, antimicrobial, anti-inflammatory, neuroprotector, antitumor agent, and hepatoprotector. Licorice's antioxidant and potent free radical scavenging activity is well documented and may be a mechanism for many of its medicinal actions (Chopra et al. 2013; Di et al. 2005; Haraguchi et al. 1998; Latif et al. 2012; Varsha et al. 2013; Vaya et al. 1998). Antibacterial activity may be connected to this quality (Sharma and Agrawal 2013), and studies have shown licorice to be strongly active against numerous gram-positive and gram-negative bacterial organisms, including tuberculosis and candida (Chopra et al. 2013; Gupta et al. 2008; Irani et al. 2010; Nitalikar et al. 2010; Varhsa et al. 2013). It also stimulates macrophage activity (Wagner and Jurcic 2002) and other immune cells (Blatina 2003; Brush et al. 2006); is effective against yeast and fungus, including drug-resistant strains of candida (Fatima et al. 2009); shows rapid activity against numerous cavity-causing bacteria (Hwang et al. 2004; Sedighinia et al. 2012); and may have antimalarial applications (Sianne and Fanie 2002). Licorice is also strongly antiviral and has demonstrated an ability to control viral replication, making it useful in treatments for SARS, HIV (Clercq 2000; Hattori et al. 1989; Ito et al. 1988), hepatitis A (Crance et al. 1990), hepatitis C (Su et al. 1984; Van Rossum et al. 1999), herpes zoster (Baba and Shigeta 1987), herpes simplex (Partridge and Poswillo 1984; Pompei et al. 1979), and cytomegalovirus (Numazaki et al. 1994). Licorice is also well-known for reducing inflammation, and one study showed that glycyrrhizin and other isolated constituents strongly reduced anaphylactic reactions in the skin, suggesting a usefulness in treatments for dermatitis and asthma (Shin et al. 2007). Glycyrrhizic acid is similar in structure to hormones secreted by the adrenal cortex and accounts for licorice's gluco-corticoid activity (Armanini et al. 1983). Licorice exerts steroid-like anti-inflammatory actions that mimic hydrocortisone, and it inhibits the production of other inflammatory markers (Ohuchi and Tsurufuji 1982; Okimasu et al. 1983).

Licorice has a protective effect in many body systems. In the nervous system, it improves sleep, enhances memory and learning, reduces pain and anxiety, and acts as an anticonvulsant. One study showed that licorice extract potentiated pentobarbital-induced sleep, increased non-REM sleep without decreasing delta activity, increased the duration of sleep, and reduced sleep latency (Cho et al. 2012). Others demonstrated significantly enhanced memory (Chakravarthi and Avandhani 2012; Dhingra et al. 2004) and learning (Ravichandra et al. 2007), possibly through antioxidant and anti-inflammatory actions, and suggested that licorice may be effective for the management of neurodegenerative conditions (Chakravarthi and Avandhani 2013; Dhingra et al. 2004). Anticonvulsant activity has also been shown by delaying the onset of induced convulsions and protecting animals against induced seizures (Ambawade et al. 2002; Nassiri-Asl et al. 2007; Yazdi et al. 2011). Furthermore, studies suggest that licorice can reduce pain (Bhandage et al. 2009) and anxiety (Ambawade et al. 2001) and protect against chronic fatigue stress (Trivedi and Sharma 2011) and other stress (Sowmya and Kumar 2010). Licorice also defends the body through antitumor and cytotoxic activity, with studies showing that isolated antioxidant compounds prevented induced colon and lung tumors (Chin 2007), inhibited tumor cells (Sheela et al. 2006), induced cell death in breast cancer cells (Jo et al. 2005), and had other cytotoxic effects (Lee et al. 2007; Rathi et al. 2009; Yoon et al. 2005). Licorice is also hepatoprotective (Al Razzuqii and Al-Hussaini 2012; Luper 1999; Nagai et al. 1991; Van Rossum et al. 2001), with studies indicating that it protects the liver from peroxidative damage (Rajesh and Latha 2004). When taken with milk thistle (*Silybum marianum*), it is protective against oxidative stress on the liver (Rasool et al. 2014). One study showed that licorice is protective to the kidneys, reducing excretion of urinary protein in induced nephritis (Fukai et al. 2003). Licorice is also beneficial in the respiratory system through demulcent and expectorating actions that ease sore throats and coughing, and loosen thick mucus (Hikino et al. 1985; Jahan and Siddique 2012; Kamei et al. 2003). One study demonstrated that it was more effective than codeine in reducing coughing without adverse effects (Saha et al. 2011). Protective effects in the digestive system include reducing symptoms of dyspepsia (Raveendra

FIGURE 77.
Licorice (*Glycyrrhiza lepidota*). Photo by author.

et al. 2012) and inhibiting ulcers (Kalaigandhi and Poovendran 2011) by reducing gastrin (Masoomeh and Kiarash 2007), increasing mucus secretion, and reducing pepsin (Adel et al. 2005). Additionally, research on licorice has shown its ability to regulate body functions by decreasing total cholesterol, triglycerides, and LDL and increasing HDL (Maurya et al. 2009); reducing blood glucose levels (Rastogi and Mehrotra 1994; Takii et al. 2000); lowering testosterone levels (Armanini et al. 1999, 2002); and acting as an anticoagulant (Mauricio et al. 1997; Mendes-Silva et al. 2003).

Grindelia squarrosa, G. spp. (Asteraceae)

GRINDELIA / GUMWEED / YERBA DEL BUEY

Grindelia is found in a variety of habitats, including grasslands, prairies, shrublands, woodlands, and coniferous forests, and prefers open areas with dry soils. A resilient and short-lived reseeding perennial, it is also often found at roadsides, waste areas, and other disturbed sites and is sometimes used in roadside revegetation projects. Grindelia is known to increase on overused grazing lands and is undesirable to livestock and most wildlife due to its tannins, volatile oils, resins, alkaloids, and other compounds. These give it an unpleasant taste and texture while also protecting the plant and providing a foundation for its medicinal actions in people. The genus *Grindelia* includes numerous species, some of which are limited to single states or adjacent states, but collectively it ranges across much of the United States. The American West is home to about seventeen species with G. *squarrosa* being the most widespread by far. G. *squarrosa* is an interesting example of plant intelligence. Its appearance varies; it may grow ray flowers (petals) to attract pollinators or may opt not to develop these structures and self-pollinate. This regulatory action is held within the genes of the plant and can be activated or not, depending on plant responses to local conditions. This strategy conserves critical resources, allows reproduction when pollinator presence is low, and likely facilities expansion into new areas where pollinators may not be present (Minsung 2008).

The recorded medicinal history of grindelia in American medicine begins in the 1800s, but it was used earlier by Native people and early colonists of the West. Numerous tribes of the plains and the western states have reported uses of grindelia, including treatments for poison oak and venomous bites, holding wounds together during healing, and reducing pain and swelling (Barrett and Gifford 1933; Bocek 1984; Camazine and Bye 1980; Cook 1930; Hart 1981, 1992; Romero, 1954; Train et al. 1941; Vestal 1952; Zigmond 1981). It has been used for blood tonification (Hedges 1986; Chesnut 1902; Merriam 1966); easing colic and stomachaches (Chamberlin 1909, 1911; Chesnut 1902; Gilmore 1913a, 1991 [1919]; Hart 1992; Murphey 1990 [1959]; Swank 1932; Train et al. 1941); calming colds, coughs, pneumonia, and tuberculosis (Chesnut 1902; Gilmore 1991 [1919]; Hart 1992; Ray 1932; Train et al. 1941); soothing urinary irritation (Beardsley 1941; Train et al. 1941); liver support (Hart 1992; Johnston 1987; McClintock 1909; Murphey 1990 [1959]); and treating venereal disease (Beardsley 1941; Blankinship 1905; Train et al. 1941). Dunmire and Tierney (1995) added to this record by discussing Pueblo

FIGURE 78. Grindelia showing ray flowers and resinous exudate (*Grindelia squarrosa*). Photo by author.

people's uses for grindelia, including many of the same applications, and also describing an archaeological find of grindelia seeds in a bowl with amaranth seeds, suggesting they may have been eaten. These traditional applications shaped its use by eclectic physicians and herbalists who followed. Grindelia was first mentioned in 1863 as a poison ivy remedy by Dr. C. A. Canfield of California and subsequently popularized by James G. Steele of San Francisco in 1875 (Lloyd 1921). Many of its applications were adopted, especially as a treatment for the urinary and respiratory systems as well as skin conditions. Grindelia's resinous flower buds are harvested when covered in their sticky white exudate and prepared as a high-alcohol tincture or infused oil, although leaves are sometimes also used for tea. These preparations serve as antispasmodics and bronchodilators for asthma and dry coughs, mucus cutters for wet coughs, diuretics for urinary conditions, anti-inflammatories for poison ivy, and bitters for improved digestion. Hoffman (2003) explained grindelia's usefulness in relieving asthma by describing its relaxant effect on the smooth muscles and cardiac muscles, which eases constriction in the lungs and calms a rapid heart rate or anxiousness. Grindelia was a common ingredient in cough syrups formulated by eclectic physicians around the turn of the twentieth century, and some modern over-the-counter cough remedies are still made from polysaccharides and flavonoids derived from grindelia. Grindelia with mullein (*Verbascum thapsus*) and wild lettuce (*Lactuca serriola*), formulated by New Mexico herbalist Mary Lou Singleton, was the first remedy that launched me into dedicated herbal studies after effectively treating my persistent pertussis-like cough. Since then, this herb has been a main character of many of my cough formulas. Grindelia is also useful for wound care, as it stimulates tissue healing, increases blood flow, reduces inflammation, and has antimicrobial activity. Curtin (1965) elaborated by describing its

Materia
Medica

113

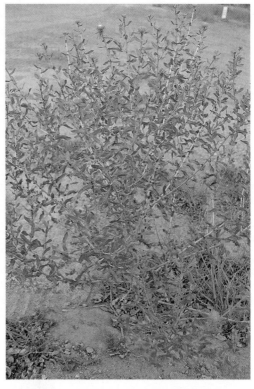

FIGURE 79. Grindelia without ray flowers showing resinous exudate (*Grindelia squarrosa*). Photo by author.

FIGURE 80. Grindelia (*Grindelia squarrosa*). Photo by author.

use as a fresh plant poultice with a rubefacient effect for treating rheumatic complaints. Additionally, grindelia's lovely botanical aroma is a personal favorite. The plant makes a wonderful infused oil for inclusion in aromatic chest balms and can be used as a natural perfume, with longer-than-expected staying power due to its sticky lingering resins.

With a long history of use for a variety of conditions, grindelia species have been the subject of scientific research exploring their therapeutic potential. The chemical composition of grindelia has been summarized by Nowak and Rychlinska (2012) and includes phenolic acids, diterpenes, methylated flavonoids, triterpenoid sapogenins, polyacetylenes, tannins, and essential oils. Grindelia species have resin levels reaching 20 percent (Timmerman 1994). Phenolic acids are widespread in medicinal plants and are thought to be responsible for their anti-inflammatory, antibacterial, spasmolytic, and antioxidant effects. Patel and Patel (2017) provided a review of studies on a number of hispidulin-containing plants. Hispidulin, a medicinal constituent found in grindelia, is a natural flavonoid that acts as a potent benzodiazepine receptor (part of the GABA receptor complex, the primary inhibitory neurotransmitter of the central nervous system) and is valued for antioxidant, antifungal, anti-inflammatory, antimutagenic, anticonvulsant, antineoplastic, antimycobacterial, antiasthma, antimicrobial, antiproliferative, and insecticidal activity

(Kavvadias et al. 2004; Lin et al. 2010). Since most of the studies summarized by Patel and Patel were conducted on extracts derived from plants other than grindelia, they are not detailed here, but they suggest that grindelia could be used to treat a variety of conditions, including cancer, osteoporosis, anxiety, neurodegenerative disease, renal disease, and inflammatory conditions. Studies conducted on grindelia leaf and flower extracts support traditional uses, including those pertaining to antimicrobial, antioxidant, and anti-inflammatory activities. One study showed that grindelia extracts have significant antibacterial activity against all tested pathogens, including *E. coli* and bacillus (Hassan et al. 2014). Another examined grindelia's array of flavonoids and hydrocinnamic acids, showing a strong inhibitory effect against enzymes associated with Alzheimer's disease and depression (Ferreres et al. 2014). Lastly, grindelia studies have shown its anti-inflammatory activity, with inhibition of nitric oxide production in macrophage cells and a reduction in tumor necrosis factor (a protein involved in systemic and acute-phase inflammation) (Verma et al. 2010).

Gutierrezia sarothrae, G. spp. (Asteraceae)

SNAKEWEED / ESCOBA DE LA VIBORA

Snakeweed is a common and wide-ranging plant on the high mesas, grasslands, and other dry, sandy, or overgrazed areas of the Mountain West and Great Plains and is a highly valued medicinal plant in many herbal traditions. A similar species, *G. microcephala*, is less frequently encountered and is limited to the Southwest. It is distinguished by having only one or two ray flowers compared to *G. sarothrae*'s three to eight ray flowers. Blooming in late summer or early fall, snakeweed brightens up the mesa at a time when few other plants are flowering, and its intoxicating scent fills the air just as we begin our transition into the darker time of year. Animals such as pronghorn, mule deer, bison, and bighorn sheep browse snakeweed. It provides cover while being a major food source for black-tailed jackrabbits, other small mammals, and small birds. Snakeweed spreads rapidly across poorly managed grazing areas and other disturbed lands, sometimes forms near monoscapes, and reduces forage availability on grasslands through allelopathy and competition with native grasses (Mayeux and Leotta 1981). I collect snakeweed along with sand sage (*Artemisia filifolia*) and often become enveloped by the aromas rising from the land while gathering these plants on wide-open desert grasslands, where transformation and alterative experiences are readily at hand. While snakeweed is currently widespread across the American West, prior to cattle grazing this native plant was less abundant than it is today. This may account for its scant presence in archaeological sites but its high importance in more modern Native American and Hispanic herbal traditions (Dunmire and Tierney 1997). Snakeweed is a frequent member of oak-juniper woodlands, desert grasslands, and other plant communities and was among the first specimens collected by Lewis and Clark along the Missouri River (Dodson 2012).

Snakeweed is plentiful and easy to gather, and is highly prized for arthritis treatments and a number of other uses. Its semi-resinous aromatic foliage and profuse golden blossoms are collected and dried to prepare soaks, liniments, infused oils, and teas. Topical remedies are used to treat arthritis, inflammation, joint soreness, and musculoskeletal pain. For this purpose, snakeweed is sometimes combined with other signature plants of the region, including datura (*Datura* spp.), creosote (*Larrea tridentata*), or sage (*Artemisia* spp.). Snakeweed is so highly valued for such treatments, in part, because it has a higher safety profile than these other plants and can be used more frequently and long term with fewer associated risks (Moore 2003). Like many other aromatic plants, snakeweed not only creates space and movement in the musculoskeletal system but also relieves stagnancy in other areas of the body, including the respiratory and female reproductive systems, making it useful as a decongestant for colds and for bringing on reluctant menses. Recent scientific research has identified various volatile compounds (Lucero et al. 2006) as well as other terpenes and flavonoids isolated in previous research (Hradetzky et al. 1987; Molyneux et al. 1980). Studies have also shown that snakeweed has cytotoxic activity against sarcoma, leukemia, and cervical cancer cells (Booth et al. 2012; Dong et al. 1987; Ulubelen et al. 1965) as well as moderate antimalarial activity (Su et al. 2016).

FIGURE 81
Snakeweed
(*Gutierrezia sarothrae*). Photo by author.

Underlying these modern applications, snakeweed has a long history of importance in traditional herbal medicine in the Southwest and on the Great Plains. Pueblo people prepare soaks, poultices, tea, or vapors as an emetic; to treat eye conditions, rattlesnake bites, bruises, colds and coughs, fevers, diarrhea, and venereal disease; and for bathing newborns, postpartum care, general purification, and other uses (Dunmire and Tierney 1995). For the Navajo, snakeweed is a "life medicine" employed in previously mentioned forms and as plant ash rubbed on the body for upset stomachs and body aches, diarrhea, fever, headaches, nervousness, cuts and scrapes, and swollen bites. The Navajo use it during childbirth for delivery of the placenta, to treat painful urination, and in ceremonies (Dunmire and Tierney 1997). Other tribes that use snakeweed include the Tewa, Keres, Jemez, Isleta, Hopi, Comanche, Paiute, Lakota, Diegueño, Blackfoot, Dakota, Cahuilla, and Kawaiisu. For these groups, it is a treatment for body aches (Camazine and Bye 1980; Elmore 1944; Taylor 1940; Train et al. 1941; Zigmond 1981), toothache (Bean and Saubel 1972), headache (Elmore 1944), diges-

FIGURE 82. Snakeweed flowers (*Gutierrezia sarothrae*). Photo by author.

tive upsets and diarrhea (Colton 1974; Hinton 1975; Robbins et al. 1916; Vestal 1952; Whiting 1939; Wyman and Harris 1951), colds and coughs (Carlson and Jones 1940; Johnston 1987; Rogers 1980; Train et al. 1941), sores and bruises (Cook 1930; Elmore 1944; Jones 1931), sprains (Train et al. 1941), measles (Train et al. 1941), venomous snakebites and stings (Elmore 1944; Swank 1932; Vestal 1952), fevers (Camazine and Bye 1980; Jones 1931; Vestal 1952), vertigo (Rogers 1980), nosebleeds (Train et al. 1941), urinary issues (Stevenson 1915), menstrual discomfort (Robbins et al. 1916), earache (Robbins et al. 1916), and venereal disease (Jones 1931). It is also used to assist in childbirth (Cook 1930; Robbins et al. 1916) and as an emetic (Swank 1932; White 1945). In Hispanic communities, where it is also highly valued, snakeweed has similar and overlapping uses, including as a treatment for arthritis, colic, and malaria; as a postpartum sitz bath or douche; and for menstrual regulation (Moore 1990).

Hypericum scouleri, H. perforatum, H. spp.
(Hypericaceae, Clusiaceae, Guttiferae)

ST. JOHN'S WORT

St. John's wort is one of many medicinal plants bridging the botanical cultures of the Old and New Worlds. The American West is home to about nine native *Hypericum* species, with *H. scouleri* being the most common. In addition, there are nine nonnative species, including the European *H. perforatum*, which is considered a noxious weed in some areas. *H. perforatum* was first recorded in North America in Pennsylvania in 1703 and was documented in many states by the early 1900s, especially in the Northwest (Sampson and Parker 1930). Today it is commonly found in a range of habitats, including numerous forest and grassland types, mountain meadows, and prairies. It is often associated with disturbance areas, such as roadsides and places that have experienced fire, logging, or grazing, and is known to form dense stands in some western landscapes. Studies have shown a high degree of morphological and

FIGURE 83
St. John's wort
flowers (*Hyperi-
cum perforatum*).
Photo by author.

phytochemical (hypericin and pseudohypericin) variation among populations in different regions (Sirvent et al. 2002; Walker 2000; Walker et al. 2001). St. John's wort is not known to provide any significant support to wildlife as forage or cover and is considered toxic to livestock as it causes photosensitivity and weakness in animals not accustomed to it.

St. John's wort is an herb with an ancient history of use in medicine and ceremony, particularly potent in wound healing and affecting the supernatural realm. Its strength was so highly regarded that King George VI named one of his racehorses Hypericum. In Europe, St. John's wort's association with defense against evil and bad magic is one of its defining characteristics going back at least to the Middle Ages (Richardson 2017). Flowers were traditionally picked on June 24, the eve of Saint John's feast day, made into floral garlands joined with vervain (*Verbena* spp.) and yarrow (*Achillea millefolium*), and strung across doorways for protection. Bonfires were lit and strewn with St. John's wort to break up the forces of evil and death during what was considered to be a dangerous time of increased activity by witches and ghosts. The protective properties of this herb were so powerful that it was also referred to as *fuga daemonium* ("devil's flight"); it was believed that the devil hated the plant so much that he stabbed the leaves repeatedly with a dagger, causing all the tiny red dots to appear on August 29, the day of Saint John's beheading (Richardson 2017). The blood of the saint further potentiated the plant's protective nature. This story explains the botanical names *Hypericum*, meaning "over an apparition" or "over an icon," and *perforatum*, or "tiny leaf punctures."

The protective magic and lore of St. John's wort help us understand this plant's medicinal uses. Flowering tops are harvested while budding and blooming and are prepared fresh as tincture or infused oil. They have also been boiled in wine, used in baths, or made into tea. During the Middle Ages, psychiatric issues were often perceived and described in terms of witchery and demonic effects upon a person; and St. John's wort has long been used in combination with other herbs, such as betony (*Stachys officinalis*), for the treatment of anxiety, depression, nervousness, and melancholy. Furthermore, the legendary wound-healing effects of St. John's wort were described by early herbal authors, from Dioscorides to Culpeper and beyond. The red dots on the leaves may be considered an expression of the Doctrine of Signatures, resembling pores on the skin and indicating the plant's usefulness in skin care and treating open wounds. St. John's wort's anti-inflammatory, astringent, vulnerary, and analgesic properties made it a favored wound care herb for knights returning from the Crusades, and the flower was an emblem for the St. John Ambulance Brigade founded in 1877 (Richardson 2017). The infused herbal oil is considered an essential remedy for burns, lesions, nerve injury, venomous bites, swellings, bruises, and other infected or inflamed traumas. Healing effects on the nervous system, along with antiviral and antispasmodic actions, bring comfort to deeper body conditions such as rheumatic pain, sciatica, varicose veins, and shingles. St. John's wort also improves digestion and metabolism by increasing tissue tone, normalizing stomach acid, improving liver functioning, and expediting elimination of wastes. Other applications include a relaxant effect in the urinary and female reproductive systems that can reduce overactive urination and bring on menses.

Herbal traditions in the American West expand upon those developed in the Old World. The Menominee, Meskwaki, Miwok, Choctaw, Iroquois, Seminole, Cherokee, Alabama, Houma, Koasati, Natchez, Montagnais, Paiute, Shoshoni, and other Native American tribes have reported using locally available species for a wide variety of applications, including kidney ailments (Smith 1923), colic (Bushnell 1909; Taylor 1940), aching feet (Train et al. 1941), fever (Hamel and Chiltoskey 1975; Herrick 1977), lung weakness and early stages of tuberculosis (Smith 1923, 1928; Speck 1917), venereal diseases (Hamel and Chiltoskey 1975; Train et al. 1941), snakebites and wounds (Barrett and Gifford 1933; Hamel and Chiltoskey 1975; Smith 1928; Train et al. 1941), nosebleeds (Hamel and Chiltoskey 1975), diarrhea (Swanton 1928; Taylor 1940), rheumatism (Taylor 1940), childbirth pain (Speck 1941), and toothaches (Speck 1941; Train et al. 1941). It has been used as an eyewash (Bushnell 1909; Swanton 1928; Taylor 1940), a laxative (Sturtevant 1965), a tonic for infants and children failing to thrive (Hamel and Chiltoskey

FIGURE 84. St. John's wort (*Hypericum perforatum*) at Cromeleque dos Almendres, a Neolithic site of standing stones in Portugal. Photo by author.

1975; Taylor 1940), and an abortifacient (Hamel and Chiltoskey 1975) and even been ground into meal as food (Barrett and Gifford 1933). St. John's wort has become an herb of choice for the often-paired afflictions of the modern computer era: back pain and carpal tunnel syndrome (Moore 2003). Living in the high desert with bitingly dry cold air in the winter months, I have found St. John's wort oil to be very useful for soothing irritated subcutaneous nerve endings in people who complain of dry itchy skin despite the skin having a healthy appearance. Every year I make fresh batches of the gorgeous burgundy-colored infused oil for use as massage oil, first-aid salve, and lip balms for the treatment of cold sores. People using these topical products commonly report feelings ranging from happiness to euphoria as an added bonus to their treatment, indicating that its mood-lifting qualities can be experienced without internal use. *H. perforatum* is an easily cultivatable plant in western gardens, preferring semi-shaded areas with moist soil. Plan accordingly, as it commonly migrates out of the place I plant it, instead creating its own spot by crowding out less fortunate plants nearby. Since St. John's wort should be prepared fresh for tinctures or freshly wilted for oils, it is highly recommended for the herbal garden despite any inconveniences its personality might cause.

RESEARCH SUMMARY Gaining widespread notoriety as a medicinal plant, St. John's wort (*H. perforatum*) has been the subject of extensive scientific research in recent decades and thus warrants a summary here. Phytochemical analysis reveals numerous active compounds, including the flavonoids rutin, quercetin, and kaemferol, as well as hypericin and hyperforin, which are believed to have the most medicinal activity (Klemow et al. 2011). Numerous studies have confirmed this plant to be just as effective as antidepressant medications for mild to moderate depression with few side effects (e.g., Apaydin et al. 2016; Kalb et al. 2001; Linde et al. 1996; Philipp et al. 1999; Schrader 2000; Vorbach et al. 1997; Wheatley 1997; Woelk 2000), but consensus is lacking regarding its effectiveness for more severe presentations (e.g., Hypericum Depression Trial Study Group 2002; Linde et al. 2009; Montgomery et al. 2000; Shelton et al. 2001). Antioxidant and neuroprotective properties connected to reductions in neurotoxicity, inflammation, and digestive ailments have also been shown through research and could lead to improved treatment for neurodegenerative diseases such as Parkinson's and Alzheimer's (Mohanasundari and Sabesan 2007; Zou et al. 2010). Research also suggests that St. John's wort is a cognitive enhancer, showing significant positive effects on both reference and working memory (Ben-Eliezer and Yechiam 2016). Also useful for opium addiction, it may activate opioid receptors without initiating withdrawal symptoms (Subhan et al. 2007) and has been shown to reduce opiate withdrawal symptoms as effectively as pharmaceuticals (Feily and Abbasi 2009).

Research has also shown the virtues of St. John's wort in treating infections, wounds, inflammation, and even cancer. Hyperforin has been known since the 1950s (Schempp et al. 1999) to be antibacterial, including against all tested gram-positive strains and especially against drug-resistant strains of staph (Bystrov et al. 1975). St. John's wort is also effective against many viruses, including influenza, herpes, and HIV, and it inactivates enveloped viruses (Diwu 1995; Holden 1991; Meruelo 1993; Mishenkova et al. 1975; Tang et al. 1990). Studies have also shown it to be anti-inflammatory, gastroprotective (Zdunic et al. 2009), an effective topical remedy for psoriasis (Mansouri et al. 2017), and useful in wound care, with topical applications improving tissue regeneration and speeding healing (Yadollah-Damavandi et al. 2015). St. John's wort is known to have an array of anticancer properties, including inhibiting tumor cell growth, inducing programmed cell death (Schempp et al. 2002), and slowing the growth of cells from neoplastic tissues (mesothelioma, melanoma,

FIGURE 85. St. John's wort (*Hypericum perforatum*). Photo by author.

carcinoma, sarcoma, leukemia, and others) (Fox et al. 1998; Hostanska et al. 2003). Furthermore, in photodynamic therapy, a photosensitizing agent such as St. John's wort is combined with specific wavelengths of light to kill cancer cells and shrink tumors. Studies suggest that St. John's wort may be useful in melanoma and lymphoma treatments of this type (Fox et al. 1998; Kleemann et al. 2014). Another study suggests its potential usefulness in a variety of oncological conditions both as a diagnostic marker and a treatment due to the accumulation of hypericin in neoplastic tissue and St. John's wort's antitumor properties, but the study also warned of its potential to interfere with anticancer drugs (Jendzelovska et al. 2016). Additional cancer studies showed St. John's wort's cytotoxic activity in conjunction with laser irradiation against prostatic, urinary, bladder, carcinoma, and pancreatic cancer cell lines (Colasanti et al. 2000; Liu et al. 2000; Kamuhabwa et al. 2000).

Herb–drug interactions with St. John's wort have been extensively studied. The herb has been found to have potentially significant interactions with a variety of drugs, including immunosuppressants, anticancer compounds, cardiovascular medications, oral contraceptives, and lipid-lowering drugs (Soleymani et al. 2017). Specific medications reported to interact with St. John's wort include fexofenadine, digoxin, and other digitalis drugs; Gleevec, amitriptyline, ivabradine, cyclosporin, verapamil, benzodiazepine, warfarin, voriconazole, SSRIs, and numerous herbs with sedating actions (Klemow et al. 2011). Interactions with pharmaceuticals may occur due to St. John's wort's ability to induce digestive or hepatic enzymes that remove drugs from the body or convert them to inactive forms (Klemow et al. 2011). Interactions may result in either potentiating the drug or reducing its effectiveness (Parker et al. 2001). Negative drug interactions were found to be associated with the chemical hyperforin and may be reduced by limiting hyperforin intake to less than one milligram daily (Chrubasik-Hausmann et al. 2018; Soleymani et al. 2017).

Juniperus monosperma, J. spp. (Cupressaceae)

JUNIPER / SABINA

To walk among juniper's powerfully aromatic branches with ancient soils underfoot and the passing clouds brushed upon the bright blue sky overhead is a transformative medicine all its own. Juniper is among the most widespread and habitat-defining plants in the American West, and ethnobotanists William Dunmire and Gail Tierney (1995) and Daniel Moerman (1998) list more uses for it than any other plant. Often mistaken for cedars, junipers are actually part of the cypress family. Numerous species inhabit vast middle-elevation acreages of the West, with populations increasing and expanding into grasslands and others found across the United States. These large, woody, drought-tolerant, aromatic shrubs are a reliable and dominant character in the piñon-juniper woodlands and play varying roles in a number of other plant communities across the West. They create good habitat and forage for mule deer, bighorn sheep, bison, wild horses, pronghorn, coyotes, bobcats, badgers, porcupines, rabbits, mice, voles, wood rats, squirrels, and numerous bird species. Additionally, seventeen other plant species have been identified only in association with piñon-juniper plant communities (Goodrich et al. 1999). As predicted higher temperatures and prolonged drought continue to unfold and plant communities respond, hearty drought-tolerant shrubs like juniper will likely become more important ecologically and medicinally.

Many juniper species are used medicinally, with alligator juniper (*J. deppeana*) being a notable exception, and uses are extensive. Teas, made from berries or leaves, have a distinct and potent aroma and flavor, often eliciting strong reactions, from enjoyment to distaste. Herbalists often use juniper

FIGURE 86. Juniper (*Juniperus monosperma*). Photo by author.

berry tincture or tea as an antiseptic diuretic for urinary tract infections and inflammations. Some include juniper in digestive formulas as a carminative and to increase gastric secretions. Some use it in topical oils for eczema or psoriasis, or use the leaves and berries in incense. Many other applications for this potent and abundant remedy stem largely from its combination of purifying, protective, and relaxant characteristics. Juniper's dense woody physical structure, enduring and reliable nature, and pungent aromatic foliage embody its enchanting and transformative power as described in chapter 4. Although we might think of pedicularis for muscle relaxation and alterative experiences, juniper is far more common and can also be used both internally and topically for similar purposes. I value juniper most as a relaxant and aromatic massage oil or a protective alcohol- and glycerin-based spray that eases the mind and body, supports those experiencing vulnerability, and can even alleviate emotional trauma. Juniper's purifying and anti-inflammatory actions are also helpful for relieving chronically inflamed skin conditions such as eczema and psoriasis.

In documented Native American herbal practice, juniper is legion. Uses summarized here are limited to southwestern species and tribes, including the

Navajo, Hopi, Zuni, Paiute, Shoshoni, Apache, Diegueño, Gosiute, Jemez, Keres, and Havasupai. Juniper berry tea is a diuretic (Mahar 1953; Train et al. 1941). Leaf tea and other preparations are used for clearing colds and coughs (Chamberlin 1911; Mahar 1953; Reagan 1929; Train et al. 1941; Vestal 1952; Weber and Seaman 1985), treating fevers (Mahar 1953; Romero 1954; Train et al. 1941; Vestal 1940, 1952), calming digestive problems such as diarrhea and constipation (Colton 1974; Cook 1930; Mahar 1953; Swank 1932; Train et al. 1941; Vestal 1952), and soothing general aches and pains (Bocek 1984; Camazine and Bye 1980; Colton 1974; Fowler 1989; Mahar 1953; Train et al. 1941; Wyman and Harris 1951). Juniper is used to treat high blood pressure and as a blood tonic (Bocek 1984; Train et al. 1941). Juniper bark baths soothe itchy bites or sore feet (Jones 1931), and heated twigs have been applied as a topical treatment for measles, smallpox, bruises, wounds, and swelling (Colton 1974; Mahar 1953; Robbins et al. 1916; Train et al. 1941). Burning branches is a treatment for colds and offers general pleasantness (Mahar 1953; Train et al. 1941). Juniper has many associations with the birthing process (Colton 1974; Jones 1931; Vestal 1952; Stevenson 1915) and with death (Colton 1974; Swank 1932). Tea serves as both a mother's muscle relaxant (Reagan 1929) and as a cleansing bath or steam for mother and baby (Robbins et al. 1916). Plants or ashes may be rubbed on newborns (Jones 1931; Colton 1974), and tea or smoke is sometimes used to aid difficult births (Vestal 1952). Juniper plays a major role in general gynecological care, including teas for postpartum health (Camazine and Bye 1980; Cook 1930; Stevenson 1915; Vestal 1952), contraception (Camazine and Bye 1980), venereal disease (Train et al. 1941), and menstrual regulation (Mahar 1953; Train et al. 1941; Vestal 1952). Juniper's association with cleansing and purification is strong and includes diaphoretic baths and teas (Bocek 1984; Mahar 1953; Swank 1932; Vestal 1952), emetic and laxative leaf and twig teas (Colton 1974; Jones 1931; Swank 1932; Vestal 1952), and protecting against negativity or evil spirits (Colton 1974; Swank 1932; Vestal 1952). Additional uses include cooking the berries with meats and stews, adding calcium-rich burned juniper ash to bread flour, cutting wood for fuel and construction, and using other plant parts for basketry, dye making, body paint, bows, mats, diapers, menstrual pads, and prayer sticks. Hispanic communities adopted many similar uses, including treating urinary infections, stimulating digestion, soothing stomachaches, and assisting in birthing and postpartum care (Curtin 1965; Moore 1990). Juniper is contraindicated for kidney infections, chronic kidney weakness, and pregnancy due to its vaso-dilating effect on the uterus.

Scientific research supports traditional uses and highlights juniper's potential in other therapeutic treatments. Phytochemical analysis has identified a number of *J. communis*'s active compounds, including numerous terpenes, phytosterols, and flavones (Bais et al. 2014), with a detailed phytochemical and pharmacological summary provided by Al-Snafi (2018b). Numerous studies have shown juniper's antibacterial and antifungal activity against staph, strep, *E. coli*, tuberculosis, and several drug-resistant bacteria strains (Al-Snafi 2018b; Fierascu et al. 2018; Gordien et al. 2009; Haziri et al. 2013; Modnicki and Labedzka 2009;

Pepeljnjak et al. 2005; Rezvani et al. 2009; Sati and Joshi 2010; Sela et al. 2013). Juniper extracts exhibit strong scavenging and chelating antioxidant action (Al-Snafi 2016; Elmastas et al. 2006; Fierascu et al. 2018; Hoferl et al. 2014; Miceli et al. 2009; Stoilova et al. 2014; Ved et al. 2017), hepatoprotective activity (Manvi 2010; Singh et al. 2015; Ved et al.), and neuroprotective properties against Parkinson's-like symptoms (Rana and Bais 2014), along with offering an increase in working memory (Cioanca et al. 2014). Juniper's anti-inflammatory and analgesic properties have been demonstrated through studies showing reduced prostaglandin and other inflammatory markers (Han and Parker 2017; Schneider 2004; Tunon et al. 1995), antiarthritic actions (Bais et al. 2017), and significant central analgesic activity (Banerjee et al. 2012). Antidiabetic, antihyperlipidemic (Manvi 2010), and antihypercholesterolemic properties (Akdogan et al. 2012) have also been observed through significant hypoglycemic activity (Sanchez et al. 1994); major reductions in blood glucose, total cholesterol, triglyceride, and LDL; and an increase in HDL (Banerjee et al. 2013). Gastrointestinal studies showed that juniper has significant antiulcer activity, with improved healing by reducing the volume and acidity of gastric secretions (Pramanik et al. 2007). In the urinary system, juniper shows antilithic activity by significantly reducing stones comprised of calcium oxalate, calcium hydrogen phosphate, magnesium ammonium phosphate, and ammonium urate (Barzegarnejad et al. 2014). Furthermore, Juniper may have antifertility properties as seen through antiprogestational (Pathak et al. 1990) and abortifacient effects when administered on days fourteen through sixteen of pregnancy (Agrawal et al. 1980). Lastly, juniper has shown cytotoxicity against human breast cancer cell lines (Benzina et al. 2015; Ghaly et al. 2016), human pulmonary adenocarcinoma (De Marino et al. 2011), and human neuroblastoma (Lantto et al. 2016). Given this large volume of evidence highlighting juniper's diverse protective and healing properties, it is no surprise that is has been so highly regarded by the people who live alongside this remarkable yet ordinary shrub.

Larrea tridentata (Zygophyllaceae)

CREOSOTE / CHAPARRAL / HEDIONDILLA / GOBERNADORA

Creosote has long been recognized as a source of medicine by many cultural groups and has more recently been the subject of scientific research confirming old uses and illuminating new potential. An important plant in many herbal traditions, creosote is known as hediondilla in Spanish traditions, gobernadora in Mexican communities, and chaparral among modern herbalists. Ranging across the greater Southwest, creosote is found in all the major deserts and is a dominant plant in the Chihuahuan Desert, sometimes forming expansive, nearly monotypic stands where overgrazing has occurred. A detailed discussion of creosote's ecological considerations and implications for its medicinal actions is included in chapter 2. Creosote provides shelter for numerous animals, including the desert tortoise and the kangaroo rat, which make use of shade created by its branches in the desert. Many small mammals, including black-tailed jackrabbits and wood rats, browse its leaves or eat its seeds. Becoming acquainted with creosote brings the seeker into vast desert basins, where unrelenting heat, the penetrating aroma of creosote leaves, and the humbling exposure of standing under endless blue skies and unyielding sun may converge to create an altered state of awareness.

Until the historic cattle-grazing era, which largely relegated creosote to the category of invasive shrub, it enjoyed a long history of being valued by local people as an important resource for making medicine and items of material

FIGURE 88. Creosote leaves and flowers (*Larrea tridentata*). Photo by author.

culture. Dried leaves, flowers, seeds, and twigs are prepared as a 75 percent tincture, infused oil, salve, soak, liniment, poultice, or purifying smoke (not inhaled). Scientific research going back decades has isolated a number of chemicals believed to be responsible for creosote's powerful medicinal actions, including NDGA and individual ligans and flavonoids. Creosote is most often used as a topical because it is so potent; it is unpalatable to most people, and long-term or regular internal use can have negative health effects due to the extra work required by the liver to process the herb. Creosote's stimulating effect on the liver, however, makes it a useful remedy for the easement of arthritis and other joint pains, as well as for allergies and other autoimmune conditions where bodily purification is called for. Furthermore, creosote's powerful dispersive effect and potent activity against a number of stubborn microbes, including fungi, yeast, bacteria, and protozoa, make it a useful first aid herb or an excellent addition to formulas for serious illnesses such as bronchitis, tuberculosis, *E. coli*, staph, and MRSA (Lambert et al. 2012; Martins et al. 2013: Quiroga et al. 2004; Schmidt et al. 2012; Snowden et al. 2014). I find creosote to be essential for treating athlete's foot and other fungal infections and it is useful in formulas to clear other unrelenting infectious or inflammatory conditions. For athlete's foot, toenail fungus, or similar infections in other areas of the body, I prepare an infused antimicrobial liquid soap, salve, or soak. The infused liquid soap is also very helpful for cases of acne or tinea barbae (a fungal infection in facial hair).

FIGURE 89. Creosote (*Larrea tridentata*). Photo by author.

Recent studies have also shown creosote's potential in treatments for breast cancer and melanoma as well as its antioxidative and anti-inflammatory chemoprotective applications for skin cancer (Lambert et al. 2005; Rahman et al. 2011; Van Slambrouck et al. 2007). This plant's fifty-plus-year history of phytochemical and medicinal research focused on antimicrobial and antitumor properties seems to fit its stubborn and relentless nature along with its propensity to spread across the land, altering ecology along the way.

Indigenous people of the American Southwest and Mexico used creosote for a variety of ailments. It was widely used and often regarded as a panacea (Curtin 1984 [1949]; Train et al. 1941). Uses documented from the Papago, Paiute, Cahuilla, Yavapai, Pima, Mahuna, Kawaiisu, Hualapai, Diegueño, Isleta, and Shoshoni include treatments for arthritis and body aches (Bean and Saubel 1972; Castetter and Underhill 1935; Curtin 1984 [1949]; Gifford 1936; Hedges 1986; Jones 1931; Train et al. 1941; Zigmond 1981), colds and respiratory conditions including asthma and tuberculosis (Barrows 1967 [1900]; Bean and Saubel 1972; Curtin 1984 [1949]; Murphey 1990 [1959]; Train et al. 1941; Watahomigie 1982), dandruff (Curtin 1984 [1949]), burns, and wounds

(Bean and Saubel 1972; Castetter and Underhill 1935; Train et al. 1941). It was used for toothaches and as a mouthwash or gargle (Curtin 1984 [1949]), for bowel and gastric complaints (Bean and Saubel 1972; Curtin 1984 [1949]; Romero 1954; Train et al. 1941), and as a purifying emetic for treating fevers and other ailments (Bean and Saubel 1972; Castetter and Underhill 1935; Curtin 1984 [1949]). It also treated venereal disease (Gifford 1936; Train et al. 1941) as well as menstrual cramps and irregularities (Bean and Saubel 1972; Castetter and Underhill 1935; Romero 1954). Creosote leaves were powdered and applied to a newborn's navel or to the mother to induce milk flow. They were used as bedding to ease postpartum cramps (Castetter and Underhill 1935). The Seri of Sonora, Mexico, prepared creosote either as a hot leaf or ash poultice, a tea soak, or a purifying smoke or steam of leafy branches for those experiencing postpartum discomfort, headaches, stingray wounds, or other pains (Felger and Beck Moser 1985). The Hispanic herbal tradition continued many of these same uses, especially as a poultice, soak, or salve (mixed with oshá, tobacco, and/or trementina de piñon) for arthritis, skin or saddle sores, and ringworm. Creosote tea has also been used as an antiseptic for urinary inflammations. Internal use may be contraindicated for people taking prescription drugs due to its stimulating effects on the liver.

Ligusticum porteri, L. spp. (Apiaceae)

OSHÁ / CHUCHUPATE / BEAR ROOT

Oshá strongly characterizes the central role that botanical relationships can play in the life and culture of a region. It is a primary medicinal plant of the Southwest that is known to be widely used by inhabitants of its natural range and beyond. Its earliest documented use is represented by a medicine bundle containing oshá and other medicinal plants found in southeastern Utah and dated between two hundred and six hundred years ago (Harrison 2000). The name oshá may be derived from the Spanish word *oso* or from Native American words for "bear," as it is a known medicinal plant for bears, which dig the roots and rub them on their bodies (Bowen 1895; Costa-Neto 2012). Oshá inhabits moist meadows and forests in subalpine and montane areas of the southern Rocky Mountains and other mountain ranges of the American Southwest and northern Mexico. The plant's preference for open meadows and its pattern of setting more seed in these habitats could potentially facilitate its migration into new areas as forests experience increased large-scale disturbances such as fires and bark beetle outbreaks. Distinct chemotypes in oshá populations have been observed in Colorado, with Front Range samples containing more than twice as much (Z)-ligustilide (a major medicinally active constituent) than those from the Western Slope (Smith et al. 2018). When identifying oshá, take care not to confuse it with other members of this plant family, some of which contain deadly toxins, such as poison hemlock (*Conium maculatum*) and water hemlock (*Cicuta maculata*). Guidance on differentiating these species is provided in the American Herbal Pharmacopoeia oshá monograph (2018).

Highly esteemed in indigenous cultures and Hispanic herbal traditions, oshá has become a popular and sought-after herbal remedy, with interest rising around the world. This high-profile image combined with it being notoriously difficult to cultivate has contributed to concerns about conservation and sustainable harvest. The nonprofit organization United Plant Savers includes oshá on its "at risk" list, and Moore (2003) suggested that harvest pressure could be reduced by using *L. grayii* and *L. filicinum* as suitable substitutes. I use herbs such as grindelia (*Grindelia squarrosa*), sage (*Salvia officinalis*), and bee balm (*Monarda fistulosa*) as substitutes for most respiratory applications, reserving oshá for more acute situations only. Nevertheless, unregulated root harvest from wild populations is part of the reality of oshá, as such practices stand at the heart of local ancestral herbal traditions and market demands motivate commercial wildcrafters. According to Kindscher et al. (2019), most harvesting occurs on us Forest Service lands with no permit. The Kindscher et al. study harvested oshá at variable rates (0 percent, 33 percent, 66 percent, and 100 percent) from multiple montane plots in southern Colorado and observed recovery rates with the purpose of helping to guide policy for sustainable harvest of wild populations on public lands. The study suggested that oshá populations can recover quickly to preharvest conditions at lower rates of harvesting (33 percent) and may be facilitated by rhizomatous remains that resprout after harvesting (Kindscher et al. 2013). The rate of recovery slowed as harvesting increased to 66 percent, and the full 100 percent harvest resulted in significant impacts after five years of observation. Based on these results, a recommendation of a 50 percent rate of harvesting mature plants over ten years was proposed.

With potent and reliable medicinal actions and a long history of use, oshá is considered an indispensable remedy in many apothecaries. Prepared as a

top to bottom

FIGURE 90
Oshá flowers
(*Ligusticum porteri*).
Photo by author.

FIGURE 91
Oshá flowers
(*Ligusticum porteri*).
Photo by author.

fresh or dry root tincture, syrup, elixir, essential oil, powder, smoke, or infused honey, or simply chewed, oshá is a top remedy for colds, coughs, sore
throats, fevers, and other viral infections. Its diaphoretic, anesthetizing, expectorating, and detoxifying effects make it useful for early stages of infection
or as a preventive. Moore (2003) reported that oshá root increased bronchial
capacity and significantly reduced the adverse effects of high altitude. Oshá
is also useful as a bitter digestive remedy and as an antibacterial and styptic
for wound care. Wood (2009) compared oshá to angelica (*Angelica* spp.) as a
warming root with anti-inflammatory and expectorating actions in the lungs,
as stimulating and nutritive for enhanced digestive health, and as calming
for the nervous system. On his website, herbalist 7Song indicated moxa-like
applications of oshá for necrotic spider bites and other venomous encounters
as well as chewing the root for smoke inhalation from wildfires.

Many indigenous groups across the western states and traditional Hispanic
communities of the Southwest have reported uses for oshá and some have
even regarded it as a panacea (Garth 1953; Smith 1923) or cultural cornerstone.
Locally available *Ligusticum* species have been used for colds and respiratory
conditions, including hemorrhages (Garth 1953; Gifford 1967; Goodrich and
Lawson 1980; Hart 1992; Train et al. 1941), and for earaches (Hart 1992), cardiac complaints (Hart 1992), and seizures (Hart 1992. They have been used
to stimulate appetite and treat digestive disorders (Garth 1953; Schenk and
Gifford 1952; Sturtevant,1955), build the blood (Goodrich and Lawson 1980),
and ease bodily aches and pains (Camazine and Bye 1980; Garth 1953). Oshá
roots have long been used for good luck, warding off rattlesnakes, protective
magic (Curtin 1957), and reviving entranced or possessed people (Turner et
al. 1980), and the seeds and leaves can be used as a dried herb or vegetable for
culinary purposes (Ager and Ager 1980; Anderson 1939; Baker 1981; Castetter
and Opler 1936; Garth 1953; Hamel and Chiltoskey 1975; Heller 1953; Jones
1983; Perry 1975; Rousseau 1946; Witthoft 1977). Curtin (1965) observed that
the Apache, as well as Spanish settlers, smoked oshá stems as a cigarette
substitute and chewed the roots to quit smoking tobacco. Oshá is deeply
rooted in the culture of New Mexico. According to Curtin, "There is hardly
a native house in New Mexico, be it Indian or Spanish-American, without a
small store of the root" (1965:139). Northern New Mexican herbalist Leticia
Gonzales (personal communication 2018) recalled her relationship with oshá:
"Oshá has been with my family and the people for so long, we don't remember a time without it. I grew up on strong, bracing, pungent, decoctions of it

FIGURE 92 *opposite* Oshá (*Ligusticum porteri*). Photo by author.

for my lungs; my brother was given oshá in a bottle for colic; the *viejitos* and *abuelos* smelling of oshá in the winter months from the pieces they chewed and kept in their front shirt pockets."

Research supports many of these traditional uses, and phytochemical analysis of *Ligusticum porteri* and other *Ligusticum* species has revealed a wide array of constituents, including high levels of phthalides (ligustilide and butylidenephthalide) (Brindis et al. 2011; Cegiela-Carlioz et al. 2005; Rivero et al. 2012; Yang et al. 2012) and phenolic compounds (ferulic acid) (Ou and Kwok 2004). Phthalides are associated with sedating and antispasmodic actions (Leon et al. 2011) as well as antioxidant, anti-inflammatory, antitumor, antiproliferative, and immune-stimulating actions (Yang et al 2012). Ferulic acid is a potent antioxidant (Turi and Murch 2013) known to have numerous protective medicinal effects for those suffering from cancer, diabetes, and cardiovascular and neurodegenerative ailments (Ghatak and Panchal 2010). It also has antimicrobial, anti-inflammatory, and cholesterol-lowering actions (Ou and Kwok 2004). Oshá's antimicrobial activity has been observed against a number of organisms, including *E. coli*, listeria, salmonella, and staph (Andrade-Ochoa et al. 2013). One study (Cegeila-Carlioz et al. 2005) suggested that oshá may significantly increase the effectiveness of certain antibiotic drugs against drug-resistant bacterial strains. Mooney et al. (2015) noted that oshá's inhibitory effect on *Bacillus cereus* was lower in plants growing in high-light environments such as open meadows. This finding makes sense, as plants growing in darker conditions would naturally encounter greater microbial growth and would need to produce more defensive chemicals for their own health. Other observations from oshá studies include immune-modulating effects and antioxidant activity (Nguyen et al. 2016), gastroprotective and antiulcer effects (Velazquez-Moyado et al. 2015), analgesic properties similar to the drug dipyrone (Deciga-Campos et al. 2005; Juarez-Reyes et al. 2013), and significant antihyperglycemic actions accompanied by increased insulin secretions (Brindis et al. 2011).

Mahonia repens, M. spp. (Berberidaceae)

OREGON GRAPE / CREEPING BARBERRY

Mahonia repens is a woody evergreen groundcover of the American West and northern plains, most commonly encountered in the understory of middle-elevation coniferous forests. Larger *Mahonia* species of the Southwest include *M. fremontii* and *M. haematocarpa*, and to a lesser extent *M. trifoliata*. Additional species, including *M. nervosa* and *M. aquifolium*, which are commonly sold in herbal commerce, range across other western states. *M. repens* is known to respond positively to disturbance events such as fires and logging, often resprouting from deeply rooted rhizomes and increasing in density with the additional sunlight. It is an important plant for wildlife, providing fall and winter leaf and berry forage for deer, elks, bighorn sheep, mountain goats, bears, and a variety of small mammals and birds. *Mahonia* is also valuable for restoration of disturbed areas due to its ability to spread on dry rocky slopes, effectively controlling erosion. As a medicinal plant containing isoquinoline alkaloids, otherwise known as berberine, it plays an important role in sustainable herbal practice, serving as a suitable substitute for the highly popular and threatened root medicine goldenseal (*Hydrastis canadensis*).

In modern American herbal traditions, the use of Oregon grape is widespread, most often for microbial infections. While it is typecast as nature's antibiotic, there are many other reasons to keep this herb in one's apothecary, as revealed by a more detailed understanding of its workings. Numerous western Native American groups reported using Oregon grape for upset digestion (Barrett and Gifford 1933; Blankinship 1905; Chesnut 1902; Gunther 1973; McClintock 1909; Murphey 1990 [1959]; Nickerson 1966; Ray 1932; Train et al. 1941; Watahomigie 1982; Weber and Seaman 1985), vomiting (Ray

1932), hemorrhage (McClintock 1909; Murphey 1990 [1959]), venomous bites and wound healing (Barrett 1952; Hart 1992; Vestal 1952), pulmonary or venereal diseases and other microbial infections (Gill 1983; Gunther 1973; Hart 1992; Hellson 1974; Ray 1932; Romero 1954; Schenck and Gifford 1952; Train et al. 1941; Turner et al. 1990; Zigmond 1981), and chronic inflammation such as arthritis (Barrett and Gifford 1933; Elmore 1944; Hart 1992; Train et al. 1941; Turner et al. 1990; Weber and Seaman 1985). It was used as an eyewash (Basehart 1974; Ray 1932; Turner et al. 1980, 1990), a mouthwash (Gunther 1973), a sore throat gargle (Gunther 1973),

FIGURE 93. Oregon grape ground cover in flower (*Mahonia repens*). Photo by author.

a laxative (Turner et al. 1983, 1990; Vestal 1952; Watahomigie 1982; Weber and Seaman 1985), a kidney tonic (Blankinship 1905; Hart 1992; Hellson 1974; Turner et al. 1980), a liver tonic (Watahomigie 1982), and a blood tonic (Baker 1981; Chesnut 1902; Gunther 1973; Mahar 1953; Merriam 1966; Nickerson 1966; Palmer 1975; Reagan 1936; Train et al. 1941; Turner et al. 1980, 1900). These uses correlate strongly with current applications. The eclectic physician Finley Ellingwood (1919) listed *M. aquifolium* as an alterative for dry scaly skin conditions, such as psoriasis, eczema, and acne, that originate from systemic imbalances related to poor digestion and disordered blood. Herbalist Matthew Wood (2009) elaborated on this by describing the plant's ability to increase digestive secretions, improve nutrient absorption, increase bile secretions from the gall bladder, and stimulate liver functioning. These combined actions effectively build and clean the blood while tonifying the mucus membranes, thus acting as a broad-spectrum antimicrobial by modifying the internal environment of the body. Oregon grape's stimulating actions on the digestive system and liver help to build nutrients for cellular repair, clear toxins and waste from the body, and increase protective and moistening secretions, all contributing to its usefulness in treating chronic skin conditions. I frequently include Oregon grape in formulas for other types of chronic inflammation, too, especially those triggered by Epstein-Barr virus or other microbial infections, and for folks with contraindications to licorice (*Glycyrrhiza* spp.). The antimicrobial effects described above make Oregon grape an excellent herb for the treatment of gram-positive and gram-negative bacteria, fungal infections including candida and athlete's foot, and digestive trouble caused by bacterial food poisoning or amoebic infections such

FIGURE 94 Oregon grape shrub (*Mahonia fremontii*). Photo by author.

as giardia (Moore 2003). For the latter, I often combine Oregon grape with small amounts of tree of heaven (*Ailanthus altissima*). Additionally, it is anti-inflammatory for liver diseases, mildly stimulating to the sluggish thyroid, and a useful eyewash for conjunctivitis (Kane 2011). Prepare roots as a tincture, make a tea, or use a diluted tincture as a topical wash or soak. Oregon grape is contraindicated for people taking prescription drugs due to the stimulating effect on the liver.

FIGURE 95
Oregon grape leaves (*Mahonia fremontii*). Photo by author.

RESEARCH SUMMARY Scientific research on *Mahonia* species has focused largely on antimicrobial, anti-inflammatory, antioxidant, and anticancer activities. Numerous alkaloids, including magnoflorine, isocorydine, corydine, isoboldine, berbamine, berberine, palmatine, magnoflorine, jatrorrhizine, isocorydine, corytuberine, columbamin, and corytuberine (Slavik et al. 1985), and many other compounds (He et al. 2008; Lu et al. 2009) have been identified. Some alkaloid-producing proteins are root specific, and other alkaloid content was found to be much higher in the roots than in other parts of the plant (Zhu et al. 2015). A review of *Mahonia*'s phytochemistry and pharmacological uses was provided by He and Mu (2015). Antimicrobial research has shown *M. leschenaultii* and *M. manipurensis* to have potent antibacterial and antifungal activity against numerous pathogenic organisms (Duraiswamy et al. 2006), including gram-positive and gram-negative bacteria (Pfoze et al. 2011). *M. aquifolium* has been shown to significantly inhibit MRSA (Wendakoon et al. 2012). Antifungal activity is strongly associated with the alkaloid jatorrhizine (Vollekova et al. 2003). *Mahonia* has also been shown to inhibit influenza (Zheng et al. 2003) and has showed immuno-stimulating activity (Galle et al. 1994).

Other research has focused on Mahonia's notable antioxidant activity (Bezakova et al. 1996; Gunduz 2013; Hu et al. 2011; Yu et al. 2008) and associated anti-inflammatory, analgesic, and protective effects (Chao et al. 2009). One study showed that *M. leschenaultia* protected the kidneys, likely through antioxidant action (Palani et al. 2010b), and another reported pain relieving, anti-inflammatory, and hepatoprotective activity by reducing inflammation and necrosis in liver cells, with these actions attributed to antioxidant free radical scavenging activity five times higher than vitamin C (Chao et al. 2013).

FIGURE 96
Oregon grape
flowers (*Mahonia
aquifolium*).
Photo by author.

Further studies have shown a reduction in lung inflammation (Hu et al. 2016) and significant anti-inflammatory action through inhibition of nitric oxide production, also indicating antioxidant activity (Zhang et al. 2011). Clinical trials with *M. aquifolium* herbal products reported significant reduction of the severity of chronic inflammatory psoriasis symptoms and improvements in quality-of-life ratings with few side effects (Bernstein et al. 2006; Gieler et al. 1995; Gulliver and Donsky 2005).

Studies also suggest that *Mahonia* species may have a role in treatments for cancer, neurodegenerative diseases, diabetes, and respiratory illnesses. Anticancer research shows potential for *Mahonia* as an antiproliferative or inhibitory agent against a leukemia cell line (Hajnicka et al. 2002), a liver cancer cell line (Cong et al. 2011), colon cancer (Hu et al. 2011), human lung cancer cells (Wong et al. 2009), and myelogenous leukemia cells (Jing 1996). *Mahonia bealei* inhibited an enzyme associated with early onset of dementia, showing a synergistic effect when combined with *Coptis chinensis* and *Phellodendron chinense* (Kaufmann et al. 2016). *M. leschenaultia* reduced hyperglycemia and hyperlipidemia, showing potential for diabetes treatments (Palani et al. 2010a). Another study demonstrated that *M. aquifolium*'s antitussive effects greatly exceeded those of codeine (Saraswathy et al. 2014). Colletively, these investigations show an enormous potential for *Mahonia* in a wide variety of therapeutic roles.

Marrubium vulgare (Lamiaceae)

HOREHOUND / MARRUBIO

An herb of Old World traditions, horehound is nonnative but naturalized in many areas across the United States. An aromatic and potentially invasive member of the mint family, it is commonly encountered in drier habitats of the Mountain West and frequents disturbed land of any sort. Horehound has a weedy character, with a willingness to grow out of cracks in concrete, and spreads easily by producing burrs that readily catch on clothing, hair, and fur. Although it is abundant in some wild areas, its cultivation is easy, and this herb adds a touch of long-lasting silvery-green color and attracts bees to the garden. While its scent, appearance, and character are often described in less than flattering terms, I nevertheless find it an upstanding member of my apothecary and have come to associate its unique medicinal aroma with healing.

Horehound has been esteemed since ancient times. Discussed by Hippocrates, Dioscorides, and Pliny, it was also held in high regard by Egyptians, Romans, medieval Europeans, and others for its medicinal actions as well as its protective magic (Grieve 1971 [1931]). In the Old World, it has long been a staple of treatments for colds, coughs, and fevers. Horehound's expectoration is part of its strategy to help the body overcome an infection by clearing old stagnant phlegm and stimulating fresh secretions with new immunological cells that alter the microbial environment (Wood 2008). Hoffman (2003) explained its expectorating action for nonproductive coughs through its re-laxant effect on the smooth muscles of the lungs and airways and its ability to promote mucus production. I have found horehound to be essential for childhood asthma and have combined it with licorice (*Glycyrrhiza* spp.) and other herbs for custom honey-based formulations to great effect. Additionally, horehound is very bitter. It promotes digestion by stimulating secretions and peristaltic action, and it increases bile production in the gallbladder. Leaves are prepared as tincture, syrup, infused honey, cough drops, or tea, albeit an extremely bitter-tasting one. Moore (1990) indicated warm horehound tea combined with honey and oshá for respiratory conditions and cold horehound tea for digestive applications. Curtin (1965) reported its use as a footbath for frostbite and rheumatic complaints, and as a powdered disinfectant for wound care. Wood also indicated it specifically for androgen-related issues of the female reproductive system. Moore (2003) warned against prolonged use due to its potential to cause hypertension in people prone to that condition.

FIGURE 97 Horehound (*Marrubium vulgare*). Photo by author.

Modern research on horehound validates many of these traditional uses and also suggests a role in other therapeutic treatments. Phytochemical analysis shows that marrubiin is a primary medicinal compound extracted from aerial parts, along with numerous other constituents, including flavonoids, steroids, terpenoids, tannins, saponins, and volatile oils (Lodhi et al. 2017). Lodhi et al. provide a detailed summary of existing research regarding the phytochemical analysis and medicinal actions of horehound, including studies validating its analgesic, antispasmodic, gastroprotective, antihypertensive, antidiabetic, antihyperlipidemic, hepatoprotective, immunomodulating,

top to bottom

FIGURE 98. Horehound flowers
(*Marrubium vulgare*). Photo by author.

FIGURE 99. Horehound burr
(*Marrubium vulgare*). Photo by author.

antioxidant, mosquitocidal, and antiprotozoal effects. It has shown anticancer activity in human colorectal, breast, cervical, prostate, and other cancer cell lines and antimicrobial action against numerous gram-positive and gram-negative bacterial, fungal, and mycobacterial strains. Horehound leaf extract also shows strong anti-oxidant activity (Kadri et al. 2011; Matowski et al. 2008; Orhan et al. 2010), with improved fibroblast growth, and can be an effective treatment for wounds (Amri et al. 2017). Root extracts demonstrated anti-inflammatory activity for the heart (Yousefi et al. 2014) along with vas-orelaxant and antihypertensive actions (Vergara-Galicia et al. 2013). Other studies reported antispasmodic and potent analgesic action, stronger than some pain-reliev-ing drugs (De Jesus et al. 2000), and also antibacterial action against *H. pylori* (Robles-Zepeda et al. 2011), strep (Warda et al. 2009), *E. coli*, proteus, and others (Masoodi et al. 2008), with particular effectiveness against gram-positive organisms (Zarai et al. 2011). Eth-nobotanical studies have reported horehound's use for the treatment of diabetes within its original Old World range (e.g., Barkaoui et al. 2017; Rachid et al. 2012), and research shows a significant reduction in blood glu-cose levels, total cholesterol, triglycerides, and other hyperglycemic and hyperlipidemia markers (Elberry et al. 2015). Studies have also observed hepatoprotective (Akther et al. 2013) and abortifacient (Aouni et al. 2017) activity in horehound extracts.

Monarda fistulosa (Lamiaceae)

BEE BALM / OREGANO DE LA SIERRA

Bee balm's medicinal benefits are myriad and wide-ranging but almost always relate to movement of fluids and energy in the body. This has long been one of my favorite and most beloved medicinal herbs; many aspects of this plant are described in chapter 2. Observing and getting to know that wild bee balm stand in the Sandia Mountains illuminated this plant's power to enliven any place with its own radiating beauty and ability to draw in pollinators, fostering a vital system of interconnections among plants, animals, people, and the land. I was initially so moved by bee balm's intimate relationship with the pollinators that I did not harvest its flowers from my own garden for several years. This plant is, of course, healing to us too. Acting beneficially in many body systems, including the digestive, immune, lymphatic, respiratory, and nervous, this plant has many applications borne out through both generations of herbal practice and scientific research. Recent studies have isolated and identified many of bee balm's aromatic and medicinal compounds (Zamureenko et al. 1989). But bee balm is not homogeneous in its phytochemistry and includes numerous different chemotypes, or differing chemical constituents produced within the same species (Keefover-Ring 2008). For example, one study showed that southern *M. fistulosa* populations from Colorado had higher amounts of most terpenes than plants from the northern Rockies and that terpene levels were similar in the flowers and leaves, reaching their peak production in mid-July (Keefover-Ring 2008). That same study identified carvacrol, thymol, and linalool chemotypes in southern Colorado in both mixed and monotypic stands.

This complex array of chemical compounds contributes to bee balm's essential role in the Western apothecary. Its leaves and flowers can be prepared as fresh plant tincture, tea, infused honey, elixir, syrup, or glycerite. The wilted herb can be used for infusing oils, and the dried herb is often used for diaphoretic teas or carminative culinary seasonings. Bee balm's spicy oregano-like flavor creates a warming sensation, but like most other mint family members, it also has a diffusive, cooling effect. Moore (2003) recommended bee balm for delayed menses, fevers, coughs, sore throats, indigestion, and upset stomachs. Pueblo people across New Mexico and Arizona used bee balm in a variety of ways, including for seasoning meats and stews, and also for the treatment of stomachaches, fevers, wounds, and headaches. It was used as an eyewash and for recovery from heart attacks (Dunmire and Tierney 1997). Many other western tribes used bee balm in similar ways and as a treatment for measles (Hamel and Chiltoskey 1975); aching kidneys (Hart 1992; Hellson 1974); swollen neck glands (Hellson 1974); upset stomachs, gas, bloating, and abdominal pain (Hamel and Chiltoskey 1975; Hart 1992; Herrick 1977; Hoffman 1891; Reagan 1928; Smith 1928; Wyman and Harris 1951); rheumatic pain (Swanton 1928); headache (Elmore 1944; Gilmore 1933; Hamel and Chiltoskey 1975; Herrick 1977; Hocking 1956; Smith 1928; Robbins et al. 1916; Vestal 1952); worms (Densmore 1932); colds and fevers (Arnason et al. 1981; Densmore

FIGURE 100 Bee balm flower (*Monarda fistulosa*). Photo by author.

1918; Gilmore 1933; Hamel and Chiltoskey 1975; Hart 1992; Herrick 1977; Murphey 1990 [1959]; Robbins et al.; Smith 1928, 1923, 1932; Tantaquidgeon 1942, 1972; Taylor 1940; Vestal 1952); cough and respiratory problems (Hart 1992; Hellson 1974; Rogers 1980; Smith 1932; Vestal 1952); heart trouble (Hamel and Chiltoskey 1975); and wounds, boils, burns, and other skin inflammations (Densmore 1928; Gilmore 1991 [1919]; Hellson 1974; Rogers 1980; Vestal 1952; Vestal and Schultes 1939). It was used to promote restful sleep (Hamel and Chiltoskey 1975); as an eyewash (Hart 1992; McClintock 1909; Robbins et al. 1916; Rogers 1980); for the movement of fluids through diuresis or induced perspiration (Hamel and Chiltoskey 1975; Swanton 1928; Taylor 1940); to treat delirium (Swanton 1928; Taylor 1940); to expel afterbirth (Hart 1992); as protection against ghosts (Herrick 1977, Swanton 1928); and as perfume (Grinnell 1972; Vestal and Schultes 1939). Bee balm is one of my preferred herbs for the dispersal of respiratory congestion and protection against and/or treatment of active lung infections. Its antiviral, diaphoretic, and anesthetic actions also make it useful for the treatment of ordinary colds accompanied by fevers or sore throats. The most common use of this herb in my house, however, is for the treatment of mosquito and ant bites. Its dispersive, warming, and anesthetic properties are amplified by vigorous rubbing of the infused oil or salve, which calms the desire to scratch, alleviates pain, and reduces inflammation for quick relief and expedited healing. With antibacterial, antiviral, antifungal, styptic, anesthetic, and anti-inflammatory effects, bee balm is a broadly useful ingredient in all-purpose first aid salves.

FIGURE 101 Bee balm (*Monarda fistulosa*). Photo by author.

Scientific research adds to our understanding of bee balm's medicinal applications. Recent studies have shown it to be an effective mosquito repellant and protection against yellow fever, comparable to the commonly used pesticides deet and rotenone (Johnson et al. 1998; Tabanca et al. 2013). This plant's antibacterial, anticandidal, antifungal, and anti-inflammatory properties have been supported by research demonstrating its effectiveness against a range of microorganisms, including *E. coli*, *P. aeruginosa*, *Proteus vulgaris*, staph, *B. subtillis*, and penicillium (Zhilyakova et al. 2009). Bee balm's thymol has shown strong antioxidant action by scavenging free radicals produced through oxidation that seek to steal electrons from lipids in cell membranes, causing cell damage (Meeran and Prince

2012). Since antioxidant herbs protect the heart and have far-reaching health benefits, this research supports San Juan Pueblo's use of bee balm in post-heart attack treatments and suggests a role in many other health treatments.

Opuntia spp. (Cactaceae)
PRICKLY PEAR / NOPAL

Prickly pear is an iconic figure of desert landscapes of the American South-west and Mexico, and also features strongly in the culture of the region. It is the most widespread of all cacti and is broadly distributed across the Ameri-cas, with *Opuntia* species ranging almost to the Arctic Circle in the north and nearly to the southern tip of South America. They are surprisingly cold toler-ant, with some species, such as *O. fragilis*, able to withstand temperatures as low as -58°F by remaining low to the ground and reducing the water content in their cells (Ishikawa and Lawrence 1996; Loik and Park 1993). More than two dozen species live in the American West, with *O. polyacantha, O. phaea-cantha, O. macrorhiza, O. engelmannii*, and *O. fragilis* having the largest dis-tributions. Prickly pear is commonly found in dry grasslands, shrublands, woodlands, and foothills. *Opuntia* species may have infrataxa, or subspecies varieties, and may cross-hybridize, making species-specific identification difficult. Wildlife including pronghorn, deer, javelinas, and numerous small mammals and birds rely on prickly pear for seasonal forage. Cochineal insects hosted by prickly pear are the source of a bright red dye that was valued by Native people and eventually became a commodity of the Spanish colonial era. Prickly pear also featured prominently in the tribulations of the Corps of Discovery and was described by Meriwether Lewis as "one of the beauties as well as the greatest pests of the plains" (Moulton 1987:383).

Prickly pear's relationship with humans is based in its use as a highly nu-tritious and health-promoting wild food, and it has played an important role in the region's ancestral and modern culinary and healing traditions. The word *nopal* is derived from the language of the Aztecs, and the plant features strongly in Aztec lore and culture (Curtin 1965). Ethnobotanical sources and wild foraging guides provide a significant body of information regarding its historic and current uses in food preparation and beverage making, including working with both pads and fruits (e.g., Castetter 1935; Kane 2019; Kindscher 1987; Moerman 1998; Slattery 2016; Thayer 2010). Prickly pear fruits add beau-tiful color and delicious flavor to desserts and drinks, and the juice tastes good simply diluted with water or added to herbal teas. Although there are many effective methods of dealing with the glochids, I favor the soak and peel technique, as I often harvest these fruits from urban areas where they

FIGURE 102. Prickly pear (*Opuntia polyacantha*) showing flower color variations. Photo by author.

are commonly planted in residential neighborhoods. This technique is useful for reducing exposure to air pollution and other possible contaminants, but it is nevertheless wise to choose harvesting locations in less-trafficked areas where you are confident herbicides are not being used.

Although most ethnobotanical information describes culinary preparations, there are also documented traditional medicinal uses from wide-ranging indigenous groups, mostly pertaining to topical uses. Local *Opuntia* species were prepared for the treatment of burns and wounds (Bean and Saubel 1972; Camazine and Bye 1980; Cook 1930; Gilmore 1991 [1919]; Hart 1992; Hocking 1956; Palmer 1975; Romero 1954; Swank 1932, Train et al. 1941; Turner et al. 1980; Watahomigie 1982), and spines were used for puncturing abscesses or cleaning infected eyelids (Basehart 1974; Vestal and Schultes 1939). *Opuntia* was also applied to snakebites (Kraft 1990) and warts (Tantaquidgeon 1942). It was used to treat inflamed skin, swollen glands, and rheumatic complaints (Bocek 1984), and as a poultice for encouraging milk flow in mothers (Curtin 1984 [1949]). Midwives used prickly pear for the facilitation of childbirth and as a lubricant to aid in the delivery of a retained placenta (Gunther 1973; Vestal 1952). Keres men ate thorn coverings to strengthen themselves for war (Swank 1932). *Opuntia* was consumed internally for constipation, diarrhea, and stomachaches (Akana 1922; Bean and Saubel 1972; Buskirk 1986; Curtin 1984 [1949]; Hart 1992; Whiting 1939).

Prickly pear's healing potential has been rediscovered and expanded in recent decades as diet-related health conditions such as diabetes and high cholesterol have become more widespread. The filleted pads can be applied as a poultice and covered with a clean cloth

FIGURE 103. Prickly pear (*Opuntia polyacantha*) showing flower color variations. Photo by author.

for a drawing and cooling effect similar to that of aloe vera gel. Preparations suitable for internal use include well-strained tea made from the flowers or juice from the fruits (tunas), which can be used fresh, preserved with 25 percent alcohol, frozen, or further processed into a syrup or elixir. The juice is an anti-inflammatory diuretic, helpful for easing the symptoms of painful urination (Moore 1989). Fresh juice is also indicated as a hypoglycemic treatment that reduces LDL cholesterol and triglycerides. Moore noted that, unlike other hypoglycemic herbs, prickly pear produces this effect only in people with high blood sugar and will not affect those with normal levels. Kane (2011) reported that when taken before meals, prickly pear reduces blood sugar by 15 to 20 percent for people with non–insulin dependent diabetes by means of its soluble fiber content slowing down sugar uptake. It positively affects LDL cholesterol in the same manner. Prickly pear also cools digestive heat, relieves symptoms of acid reflux and stomach upsets, and enhances the mucosa for a protective and healing effect on ulcers (Kane 2011). Furthermore, its flowers are prepared for capillary weakness with inflamed mucosa in conditions such as colitis, asthma, and vaginitis, and also to aid in excreting uric acid as a preventative treatment for gout.

FIGURE 104. Ripe prickly pear fruits. Photo by author.

RESEARCH SUMMARY Research involving different *Opuntia* species extracts derived from flowers, powdered pads, fruits, and roots has validated traditional uses and illuminated a variety of potential protective and therapeutic applications, especially in the treatment of chronic health conditions. Due to the rise in chronic illnesses across many cultures and the importance of developing better treatments for these ailments, a significant body of research has evolved; a detailed summary of this study is included here. Phytochemical analysis reveals that *Opuntia* contains alkaloids, carbohydrates, fats, oils, flavonoids, phenolics, tannins, steroids, and saponins (Chichonyi Kalungia et al. 2018; Ramyashree et al. 2012). Many review articles summarize *Opuntia*'s notable chemical compounds and pharmacological uses (e.g., del Socorro Santos Diaz et al. 2017; Kaur 2012; Nazareno 2015; Osuna-Martinez et al. 2014; Sharma et al. 2015).

Much research has focused on *Opuntia*'s role in treating the widespread and chronic health issues associated with cardiovascular disease, diabetes, and obesity. Prickly pear is known to have significant atherosclerosis-inhibiting, lipid-lowering (Budinski et al. 2001; Khouloud et al. 2017; Osoria-Esquivel et al. 2012), and hypotensive actions (Saleem et al. 2005). Research suggests that antiatherogenic properties and cholesterol-lowering activity may be associated with *Opuntia*'s high antioxidant content and its ability to prevent oxidative stress (Keller et al. 2015; Osuna-Martinez et al. 2014). The ability to lower LDL and total cholesterol could originate from prickly pear's high dietary fiber content (Wolfram et al. 2002) or its inhibition of pancreatic enzymes (Padilla-Camberos et al. 2015). *Opuntia* has also been shown to reduce atherosclerotic lesions (Garoby-Salom et al. 2016). Prickly pear inhibits enzymes that serve as biological markers for diabetes (Chahdoura et al. 2017), improves blood glucose and insulin levels (Chahdoura et al. 2017; Lopez-Romero et al. 2014), and demonstrates antioxidant activity in the liver (Chahdoura et al. 2017). The mechanism for hypoglycemic action is not certain but may be due the presence of dietary fiber and mucilage believed to slow the absorption of glucose (Frati-Munari et al. 1988), or it may involve stimulating insulin secretion through action on the pancreas (Butterweck et al. 2011) or antioxidant activity marked by the reduction of nitric oxide (Berraaouan et al. 2015; El-Razek et al. 2012). Studies have also shown *Opuntia* to outperform a common diabetes medication in lowering blood glucose (Kalungia et al. 2018) and also to slow the progression of cataracts, a common side effect of diabetes (El-Razek et al. 2012). Another common health condition associated with diabetes is obesity, and prickly pear has demonstrated that animals fed a high-fat diet along with *Opuntia* extract gained less weight and had lower levels of circulating cholesterol, LDL cholesterol, and HDL cholesterol than those that did not consume *Opuntia* (Rodriquez-Rodriquez et al. 2015). Human clinical trials support this outcome, with results showing lower body mass index, body fat composition, and waist circumference (Grube et al. 2013), as well as *Opuntia* fibers binding dietary fat and increasing its excretion (Chong et al. 2014; Uebelhack et al. 2014).

Additional research has investigated *Opuntia*'s role in a number of other therapeutic applications, including wound care, pain management, mitigating microbial infections, cancer treatments, improving digestive health, and reducing toxicity. Useful for healing wounds (Deters et al. 2012), reducing inflammation (Deters et al. 2012; Izuegbuna et al. 2019; Loro et al. 1999; Park et al. 2001), and managing pain (Loro et al. 1999; Park et al. 2001), prickly pear could play an important role in the treatment of acute injuries, chronic pain, and neurological damage. *Opuntia* is neuroprotective through antioxidant action (Dib et al. 2014; Izuegbuna et al. 2019) that reduces free radical neuronal damage (Wie et al. 2000) and inhibits nitric oxide production (Lee et al. 2006). It may also increase long-term memory (Kim et al. 2010) and

FIGURE 105   Prickly pear (*Opuntia phaeacantha*). Photo by author.

serve as an antidepressant (Ismail Owens et al. 2010; Park et al. 2010). It can reduce hangover symptoms through anti-inflammatory action (Wiese et al. 2004). Prickly pear also demonstrates antiviral activity by inhibiting the replication of DNA and RNA viruses, including herpes, influenza, and HIV (Ahmad et al. 1996), and shows antimicrobial action against pathogens contributing to acne (Desai 2015). Numerous antimicrobial endophytic fungi species found in *Opuntia* have been identified. They contribute not only to the plant's survival but also to its medicinal actions (Ratnaweera et al. 2015; Silva-Hughes et al. 2015). In the digestive system, prickly pear has a protective effect that may be attributed to mucilage defending the mucosa as well as pectin polysaccharides assisting in mucosa regeneration (Galati et al. 2003; Trachtenberg and Mayer 1981). This activity reduces gastric lesions, prevents a decrease in gastric mucus (Kim et al. 2012), alleviates constipation (Han et al. 2017), and positively alters gut microbiota, leading to benefits such as improved cognition and liver health (Sanchez-Tapia et al. 2017). *Opuntia* is also protective for the liver and kidneys, showing significant hepatoprotective and healing activity in cases of acetaminophen-induced liver toxicity (Gonzalez-Ponce et al. 2016) and significantly reducing toxicity in the kidneys (Hfaiedh et al. 2018). Cancer research has shown *Opuntia* to be cytotoxic or inhibitory against human colon and prostate cancer cells (Antunes-Ricardo et al. 2014; Chavez-Santoscoy et al. 2009; Kim et al. 2014; Naselli et al. 2014; Serra et al. 2013), human chronic myeloid leukemia cells (Sreekanth et al. 2007), breast and hepatic cancer cells (Chavez-Santoscoy et al. 2009; Kim et al. 2014), brain cancer (Hahm et al. 2010), and cervical cancer (Hahm et al. 2010). *Opuntia* may also be useful in lowering fertility by reducing sperm count without effecting libido or testosterone levels, an effect that was reversed after discontinuance of the treatment (Ramya et al. 2015).

Pedicularis spp. (Orobancaceae)

PEDICULARIS / BETONY / LOUSEWORT

Pedicularis plants undoubtedly have a deeply alluring quality that has drawn the attention of herbalists and plant lovers of all kinds. Some seek recovery for overworked muscles or the relaxation of tension in the body. Others are searching for the more subtle shifts and openings that relaxation in the physical body can bring to the mind and spirit. Indeed, the sheer beauty and mysterious underground workings of these varied plants are captivating for anyone acquainted with pedicularis. Our local species have been both good medicine and tremendous sources of inspiration and learning for me over the years, an ecological and personal relationship detailed in chapter 4. Ranging from open prairies to semiarid foothill woodlands to alpine mountain meadows, pedicularis draws us into wild and less-trodden landscapes where the gateways beckon our entry and exploration.

The genus *Pedicularis* includes more than six hundred species, found in prairie, montane, subalpine, alpine, and tundra environments across the Northern Hemisphere. Of those, forty species are found in North America, and several western species are briefly described below. Pedicularis prefers habitats with undisturbed soil and moderate availability of minerals and water. It generally avoids habitats with extreme environmental conditions, such as high stress and disturbance, and avoids nutrient-dense wet areas with high levels of aboveground vegetative competition (Těšitel et al. 2015). The genus *Pedicularis* was previously grouped with the Scrophulariaceae family until its parasitic members were relocated to the Orobanchaceae family, where it resides today. This large genus is generally characterized by varied morphological differences, particularly in the upper lip of the corolla. Genetic and biogeographical studies suggest that all pedicularis species originated in Asia, migrating to North America when the Bering Land Bridge was open during the Miocene (about 24 to 5 million years ago). The genus subsequently dispersed across North America from ancestral Rocky Mountain and southern Cascade range populations, and eventually reached Europe from populations in the eastern half of the continent (Robart et al. 2015).

FIGURE 106 *above* *Pedicularis groenlandica* growing along with monkeyflower (*Mimulus* sp.) in a wet open meadow at high elevation. Photo by author.

FIGURE 107 *left* *Pedicularis procera* growing in semi-open forested areas. Photo by author.

Pedicularis plants are fascinating ecologically and may even be considered keystone species due to their important role in facilitating biodiversity. As hemiparasitic plants, they produce underground structures called haustoria, which create a direct connection between the xylem of the host and that of the parasite (Piehl 1963). Pedicularis and other root hemiparasites produce their own chlorophyll and can thus survive on their own but may obtain additional resources through root connections to host plants. These interactions vary depending upon the species of pedicularis and the host plants, which commonly include asters, oaks, conifers, and grasses (Ai-Rong Li 2012) as well as a wide variety of potential hosts from at least eighty different plant species in thirty-five families (Piehl 1963). The transfer of secondary resources such as water, minerals, and alkaloids from nearby plants is well established (Schneider and Stermitz 1990) and has larger implications for the ecosystem in which pedicularis makes its home. Pedicularis clearly benefits from this relationship, but there is also evidence that this phenomenon has a wide-reaching ripple effect. While this hemiparasitic relationship can negatively impact the

FIGURE 108
Pedicularis race-mosa growing in the forest under-story. Photo by author.

growth of the host plant, it is also associated with greater plant diversity in the bioregion (Hedberg et al. 2005). Pedicularis may inhibit the growth of plants with a propensity to dominate the landscape, such as goldenrod (*Solidago* spp.) or grasses, while its pollen-rich flowers attract bees and hummingbirds to the area for increased pollination and reproduction of other important species (Hedberg et al. 2005). In fact, other flowering plants are likely to produce more fruits and set more seeds when growing in close proximity to pedicularis (Laverty 1992). In addition to curtailing the growth of dominating host plants and promoting the biomass and reproduction of other plants, pedicularis also contributes to species diversity by reallocating nitrogen and other nutrients to neighboring plants through decomposition (Demey et al. 2013). These combined qualities make pedicularis an important element in ecological restoration projects (DiGiovanni et al. 2016).

Aside from their ecological importance, pedicularis species are known in herbal medicine traditions wherever they grow. Native American tribes including the Washo, Thompson, Catawba, Chippewa, Cherokee, Iroquois, Menominee, Meskwaki, Ojibwa, Potawatomi, Shoshoni, Eskimo, and Inu-piat have reported a number of uses, including treatments for bodily aches and pains (Herrick 1977); cuts, scrapes, and swellings (Smith 1928, 1933; Train et al. 1941); diarrhea, digestive pains, and disorders (Arnason et al. 1981; Hamel and Chiltoskey 1975; Speck 1937; Train et al. 1941); and tuberculosis (Grinnell 1972; Hamel and Chiltoskey 1975; Hart 1981; Herrick 1977). Pedicularis has been used in delousing animals (Hamel and Chiltoskey 1975); heart healing and blood building (Gilmore 1933; Herrick 1977); and treating sore throats (Arnason et al. 1981). It has been used as a general tonic, an aphrodisiac, and a love charm (Smith 1923, 1928, 1932) and prepared as food (Ager and Ager 1980; Anderson 1939; Heller 1953; Jones 1983; Perry 1975; Porsild 1953; Waugh 1916). Employed by modern herbalists mainly for its muscle relaxant properties, pedicularis is typically used in formulas for general relaxation or recovery from physical injury. Phytochemical analysis has been done primarily on Asian species but identifies a number of common constituents, including iridoid glycosides, phenylpropanoid glycosides, lignans, glycosides, flavonoids, and alkaloids (Mao-Xing Li 2014). The synergistic effects of pedicularis's many constituents result in additional properties: it is antitumor, hepatoprotective, antioxidative, protective to red blood cells, antibacterial, and cognition enhancing (Gao et al. 2011; Mao-Xing Li 2014). Recent research gives implications for broader uses in medicine. Specifically, pedicularis has been shown to have antimicrobial activity against a number of pathogens, including *P. aeruginosa*, *S. aureus*, *S. epidermidis*, *P. olympica*, *P. vulgaris*, *E. coli*, *K. pneumoniae*, *C. albicans*, and *M. luteus* (Dulger and Ugurlu 2005; Khodaie et al. 2012; Yuan et al. 2007). Significantly, it has also demonstrated the ability to repair DNA and to lower levels of glucose and other diabetic markers (Chu 2009; Yatoo et al. 2016). Not surprisingly, pedicularis has been used to increase endurance in athletes by reducing muscle fatigue (Zhu et al. 2016). This combination of traits makes pedicularis a useful component in a wide variety of disease prevention and treatment formulas.

Due to its hemiparasitic nature, pedicularis can take on additional phytochemicals and healing characteristics by absorbing resources from neighboring host plants. This could be a drawback in the case of host plants with toxic compounds, such as some *Senecio* species (Schneider and Stermitz 1990). Finding pedicularis among aspen stands, however, is like harvesting two herbs in one, as the aspen subtly shifts the energy and properties of the pedicularis, increasing its anti-inflammatory and pain-relieving nature. This hemiparasitic trait, however beneficial medically, is also what makes pedicularis truly wild and difficult to cultivate.

Working with pedicularis draws the practicing herbalist into the prairies and mountains to harvest and craft remedies born of wild places. Since pedicularis is not cultivated, we must obtain this medicine through wildcrafting in places where it grows abundantly. Before harvesting, make sure you have an undoubted identification not only for pedicularis but also for any potential host plants in the vicinity. Also be certain that wild populations in your area are stable and healthy, and that the stand you are visiting is robust. Leave lots of flowers and avoid disturbing roots to maintain healthy wild populations. This is a low-dose herb, so you will not need to take much. Tinctures are best prepared fresh in the field with leaves and flowers. Wilted or freshly dried herb is appropriate for other preparations, such as infused oils, salves, and smoke blends. These help with injured or overworked muscles, encourage restful sleep, release tension residing deep within the body, and allow us to see things in a new light. These plants also offer something more profound—almost magical. This experience is illuminated by spending time in the places where these plants grow and is exemplified by each particular species. Although species are used interchangeably, subtle differences may be ascertained through knowing each one individually.

Pedicularis groenlandica   **ELEPHANT HEAD BETONY**

FIGURE 109
Pedicularis groen-landica. Photo by author.

Think of this species when the release of gripping tension is needed to relieve physical or energetic stagnancy and to promote movement in the musculature, heart, and mind. Thriving in open wet meadows and boggy habitats of higher elevations, *P. groenlandica* is suited to the person who needs to let go, stop being bogged down, and move on from problems or obstacles that may be holding them back.

Pedicularis racemosa   **PARROT BEAK / SICKLETOP BETONY**

FIGURE 110
Pedicularis race-mosa. Photo by author.

This plant inhabits the forest edges, acting as liaison between worlds, an intermediary between light and dark. Just as its parasitic roots spread underground, subtly shifting the energy of the forest ecosystem, it infiltrates the heart and implants trust and faith where fear, distrust, or other difficult emotions may reside. Working with it as plant medicine provides more than relief from musculoskeletal aggravations; it also helps bridge the disparities in our lives by connecting us with lost parts of ourselves. It summons, from our own depths, the aspects of our being that we have ignored and helps us be more complete individuals and more holistic practitioners. *P. racemosa* ultimately invites us to discover the unexplored magic within ourselves.

Pedicularis procera FERN LEAF / GIANT BETONY

P. procera is the largest of the species discussed here. Its flowering tops can be seen
rising through the forest vegetation, drawing
us into connection. It is a favorite for remedies that relax the muscles and alleviate pain,
allowing us to accept ourselves as we are and

FIGURE 111
Pedicularis procera.
Photo by author.

let go of what we need to shed. This species encourages us to stand tall with
confidence and be relaxed in who we are.

Pedicularis centranthera DWARF BETONY

This species prefers semiarid lower-elevation pine and oak forests and is usually seen growing in pine needle mulch. It is adapted to these warmer, drier
elevations, with an ability to shed its aboveground parts, return underground,
and disappear during the hottest and most
stressful time of year. *P. centranthera* exemplifies the strategy of retreating periodically to
engage in recuperation and restoration, and by
using it we can maintain our endurance and a
balance between the inner and outer worlds.

FIGURE 112.
*Pedicularis
centranthera.*
Photo by author.

Pedicularis parryi PARRY'S BETONY

The cacophonous riot of shapes, colors, and tex-
tures of the varied flowering plants in an alpine
meadow stand as a testament to the biodiversity-
facilitating powers of *Pedicularis parryi* (see Figure
32). This species grows in open high-altitude meadows, shining light on issues we may be holding on
to but do not have the clarity to understand or process. *P. parryi* is more direct in its workings than
the other forest species and may be best suited to
those of us with more concrete ways of perceiving the world and those who are less able to shift
with the more subtle workings of other pedicularis
species.

FIGURE 113.
Pedicularis parryi.
Photo by author.

Pedicularis bracteosa **BRACTED BETONY**

Growing on the edge of dark and wild forests inhabited by saxifrages and orchids, *P. bracteosa* helps
create an ambiance of wild flowing vitality and an
entrancing mood of introspection, beckoning one
to look inward—into the forest and into ourselves.
It is almost as if the underground haustoria are
penetrating us, drawing us into the vibrational and
energetic world of life in the forest, making us one
with the landscape and opening us to a new world
of discovery.

Pinus edulis, P. ponderosa, P. spp. (Pinaceae)

PIÑON PINE / PONDEROSA PINE / AND OTHERS

The American West is home to more than twenty different native pine species that have been used for medicine making and other purposes. Ponderosa pine (*Pinus ponderosa*) is among the most widely distributed and most
common across the region. Piñon pine (*Pinus edulis*) is a plant of the Four
Corners states (New Mexico, Colorado, Utah, and Arizona) and is one of the
plants I most strongly associate with the land and culture of the Southwest.
Its rich green tones dot the landscape and contrast with the rugged red soils
of the Colorado Plateau to create one of the iconic southwestern vistas. This
slow-growing conifer resides in lower, more arid elevations, from about four
thousand to nine thousand feet, and may take seventy-five to two hundred
years or more to reach maturity. Its resin, or pitch, like that of other pines, is
a prized medicine, and the nuts have been a staple of the region's food since
the earliest human settlements. Like other coniferous forests, this woodland habitat has seen significant losses over recent years. Persistent drought,
massive wildfires, and bark beetle outbreaks have devastated vast acreages
of piñon pines. (See chapter 2.) Research suggests that climate, rather than
grazing or other land uses, is the biggest factor in determining the health and
distribution of piñon populations (Barger et al. 2009). As discussed in chapter
1, predicted higher temperatures coupled with longer drought periods are
likely to result in negative impacts, beginning with slow regeneration after
the recent mass die-offs and longer-term declines in populations across the
region (Barger et al. 2009). Piñon and its associated plant communities create
good habitat for deer, elks, pronghorn, wild horses, small mammals, coyotes,

mountain lions, bobcats, goshawks, and numerous other bird species. Piñon nuts are an important food source for many birds and small mammals, especially Clark's nutcracker, scrub jays, piñon jays, chipmunks, and squirrels. Additionally, piñon-juniper woodlands host a number of other plants, including seventeen species identified only from this habitat (Goodrich et al. 1999).

Piñon stands at the center of culinary and herbal traditions wherever it grows, and evidence of its use goes back at least eight thousand years on the Colorado Plateau (Janetski 1999). Piñon nuts have been found at nearly all ancestral Pueblo archaeological sites, were a valuable commodity for Spanish colonists, and can be purchased from local harvesters from roadside pickup trucks today (Curtin 1965; Dunmire and Tierney 1997). Although good crops occur only every four to seven years, and eighteen months are required for the nuts to develop, it is well worth the wait. This high-caloric wild food has high levels of protein and unsaturated fats and contains carbohydrates, vitamins, and minerals along with all twenty amino acids, making it a complete protein (Dunmire and Tierney 1995; Janetski 1999). It was one of the most important food sources for people of the Colorado Plateau in part because it contains tryptophan, an important amino acid that is missing from a corn-based diet (Castetter 1935; Janetski 1999). The nuts are best harvested around the time of first frost in the fall and can be eaten raw, roasted, or ground into flour (Castetter 1935; Dunmire and Tierney 1995; Janetski 1999).

FIGURE 115
Piñon pine (*Pinus edulis*). Photo by author.

FIGURE 116
Piñon pine
(*Pinus edulis*)
needles and
cone. Photo by
author.

FIGURE 117 Piñon
pine (*Pinus edulis*)
resin. Photo by
author.

For medicinal purposes, its needles, inner bark, and pitch are collected, with the resinous pitch forming the foundation of one of the finest aromatic herbal oils. This infused oil is excellent on its own but combines well with other infused oils, such as arnica, pedicularis, snakeweed (*Gutierrizia sarothrae*), and datura, for relaxation of muscular tension and treating arthritis or deep body injury. Pines have varying aromas, with piñon imparting a citrus tone and ponderosa more reminiscent of vanilla, but both are resinous and provide a tension-melting warming effect when rubbed into the body. Trementina de piñon, a New Mexican herbal specialty, is prepared by warming fresh pitch and using as is or further processing into a salve. This famous remedy causes local inflammation to bring splinters to the surface for easier removal and is also used for aches and pains.

Spanish New Mexicans sometimes added native tobacco and salt to piñon pitch and applied it topically for headaches. Puebloans used the pitch similarly, but they often mixed it with tallow to draw out infections from wounds, or they simply chewed and swallowed a small piece to clear up head colds (Camazine and Bye 1980; Dunmire and Tierney 1995; Jones 1931). Sometimes the pitch was added to boiling water as a tea to expel worms or parasites (Janetski 1999). Navajo people burned the pitch to treat colds and also used it as glue for broken pots and to seal woven baskets or jugs (Dunmire and Tierney 1997; Vestal 1952). Hopi and Tewa people applied resin to the forehead to protect against sorcery (Colton 1974; Whiting 1939). The Zuni and other southwestern tribes used piñon in similar ways and also used needle tea or an inner bark decoction as an expectorant and a diaphoretic for fevers, flu, and syphilis (Camazine and Bye 1980; Stevenson 1915). Modern scientific research supports many of these historic medicinal uses. Numerous terpenes and other compounds have been identified in piñon (Mirov and Iloff 1956). One study found that ponderosa pine has high levels of beta-pinene and inhibits the growth of three *Fusarium* fungal species (Krauze-Baranowska et al. 2002). Another study confirmed that the terpenes in ponderosa's aromatic resin have broad antimicrobial activity against fungi and gram-positive bacteria such as staph and strep (Himejima et al. 1992).

Populus deltoides wislizenii, Populus spp. (Salicaceae)

COTTONWOOD / ALAMO

Cottonwoods, with the golden glow of their leaves fluttering in the fall breeze and the elegant forms of their massive, curvaceous, branching trunks in winter, are among the most striking trees anywhere. Although cottonwoods are found along many rivers across the United States, they are a defining symbol of western rivers and the cultures that thrive along these waterways. The Rio Grande bosque's cottonwood forest mosaic in New Mexico has been in existence in some form for at least two million years and is one of the largest ecosystems of this type in North America (Crawford et al. 1996). These large, fast-growing riparian matriarchs stand at the center of the human settlements and rich valley cultures that have evolved along the river. Large-scale water diversions and flood control efforts of the last century have unfortunately significantly impacted cottonwoods, resulting in a sharp decline of their populations over the last several decades (Molles et al. 1998). Current and future ecological considerations for cottonwood and the riparian floodplain are covered in chapter 2; other important aspects of this medicinal tree are discussed in chapter 4. Additionally, many cottonwood species play an important role for bees in the production of antioxidant, antimicrobial, and anti-inflammatory propolis. Studies have shown that *P. nigra* (a nonnative), *P. balsamifera*, and *P. deltoides* are preferred foraging species for bees, which collect the bud exudates (Dudonne et al. 2011; Wilson et al. 2013).

FIGURE 118
Cottonwood tree
(*Populus deltoides wislizenii*). Photo by author.

Cottonwood's nurturing character transcends its ecological role in the riverside forest and provides for medicine, food, and culture. Its primary use in Pueblo, Hispanic, and other regional herbal traditions is as a salicin-containing anti-inflammatory pain reliever for arthritis, sports injuries, headaches, and fevers. Cottonwood also serves as an antimicrobial for wounds, a diuretic, and a digestive bitter. A bud tincture makes an effective expectorant for coughing and thick mucus. Caution is recommended when using anticoagulant drugs or for people with aspirin sensitivity. Collect leaf buds in late winter for tincture or infused oil, inner bark in late fall or early spring for decoctions (thick outer bark is inert), and leaves in summer for tea. Leaves are milder in action than the bark but are far less bitter and more palatable. Gathering cottonwood buds (see Figure 46), which develop their peak resin content in March in the Southwest, is a significant event in my annual calendar as it marks the final act of winter and heralds the transition into the spring growing season. Collecting the buds individually is a meditative act that makes space for contemplations regarding the change of seasons, the passage of time, and where life is headed as we move into a new cyclic phase in the landscape and in ourselves.

In the Southwest, cottonwoods have long characterized the land and the people who settled along the river valleys. Pueblo people and many other tribes across the United States have employed cottonwood's anti-inflammatory powers by chewing leaves for toothaches, applying poultices or buds melted in tallow to skin abrasions and wounds, and using the tree for general pain relief (Bean and Saubel 1972; Black 1980; Bushnell 1909; Chandler et al. 1979; Curtin 1984 [1949]; Densmore 1928; Dunmire and Tierney 1995; Gilmore 1933; Hamel and Chiltoskey 1975; Hart 1992; Hedges 1986; Herrick 1977; Hinton 1975; Kari 1985; Mechling 1959; Reagan 1928; Rousseau 1946; Smith 1929, 1923, 1932; Tantaquidgeon 1942; Turner 1973; Zigmond 1981). Indigenous people also used it to treat respiratory ailments with catarrh (Curtin 1957; Gunther 1973; Hart 1992; Kari 1985; Smith 1932; Train et al. 1941; Turner 1973), venereal disease (Hamel and Chiltoskey 1975; Hart 1992; Train et al. 1941), and stomach disorders (Hamel and Chiltoskey 1975; Train et al. 1941) and used its thick, curved bark as splints for broken bones. Cottonwood also provided fresh edible catkins each spring as well as cotton and buds for chewing gum (Dunmire and Tierney 1995; Castetter 1935; Castetter and Opler 1936; Elmore 1944; Hrdlicka 1908; Jones 1931; Reagan 1929). As Spanish settlers began moving up the Rio Grande Valley, transforming it into farmland, they too

FIGURE 119
Cottonwood
leaves (*Populus
deltoides wisli-
zenii*). Photo
by author.

found comfort in the cottonwood forests and came to integrate cottonwoods into their plant medicine traditions. Hispanic communities used cottonwood very similarly to their Pueblo neighbors but with some additions, such as boiling bark to treat fevers, arthritis, and diarrhea (Moore 1990). Burned bark and leaf ashes were also mixed with cornmeal and made into poultices for skin abscesses (Curtin 1965; Moore 1990). Leaf buds were infused into oil and applied to cracked skin, burns, and wounds (Moore 1990). The resinous oil created from cottonwood buds is a personal favorite remedy that also makes wonderfully warming massage oil for sore muscles and other bodily aches. Unlike arnica, it can be used on broken skin. The smell is enchanting, the experience is comforting, and it has a way of making you feel cared for.

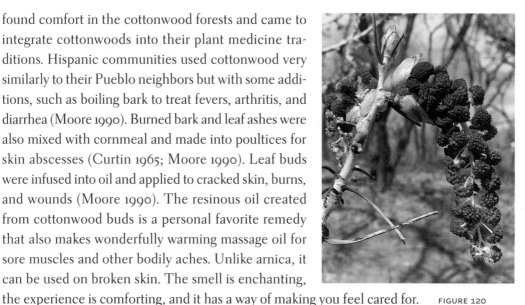

FIGURE 120
Cottonwood catkins (*Populus deltoides wislizenii*). Photo by author.

Scientific research has been conducted on a variety of *Populus* species and has centered largely on anti-inflammatory activity. Primary compounds identified for *Populus* species include an array of terpenes, flavonoids, and phenolic acids (Belkhodja et al. 2016; Dudonne et al. 2011; Isidorov and Vinogorova 2003; Kurkin et al. 1990; Si et al. 2009). Studies investigating the effectiveness of *Populus* species for the treatment of inflammatory conditions have revealed *P. alba* essential oil to be a protective agent against osteoarthritis (Belkhodja et al. 2017), *P. deltoides* leaf extract to be anti-inflammatory through the inhibition of nitric oxide and tumor necrosis factor alpha (Jeong and Lee 2018), and *P. davidiana* bark extract to also be anti-inflammatory (Zhang et al. 2006). In another study, *P. nigra* flower bud extract showed moderate antioxidant activity, strong anti-inflammatory action, and hepatoprotection against toxicity, and it acted as a vasorelaxant (Bebbache-Benaida et al. 2013). *P. ussuriensis* bark extract also showed potent antioxidant activity (Si et al. 2011). Research also found that *P. balsamifera* extract containing the phytochemical salicortin reduces whole-body fat and hepatic triglyceride levels and modulates glucose regulation and lipid oxidation, suggesting a potential new use of cottonwood medicine in antiobesity treatments (Harbilas et al. 2013).

Potentilla hippiana, P. pulcherrima, P. spp. (Rosaceae)

POTENTILLA / CINQUEFOIL / TORMENTIL

Potentilla, or cinquefoil, is another plant that bridges cross-continental biological and cultural worlds. It is impressively diverse and adaptable, with about fifty-seven species native to the western United States and an additional

FIGURE 121
Cinquefoil (*Po-tentilla thurberi*)
flower. Photo by
author.

six nonnative species making their homes in wide-ranging habitats, including forests, woodlands, sagebrush flats, and grasslands. Some species, such as *P. glandulosa*, are known to establish or spread after disturbances, such as fires, logging, and grazing, and could expand their range in coming years. Some species are also highly valued by browsing animals such as mule deer, white-tailed deer, elks, and Rocky Mountain goats and are also of great importance to a wide range of small mammals for forage and cover. The ecological role of potentilla species has not been fully explored, but one study revealed potential allelopathic activity of *P. fulgens* from India, as it significantly reduced seed germination of food crops (Nazir et al. 2007). Another study illuminated the role of environmental factors that can influence phytochemical production and observed that higher altitude and longer exposure to sunlight correlated to higher production of flavonoids, rutin, and phenolic compounds, along with increased antioxidant activity (Liu et al. 2016). In the Southwest, I often find *P. hippiana* and *P. pulcherrima* abundant in mountain meadows and have occasionally harvested from large stands. It is also an easy herb to cultivate, preferring open sunny areas in the home garden. The small yellow flowers and silvery leaves add a unique brightness to any meadow or yard, and the striking red flowers of *P. thurberi* are especially surprising and beautiful.

Cinquefoil is a medicinal plant of both the Old and New Worlds and an herb of potent magic, strength of character, and love potions. It was described by Theophrastus of ancient Greece in the third century BCE and was named for its five leaflets (*cinq feuilles* in French), which are said to represent the five senses (Richardson 2017). As a magical herb of the Middle Ages, it was used to invoke the supernatural world, to guard against witches (who apparently also used it), and in divination practices. One gruesome old recipe called witch's ointment calls for cinquefoil, wolfsbane, fat from children dug out of their graves, and wheat flour (Grieve 1971 [1931]). Wood described the magical properties of cinquefoil: "This is in fact the single most reliable indication I know in herbalism: tormentil . . . has never failed in any instance I am aware of to resolve employment, boundary, or legal tension" (2008:399–40). He suggested placing leaves or spraying tincture on documents or locations related to the conflict or interference. Cinquefoil has also served as a symbol of power, loyalty, and fortitude and was incorporated into the architecture of churches, stonework, and woodcarvings well into the 1500s. Prior to the introduction of the potato in the 1500s, it was an important root crop with a starchy turnip-like flavor. It was eaten boiled or baked, and was ground for breads and cereals.

As a medicinal plant, cinquefoil has uses similar to those of other rose family members and often finds its way into formulas for wound healing, oral health care, digestive ailments, and respiratory treatments. The root, leaves, and flowers are prepared as tea, tincture, powder, lotion, infused vinegar, and wine. Famed as an astringent herb, cinquefoil also stops bleeding, relieves pain, and heals soft tissue. It makes an excellent treatment for wound healing, hemorrhoids, swellings, lumps, bruises, and other inflammations. Also being slightly mucilaginous, cinquefoil is useful prepared as a mouthwash or gargle for mouth sores, swollen tonsils, and sore throats. In the digestive system, it calms diarrhea, bowel spasms, and symptoms of colitis and is also commonly used for regulating menstrual flows, treating fevers, and calming coughs. Old World and New World species have been used in much the same way, and many of the more common cinquefoils have been described by American

FIGURE 122
Cinquefoil (*Potentilla pulcherrima*) flower. Photo by author.

herbalists, who added treatments for poison oak and other uses related to its antioxidant content. Although not widely documented in the ethnobotanical record, cinquefoil has some reported uses among indigenous groups, including the Okanagan-Colville, Chippewa, Iroquois, Gosiute, Thompson, Cherokee, and Navajo. These groups have used it for wound care (Chamberlin 1911; Densmore 1928; Turner et al. 1980, 1990; Wyman

FIGURE 123
Cinquefoil (*Potentilla pulcherrima*) compound leaves. Photo by author.

and Harris, 1951), fever (Witthoft 1947), and diarrhea and digestive upsets (Densmore 1928; Herrick 1977). It was made into a tea for labor and post-childbirth care (Turner et al. 1980). Its powdered roots were applied in the nostrils or on the temples for headaches (Densmore 1928). It was used as a stimulating tonic (Perry 1952; Steedman 1928), a venereal disease treatment (Turner et al. 1988; Vestal 1952), and an antidote for bewitchment (Swanton 1928). For the Navajo, cinquefoil is a "life medicine" (Vestal 1952).

Recent research adds to our understanding of this plant, and much of it has focused on antioxidant and anticancer activity of a variety of species. Studies have shown that phenolic compounds, flavonoids, saponins, triterpenoids, and tannins

FIGURE 124 Cinquefoil (*Potentilla pennsylvanica*). Photo by author.

in numerous potentilla species have strong antioxidant and metal chelating action, along with anti-inflammatory activity (Grochowski et al. 2017; Jang et al. 2011; Uysal and Aktumsek 2015; Uysal et al. 2019; Walia et al. 2018). Many species exhibit potential for use in cancer prevention and treatments, showing high antiproliferative action against a human breast cancer cell line (Uysal et al. 2017), cytotoxicity to a human osteosarcoma cell line (Wan et al. 2016), significant antiproliferative action on a human urinary bladder cancer cell line (Zhang et al. 2018), and antitumor activity in human liver carcinoma, breast cancer, and colon carcinoma cell lines (Zhang et al. 2017). Potentilla also demonstrates usefulness in a variety of immunological applications, including stimulating immune activity by increasing production of T lymphocytes and white blood cells (Ang et al. 2014), anthelmintic activity (Roy et al. 2010), and antibacterial and antifungal activity (Wang et al. 2013). Additionally, potentilla shows vasoconstriction and anti-inflammatory effects similar to hydrocortisone (Wolfle et al. 2017), anticavity activity by inhibiting oral bacteria and biofilm production (Tomczyk et al. 2010), hepatoprotective action (Morikawa et al. 2018), and antidiabetic activity by improving glucose uptake (Wang et al. 2019).

Prosopis glandulosa torreyana, Prosopis spp. (Fabaceae)

MESQUITE

Mesquite is a common shrub of desert grasslands and scrublands below five thousand feet in elevation. Its name was likely derived from the Aztec *mizquitl* and modified by Spanish colonists. *P. glandulosa* includes three varieties, which are collectively distributed across the greater American Southwest and northern Mexico. *P. glandulosa torreyana* is western honey mesquite. The Southwest is also home to *P. pubescens*, or screwbean mesquite, and *P. velutina*, or velvet mesquite. Mesquite provides cover and forage for a wide variety of wildlife and serves as a migratory corridor for birds along the Rio Grande, where it hosts as many as thirty-eight bird species (Sosebee and Dahl 1979). Mesquite is also highly desert adapted. Shrubs commonly have forty-foot-long taproots if there is subsurface water. The longest recorded roots reached 190 feet (Sosebee and Wan 1989). In areas with no subsurface water source, mesquite can grow lateral roots up to sixty feet from its center (Sosebee and Wan 1989). Roots also host nitrogen-fixing bacteria and interact with arbuscular mycorrhizae (Bainbridge, 1990). This underground activity is often detrimental to grasses but may assist other plant growth by improving soil conditions (Ansley and Jacoby 1998; Barnes and Archer 1996).

Mesquite has an interesting natural history that has oscillated in accordance with changing conditions. It is theorized that mesquite's density within its range has ebbed and flowed over thousands of years (Dodson 2012). It was likely dispersed with greater frequency during the Pleistocene, co-occurring

FIGURE 125 Mesquite shrub (*Prosopis glandulosa torreyana*). Photo by author.

with browsing megafauna that would likely have eaten it and spread the seeds (Mooney et al. 1977). During subsequent prehistoric human occupation of the region, mesquite density was likely reduced as people harvested the pods in large quantities and collected the wood for fuel and construction (Bell and Castetter 1937; Felger 1977). Early American explorers in New Mexico and Texas described vast expanses of rich grasslands in areas now dominated by mesquite (Brown and Archer 1987), and studies in Texas and New Mexico have documented a significant increase of populations during the last 150 years (Buffington and Herbel 1965; Humphrey 1974). Mesquite's density expanded rapidly after grazing animals were introduced and wildfires were suppressed. Once relegated primarily to drainages, mesquite now encroaches on grasslands and in some areas may form dense thickets. Its northward expansion is limited primarily by cold sensitivity.

Mesquite has had a long relationship with people who inhabit its range, serving as one of the most important wild foods for Native people of the Southwest (Bell and Castetter 1937; Felger 1977). Analysis reveals that its seeds and pods contain protein, carbohydrates, fat, fiber, amino acids, and various minerals (Harden and Zolfaghari 1988), and they can be pounded into flour and made into a wide variety of foods and fermented beverages. Its flowers and gum have been used in specialty foods; its leaves, roots, pods, and gum have been made into medicinal preparations for the treatment of eye and ear infections (Basehart 1974; Bean and Saubel 1972; Buskirk 1986; Curtin 1984 [1949]; Hinton 1975; Jones 1931; Robbins et al. 1916; Russel 1908; Swank 1932; Train et al. 1941), fevers (Hinton 1975), burns and wounds (Bean and Saubel 1972; Castetter and Underhill 1935; Curtin 1984 [1949], 1957; Russel 1908), enuresis (Basehart 1974), and stomach acid (Carlson et al. 1940; Curtin 1984 [1949]). The plant has also been used for menstrual regulation (Curtin 1984 [1949]).

Many of these traditional uses continue today in modern wild food foraging and herbal practices. Mesquite is one of my favorite wild foods, as it imparts a deliciously unique flavor to a variety of recipes ranging from cookies to quiche crusts. The flavor is distinct and robust, so I typically keep mesquite to about 20 or 25 percent of the total flour required by the recipe to prevent it from overwhelming the other ingredients. This moderation in cooking and baking is a good idea, since too much mesquite can cause indigestion marked by gas and bloating for some people. Leaves, flowers, pods, and bark are also harvested to make medicinal preparations, including astringent and antimicrobial wound care washes, eyewashes, and teas for the treatment of diarrhea, stomach ulcers, colitis, and other digestive inflammations. Moore

(1998) described the process for harvesting and preparing the mucilaginous gum, which is sometimes present on the bark. Dissolved in warm water, this gum is useful for easing hot inflammation in the digestive system by restoring the intestinal mucosa and treating peptic ulcers, as well as for soothing sore throats (Moore 1989, 1990). Moore also provides a recipe for making mesquite molasses from the pods.

Modern research has been conducted on numerous *Prosopis* species from the Americas, Asia, and Africa and has confirmed traditional uses and illuminated new potential applications. An array of phytochemicals, including tannins, steroids, flavonoids, terpenes, phenols, and alkaloids, have been identified, and *Prosopis* extracts have demonstrated wide-ranging medicinal actions for pain and inflammation relief, controlling blood sugar and cholesterol, treating microbial infections, easing coughs and respiratory constriction, and maybe even cancer treatments. These numerous studies were summarized by Garg and Mittal (2013) and Henciya et al. (2017). Lajnef et al. (2015) found that seed extracts contain fatty acids, including oleic and palmitic acids, and phenols that exhibit antioxidant properties. A significant body of research confirms *Prosopis* species' broad antimicrobial actions (e.g., Napar et al. 2012; Preeti et al. 2015; Rahman et al. 2011; Raut 2014), including antibacterial effects from leaf (strongest), pod, and flower extracts comparable to antibiotic drugs (Singh and Verma 2011). Studies show potent activity against a number of bacterial strains, including staph, bacillus, and salmonella, and drug-resistant strains of candida, *E. coli*, and strep (Khan et al. 2010; Singh and Verma 2011). Leaf and pod extracts have also shown antimalarial activity (Batista et al. 2018), and compounds synthesized from *Prosopis farcta* have shown cytotoxic effects on colon cancer cells (Miri et al. 2018). Additionally, *Prosopis* extracts have beneficial effects on cardiovascular, respiratory, and digestive functioning. The plant is cardioprotective, reduces blood pressure and water retention (Huisamen 2013), increases HDL cholesterol while decreasing LDL cholesterol (Omidi et al. 2013), and significantly reduces total cholesterol, triglycerides, and lipoproteins (Saidi et al. 2016). Studies have also shown *Prosopis* to be an effective digestive antispasmodic, bronchodilator, and vasodilator (Janbaz et al. 2012). It is antidiabetic by significantly increasing insulin levels and also moderately decreasing blood glucose levels (George et al. 2011).

Rosa woodsii, R. spp. (Rosaceae)

ROSE / ROSA DE CASTILLA

Roses and people have an ancient and enduring connection, spanning multiple continents
and innumerable cultures. Celebrated in both
the Old and New Worlds, wild and cultivated
roses have been uniting herbal traditions for
thousands of years. Several common Old
World species have naturalized across the
United States, and the American West is home
to approximately thirteen native *Rosa* species,
with *R. woodsii* being the most widespread.
Woods' rose is found in wide-ranging habitats, including a variety of forests and grasslands, mountain meadows, prairies, riparian
areas, shrublands, and roadsides. It provides
important forage, nesting sites, and cover for

FIGURE 127. Rose (*Rosa woodsii*).
Photo by author.

a wide variety of wildlife, such as small and large mammals and birds. Rose
hips are high in energy, protein, vitamin C, and other nutritive elements and
are a sustaining food for many animals in winter, while rose leaves support
wildlife from spring through fall. Rose is also a highly successful plant for
the restoration of disturbed areas, and its rhizomatous structure is effective
for mitigating erosion. *R. woodsii* has many variations and now includes numerous plants once considered distinct species. It is also known to hybridize
with other *Rosa* members.

   Roses are one of the most prominently placed plants in natural and cultural history, with fossils dating back to the Eocene (56–34 million years ago)
(DeVore et al. 2007) and stories of roses in all major religions of the world.
Four-thousand-year-old Minoan frescos in Crete depict Roses and in the
seventh or eighth century BCE. Homer described in the *Iliad* how Aphrodite healed wounds with rose oil. Ancient Greeks associated roses with love
and believed that they sprang forth from the blood of Adonis (Grieve 1971
[1931]). The Greek poet Sappho named roses the "queen of flowers." The
word *rose* may originate from the Greek word for red, *rodon* (Grieve 1971
[1931]). Roses were widely used throughout the Old World. They have been
cultivated since ancient times, with writers such as Horace and Pliny describing their horticulture. Ancient Romans saw roses as a symbol of pleasure and
used them for celebratory decorations, floated rose petals in wine, and wore

rose garlands around the head to guard against the ill effects of intoxication. They were worn by brides and grooms at weddings and also by gods and goddesses, including Cupid, Venus, and Bacchus. Roses were scattered at feasts, tossed at victors, and affixed to warships in battle. Cleopatra is said to have ordered a rose petal carpet for Mark Antony (Richardson 2017). According to Christian lore, roses were white until stained by the blood of Christ and the flowers emerged from places where his blood dripped from the crown of thorns (Richardson 2017). Rosary beads, so named in 1208, were originally made from pressed rose petals, and the golden rose was conferred upon devoted church members by the pope. In 850 CE, Charlemagne's son planted a rose in Hildesheim, Germany. Still growing today, it is believed to be the oldest living rose in the world (Richardson 2017).

The Old World medicinal history of roses can be characterized by pan-cultural use and an astounding array of preparations, with rose water and otto of roses (essential oil) among the most legendary. An official plant of most pharmacopeias, roses are best collected as flower buds just prior to opening. Other parts, including the hips, leaves, thorns, and galls, have also been used. Although numerous species are native to Europe and the British pharmacopeia specifically lists *R. gallica*, most modern roses are hybrids, and cultivated aromatic plants have long been a primary source for herbal preparations. The use of rose water dates to the tenth century, and Grieve (1971 [1931]) says that otto of roses was discovered around the turn of the seventeenth century during a royal wedding, when the couple was rowing through rose water canals and noticed the summer sun separating the rose oil from the water. They skimmed this pure essential oil from the water's surface. According to Mahaddese (2016), however, rose essential oil was extracted by Avicenna, a famous Iranian scientist, in the tenth century and

FIGURE 128 Rose thicket (*Rosa woodsii*). Photo by author.

Materia
Medica

165

was used for the treatment of various conditions. Large-scale production of the essential oil began during the 1600s, and by the end of the century it had spread to Europe by way of the Turkish Empire (Grieve 1971 [1931]).

Other preparations include confections of petals in sugar, fluid extracts in glycerin and diluted alcohol, syrup, infused honey, ointment of rosewater or cold cream, cordials, infused vinegar, electuaries, potpourris, incense, tea, tinctures, elixirs, adornments, and a long list of foods and alcoholic spirits. Cooling and drying, roses are known for clearing heat, phlegm, and inflammation, and remedies are helpful for both chronic and acute conditions. While known primarily as astringent herbs, roses have a variety of medicinal actions and are commonly used for treating the circulatory, respiratory, and digestive systems and are found in products for the skin and other soft tissues. Roses have a long association with passion and the heart and also serve to increase circulation through diuresis, reduce heart inflammation, and support the emotional heart during difficult times. Roses' drying action and expectoration also help to clear colds and support the respiratory system by calming wet coughs, reducing excess secretions, opening up constriction in the airways, soothing sore throats, and promoting rest and sleep. High in vitamin C, roses have been long used as a cold preventative, and rose petal conserve was considered a specific for tuberculosis in the Middle Ages. In the digestive system, roses ease upset stomachs, reduce nausea, astringe diarrhea, move constipation, calm heartburn, and soothe irritable bowels and all manner of hot digestive inflammations. Few other plants have been as revered as roses for healthy skin. With cooling, drying, anti-inflammatory, and antioxidant actions, they are commonly used in skin creams and other soft-tissue remedies, including first aid balms, eyewashes, and mouthwashes. Roses are also prescribed for kidney and bladder ailments, yeast infections, excess vaginal discharge, menstrual irregularities (including heavy flows), arthritis, and joint pain. Deeply nourishing, fortifying, and revitalizing, roses are the remedy of choice for folks with existential woes and heavy hearts; those who are deeply fatigued, overwhelmed, or broken down; and people who suffer from stress and tension-induced headaches, anxiety, or depression. Throughout the history of humanity, roses have been consistently thought of as the remedy of our time.

Medicinal uses among indigenous groups and practicing herbalists in the New World are consistent with those already described but include some ethnobotanical additions. Applications described by wide-ranging Native American tribes include remedies for coughs and colds (Bocek 1984; Leighton 1985; Train et al. 1941; Turner et al. 1990); fevers (Bocek 1984; Hedges

1986; Kari 1985; Romero 1954); sore throats (Bocek 1984; Gunther 1973; Hart 1992; Leighton 1985; Theodoratus 1989; Turner et al. 1990); diarrhea, heartburn, colic, and other digestive problems (Barrett and Gifford 1933; Bocek 1984; Hamel and Chiltoskey 1975; Hart 1981, 1992; Johnston 1987; Kari 1985; Mahar 1953; McClintock 1909; Romero 1954; Rousseau 1945a; Smith 1923, 1928, 1929,

Train et al. 1941; Turner et al. 1990; Witthoft 1947); and worms (Taylor 1940). Roses have been used to make eyewash (Carrier Linguistic Committee 1973; Densmore 1928; Gilmore 1913b, 1991 [1919]; Gunther 1973; Hart 1992; Herrick 1977; Hoffman 1891; Leighton 1985; Smith 1929; Steedman 1928; Turner 1973); to treat skin inflammations and diseases, beestings, bleeding wounds, and burns (Bocek 1984; Densmore 1913, 1928; Gilmore 1991 [1919]; Gunther 1973; Hart 1992; Mahar 1953; Reagan 1928; Smith 1928, 1929; Swank, 1932; Train et al. 1941; Turner et al. 1980, 1990); to ease difficult births (Gunther 1973; Herrick 1977; Turner et al. 1990); and for postpartum recovery (Turner et al. 1990). Roses have treated bodily aches and pains (Bocek 1984; Nickerson 1966; Smith 1933), convulsions (Densmore 1913), and venereal disease (Gunther 1973; Turner et al. 1990). They have been used to strengthen the blood (Kari 1985), as good luck charms (Turner et al. 1980, 1990), and as protection against ghosts and ill will (Hart 1992; Palmer 1975; Turner et al. 1980, 1990). Roses have also been used in hair and body washes and oils. The hips have been incorporated into a variety of wild foods. While *Rosa* species seem relatively common in the wild, it is important to remember that they serve as forage for wildlife, including bears, which eat them to prepare for hibernation. Since roses are easily cultivated in my western garden, I supplement wild harvests with backyard or neighborhood harvesting. Exquisite dryland roses forming elegant plumes have particular appeal for me, and I occasionally add the flowers of cliffrose (*Purshia stansburiana*) and Apache plume (*Fallugia paradoxa*) to topical preparations for the hair and skin. These latter species seem to have an added effect when the characteristics of flexibility and resiliency are needed, and the infused oil can be added to balms with other appropriate herbs for this purpose.

RESEARCH SUMMARY   Due to the enormous popularity and long history of roses in medicine, cosmetics, culinary arts, and gardening, a large body of research has been accumulated for this plant and warrants summary here. Numerous animal studies and human clinical trials have been done using primarily hips and petals of several rose species, including *R. canina*, *R. multiflora*,

FIGURE 130
Rose hips (*Rosa woodsii*). Photo by author.

R. damascena, *R. rugosa*, and *R. laevigata*. Scientific research has confirmed rose's beneficial activity in wide-ranging medical conditions and has identified a large number of active compounds, including ascorbic acid, phenolic acid, fatty acids, terpenes, glycosides, flavonoids, vitamin C, kaempferol, quercetin, and geraniol (Boskabady et al. 2011; Marmol et al. 2017). Rose hips have been shown to reduce inflammation and provide relief from symptoms of rheumatoid arthritis (Cohen 2012; Kharazmi and Winther 1999; Rein et al. 2004; Warholm et al. 2003), and their antioxidant activity may help restore bone mineral density for the prevention and treatment of osteoporosis (Marmol et al. 2017). Studies have also demonstrated the ability of rose hips and petals to significantly reduce blood glucose levels and improve pancreatic functions in the treatment of diabetes (Gholamhoseinian et al. 2012; Konate et al. 2014; Orhan 2009). Promoting cardiovascular health, rose may be useful in the treatment of hyperlipidemia by significantly lowering triglycerides and free fatty acids (Niominya et al. 2007) while also reducing total cholesterol and plaque formation (Gholamhoseinian et al. 2012) and increasing heart rate and contractility (Boskabady et al. 2011). In the treatment of obesity, rose hips increase lipid metabolism and decrease fat accumulation (Nagatomo et al. 2013; Ninomiya et al. 2013). Digestive ailments resulting in diarrhea have been significantly alleviated by roses through improved absorption of water and electrolytes (Rao and Gurfinkel 2000), and peptic ulcers, often caused by *H. pylori*, have been treated by rose's ability to prevent gastric mucosa erosion (Lattanzio et al. 2011). Rose is also supportive to the liver and kidneys, strengthening liver cell membranes to prevent toxicity (Sadeghi et al. 2016) and reducing inflammation and calcium oxalate concentrations in the kidneys for the prevention of urinary stones (Tayefi-Nasrabadi et al. 2012). In the respiratory system, rose acts as a bronchodilator, antitussive, and smooth muscle relaxant (Rakhshandah et al. 2010; Shafei et al. 2010) to relieve coughing and lung constriction. Roses have also reduced painful menstruation in clinical trials (Bani et al. 2014).

In the nervous system, rose has proven its ability to improve spatial and long-term memory (Esfandiary et al. 2015) and protect against neuronal damage (DeToma et al. 2011; Semwal et al. 2016), making it a promising therapy for Alzheimer's disease. Rose generally increases cognition in dementia patients, relieves depression, and treats behavioral issues through its antioxidant effects (Dolati et al. 2010; Esfandiary et al. 2018; Mophammadpour et al. 2014). It also enhances libido (Farni et al. 2015; Momeni et al. 1991). In epilepsy treatments, rose hips act as an anticonvulsive (Ashrafzadeh et al. 2007; Homayoun et al. 2015; Hosseini et al. 2011). For treatment of anxiety and depression, volatile rose oils stimulate the central nervous system, increasing the release of serotonin for a relaxant and mood-lifting effect (Hongratanaworakit 2009; Sánchez-Vidaña et al. 2017). Roses have long been a prized herb for skin care, and rose root extracts have been shown to be anti-inflammatory for skin injuries and chronic skin conditions, with antioxidant and anti-inflammatory activity also helping reduce skin damage due to aging and UV exposure (Marmol et al. 2017; Park et al. 2014; Phetcharat et al. 2015). Rose's quercetin was also found to reduce melanin content in melanoma cells (Fuji et al. 2009) and minimize age-related deterioration of the skin by reducing the depth of wrinkles, improving skin elasticity, and increasing cell longevity (Phetcharat et al. 2015).

Rose has been widely studied for its applications in the treatment of infectious disease and cancer. The antimicrobial activity of rose has been well documented and includes antiviral actions inhibiting hepatitis C and HIV; antifungal activity against candida; and antibacterial activity against a large number of microbes, including *H. pylori*, staph, and UTI bacterial strains (studies summarized by Marmol et al. 2017 and Mahaddese 2016). It is selective in the gut, inhibiting pathogenic bacteria while protecting beneficial bacteria (Kamijo et al. 2008). Roses also, in some cases, potentiate the effects of antibiotic drugs (Shiota et al. 2004). Clinical trials also confirm rose petals to be effective as mouthwashes and eyewashes for treatment of ulcers, conjunctivitis, and other infections (Biswas et al. 2001; Hoseinpour et al. 2011; Mitra et al. 2000). It is worth noting that while numerous studies and clinical trials have shown rose petals to be antimicrobial against a long list of pathogens, some studies were conducted on *Rosa* species while others were conducted on different plants that share the active ingredient geranoil but may not have the same synergistic effects. Numerous studies have shown rose to be antiproliferative against prostate, esophageal, gastric, pulmonary, ovarian, lung, breast, cervical, and other cancer cell lines (e.g., Chen et al. 2014; Guimarães et al. 2014; Jimenez et al. 2016; Khatib et al. 2013; Kooti et al. 2017; Lee et al. 2008; Liu et al. 2012; Tumbas et al. 2012; Venkatesan et al. 2014; Zamiri-Akhlaghi et al. 2011; Zhamanbayeva et al. 2016; Zu et al. 2010). Rose's use in the treatment of estrogenic tumors is debated, however, as phytoestrogens could cause an increase in tumor growth (Guimarães et al. 2014; Tumbas et al. 2012; Uifălean et al. 2016).

Rudbeckia laciniata (Asteraceae)

CUTLEAF CONEFLOWER

Cutleaf coneflower is a familiar character of streamside habitats throughout the Rocky Mountains and across other areas of the United States. The species includes several subvarieties and is considered to be a nonnative invasive plant in parts of Asia. Although I have not observed invasive behavior in local habitats, three known phytotoxic sesquiterpenes have been discovered in its roots (Fukushi et al. 1998) and could contribute to its spread in other regions of the world. Large stands may form in areas with reliable perennial streams, and some have proposed cutleaf coneflower as a substitute for wild echinacea. Although it is locally abundant in cooler, wetter regions of its range, I have noticed certain streams in familiar desert mountains running with less water and less cutleaf coneflower. This plant is easy to grow in open sunny spots in the western garden, and with a little extra water, it will add rays of golden sunshine and lots of insects to your yard.

The role of cutleaf coneflower in herbal practice has been eclipsed or obscured by another plant. Herbalists (and early eclectic physicians) often describe cutleaf coneflower as a substitute for the well-known medicinal herb echinacea and say little else about it. The comparison with echinacea, another coneflower, is fair, as they do have significant overlap in medicinal character, but that does not tell the whole story. Echinacea has a large volume of anecdotal information and evidenced-based research behind it and has been described by innumerable botanical authors (e.g., Foster 1991; Kindscher 2016; Moore 2003), so I shall not repeat that material here. Despite standing in the shadow of a much more famous relative, cutleaf coneflower has its own unique identity and an important place in the apothecary. Cutleaf coneflower is stimulating to the organs of elimination, promoting digestion, and urinary and liver functioning (Moore 2003). It is also moistening and encouraging to the lungs. These actions help clear the body of toxins and waste, reduce inflammation, lessen bodily aches, and clear infections. Both herbs are notable for their roles in modulating immune response, but I use them distinctly. When I have that first vague feeling of coming down with an illness, before the symptoms manifest in any discernable way, this is the time to mix up some

FIGURE 131. Cutleaf coneflowers (*Rudbeckia laciniata*). Photo by author.

echinacea and vervain (*Verbena* spp.)
and take frequent doses throughout
the day. Cutleaf coneflower works
better as a tonic for healthy immune
functioning, restoring balance in this
system and managing chronic inflammation. In other words, use echinacea
in short bursts for prevention, early
onset, or acute situations, and call on
cutleaf coneflower for ongoing maintenance, foundational shifting of the
immune system, or convalescence
after prolonged illness. Prepare tincture or tea made from leaves, flowers,
and roots. A few additional uses have
been documented from the Cherokee
and Chippewa, including as a burn
or wound poultice (Densmore 1928),
a root tea for indigestion (Densmore
1928), and eating shoots and leaves
as a spring vegetable (Castetter 1935;
Perry 1975; Witthoft 1977). The leaf
tea is also a long-standing traditional
remedy in New Mexico for gonorrhea
and menstrual stagnancy (Curtin 1965;
Moore 1990).

FIGURE 132. Cutleaf coneflower (*Rudbeckia laciniata*). Photo by author.

Surprisingly little research has been done on *Rudbeckia laciniata*'s medicinal activity. Phytochemical analysis has identified compounds including
lignans (Lee et al. 2013), sesquiterpenes (Bohlmann et al. 1978; Fukushi et al.
1994, 1998; Jakupovic et al. 1986), triterpenes (Bohlmann et al. 1978), flavonol
glycosides, and quinic acid derivatives (Lee et al. 2014). A study by J. Lee et al.
(2014) found that although phenolic/flavonoid content in *Rudbeckia laciniata*
was low compared to other Asteraceae plants studied, it exhibited the strongest inhibitory effects against elevated nitric oxide production in macrophage
cells, which has been implicated in numerous disease processes. Clearly,
additional research is needed on this plant to gain a better understanding of
its role in disease prevention and treatment and to illuminate other potential
applications, such as wound care.

Scutellaria lateriflora, S. spp. (Lamiaceae)

SKULLCAP

At least a dozen *Scutellaria* species are native to the American West, with *S. lateriflora* and *S. galericulata* being the most widespread and most commonly used in regional herbal practice. These two species grow in moist places along mountain streams, and I have found the former easy to cultivate in moist shady areas of my garden. Be sure to avoid collecting threatened species with very limited ranges, such *as S. montana* and *S. ocmulgee*, both found in small areas of southern states. The botanical name *Scutellaria* is derived from the Latin *scutella*, meaning "small dish," a reference to the calyx, and *lateriflora*, describing flowers that form along the side of the stem. Herbalists and plant practitioners often work with species that are locally available, using them interchangeably, but their chemistry may be variable (see below) and could result in differences in medicinal actions. Moore (2003) described subtle variations in medicinal effects among various species, with *S. galericulata* being the most anti-inflammatory, *S. nana* having anesthetizing action, *S. resinosa* and *S. wrightii* acting as peripheral vasodilators, and *S. californica* having the strongest bitter action. The well-known and much more widely researched Chinese Baikal skullcap, *S. baicalensis*, is significantly different from other skullcaps and not used in the same ways (Cech 2000).

FIGURE 133 Skullcap (*Scutellaria lateriflora*). Photo by author.

Considered by many herbalists to be a premier nervine (e.g., Gladstar 2001; Grieve 1971 [1931]; Hoffmann 2003), skullcap is fortifying and restorative to the central nervous system. The whole plant or leaves and flowers can be prepared as tea or tincture. As with many nervines, fresh plant tinctures in 190-proof alcohol are preferred. As a tonic, skullcap is usually combined with complementary herbs to create the desired effects. Skullcap's most notable action is calming irritability or the overstimulation of nerves, which often results in physical discomfort, pain, or a sense of agitation and restlessness. Common uses include calming tension and fear, and treating mild seizures, exhaustion, depression, anxiety, insomnia, nightmares, restlessness, and other symptoms of unmanaged stress or nervous depletion. Skullcap is also useful for those transitioning off sedative drugs. Eclectic physicians indicated skullcap for nervous disorders such as twitching, irregular muscular movements, tremors, and shakes (Ellingwood 1919) and for heart disorders with an intermittent pulse stemming from nervousness (Felter 1922). For best success in the management of chronic nervous system issues, Moore (2003) recommends skullcap and the simultaneous removal of refined sugar from the diet. I have found skullcap to have mild to moderate bitter actions, making it a particularly compatible remedy for stressed-out people with a low appetite, poor digestion, or a chronic upset stomach. I combine it with other herbs, including catnip (*Nepeta cataria*), chamomile (*Matricaria chamomilla*), vervain (*Verbena* spp.), motherwort (*Leonurus cardiaca*), lemon balm (*Melissa officinalis*), or the drop-dose herb pulsatilla (*Pulsatilla patens*), for kids and others with difficulty accepting transitions, stage fright, or other situational nervousness. Additionally, uses have been documented among the Miwok, Mendocino, Cherokee, Delaware, and Oklahoma tribes, including treatments for chills and fevers (Chesnut 1902) and coughs and colds (Barrett and Gifford 1933). Tribes also used it to encourage menstruation (Hamel and Chiltoskey 1975), calm nerves (Hamel and Chiltoskey 1975), expel afterbirth (Hamel and Chiltoskey 1975; Taylor 1940), and promote kidney health (Hamel and Chiltoskey 1975). It has been used as a laxative (Tantaquidgeon 1972), and an eyewash (Barrett and Gifford 1933). Although it is generally considered safe, oversensitivity to or overuse of skullcap can cause side effects, such as dizziness, giddiness, confusion, or lack of mental clarity (Cech 2000). Other cautions regard the roots, which can cause menstrual spotting or increase liver enzymes, potentially affecting the processing of medications (Moore 2003). Take care to purchase any skullcap products or herb materials from reputable sources to avoid adulteration with the herb germander (genus *Teucrium*), a persistent problem that has been documented since the early twentieth century and may remain a danger (Foster 2012). In fact, this contamination has caused skullcap to be falsely accused of liver toxicity in the past.

The *Scutellaria* genus includes at least 350 to 400 members worldwide (Paton 1990). More than 295 compounds have been identified through phytochemical analysis of the genus (Shang et al. 2010), and although many species have a large number of compounds in common, they may occur at significantly different rates among the various species (Islam et al. 2010; Kim et al. 2014), possibly producing a range in medicinal effects. For example, one study found that antioxidant activity in sixteen *Scutellaria* species varied considerably (Vaidyea et al. 2014). Therefore only studies involving *S. lateriflora* will be discussed here. Upton's (2012) monograph provides a summary of scientific information for *S. lateriflora*.

Skullcap is known for calming nervous system agitation, and much research on this plant has focused on its effects on mood, anxiety, seizures, neurodegenerative disease, and cancer. Studies have shown *S. lateriflora* to have beneficial effects on mood and anxiety, and although the bioactive compounds and pharmacological activity of skullcap have yet to be fully investigated, its anxiolytic mechanism is believed to be interaction with benzodiazepine receptors in the brain and modulation of GABA activity (reducing neural activity in the central nervous system, which may reduce feelings of fear or anxiety) (Awad et al. 2003). One clinical trial showed skullcap to be beneficial for reducing anxiety without overt side effects, and no drug interactions were reported (Wolfson and Hoffman 2003). Another trial found no significant impact on anxiety but a substantial beneficial impact on general mood without side effects (Brock et al. 2014). Skullcap may also have antioxidant and neuroprotective qualities, as reported by Silva et al. (2005), who observed *S. lateriflora* extract to be highly efficacious in scavenging free radicals and reducing lipid peroxidation. Another study reported that skullcap extract and the flavonoids baicalein and baicalin reduced the incubation and advancement of prion disease in animals, which could lead to more effective treatments for neurodegenerative diseases such as Alzheimer's and Parkinson's (Eiden et al. 2012). A study showing the cessation of induced seizures in animals taking a combination extract of skullcap, datura (*D. stramonium*), and gelsemium (*G. sempervirens*), and the return of seizures upon stopping treatment, suggests the usefulness of skullcap in epilepsy therapeutics (Peredery and Persinger 2004). Furthermore, thirteen species of *Scutellaria* were assessed for the bioactive flavonoids apigenin, baicalein, baicalin, chrysin, scutellarein, and wogonin and tested for antitumor activity against brain, breast, and prostate cancers, with results showing that plant extracts and individual flavonoids are effective against brain and breast cancer, with some species having potent anticancer activity (Parajuli et al. 2009). A review by Patel et al. (2013) summarizes research on the antitumor activity of *Scutellaria* species on breast, prostate, ovarian, brain, and other cancers. Lastly, *S. lateriflora* extract has been found to be antimicrobial, with activity against *E. coli* and candida (Bergeron et al. 1996).

Solidago canadensis, *S.* spp. (Asteraceae)

GOLDENROD

Goldenrod includes a large number of species, some having extensive ranges across the United States. Many of the species have several recognized varieties, making species-specific identification challenging. The genus name

FIGURE 134. Goldenrod
(*Solidago canadensis*).
Photo by author.

FIGURE 135. Goldenrod
(*Oligoneuron rigidum*).
Photo by author.

Solidago is from the Latin words *solidus* and *ago*, meaning "to make whole," a reference to its healing powers. Goldenrod is found in a wide variety of habitat types with moderate moisture and may be a dominant or co-dominant species, especially in disturbed areas. It is known to have some allelopathic activity, inhibiting the seedlings of other herbaceous species (Werner et al. 1980), an adaptation that may become more pronounced outside its native range, where it is sometimes considered an invasive species (Yuan et al. 2013). Goldenrod is a persistent and long-lived plant, with one stand in Iowa thought to be more than one hundred years old (Werner et al. 1980). In its native range, goldenrod serves as forage for white-tailed deer and is an important nectar source for bees and other insects. *Solidago* species are easy to grow in western gardens. They provide a bright splash of golden color and a willingness to colonize areas where other plants may be reluctant to thrive. Due to goldenrod's assertive spreading rhizomes, be sure to plant it where it will not overtake other garden plants.

Goldenrod finds its place in herbal traditions as an herb of respiratory and urinary formulas, but is also useful in a number of other applications. Considered a top remedy for mucus in the upper respiratory system, its leaves and flowers are commonly included in formulas for head colds as either a tea or tincture. Goldenrod's aromatic oils and associated dispersive properties can help clear lingering infections and alleviate allergies, especially those with red irritated conjunctiva (Wood 2008). In urinary formulas, goldenrod serves as an astringent, diuretic, antiseptic, and anti-inflammatory, alleviating bladder infections and lower-body edema or skin conditions. Wood specifically indicated goldenrod for people working through emotions and with tired lower backs and feet, which suggests depleted or overwhelmed kidneys. Goldenrod's bitter, astringent, and carminative actions help reduce symptoms of indigestion, including

gas, bloating, and diarrhea, while also promoting scar tissue formation for healing gastric ulcers (Grieve 1971 [1931]). Goldenrod can be included in wound-healing remedies as a cooling yet stimulating antiseptic, styptic, anti-inflammatory, and vulnerary herb. I often combine Goldenrod with other herbs in topical remedies such as liniments, oils, and balms for sore or overworked muscles, and I have known herbalists to use goldenrod as a spirit-lifting herb, particularly during dark times of year. I consider goldenrod's drying effects to be valuable for allergy season, when the head feels full of fluid and the eyes are excessively watery. Native American groups, including the Cahuilla, Diegueño, Kawaiisu, Miwok, Iroquois, Meskwaki, Okanagan-Colville, Potawatomi, Shuswap, Thompson, Chippewa, Menominee, Keres, Delaware, Oklahoma, Cree, Mahuna, Alabama, Blackfoot, Algonquin, Zuni, and Navajo, reported a variety of uses for goldenrod, including as a hair rinse (Densmore 1928; Hedges 1986) and a gynecological wash (Bean and Saubel 1972). It has been used to treat toothaches and other oral health problems (Barrett and Gifford 1933; Hamel and Chiltoskey 1975; Swanton 1928; Taylor 1940), jaundice (Herrick 1987; Speck 1941), and venereal diseases (Herrick 1987; Steedman 1928). It has been made into washes or poultices for wounds, including burns and stings (Barrett and Gifford 1933; Bocek 1984; Densmore 1928; Herrick 1987; Romero 1954; Smith 1928; Zigmond 1981); used to restore appetite (Steedman 1928); and used to ease digestive upsets, including nausea and constipation (Densmore 1928; Herrick 1987; Swank 1932). Goldenrod has treated kidney conditions (Herrick 1987); heart disease (Black 1980); colds and flu (Hamel and Chiltoskey 1975; Swanton 1928; Turner et al. 1980); sore throats and congestion (Densmore 1928; Hellson 1974; Stevenson 1915); sprains, strained muscles, and other bodily pains (Densmore 1928; Stevenson 1915); diarrhea (Hamel and Chiltoskey 1975; Tantaquidgeon 1972; Turner et al. 1980, 1990); fevers (Densmore 1928; Hamel and Chiltoskey 1975; Smith 1933; Tantaquidgeon 1942, 1972; Turner et al. 1980; Witthoft 1947); headaches (Densmore 1932); convulsions (Densmore 1928); neuralgia (Hamel and Chiltoskey 1975); diuresis (Densmore 1928); hemorrhage (Densmore 1928; Herrick 1987); and labor difficulties (Densmore 1928). Ethnobotanical investigations have documented uses for *S. microglossa* in Brazil for a variety of conditions, including wounds, acne, bruises, and stomach-related ailments (Bieski et al. 2012), and the use of *S. virgaurea* in northern India for kidney issues, asthma, throat infections (Pala et al. 2010), rheumatism, and wound care (Dangwal et al. 2013).

Recent research on goldenrod has investigated antimicrobial and anti-inflammatory activity, along with other potential uses. The herb is known to contain a number of phytochemicals, including flavonoids, saponins, carotenoids, terpenes, lignans, and coumarins (Huang et al. 2013; Vila et al. 2002). Three species of goldenrod have shown strong activity against both gram-positive and gram-negative bacteria, including staph, *E. coli*, pneumonia, and salmonella, as well as antifungal activity against candida (Frey and Meyers 2010; Kolodziej et al. 2011; Morel et al. 2006; Vila et al. 2002). Researchers have observed pain-relieving effects through local and systemic anti-inflammatory activity (Tamura et al. 2009), muscle relaxation from antispasmodic actions (Kissman and Groth 1999), and a reduction in the nervous system's response to both inflammatory and noninflammatory sources of pain (Malpezzi-Marinho et al. 2019). Studies have shown goldenrod to promote cicatrization, or the formation of scar tissue in wound healing, which may be useful in cutaneous healing as well as the treatment of gastric ulcers (Neto et al. 2004). Digestive benefits of goldenrod extracts include gastroprotective activity through regeneration of gastric mucosa and a reduction in volume and acidity of gastric secretions (de Barros et al. 2016). Additionally, goldenrod has exhibited hypoglycemic activity (Santos et al. 2006), moderate hypolipidemic actions (Huang et al. 2013), and antioxidant powers, potentially useful for the prevention of neurodegenerative diseases (Paun et al. 2016).

Sphaeralcea angustifolia, S. coccinea, S. spp. (Malvaceae)

GLOBEMALLOW / YERBA DE LA NEGRITA

The captivating tiny orange flowers of local globemallows were among the first wildflowers to ensnare my heart. Since then I have gotten to know many species, blooming in varied colors and growing in a wide variety of environments, making globemallow one of the most reliably abundant native medicinal herbs in the Southwest. The genus (primarily *S. coccinea*) ranges across the Mountain West, but most species prefer the drier soils of the greater Southwest and southern plains. Due to their propensity for cross-hybridizing, it can be very difficult to differentiate individual species. Globemallows have a close relationship with native desert bees, whose lives unfold in harmony with the coming of unpredictable rains that spur this plant's seeds to germinate, summoning the bees to gather nectar and to facilitate pollination. *S. coccinea* also provides important forage for numerous animals, including pronghorn,

FIGURE 137
Globemallow
(*Sphaeralcea
angustifolia*) can
have a long and
leggy structure.
Photo by author.

deer, bighorn sheep, bison, prairie dogs, jackrabbits, gophers, wood rats, mice, squirrels, and some and insect bird species. It is adapted to a broad range of soil types, is highly drought resistant, spreads by rhizomes, and establishes well on disturbed soils. As a result, it is useful in restoring arid and semiarid habitats and areas that have experienced wildfire, especially short-grass and mixed-grass prairies, piñon-juniper woodland, and sagebrush ecosystems.

Globemallow has a long history of use in the Southwest. It is found regularly at archaeological sites, including Chaco Canyon, where it is more frequently found in ceremonial kivas than in residential or food prep rooms, suggesting ritual and/or medicinal usage (Dunmire and Tierney 1997). Ethnobotanical records show many uses for globemallow among Native American and Hispanic communities, with a focus on treating the digestive and respiratory systems as well as wound care and treatment of inflammation. Tribes from the plains and Southwest, including the Shoshoni, Navajo, Pima, Kiowa, Keres, Cheyenne, Lakota, Comanche, Dakota, Gosiute, Havasupai, and Hopi, have described using globemallow to treat upset stomachs and diarrhea (Colton 1974; Curtin 1984 [1949]; Fewkes 1896; Russell 1908; Train et al. 1941; Whiting 1939); coughs and colds (Hocking 1956; Train et al. 1941); wounds, swellings, and rheumatic complaints (Carlson and Jones 1940; Gilmore 1991 [1919]; Murphey 1990 [1959]; Robbins et al. 1916; Train et al. 1941; Vestal 1952; Wyman and Harris 1951); and venereal disease (Train et al. 1941). Pueblo people pounded globemallow roots and mixed them with saltwater to make an infection- or venom-drawing poultice or a hard cast for broken bones. They rubbed globemallow leaves on sore muscles for a rubefacient effect (Dunmire and Tierney 1995). The Navajo consider globemallow to be a "life medicine" and use the roots to stop bleeding; to treat skin ailments, indigestion, poor appetite, coughs and colds, and rabies; to strengthen the voice; and to heal diseases enacted by witchcraft (Dunmire and Tierney 1997; Elmore 1944; Hocking 1956; Vestal 1952; Wyman and Harris 1951). According to Gilmore (1991 [1919]:51), the Dakota chewed *S. coccinea* and rubbed the paste over their hands and arms. This mucilaginous application protected the skin, allowing a person to remove a piece of hot meat from boiling soup, "to the mystification and wonderment of beholders." Early Hispanic herb traditions included many of the same uses, plus a globemallow bath for babies with thrush or chronic diaper rash, and a hair and scalp rinse made from mashed globemallow leaves and flowers (Curtin 1965; Moore 1990).

This plant's close relationship with humans carries over into modern herbal traditions, where it is used for a variety of health complaints, including chronic inflammation, skin conditions, respiratory ailments, digestive problems, and urinary irritations. Globemallow is prepared as a tea made from leaves and flowers (and strained through a cloth to catch potentially irritating tiny hairs), and as a poultice, bath, or tincture. I prepare the latter by making a double-strength infusion preserved with 25 percent alcohol. If a high-mucilage preparation is desired, a cold infusion is best. Additionally, I collect roots and grind them into powder to make a gelatinous substance mixed into water, tea, or juice to alleviate throat irritations or mixed into cosmetic clays for topical soft-tissue healing. As a cooling and demulcent anti-inflammatory that stimulates macrophage activity and promotes healing, globemallow is useful whenever there is hot inflamed soft tissue (Moore 2003). This includes chronic or poorly healing infections, dry coughs, sore throats, urinary infections, hemorrhoids, ulcers, splinters, abscesses, rashes, bites, and stings. Globemallow is an effective tonic herb for immune system imbalances, such as autoimmune conditions; it can help reduce inflammation and coordinate effective immune functioning without overexciting the system. Because it is so reliable and effective in this regard, it has become one of the most used herbs in my apothecary. Likewise, its immuno-modulating effects are useful

FIGURE 138. Globemallow (*Sphaeralcea coccinea*) can have a short and compact form. Photo by author.

FIGURE 139.
Globemallow
flower (*Sphaeral-
cea angustifolia*).
Photo by author.

for people with sluggish systems who get sick often or have illnesses that linger without resolution. I consider globemallow to be an essential herb of our time—one willing to grow in a variety of habitats and adapted to the hotter, drier, and more inflamed environmental conditions of the modern era. Serving as a reminder of our interconnectedness with the environment, globe-mallow offers us the remedy of balance during a period of upheaval, disequilibrium, and rapid change.

Scientific research has confirmed some of globemallow's medicinal appli-cations. Anti-inflammatory compounds identified in *S. angustifolia* include scopoletin, tomentin, and sphaeralcic acid and account for its antiarthritic activity (del Pilar Nicasio-Torres et al. 2017). Its leaves and flowers have been found to inhibit pro-inflammatory molecules, including interleukin and tumor necrosis factor (Garcia-Rodriguez et al. 2012). Studies on *S. angustoflia* have also yielded an antiprotozoal compound, tiliroside, with antiamoebic and antigiardial activity, useful in the treatment of infectious digestive dis-orders (Calzada et al. 2017). Additional studies suggest that *S. angustifolia* has cytotoxic activity against cervical cancer cells (Booth et al. 2012). With such wide-ranging and important medicinal applications, the potential for more popular use of this herb is enormous. Fortunately, the possibility for high-yield cultivation of globemallow has already been investigated, with successful cultivation experiments in New Mexico's desert and mountain environments (Kleitz et al. 2008).

Trifolium pratense (Fabaceae)

RED CLOVER

Common throughout the American West, red clover is among the most widely distributed weedy medicinal herbs in the world and has great influ-ence wherever it spreads. The word *clover* is likely derived from the Latin *clava*, meaning "club," and the botanical name *Trifolium pratense* refers to the three-lobed leaves growing in meadows. Its presence is usually detected wherever agriculture or equestrian activities take place. Red clover exempli-fies the virtues of working with weeds. They are reliably abundant, available wherever you go, co-evolving along with large swaths of humanity, and keep-ers of health in the most generous ways. The addition of nonnative weedy plants to our apothecaries also imbues us with their adaptability, persistence, and endurance while helping protect wild populations of native plants that may be more vulnerable to harvest. Although red clover is relatively easy to find growing wild, it is also a nice herb to have in the garden, as it fixes nitrogen in the soil and adds lovely long-blooming color even after most flowers are gone in the fall. Adding horse manure while preparing new garden beds will most likely assure an adequate crop of an herb that is surprisingly expensive to purchase.

Old World tales of red clover abound. Legend has it that Saint Patrick, arriving in fifth-century Ireland, used three-lobed red clover leaves to explain the Holy Trinity concept to the king and people, successfully converting them to Christianity (Richardson 2017). This led to the clover's frequent use in church architecture, its representation of Saint Patrick's Day, and the trefoil as a form of the Celtic cross. Red clover has had a strong association with magic, protection, fertility, and well-being since Druid times. Stories tell how this plant opens one's eyes to the faerie world and grows wherever elves live, being potentiated by their presence (Richardson 2017). Starting in the 1600s, farmers planted it in their fields to increase soil fertility (by fixing nitrogen), grow more nutritious grasses, and fatten their cows. They also kept it in their stables to protect the animals from witchcraft. Clover leaves with more than three lobes have long been associated with luck and fortune: four lobes for good luck, five for fame, six for riches, and seven for prosperity. Four-leaf clovers were said to bring safe travels when worn in the shoes, bring dreams of your true love when kept under the pillow, and enable identification of anyone casting evil spells on you (Richardson 2017).

As an alterative medicinal herb, clover has far-reaching benefits and uses. Red clover flowers are harvested and can be prepared as a tea, tincture, vinegar, syrup, wine, poultice, or compress. These remedies are used in the treatment of chronic or acute respiratory weakness or illness, blood and skin purification, and the treatment of tumors. Clover syrup or tea strengthens the lungs and acts as an antispasmodic and expectorant in treatments for colds, bronchitis, or whooping cough. Red clover's ability to cleanse waste from the blood and to move the blood and lymph fluids, and its cooling and moistening effect on dry tissues, makes it a common ingredient in formulas, poultices, and compresses for all types of skin conditions, including sores, acne, eczema, psoriasis, swollen glands, mastitis, ulcers, and cold sores. It is also high in mineral content and is especially rich in calcium, nitrogen, and iron, making it a valuable nutritive tonic, especially when combined with herbs such as oats (*Avena sativa*) and nettles (*Urtica dioica*). These nutritive qualities, combined with its ability to inhibit abnormal cell growth and regulate hormones, have made red clover a commonly used herb for the treatment of tumors, cysts, fibroids, cancer, and menopausal imbalances.

The Old World tradition of medicinal uses largely carried over to Euro-American practitioners. But documented uses of red clover among indigenous American groups are limited, with Algonquin, Cherokee, Rappahannock, Shinnecock, and Thompson tribes reporting its use as a blood tonic (Herrick 1877; Speck et al. 1942) and a treatment for cough and fever (Black 1980; Hamel and Chiltoskey 1975), menopause symptoms (Herrick 1877), and cancer (Carr and Westey 1945; Turner et al. 1990). I use red clover similarly and also include the blossoms in smoke blends, especially combined with mullein (*Verbascum thapsus*) and sage (*Salvia officinalis*), for shortness of breath. Combined with other nervine or sedating herbs, such as passionflower (*Passiflora incarnata*), chamomile (*Matricaria chamomilla*), and oats (*Sativa avena*), it also makes a soothing and relaxing tea. Recent scientific research has illustrated new aspects of red clover, with a strong focus on its estrogenic effects (Burdette et al. 2002). Studies have shown its effectiveness for reducing hot flashes, with women in clinical trials averaging more than three and a half fewer per day than those taking a placebo (Myers and Vigar 2017). It has also assisted postmenopausal women with symptoms such as reduced libido, mood imbalances, impaired sleep, tiredness, and hair and skin conditions (Lipovac et al. 2011) while improving quality of life (Ehsanpour et al. 2012). It has been shown to counteract estrogen-deficiency-induced osteoporosis by increasing bone strength and mineral density (Cegiela et al. 2012) and has shown protective effects by preventing bone loss (Zhou et al. 2010). Studies have also revealed red clover's strong antioxidant effects (Esmaeili et al. 2015; Kaurinovic et al. 2012; Kolodziejczyk-Czepas et al. 2013) and documented its ability to significantly lower serum triglyceride, serum total cholesterol, liver triglyceride, and liver cholesterol levels for potential diabetes and cardiovascular disease treatments (Qiu et al. 2012). Red clover is not recommended for people taking methotrexate (Orr and Parker 2013) or hormonal drugs (Kargozar et al. 2017).

Usnea spp. (Parmeliaceae)

USNEA / OLD MAN'S BEARD

Usnea is a fruticose lichen that grows on trees throughout the Northern Hemisphere, mostly on conifers in the Southwest. *Usnea longissima, U. florida, U. diffracta*, and *U. barbata* are all commonly used in herbal commerce, but most practitioners simply gather locally available species. The estimated 360-plus usnea species (Prateeksha et al. 2016) can be identified by their characteristic internal central axis, which looks like a tiny elastic cord that is usually white; this distinguishes usnea from other lichens. Usnea and other lichens are part of the fungal kingdom but are formed through a symbiotic relationship between fungi, algae, and/or cyanobacteria, an ancient and mutually beneficial relationship that likely developed around 400 to 600 million years ago (Taylor et al. 1995; Yuan et al. 2005). Studies have shown that usnea also hosts an array of endolichenic fungi (He and Zhang 2012) that help it survive and add to its medicinal actions (Paranagama et al. 2007). Usnea species are highly sensitive to air pollution (McCune and Geiser 1997) and prefer the company of old growth trees (Cabrera 1996). They are therefore negatively impacted by industrial development and forestry practices.

FIGURE 141. Usnea growing on tree bark. Photo by author.

U. longissima, for example, was once widespread around the Northern Hemisphere and common throughout much of its large range (Keon 2002), but it has become extirpated or endangered globally due to impaired air quality and habitat loss (Derr et al. 2003).

Although left out of many modern herbals, usnea has a long history of therapeutic use around the world. Crawford (2014) documented the traditional uses of fifty-two lichen genera in geographically diverse regions, with usnea species being the most commonly used. Chinese medicinal references go back three thousand years (Cabrera 1996; Tilford 1997), with internal applications as an expectorant, and topical powders for the treatment of infections and wounds (Cabrera 1996; Hobbs 1986). Hobbs tells of the discovery of an Egyptian vase, more than three thousand years old, containing juniper and an imported lichen, and Hippocrates also described uses for lichen. In the American West, the Nitihaht and Makah used usnea for wound dressings (Gill 1983; Turner et al. 1983). These practices continue today, and it is additionally indicated for mucosal inflammation (Blumenthal et al. 1998) and infections of the urinary and respiratory systems (Hobbs 1986). I have found usnea to be an indispensable remedy for infections of various kinds but most especially those with fungal and bacterial organisms. It has the ability to keep infections from widening out to other areas of the body and is an appropriate addition to upper-respiratory formulas to prevent a cough or lung infections from developing. I include usnea in antimicrobial formulas for candida, athlete's foot, colds, and a multitude of external and internal infections. While walking through the forest, look for downed branches with usnea growing on them or collect pieces sparingly from live trees and prepare a tincture. There are a variety of methods for tincture preparation, including the application of heat and a double extraction process.

RESEARCH SUMMARY It is fitting that lichens, with a long history of use and wide distribution around the world, have been the subject of numerous studies validating traditional uses. Research on usnea has been fairly extensive and has focused largely on antimicrobial, antioxidant, anticancer, and anti-inflammatory activity. Although a variety of compounds have been identified from usnea species, including depsides, anthraquinones, dibenzofurans, steroids, terpenes, fatty acids, and polysaccharides (Laxinamujila et al. 2013), usnic acid and phenolic content are among the most important medicinally active components. A detailed review of usnea's ethnobotany, phytochemistry, and pharmacology was provided by Prateeksha et al. (2016).

Much of the research on usnea highlights its effectiveness against a number of infections as well as its antioxidant prowess. Antimicrobial research has shown a number of species, including *U. lapponica, U. longissima, U. ghattensis, U. intermedia, U. fillipendula, U. fulvoreagens, U. florida, U. barbata, U. rigida,* and *U. undulata,* to be potently active against a large number of bacteria, including both gram-positive and gram-negative organisms and the drug-resistant MRSA (Rauf et al. 2011; Ohran et al. 2016; Shrestha et al. 2014; Shrestha and St. Clair 2013; Srivastava et al. 2013; Sultana and Afolayan 2011). Other studies have demonstrated significant antifungal activity, sometimes exceeding the efficacy of standard antifungal medications (Sasidharan et al. 2014), for a number of species including *U. barbata, U. albopunctata, U. florida, U. hirta,* and *U. subflorida* (Cansaran et al. 2006; Hong et al. 2008; Madamombe and Afolaya 2003; Nishanth et al. 2015). Research has also shown strong antioxidant activity that is often accompanied by other medicinal actions. For example, *U. complanata* displays a high degree of antioxidant activity through nitric oxide reduction, free radical scavenging, and inhibition of lipid peroxidation, and is

top to bottom

FIGURE 142
Bird nest made
from usnea.
Photo by author.

FIGURE 143
Usnea close-up.
Photo by author.

also widely antibacterial, antifungal, and cardioprotective through enzyme inhibition (Mahadik et al. 2011). Other studies have shown *U. ghattensis*'s antioxidant activity to exceed levels known for synthetic antioxidants and the species also exhibits strong hepatoprotective activity (Behera et al. 2005; Verma et al. 2008). *U. longissima* has demonstrated significant antiulcerative effects (Halici et al. 2005) and antigenotoxicity (Agar et al. 2011; Odabasoglu et al. 2004) accompanied by antioxidant activity. Other species known to possess powerful antioxidant actions include *U. undulata* (Susithra et al. 2011) and *U. pictoides* (Pavithra et al. 2013; Sharma and Kalikotay 2012). Depsidones isolated from *U. articulata* surpassed quercitin in antioxidant scavenging activity (Lohezic-Le Devehat et al. 2007).

Further investigations illuminate usnea's potential role in the prevention and treatment of various cancers and also highlight its inflammation and pain-relieving capabilities. Research has shown a number of usnea species to have inhibitory or cytoxicity effects against a number of cancer cell lines. Compounds isolated from endolichenic fungal organisms on *U. cavernosa* were found to inhibit migrations of human breast and prostate cancer cells (Paranagama et al. 2007). Other isolated compounds from *U. longissima* inhibited the growth of human hepatoma cells (Yu et al. 2016). *U. fasciata* demonstrated antineoplastic action against sarcoma and Ehrlich tumor cells, with near 90 percent inhibition rates with fractions containing raffinose (Periera et al. 1994). Other investigations showed that *U. fillipendula* inhibited lung, liver, and brain cancer (Ari et al. 2014); *U. subcavata* was significantly cytotoxic against melanoma (Brandao et al. 2013). *U. barbata* displayed anticancer activity against human melanoma and colon carcinoma (Rankovic et al. 2012) and reduced leukemia and endometrial carcinoma cell counts (Cardarelli et al. 1997; Kristmundsdottir et al. 2002). *U. blepharea* was cytotoxic against leukemia cells (Maulidiyah et al. 2015). Additional research on usnea reveals its anti-inflammatory and pain-relieving actions, often linked to its usnic acid content (Jin et al. 2008). *U. barbata* and *U. hirta* have demonstrated anti-inflammatory, analgesic, and fever-reducing effects comparable to or surpassing those of inflammation-reducing and pain-reliving medications (Dobrescu et al. 1993). The phenolic compound longissimone isolated from *U. longissima* also exhibited potent anti-inflammatory activity comparable to aspirin (Choudhary et al. 2005). Another study showed that diffractaic acid and usnic acid are associated with analgesic and antipyretic activity in *U. diffracta* (Okuyama et al. 1995). Lastly, usnea shows potential cardioprotective actions by reducing the formation of blood clots through antiplatelet activity (Lee and Kim, 2005).

Verbena hastata, V. macdougalii, V. spp. (Verbenaceae)

VERVAIN / VERBENA

Vervain is one of many plants that link cultural and biological realms while also highlighting the commonality of herbal traditions across continents. *Verbena officinalis*, a central plant in Old World traditions, has migrated to North America, joining approximately sixteen species native to the American West. While many of these species have ranges limited to a small number of adjacent states or counties, some, such as *Verbena hastata*, *V. stricta*, and *V. bracteata*, are found across the United States. *V. macdougalli* is a local favorite in my area and the species I work with most. *V. macdougalii* is similar to *V. hastata* but is noticeably hairier, prefers habitats with drier soils, and is often found along roadsides or in open middle-elevation meadows. It is also important ecologically as it attracts a large variety of native bee species.

Embodying highly sacred and magical properties in Europe, vervain has long enjoyed an esteemed place in Old World botanical traditions. Spanning Mesopotamian, Greek, Roman, medieval, Druid, and modern cultures, this herb was placed on altars; woven into crowns; and used to evoke enchantments, protect against evil, and heal a variety of ailments (Richardson 2017). The ancient Greeks believed that vervain purified Zeus's table before celebrations and that it was woven into Aphrodite's crown. Vervain's use in love charms persisted well into medieval times; its aphrodisiac effects were said to be powerful enough to reconjure lost love and convert enemies. The Romans considered it a sacred, purifying plant, which was used in ceremonies and celebrations, including the altar-decorating festival of Verbenalia. Messengers, heralds, and ambassadors all wore vervain as a badge of office, and military leaders wore it for protection in battle. During the Middle Ages, witches used it for dark magic while others strung it along doorways with St. John's wort (*Hypericum perforatum*) and yarrow (*Achillea millefolium*) for protection against witchcraft. The Welsh called it devil's bane, dipped it in holy water and sprinkled it around church buildings for protection, and also prepared it as incense for exorcisms. Vervain was also held in high regard by the Druids, who engaged in ceremonies and left offerings before its harvesting. Christian stories tell us that vervain was present at Christ's crucifixion and was used to heal his

FIGURE 144
Vervain flowers
(*Verbena macdougalii*). Photo by author.

wounds (Grieve 1971 [1931]). Few other plants share such a revered and enduring place in herbal lore.

In the Old World, vervain was used medicinally in a wide variety of ways, including to treat urinary, digestive, respiratory, and nervous system issues. Nicolas Culpeper (2018 [1653]) identified vervain as a top remedy for ailments arising from cold conditions in the body. In the urinary system, it treats edema and clears urinary stones though diuresis. This legendary (and oft forgotten) use may be the origin of the word *vervain*, from the Celtic *ferfain*, meaning "to drive away" (*fer*) "a stone" (*faen*) (Grieve 1971 [1931]). In the digestive system, vervain provides the stimulation characteristic of all bitter herbs and also astringes diarrhea, calms gall bladder inflammation, clears worms, and generally purges the digestive tract. Vervain also has beneficial effects on the respiratory system: its heating and relaxing nature helps clear colds, ease sore throats and coughing, ease chills associated with fevers through diaphoresis, boost the lungs, and counteract shortness of breath by reducing inflammation. Tonifying to the nervous system, vervain has a history of use in the treatment of headaches and depression.

FIGURE 145. Vervain (*Verbena macdougalii*). Photo by author.

It is very effective for relaxing tension through antispasmodic action, which can augment the healthy flow of fluids and energy in the body, creating a beneficial health cascade. It follows the pattern of other magical herbs that were once famed for protecting against evil influences that are now recognized as biological or medical conditions of the nervous system in modern paradigms. Vervain has also been used in to treat chronic skin inflammations, venomous bites, hemorrhoids, and bleeding wounds. It has been included in mouthwashes and vinegar-based skin cleansers. Vervain can be prepared as distilled-water eyedrops for strengthening the optic nerve and clarifying vision. Furthermore, it has been used as a galactagogue and a remedy for malaria, plague, jaundice, and gout. It was one of Bach's original flower essences. From the time of Dioscorides to Culpeper, vervain was bruised and worn around the neck to ease headaches, conjure protection, and bring good luck (Richardson 2017). Vervain is at the center of Old World botanical culture; its protective symbolism and healthful power have manifested in long-standing and widely practiced traditions such as the sprinkling of vervain-infused water at a gathering to enliven the guests and make them happy.

New World uses of vervain tend to be more limited among modern herbalists, with a stronger focus on nervous system applications, but ethnobotanical studies show a history of much broader use. Its leaves and flowering stalks have been gathered for teas, tinctures, and elixirs. The Navajo, Cherokee, Chippewa, Dakota, Delaware, Oklahoma, Iroquois, Mahuna, Menominee, Concow, Costanoan, Houma, Meskwaki, and Omaha tribes all described uses for local species, including as an emetic (Hamel and Chiltoskey 1975), an anthelmintic (Herrick 1977), a snuff for nosebleeds (Densmore 1928), drops for earaches (Herrick 1977), and treatments for breast complaints (Hamel and Chiltoskey 1975). Vervain has also been used to treat difficulties of menses and childbirth (Hamel and Chiltoskey 1975; Smith 1928), wounds (Vestal 1952), digestive problems (Gilmore 1991 [1919]; Hamel and Chiltoskey 1975; Romero 1954), coughs and colds (Hamel and Chiltoskey 1975; Herrick 1977), fever (Bocek 1984; Hamel and Chiltoskey 1975; Romero 1954; Tantaquidgeon 1942; Vestal 1952), and urinary disorders (Smith 1923; Speck 1941). It has edible seeds (Rousseau 1945a) and properties that supposedly encourage obnoxious people to leave (Herrick 1977). Moore (2003) uses vervain as a palliative for the onset of colds and as a remedy for insomnia rooted in a nervous stomach or swirling thoughts. He also indicates it for sprains and deep bruising due to its positive effects on blood flow. Additionally, he describes its usefulness for recovering alcoholics with blood sugar, emotional, and circulatory imbalances.

Recent scientific research confirms some of vervain's medicinal uses and adds new potential applications to the already lengthy list. Phytochemical analysis from *V. littoralis* has isolated a number of compounds, including an array of iridoids that have shown antibacterial, increased peristaltic, and antioxidant activity (Castro-Gamboa and Castro 2004). Studies on *Verbena officinalis* suggest antitumor activity (Kou et al. 2013); the constituent citral, in particular, has demonstrated cytotoxicity in leukemia (De Martino et al. 2009). Furthermore, *V. officinalis* leaves, roots, and especially stems show strong activity against a wide variety of gram-positive and gram-negative bacteria, with greater efficacy than amoxicillin against some bacterial strains (Ahmed et al. 2017). *V. officinalis* has also demonstrated the ability to decrease the duration and severity of seizures (Rashidian et al. 2017), reduce symptoms of anxiety, and encourage onset of sleep while increasing sleep duration (Khan et al. 2016). Additionally, its phytochemicals hastatoside and verbenalin have been shown to increase REM sleep as well as delta wave activity during non-REM sleep phases (Makino et al. 2009). These collective studies support many of the historical applications of vervain for nervous system, digestive system, and acute illness and also highlight its potential usefulness in cancer treatments.

I have cultivated and wildcrafted *V. macdougalli*, using leaves and flowers prepared primarily as tincture. As others have noted, the roots are more likely to produce emetic results, and I find the tea too bitter for most American palates, especially children. Having repeatedly tested Moore's suggestion to use vervain at the onset of colds, I can verify that as one of this plant's greatest and most reliable applications. In this case, I combine vervain with echinacea and use them in small but frequent doses at the earliest sign of malaise. I have also found vervain to be particularly useful for imbalances (whether caused by stress, hormone fluctuations, or other points of origin) that result in bossy, overcontrolling, or nit-picky behavior. An ambassador from the historical herbal world, vervain is without a doubt a widely useful plant in the apothecary as well as an easy-to-cultivate and beautiful garden herb for western herbalists.

Viola canadensis, V. odorata, V. spp. (Violaceae)

VIOLET

Numerous *Viola* species range across the Old World and the New, with many associated botanical traditions rooting across continents. The nonnative species *V. odorata, V. arvensis,* and *V. tricolor* can be found in many us states, and the American West is home to more than thirty native species, with some having limited ranges and others being widespread. Interestingly, most of our native violets lack the sweet aroma that endeared *Viola* species to people in the Old World. Violets are commonly pollinated by insects, especially bees, that land on lower spurred petals; some species form underground cleistogamous flowers that never open and are self-fertilizing. *Viola canadensis* is the most common wild species in my area, and *V. odorata* is easily cultivatable in moist shady areas of the western garden. Working with these two species, I primarily use violet as a demulcent for dry respiratory conditions common in the high desert, but I often substitute mallow species that are more abundant where I live. Violets are edible, but taste them first to assess the level of saponins, which can give them a soapy flavor. To encounter the gentle spirit-lifting song of violets in the Southwest, take to the mountains. There you will find

violets humming in the moist shady understory of the forests and among the miniature flower gardens of the open higher-elevation meadows.

The legacy of violet resides as strongly in mythology and historic symbolism as it does in medicinal lore. It features prominently in ancient Greek myth, which holds that the goddess Artemis once transformed a nymph into a violet to hide her from Apollo and that Zeus changed his lover Io into a cow grazing in a violet-filled meadow to protect her from Juno. Greek myth also tells us that Persephone was gathering violets when Hades captured her and returned her to the underworld. The ancient Greeks dedicated violets to Aphrodite and hung them with roses over their doorways to announce the arrival of a newborn son. Violets appeared frequently in the writing of Homer and Virgil, and the flowers were thought to calm anger, bring sleep, and fortify the heart. The Celts prized violets for cosmetic use, and Pliny recommended wearing a garland of violets to ease a headache. Christian stories tell us that violets popped up in the Garden of Eden wherever Adam's tears of repentance hit the soil (Richardson 2017). The medieval French herbalist Macer described violets as a defense against evil spirits (Grieve 1971 [1931]), and Shakespeare associated violets with death. During the early nineteenth century, Napoleon vowed to return to France with violets in the spring and supporters called him Caporal Violette (Grieve 1971 [1931]). Violets became the Napoleonic emblem, and it is said that Napoleon wore a violet in a locket on his deathbed (Richardson 2017). Highly prized for garlands, syrups, wine, conserves, confections, cordials, infused vinegars, and perfume, and as a coloring agent, violets have been cultivated and sold in Old World markets for centuries.

The medicinal use of violet in Old World herbal traditions has an ancient history associated with its cooling and moistening character and features artful remedies such as crystallized flowers. Its leaves and flowers are used to make an array of preparations, including teas, tinctures, poultices, oils, and plasters. Its roots are expectorating but also strongly emetic and purgative, while aerial parts are associated with the plant's multitude of other herbal actions. Pliny recommended a root liniment in vinegar for gout and spleen ailments, and a flower garland worn for headaches and dizziness. Culpeper (2018 [1653]) prescribed violet for purging choler (a hot dry temperament) in the seventeenth century, and the English botanist John Gerard indicated it for sore throat, headache, insomnia, reducing inflammation, and bringing comfort to the heart in his 1597 publication *Herball*, which was largely comprised of earlier writings by the Dutch scholar Rembert Dodoens. Culpeper's and Gerard's prescriptions were on target, since violet is an alterative herb with notable demulcent, anti-inflammatory, and sedating properties. Perhaps most commonly, violets have been a remedy for the respiratory system, soothing dry mucosa, calming spasmodic coughs, clearing mucus, easing sore throats, and treating serious lung ailments including pleurisy. Violets have also long been used to cool and moisten eczema and other hot, dry skin inflammations and been prepared as poultices for bruises and wounds. Additionally, violet moves lymphatic fluids to relieve swollen glands or congested breast tissue and has been used in a great many other treatments, including for constipation, epilepsy, jaundice, rheumatism, tumors, and sore eyes.

In North America, the Iroquois, Omaha, Cherokee, Thompson, Costanoan, Karok, Ojibwa, Potawatomi, Diegueño, Luiseño, Navajo, Eskimo, Blackfoot, Makah, Tolowa, Klallam, and Carrier tribes used violet in ways similar to those described above. It had an association with heart strengthening (Smith 1932, 1933), soft-tissue healing (Bocek 1984; Hamel and Chiltoskey 1975; Herrick 1977), and respiratory support (Hamel and Chiltoskey 1975; Hellson 1974; Hoffman 1891). Additional uses include the treatment of arthritis pain (Hellson 1974), stomach pain, and diarrhea (Herrick 1977; Smith 1929). It was used in a poultice for headache or sore eyes (Baker 1981; Hamel and Chiltoskey 1975; Herrick 1977), in labor facilitation (Gunther 1973), in blood building (Hamel and Chiltoskey 1975), for urinary discomfort (Hoffman 1891), for magical purposes and detecting bewitchment (Herrick 1977), as a wild food (Hedges 1986; Perry 1975; Sparkman 1908; Witthoft 1977), and as a spring tonic (Hamel and Chiltoskey 1975). American herbalists have used violet in primarily the same ways as Old World healers but with the added focus on its nutritive properties and its use in treating tumors and cancer. Herbalist Jim McDonald wrote online that violets are deeply nourishing, strengthening, and soothing; rich in minerals; and high in vitamins A, C, and E. The leaves and flowers make a delicious edible herb or nutritive tea. He also recommended violets as a replacement for those who find nettles' diuretic action too drying. Recent scientific research on *V. odorata* and *V. tricolor* suggests that proteins called cyclotides have cytotoxic or antitumor activity in

FIGURE 148
Violet (*Viola odorata*). Photo by author.

breast cancer, lymphoma, and myeloma (Gerlach et al. 2010; Svangard et al. 2004; Svangard et al. 2007). Another study demonstrated violet's antitumor activity on human glioblastoma multiforme, an aggressive form of brain cancer (Hashemi et al. 2019).

Additional research, mainly on *V. tricolor* and *V. odorata*, confirms many of violet's traditional uses and herbal actions. These plants have been found to contain numerous chemicals, including violin (an alkaloid), quercitin, methyl salicylate, saponins, mucilage, and vitamin C (Mittal et al. 2015). Violet is high in antioxidants with free radical–scavenging capabilities (Ebrahimzadeh et al. 2010) and has a relaxant effect on contractions associated with gastrointestinal, respiratory, and vascular conditions, including diarrhea, asthma, and hypertension (Janbaz et al. 2015). Studies also that show violet's anti-inflammatory actions are comparable to those of hydrocortisone in the lungs (Koocheck et al. 2003) and that violet flower syrup provides significant relief from coughing in childhood asthma (Qasemzadeh et al. 2015). Violet's vasodilating, lipid-lowering, and antioxidant actions help lower blood pressure (Siddiqi et al. 2012). In the nervous system, violet has been shown to provide significant improvements for patients with insomnia (Feyzabadi et al. 2014). Rich in antioxidants that protect neuronal cells, violet may have benefits for those suffering from neurodegenerative diseases (Mousavi et al. 2016). Studies also show that violet's antibacterial cycoltides are active against *E. coli*, staph, and other bacterial strains (Pranting et al. 2010; Zarrabi et al. 2013). Benign prostate hyperplasia symptoms, including incomplete and intermittent urination, urgency and frequency, weak stream and straining, and nocturia, were all significantly improved with a formula including *V. odorata*, *Echium amoenum* (red feathers), and *Physalis alkekengi* (strawberry groundcherry or Chinese lantern) (Beiraghdar et al. 2017). Violet's antipyretic, analgesic, and anti-inflammatory actions are supported by research on *V. betonicifolia* (Muhammad et al. 2012), and violet has been shown to be effective against acne due to its antimicrobial, anti-inflammatory, and antioxidant activity (Shirbeigi et al. 2016). Furthermore, violet is diuretic and laxative (Vishal et al. 2009), hepatoprotective, and capable of improving liver pathology (Habibi et al. 2019). It is also a mosquito repellant (Amer and Mehlhorn 2006).

Yucca spp. (Agavaceae)

YUCCA / AMOLE

Although distributed across much of the United States, yucca is one of the most iconic plants of the Southwest and features prominently in the land and

culture of the region. About a dozen species are native to the western states, with *Yucca baccata* and *Y. glauca* having the largest ranges. Some yuccas cross-hybridize and make species-specific identification difficult. Yucca species are found in dry grasslands, prairies, shrublands, woodlands, and forest habitats at lower to middle elevations. They may be browsed by deer, elks, pronghorn, and bighorn sheep, and they serve as important forage or cover for a variety of other animals, including birds, small mammals, and insects. Each yucca species is pollinated by a corresponding specialized species of *Tegeticula* or *Parategeticula* moth, a relationship that is interdependent and mutually beneficial. Yucca was of great importance to Native people and is one of few wild plants depicted in southwestern petroglyphs.

Yucca has been valued since early prehistoric times for its multitude of uses as an important fiber plant, wild food source, and medicine. Its fibers were widely used for making cordage, sandals, ropes, mats, baskets, brushes, and many other essential items (Curtin 1965; Dunmire and Tierney 1995; Moerman 1998), with such objects commonly found in archaeological sites dating back to the Archaic period and subsequent cultural phases (Dunmire and Tierney 1995). Its flowers, fruits, and stalks are edible and were important wild foods. The fruits were a dietary staple and prepared in a number of ways:

eaten fresh or dried, cooked into a paste and dried, or as a pulp mixed with other foods and made into cakes (Dunmire and Tierney 1995). Moerman (1998) summarized a long list of foods, beverages, and condiments made from yucca, and many southwestern and plains tribes reported its medicinal uses, including treatments for sprains and broken bones (Hellson 1974; McClintock 1909; Tantaquidgeon 1942), bleeding wounds and skin diseases (Hart 1981; Johnston 1987; McClintock 1909; Speck 1937; Taylor 1940; Vestal and Schultes 1939; Witthoft 1947), snakebites (Bell and Castetter, 1941), constipation (Colton 1974; Hocking 1956; Russell 1908; Whiting 1939), upset stomach and vomiting (Elmore 1944; Rogers 1980), and heartburn (Elmore 1944). It was used in purification (Whiting 1939), as a hair wash for dandruff and baldness (Gilmore 1913a; Hart 1981; Jones 1931; McClintock 1909; Rogers 1980; White 1945), for the facilitation of childbirth, and as a midwife's lubricant for removing a retained placenta (Robbins et al. 1916; Rogers 1980; Vestal 1952). Its pounded roots were once widely used as soap or shampoo. Curtin (1965) says that juice obtained from boiled and mashed young yucca shoots was used to make a wine-like beverage consumed by the northern New Mexico Penitentes. They further processed this liquid into a syrup for topical applications to relieve arthritic joints.

FIGURE 151
Yucca elata.
Photo by author.

Modern herbal practice with yucca has centered on anti-inflammatory applications. Commonly used for both acute and chronic inflammation, yucca roots may be prepared as capsules, decoction, or tincture. Herbalist Charles Kane (2011) described yucca's anti-inflammatory action in terms of the plant's saponins binding inflammatory compounds and preventing them from entering the bloodstream. He used the same saponin-binding logic to explain yucca's effect on lowering cholesterol and triglycerides. Moore (2003) indicates yucca for urethra or prostate inflammation and cautions that overdose or long-term

FIGURE 152
Yucca baccata.
Photo by author.

use may result in a laxative effect, possible intestinal cramping, or impairing the absorption of fat-soluble vitamins.

Research on yucca has focused primarily on its potential anti-inflammatory mechanisms. Phytochemical analysis has identified sesquiterpine glycosides (Benidze et al. 2018), saponins (Eskander et al. 2013), and polyphenolics (Oleszek et al. 2001; Picacente et al. 2004) present in yucca extracts. A review and discussion of yucca's possible anti-inflammatory mechanisms was provided by Cheeke et al. (2006) and outlines several possible pathways. The Cheeke et al. review noted that yucca is rich in steroidal saponins known to have antiprotozal action (Quihui-Cota et al. 2014) and polyphenolics known to be strong antioxidants and free radical scavengers. Yucca also produces anti-inflammatory activity through the reduction of nitric oxide (Cigerci et al. 2009; Oleszek et al. 2001; Picacente et al. 2004). Studies by Bingham (1975, 1976, 1978) reported a reduction of pain and swelling with the use of yucca tablets and proposed that the antiprotozoal action of yucca is the anti-inflammatory mechanism. He based this theory in part on a report by R. Wyburn-Mason (1983) that the protozoa *Naegleria* is ubiquitously present in the joints and intestines of people with arthritis. This theory is further supported by the fact that metronidazole, an antiprotozoal drug, is commonly used in arthritis treatment and the observation that inflammation in the gut and in the joints is almost always paired. Bacteria such as *E. coli* may also cause gut inflammation, and yucca's known antibacterial activity (Katsunuma et al. 2000; Wang

Materia
Medica

FIGURE 153
Yucca flower.
Photo by author.

et al. 2000) may be an additional mechanism for reducing inflammation. Furthermore, polyphenolics found in yucca, such as resveratrol (Bertelli et al. 2002; Bingham et al. 1975) and yuccaols (Marzocco et al. 2004), have known antioxidant (Oleszek et al. 2001; Piacente et al. 2004) and anti-inflammatory activity, as well as the ability to inhibit platelet aggregation (Olas et al. 2002, 2005; Southon et al. 1988), which is another known factor in inflammation. Therefore yucca's inflammation-reducing activity may be the result of combined antioxidant, antiprotozoal, and anti-bacterial activities. Other studies on yucca have highlighted additional treatment potential. For instance, yucca seed oil is high in tocotrienols, which are known to have powerful antioxidant, anticancer, cholesterol-lowering, and neuro- and cardioprotective activity (Mokbli et al. 2017). Steroidal saponins extracted from yucca have shown potent antitumor activity against human colorectal carcinoma, breast cancer, and liver carcinoma cell lines (Eskander et al. 2013). Additionally, yucca extract has been shown to be as effective as pharmaceutical drugs against giardia (Quihui-Cota et al. 2014), and compounds extracted from yucca have been recommended for the development of steroidal hormonal drugs (Kemertelidze et al. 1972) and fungicides (Kemertelidze et al. 2009).

Invasive Trees

The plants we see—whether we're walking down a sidewalk to the local store or hiking along a favorite wild trail—undoubtedly tell stories of the relationship between people and place. The balance between native and nonnative plants, in particular, tells a lot about how people have used the land and gives a glimpse into the future of place. Most anywhere we go these days, we see the effects of globalization expanding throughout human culture. And plant communities are becoming more globalized too. Many ecosystems are now a mixture of long-standing native plants with ancient connections to the land growing together with relatively new, nonnative arrivals that collectively form our ideas of what wild places are today. As discussed in chapter 1, this emerging new feature of landscapes is a defining characteristic of plant communities in the modern era. The movement of nonnative plants into new territories may manifest in a variety of ways, ranging from a species becoming highly invasive and forming expansive monoscapes to minor noninvasive plants finding occasional places among healthy native plant populations. While we can agree that these changes are undoubtedly taking place, what precisely is happening within these plant communities is not always clear. Debates about the role of nonnative plants in native plant communities continue, with enough questions remaining to make any definitive conclusions elusive. Regardless of how we feel about nonnatives in the wild, invasive plants can bring something valuable to the medicine cabinet. To better understand how they might work as herbal remedies, we must first try to understand them as plants.

In my attempt to make sense of nonnative invasive plants where I live, several questions come to mind. First, what makes a plant native? Second, what role do nonnative plants play across ecosystems in my area and in the world? Specifically, do these plants threaten native plant populations and do they harm biodiversity and ecological functioning? Third, how can I work with these increasingly available nonnative invasive plants as an herbalist? Exploring these questions will lead us into a deeper understanding of invasive nonnative plant medicine and ecology and help us develop a more constructive relationship with them as herbalists.

The question of what makes a plant native is one that may elicit some debate. I first came to ponder this question walking through expanses of creosote (*Larrea tridentata*) in the Chihuahuan Desert, where it is a widespread indicator plant. Arriving in the Southwest from ancestral populations in South America between the mid-Pleistocene and late Pliocene, creosote has been steadily advancing its range for thousands of years (Laport et al. 2012). Aided during the last 150 years by cattle grazing, creosote is now considered invasive across the grasslands of New Mexico and northern Mexico. (See chapter 2.) What makes this plant native, in my mind, is the balance it held for thousands of years with the rest of the desert plant community, the dynamic relationship it developed with humans (indigenous people, cattlemen, and herbalists), and its invasive character developing largely as a result of poorly balanced uses of the land. Author and wilderness restorer Jesse Wolf Hardin describes native plants as those that "have inhabited an area long enough to have been affected and formed by it, and have had their own effects measured ... demonstrating they take into account and accommodate the rest of the biotic community, and reflect and express the distinguishing character of place" (personal communication 2017). Despite creosote's potentially invasive nature, this definition applies. The plant was shaped by changes in the land (both climatic and human-induced), its evolving distribution was in harmony with other slowly unfolding ecological changes for most of its existence, and it has become a defining plant of its region.

Our understanding of the role that nonnative plants play across local, regional, and global ecosystems is constantly evolving as modern plant communities continue to change. For decades, invasive nonnative plants such as the infamous salt cedar (*Tamarix* spp.) have been vilified, poisoned, and scapegoated as the destroyers of ecosystems and the annihilators of biodiversity. In recent years a new perspective has emerged—that these plants are, in fact, the saviors of ecosystems that have been severely altered by humans, reinvigorating the health of these systems and increasing biodiversity. How could we change our minds so dramatically and which viewpoint more accurately represents the role of nonnative plants? It would be nice if there were a simple answer, but there is not. Every ecosystem and each plant is unique. Furthermore, one species can play different roles in different situations, as invasive plants tend to proliferate in accordance with the degree of ecosystem alteration. Therefore highly manipulated environments are more likely to see invasive species become dominant while less disturbed areas will have more intact and robust native plant populations, which may coexist with nonnative, even potentially invasive plants. We must also consider that ecosystems are continually dynamic and that the changes taking place today are still unfolding and without historical precedent. Consequently we can't accurately predict where these changes are taking any given plant community in the long term. Many plant communities are expected to experience dramatic changes as new climate conditions accelerate (higher temperatures, increased CO_2, drought, and so on) and as native and nonnative plants comingle. Some experts see evidence for increased regional-scale biodiversity in some areas (while overall global diversity declines) as floral newcomers outnumber extinctions and as ecosystem fragmentation creates opportunities for new plant taxa to evolve (Ellis et al. 2012; Suggitt et al. 2019; Thomas 2013; Velland et al. 2017; Venevskaia et al. 2013), although these gains may be temporary. Meanwhile, others have warned that invasive plants will continue to expand their ranges at the expense of natives in the coming decades and centuries (e.g., DiTomaso 2017; Elton 1958; Evans 2014; Kerns and Guo 2012; Pimm and Gilpin 1989; Westbrooks 1998). Recent research even suggests that once an invasive organism becomes established in an ecosystem, it may accelerate the decline of native species by inhibiting native mycorrhiza, making native plants more susceptible to pollution, changing soil chemistry through allelopathy and nutrient cycling, altering fire regimes, and aiding the spread of other invasive species (Binghamton University 2018; Sher and Quigley 2013; Sladonja et al. 2015; Xiao et al. 2019).

Now that nonnative, invasive plants are here to stay, what can we do as herbalists to bring them into our practice? Many of us may face a barrier. We may first have to come to a place of accepting a plant in the local environment, allowing judgments to fall away, and seeing the plant for what it is. This can be difficult when we are struggling to accept ecological change in our world, but it will open the door to knowing invasive plants as only herbalists can. This brings up another interesting question: Does the different ecological role of a nonnative plant in a new ecosystem, and our attitude toward that plant, change its functioning as medicine? All plants are native somewhere in the world and might be employed in herbal medicine traditions in their homelands. Certainly, herbalists in their native territories evolved alongside these plants and have more intimate and accepting relationships with them, based on deeper levels of knowledge, without questioning the legitimacy of their existence in the surrounding countryside. But the way these plants interact with other species and the landscape is different in their new ecosystems. I believe that how a plant functions ecologically in its daily life, how we approach plants, and our feelings about them do influence their workings as medicine. If this is true, we must learn more about nonnative invasive plants and reconsider our attitudes about and relationships with them.

Ailanthus altissima (Simaroubaceae)

TREE OF HEAVEN

Originally from Southeast Asia, this tree was introduced into North America in the 1780s as an ornamental plant (Hu 1979) and is now present on all continents except Antarctica. Tree of heaven is one of the most problematic invasive species in Europe and is also invasive in the American West, especially in urban and riparian areas, where it is often considered an unstoppable menace, sending new shoots up wherever possible. It is a prolific reproducer, capable of rapid growth, and highly tolerant of a wide variety of environmental conditions. It is also a top competitor, producing an allelopathic compound called ailanthone that is toxic to many other plant species and is also associated with anticancer activity (Heisey 1996; Lawrence et al. 1991; Mergen 1959; Sladonja et al. 2015; Wang et al. 2018). Growing in contaminated urban areas and disconnected floodplains, it can act as a remediator of damaged land and polluted air, but its propensity for sending up new shoots could prove to be a problem in ecosystems where there are not sufficient factors to limit its growth.

Similarly, tree of heaven can play a remediating role in the digestive and respiratory systems and has other potential medicinal applications. Its bark,

leaves, and root bark can be prepared as a tea or a 50 percent tincture to clear heat and dampness from the body and are useful in treatments for diarrhea and digestive upsets caused by microbes and parasites, including giardia. For the latter, it combines well with Oregon grape (*Mahonia* spp.). In the respiratory system it reduces inflammation and cleans the airways of mucus and other irritants, facilitating recovery from a variety of ailments. Recent research has illuminated a potential role for tree of heaven in the treatment of serious diseases, as an antibacterial (Zhao et al. 2005), an antimalarial (Okunde et al. 2003), and an HIV inhibitor (Chang and Woo 2003). Additionally, tree of heaven may be a useful cytotoxic and antiproliferative treatment for a variety of cancers, including breast (Wang et al. 2018), gastric (Chen et al. 2017), brain (Wang et al. 2016), ovarian (Jeong et al. 2018), liver (Wang et al. 2013; Yan et al. 2018), and cervical (De Feo et al. 2005). It also acts as a smooth muscle relaxant, lowers blood pressure, and inhibits platelet aggregation (blood clotting) (Rhaman et al. 2019). Tree of heaven has been known to cause dermatitis in some people (Kowarik and Saumel 2007) and is typically recommended in small doses or combined with other herbs to reduce any nauseating side effects. Given how terrible the plant smells, some may have trouble harvesting it without becoming nauseated.

Elaeagnus angustifolia (Elaeagnaceae)

RUSSIAN OLIVE

This tree came to the western United States from southern Europe and Asia in the 1800s. Finding a niche in the increasingly altered riparian habitats along western rivers, Russian olive has proliferated along waterways downstream from dams. Taking advantage of the new conditions, including altered water flows and lack of flood disturbances, Russian olive has become the fourth most common woody plant species in western riparian plant communities (Friedman et al. 2005; Katz and Shafroth 2003). Although it does provide forage for wildlife, nectar for pollinators, and increased levels of nitrogen in the soil, it has a tendency to become dominant or co-dominant in the landscape and is associated with reduced species richness compared to native plant communities (Evans 2014). While changes in water flow caused by dams are a primary driver in changing plant communities and the successful establishment of Russian olive, it further advances those changes by stabilizing soil surfaces and shading out seedlings of native pioneer species, such as cottonwoods (*Populus* spp.), that rely on sunny conditions and flood disturbance areas for germination.

Russian olive's role in riparian ecosystems is still poorly understood, but its range and numbers are expanding and it is available to be a part of our herbal practices. Its leaves, bark, thorns, and fruit can be harvested and prepared as a tea, tincture, or liniment. With wide-ranging traditional uses, Russian olive is an important medicinal plant in the Old World and has thus accumulated a large body of scientific research. Farzaei et al. (2015), Hamidpour et al. (2017), and Tehranizadeh et al. (2016) have summarized existing research on Russian olive's phytochemical and pharmacological aspects as well as its traditional uses. Across the Middle East and China, it has been used in remedies for upset stomachs and diarrhea, arthritis and gout, coughs and colds with fevers, asthma and respiratory infections, kidney stones, and liver disease, with no known side effects. Recent research has also shown Russian olive to be antimicrobial against a variety of pathogens, including gram-positive and gram-negative bacteria and fungal organisms; antioxidant, protecting cells from oxidative damage and delaying or reducing the risk of many degenerative diseases; effective for wound treatments, expediting healing times and reducing pain; beneficial for the cardiovascular system by optimizing blood flow and blood pressure and reducing triglycerides and cholesterol; and useful for digestive issues through its relaxant effect on the smooth muscles, protective activity against ulcers, and the reduction of gastric acid secretion. Russian olive may also be effective in treatments for oral cancer and other carcinomas by inhibiting cell proliferation, colony formation, and the spread to other areas of the body (Saleh at al. 2018). One of the most promising areas of application for Russian olive is pain relief; research has shown it to have strong analgesic action (Ahmadiani et al. 2000; Ramezani et al. 2000), reducing both acute and chronic pain with muscle relaxant and anti-inflammatory activity. Studies have shown it to be as effective as NSAIDS and steroid medications (Farahbakhsh et al. 2011) but with added gastro- and-cardioprotective properties. In high doses it produced muscle relaxant effects comparable to diazepam (Hosseinzadeh et al. 2003). Several clinical trials have shown Russian olive to be as effective as ibuprofen

in alleviating symptoms associated with osteoarthritis in the knees (Alishiri et al. 2007; Nikniaz et al. 2014; Panahi et al. 2016; Rabiei et al. 2015). The fruits are also edible, with vitamin and antioxidant content, and are a traditional appetizer in Turkey.

FIGURE 158
Salt cedar
(*Tamarix* sp.).
Photo by author.

Tamarix spp. (Tamaricaceae)

SALT CEDAR, TAMARISK

The poster child for vilified nonnative invasive plants since the early 1900s, salt cedar is the most successful nonnative tree in the western United States and has become the third most common woody plant in the region's riparian corridors (Sher and Quigley 2003). Originating in the Mediterranean and Asia, it has come to symbolize the water struggles of the Southwest by covering large areas of severely degraded riparian habitat and becoming dominant along many waterways (DiTomaso 1998; Glenn and Nagler 2005). Numerous bird species, including the endangered western willow flycatcher, use it for shelter, but overall, tamarisk forests support fewer species and fewer individuals than native forests (Sogge et al. 2008). It is an opportunistic reproducer that is tolerant of drought, heat, fires, and saline soils. Similarly to Russian olive, it stabilizes surface soils, inhibiting the germination of native riparian

trees, and it shades out native tree seedlings. It can grow in vast monotypic stands, forming dense thickets, changing soil composition, and greatly reducing the beneficial mycorrhizal community that facilitates native plant growth (Sher and Quigley 2013). Like Russian olive, tamarisk finds a habitat niche in degraded riparian ecosystems with altered flow regimes and contributes to the process of change initiated by human water use. This tree may be considered a willing colonizer of damaged ecosystems where natives are in decline, but it can also play a role in inhibiting the growth of native plants and further reducing biodiversity.

With such widespread abundance, salt cedar is worth exploring medicinally. Its bark, leaves, and galls can be harvested and used for topical applications such as wound dressings and mouthwashes, or as a tincture for small internal doses. Ethnobotanical studies in Pakistan (Marwat et al. 2009) and Saudi Arabia (Suleiman 2019) reveal traditional uses including stimulating and tonifying liver treatments for jaundice, hepatitis, and other liver disorders; astringent and antimicrobial dressings for wounds, abscesses, eczema, and skin diseases; preparations for infectious diseases, including smallpox, tuberculosis, and measles; and astringing and inflammation-reducing remedies for upset stomachs, fever, rheumatic complaints, and headaches. Recent research has shown *Tamarix* species to be effective against an array of oral bacterial organisms (Khalid et al. 2017) and other infectious pathogens, including *M. luteus* and *E. coli* (Ksouri et al. 2009). Studies also suggest that the tree's essential oil has cytotoxic activity against human breast cancer, colorectal cancer, and pancreatic carcinoma (Alhourani et al. 2018) and that the bark, leaves, and flowers all possess strong antioxidant activity (Ksouri et al. 2009; Suleiman 2019). Despite its strong medicinal attributes, most of us remain reluctant to incorporate it into our apothecaries. In many ways, salt cedar typifies the difficulty of making new relationships with invasive plants that we see replacing beloved native plants that have defined our lands and shaped our cultures for as long as we have coexisted. Salt cedar is a symbol of the process of accepting change while still fighting for what matters. Although I appreciate that awareness, its abundance in our riverside forests often makes me feel like the big-box store has moved to town and pushed the locals out of business, leaving us with a standardized nature experience.

FIGURE 160.
Siberian elm
(*Ulmus pumila*).
Photo by author.

Ulmus pumila (Ulmaceae)

SIBERIAN ELM

Another Asian tree, Siberian elm is the first tree to leaf out all over my fair city each spring. The burst of green is followed by the raining down of confetti as its seeds fill the air and germinate wherever they land, in cracks in concrete and the earthly surfaces of the surrounding natural areas. This tree is known to spread quickly in disturbed areas and will tolerate difficult growing conditions where few others can succeed. Siberian elm binds heavy metals in soil, providing remediation in polluted urbanized areas, and provides early spring nectar for pollinators. Along with Russian olive and salt cedar, Siberian elm is expected to redefine many southwestern riparian areas in the coming decades if water management practices remain unaltered (Crawford 1996). While we may view this tree with scorn, it is the only invasive tree along our riparian corridors that forms a spreading canopy to create the kind of shade that the senescing cottonwoods (*Populus* spp.) have created for eons.

This invasive tree is also a very useful and abundant medicine as well as a wild edible. The inner bark can be collected and powdered as a substitute for the medicine of the threatened and popular slippery elm (*Ulmus rubra*). They next time you find Siberian elm growing through your backyard fence or coming up along a roadway, cut off a small branch, peel off the bark, and feel its soft slippery mucilage inside. Dried, powdered, and mixed with cold water, it makes an excellent demulcent remedy for sore throats, dry coughs, and other

FIGURE 161
Siberian elm
seeds (*Ulmus
pumila*). Photo
by author.

throat irritations. Additionally, studies show that Siberian elm produces salicylic acid and other hormones that play various physiological roles for the plant, including defense signaling, and also contribute to its anti-inflammatory and analgesic effects (Huang et al. 2015). Other compounds produced by Siberian elm are known to be antimicrobial and have been shown to be effective against thirteen strains of MRSA (You et al. 2013). Recent research also suggests its potential usefulness in treatments for cervical and breast cancer, melanoma, and lymphoma (Wang et al. 2004). Gathered in the early spring while still green, the seeds are a nutritious edible and are tasty served raw on top of salads, in sandwiches, and as garnish.

As highly adaptable and opportunistic newcomers with the ability to remake entire landscapes, nonnative invasive plants often elicit both intrigue and controversy. These plants represent paradox, as they may be both passengers and drivers of change. Additionally, they invite us to explore our thoughts about a range of issues coming to a head in the modern era, including climate change, migration and immigration, globalization, the decline and restoration of relict habitats, how we will adapt to the new conditions unfolding around us, and what changes will we make to maintain a living world. Nonnative invasive plants offer the lessons of balance, moderation, using resources wisely and with gratitude, and offering reciprocity to the land that sustains us. If we take too much, we may lose more than we ever dreamed possible. Regardless of how we feel about these plants, it is in our best interest to understand them as part of our local ecosystems and to embrace them as sources of wisdom and medicine in our lives.

Bibliography

Abad, Maria Jose, Luis Miguel Bedoya, Luis Apaza, and Paulina Bermejo. "The *Artemisia* L. Genus: A Review of Bioactive Essential Oils." *Molecules* 17, no. 3 (2012): 2542–66.

Abbas, M. N., S. A. Rana, M. Shahid, N. Rana, M. Mahmoodul-Hassan, and M. Hussain. "Chemical Evaluation of Weed Seeds Mixed with Wheat Grains at Harvest." *Journal of Animal and Plant Sciences* 22, no. 2 (2012): 283–88.

Acharya, R. N., and M. G. Chaubal. "Essential Oil of *Anemopsis californica*." *Journal of Pharmaceutical Science* 57, no. 6 (June 1968): 1020–22.

Adel, M., L. A. Alousi, and H. A. Salem. "Licorice: A Possible Anti-inflammatory and Anti-ulcer Drug." *AAPS PharmSciTech* 6 (2005): 74–82.

Ager, Thomas A., and Lynn Price Ager. "Ethnobotany of the Eskimos of Nelson Island, Alaska." *Arctic Anthropology* 27 (1980): 26–48.

Agrawal, O. P., S. Bharadwaj, and R. Mathur. "Antifertility Effects of Fruits of *Juniperus communis*." *Journal of Medicinal Plant Research* 40 (1980): 98–101.

Ahameethunisa, Abdul R., and Waheeta Hopper. "Antibacterial Activity of *Artemisia nilagirica* Leaf Extracts against Clinical and Phytopathogenic Bacteria." *BMC Complementary and Alternative Medicine* 10, no. 6 (2010). doi:10.1186/1472-6882-10-6.

———. "In Vitro Antimicrobial Activity on Clinical Microbial Strains and Antioxidant Properties of *Artemisia parviflora*." *Annals of Clinical Microbiology and Antimicrobials* 11, no. 30 (2012). doi:10.1186/1476-0711-11-30.

Ahmad A., J. Davies, S. Randall, and G. R. Skinner. "Antiviral Properties of Extract of *Opuntia streptacantha*." *Antiviral Research* 30 (1996): 75–85.

Ahmadiani A., J. Hosseiny, S. Semnanian, M. Javan, F. Saeedi, M. Kamalinejad, and S. Saremi. "Antinociceptive and Anti-inflammatory Effects of *Elaeagnus angustifolia* Fruit Extract." *Journal of Ethnopharmacology* 72 (2000): 287–92.

Ahmed, Dildar, Kamal Ahmed Qasim, Chaudhary Muhammad Ashraf, and Husnul Maab. "*Verbena officinalis* a Herb with Promising Broad Spectrum Antimicrobial Potential." *Cogent Chemistry* 3, no. 1 (2017).

Akana, Akaiko. *Hawaiian Herbs of Medicinal Value*. Honolulu: Pacific Book House, 1922.

Akdogan, M., A. Koyu, M. Ciris, and K. Yildiz. "Anti-hypercholesterolemic Activity of J. communis Oil in Rats: A Biochemical and Histopathological Investigation." *Biomedical Research* 23, no. 3 (2012): 321–28.

Akharaiyi, F. C. "Antibacterial, Phytochemical and Antioxidant Activities of *Datura metel*." *International Journal of PharmTech Research* 3, no. 1 (2011): 478–83.

Akkari, H., K. Rtibi, F. B'chir, M. Rekik, M. Aziz Darghouth, and M. Gharbi. "In Vitro Evidence That the Pastoral *Artemisia campestris* Species Exerts an Anthelmintic Effect on Haemonchus Contortus from Sheep." *Veterinary Research Communications* 38 (2014): 249.

Akther, Nayeema, A. S. Shawl, Sarwat Sultana, B. K. Chandan, and Mymoona Akther. "Hepatoprotective Activity of *Marrubium vulgare* against Paracetamol Induced Toxicity." *Journal of Pharmacy Research* 7, no. 7 (July 2013): 565–70.

Al Razzuqii, R. A. M., and J. A. Al-Hussaini. "Hepatoprotective Effect of *Glycyrrhiza glabra* in CCl4 Induced Model in Acute Liver Injury." *Journal of Physiology and Pharmacology Advances* 2 (2012): 259–63.

Albert, Andreas, Vipaporn Sareedenchai,

Werner Heller, Harald K. Seidlitz, and Christian Zidorn. "Temperature Is the Key to Altitudinal Variation of Phenolics in *Arnica montana* L. cv. ARBO." *Oecologia* 160, no. 1 (May 2009): 1–8.

Alhourani N., V. Kasabri, Y. Bustanji, R. Abbassi, and M. Hudaib. "Potential Antiproliferative Activity and Evaluation of Essential Oil Composition of the Aerial Parts of *Tamarix aphylla* (L.) H. Karst: A Wild Grown Medicinal Plant in Jordan." *Evidence-Based Complementary and Alternative Medicine* (2018). doi:10.1155/2018/9363868.

Alishiri, G., A. Ahmadiani, Bayat Noushin, M. Kamalinezhad, A. Salimzadeh, S. Saremi, M. Miri, and A. A. Noudeh. "Efficacy of *Elaeagnus angustifolia* Extract in Treatment of Osteoarthritis of Knee: A Randomized Double Blind Placebo-Controlled Trial." *Kowsar Medical Journal* 12, no. 1 (2007): 49–57.

Allen, Craig D., and David D. Breshears. "Drought-Induced Shift of a Forest-Woodland Ecotone: Rapid Landscape Response to Climate Variation." *Proceedings of the National Academy of Sciences* 95 (1998): 14839–42.

Al-Quran, Saleh. "Used Ethnobotany of Medicinal Plants by Inhabitants of Al-Mafraq, Jordan." *Arnaldoa* 21, no. 1 (2014): 119–26.

Al-Snafi, Ali Esmail. "Medicinal Plants Affected Reproductive Systems—Plant Based Review." *Scholars Academy Journal of Pharmacy* 5, no. 8 (2016): 159–74.

——. "Chemical Constituents and Medical Importance of *Galium aparine*—a Review." *Indo American Journal of Pharmaceutical Sciences* 5, no. 3 (2018a): 1739–44.

——. "Medicinal Importance of *Juniperus communis*—a Review." *Indo American Journal of Pharmaceutical Sciences* 5, no. 3 (2018b): 1779–92.

Ambawade, S. D., V. S. Kasture, and S. B. Kasture. "Anxiolytic Activity of *Glycyrrhiza glabra* Linn." *Journal of Natural Remedies* 2 (2001): 130–34.

Ambawade, Shirish D., Veena S. Kasture, and Sanjay B. Kasture. "Anticonvulsant Activity of Roots and Rhizomes of *Glycyrrhiza glabra*." *Indian Journal of Pharmacology* 34 (2002): 251–55.

Amer, A., and H. Mehlhorn. "Repellency Effect of Forty-One Essential Oils against Aedes, Anopheles, and Culex Mosquitoes." *Parasitology Research* 99, no. 4 (2006): 478–90.

American Herbal Pharmacopoeia. *Oshá Root Ligusticum porteri J. M. Coulter and Rose and Related Species: Standards of Analysis, Quality Control, and Therapeutics.* Scotts Valley, CA: American Herbal Pharmacopoeia, 2018.

American Herbal Products Association. *Tonnage Survey of Selected North American Wild-Harvested Plants, 2006–2010.* Silver Spring, MD: American Herbal Products Association, 2012.

Amri, Bedis, Emanuela Martino, Francesca Vitulo, Federica Corana, Leila Bettaieb-Ben Kaab, Marta Rui, Daniela Rossi, Michela Mori, Silvia Rossi, and Simona Collina. "*Marrubium vulgare* L. Leaf Extract: Phytochemical Composition, Antioxidant and Wound Healing Properties." *Molecules* 22, no. 11 (2017): 1851.

Anderson, J. P. "Plants Used by the Eskimo of the Northern Bering Sea and Arctic Regions of Alaska." *American Journal of Botany* 26 (1939): 714–16.

Anderson, M. Kat. USDA-NRCS *Plant Guide.* Davis: National Plant Data Center, University of California, 2003.

Andrade-Ochoa, Sergio, Karen Giselle Chavez Villareal, Blanca Estela Rivera Chavira, and Guadalupe Virginia Nevárez Moorillón. "Antimicrobial Activity of Essential Oil of *Ligusticum porteri*." Paper presented at the Biotecnología y Bioingeniería National Congress, Cancun, Mexico, June 23–28, 2013. https://smbb.mx/congresos%20smbb/cancun13/TRABAJOS/SMBB/BiotecnologiaFarmaceutica/VIII-C40.pdf.

Ang, Hui Ying, Tamilselvan Subramani,

Swee Keong Yeap, Abdul Rahman Omar, Wan Yang Ho, Mohd Puad Abdullah, and Noorjahan Banu Alitheen. "Immunomodulatory Effects of *Potentilla indica* and *Dendrophthoe pentandra* on Mice Splenocytes and Thymocytes." *Experimental and Therapeutic Medicine* 7, no. 6 (June 2014): 1733-37.

Ansley, R. J., and P. W. Jacoby. "Manipulation of Fire Intensity to Achieve Mesquite Management Goals in North Texas." In *Fire in Ecosystem Management: Shifting the Paradigm from Suppression to Prescription: Proceedings, Tall Timbers Fire Ecology Conference,* edited by Teresa L. Pruden and Leonard A. Brennan, pp. 195-204. Tallahassee: Tall Timbers Research Station, 1998.

Antunes-Ricardo, M., B. E. Moreno-García, J. A. Gutiérrez-Uribe, D. Aráiz-Hernández, M. M. Alvarez, and S. O. Serna-Saldivar. "Induction of Apoptosis in Colon Cancer Cells Treated with Isorhamnetin Glycosides from *Opuntia ficusindica* Pads." *Plant Foods for Human Nutrition* 69, no. 4 (2014): 331-36.

Aouni, Rim, Massadok Ben Attia, Mohammed Habib Jaafoura, and Amina Bibi-Derbel. "Effects of the Hydro-ethanolic Extract of *Marrubium vulgare* in Female Rats." *Asian Pacific Journal of Tropical Medicine* 10, no. 2 (February 2017): 160-64.

Apaydin, Eric A., Alicia R. Maher, Roberta Shanman, Marika S. Booth, Jeremy N. V. Miles, Melony E. Sorbero, and Susanne Hempel. "A Systematic Review of St. John's Wort for Major Depressive Disorder." *Systematic Reviews* 5, no. 1 (September 2016): 148.

Applequist, Wendy, and Daniel Moerman. "Yarrow (*Achillea millefoilum*): A Neglected Panacea? A Review of Ethnobotany, Bioactivity, and Biomedical Research." *Economic Botany* 65, no. 2 (2011): 209-25.

Ardestani, A., and R. Yazdanparast. "Antioxidant and Free Radical Scavenging Potential of *Achillea santolina* Extracts." *Food Chemistry* 104 (2007): 21-29.

Ari, F., N. Aztopal, S. Oran, S. Bozdemir, S. Celikler, S. Ozturk, and E. Ulukaya. "*Parmelia sulcata* Taylor and *Usnea filipendula* Stirt Induce Apoptosis-like Cell Death and DNA Damage in Cancer Cells." *Cell Proliferation* 47 (2014): 457-64.

Armanini, D., G. Bonanni, and M. Palermo. "Reduction of Serum Testosterone in Men by Licorice." *New England Journal of Medicine* 341 (1999): 1158.

Armanini, D., C. Fiore, M. J. Mattarello, J. Bielenberg, and M. Palermo. "History of the Endocrine Effects of Licorice." *Experimental and Clinical Endocrinology and Diabetes* 110 (2002): 257-61.

Armanini, D., I. Karbowiak, and J. W. Funder. "Affinity of Liquorice Derivatives for Mineralocorticoid and Glucocorticoid Receptors." *Clinical Endocrinology* 19 (1983): 609-12.

Arnason, Thor, Richard J. Hebda, and Timothy Johns. "Use of Plants for Food and Medicine by Native Peoples of Eastern Canada." *Canadian Journal of Botany* 59, no. 11 (1981): 2189-2325.

Ashrafzadeh, F., H. Rakhshandeh, and E. Mahmodi. "*Rosa damascena* Oil: An Adjunctive Therapy for Pediatric Refractory Seizures." *Iran Journal of Child Neurology* 1 (2007): 13-17.

Aslantürk, O. S., T. A. Çelik, B. Karabey, and F. Karabey. "Active Phytochemical Detecting, Antioxidant, Cytotoxic, Apoptotic Activities of Ethyl Acetate and Methanol Extracts of *Galium aparine* L." *British Journal of Pharmaceutical Research* 15, no. 6 (2017). doi:10.9734/BJPR/2017/32762.

Asner, Gregory, Philip G. Brodrick, Christopher B. Anderson, Nicolas Vaugh, David E. Knapp, and Roberta E. Martin. "Progressive Forest Canopy Water Loss during the 2012-2015 California Drought." *Proceedings of the National Academy of Sciences* 11, no. 2 (2016): 249-55.

Atmaca, H., E. Bozkurt, M. Cittan, and H. Dilek Tepe." Effects of *Galium aparine* Extract on the Cell Viability, Cell Cycle and Cell Death in Breast Cancer Cell Lines." *Journal of Ethnopharmacology* 186 (2016): 305-10.

Austin, D. D., and Philip J. Urness. "Vegetal Responses and Big Game Values after Thinning Regenerating Lodgepole Pine." *Great Basin Naturalist* 42, no. 4 (1982): 512-16.

Awad, R., J. T. Arnason, V. Trudeau, C. Bergeron, J. W. Budzinski, B. C. Foster, Z. Merali. "Phytochemical and Biological Analysis of Skullcap (*Scutellaria lateriflora* L.): A Medicinal Plant with Anxiolytic Properties." *Phytomedicine* 10 (2003): 640-49.

Baba, M., and S. Shigeta. "Antiviral Activity of Glycyrrhizin against Varicella-zoster Virus In Vitro." *Antiviral Research* 7 (1987): 99-107.

Babaei, M., M. E. Abarghoei, M. M. Akhavan, R. Ansari, A. A. Vafaei, A. A. Taherian, S. Mousavi, and J. Toussy. "Antimotility Effect of Hydroalcoholic Extract of Yarrow (*Achillea millefolium*) on the Guinea Pig Ileum." *Pakistan Journal of Biological Sciences* 10 (2007): 3673-77.

Baggio, Cristiane Hatsuko, Cristina Setim Freitas, Paulo Fernando Nhaducue, Lia Rieck, and Maria Consuelo Andrade Marques. "Action of Crude Aqueous Extract of Leaves of *Achillea millefolium* L. (Compositae) on Gastrointestinal Tract." *Revista Brasileira de Farmacognosia* 12 (2002): 31-33.

Bainbridge, David A., and Virginia, Ross A. "Restoration in the Sonoran Desert of California." *Restoration and Management Notes* 8, no. 1 (1990): 3-14.

Bais S., N. Abrol, Y. Prashar, and R. Kumari. "Modulatory Effect of Standardised Amentoflavone Isolated from *Juniperus communis* L. against Freund's Adjuvant Induced Arthritis in Rats (Histopathological and X Ray Anaysis)." *Biomed Pharmacother* 86 (2017): 381-92.

Bais, Souravh, Naresh Singh Gill, Nitan Rana, and Shandeep Shandil. "A Phytopharmacological Review on a Medicinal Plant *Juniperus communis*." *International Scholarly Research Notices* 2014 (2014). doi:10.1155/2014/634723.

Baker, Marc A. "The Ethnobotany of the Yurok, Tolowa, and Karok Indians of Northern California." Master's thesis, Humboldt State University, Arcata, CA, 1981.

Banerjee, S., A. Mukherjee, and T. K. Chatterjee. "Evaluation of Analgesic Activities of Methanolic Extract of Medicinal Plant *Juniperus communis* Linn." *International Journal of Pharmacy and Pharmaceutical Sciences* 4, no. 5 (2012): 547-50.

Banerjee, S., H. Singh, and T. K. Chatterjee. Evaluation of Anti-Diabetic and Anti-Hyperlipidemic Potential of Methanolic Extract of *Juniperus communis* (L.) in Streptozotocin Nicotinamide Induced Diabetic Rats. *International Journal of Pharma and Bio Sciences* 4, no. 3 (2013): 10-17.

Bank, Theodore, P. "Botanical and Ethnobotanical Studies in the Aleutian Islands I: Aleutian Vegetation and Aleut Culture." *Botanical and Ethnobotanical Studies Papers, Michigan Academy of Science, Arts and Letters* 37 (1951): 13-30.

——. "Botanical and Ethnobotanical Studies in the Aleutian Islands II: Health and Medical Lore of the Aleuts." *Botanical and Ethnobotanical Studies Papers, Michigan Academy of Science, Arts and Letters* 38 (1953): 415-31.

Barger, Nichole N., Henry D. Adams, Connie Woodhouse, Jason C. Neff, and Gregory P. Asner. "Influence of Livestock Grazing and Climate on Pinyon Pine (*Pinus edulis*) Dynamics." *Rangeland Ecolology Management* 62 (November 2009): 531-39.

Barkaoui, M., A. Katiri, H. Boubaker, and F. Msanda. "Ethnobotanical Survey of Medicinal Plants Used in the Traditional Treatment of Diabetes in Chtouka Ait

Baha and Tiznit (Western Anti-Atlas), Morocco." *Journal of Ethnopharmacology* 198 (February 2017): 338–50.

Barnes, Paul W., and Steve Archer. "Influence of an Overstory Tree (*Prosopis glandulosa*) on Associated Shrubs in a Savanna Parkland: Implications for Patch Dynamics." *Oecologia* 105, no. 4 (1996): 493–500.

Barnosky, Anthony D., Nicholas Matzke, Susumu Tomiya, Guinevere O. U. Wogan, Brian Swartz, Tiago B. Quental, Charles Marshall, Jenny L. McGuire, Emily L. Lindsey, Kaitlin C. Maguire, Ben Mersey, and Elizabeth A. Ferrer. "Has the Earth's Sixth Mass Extinction Already Arrived?" *Nature* 471 (2011): 51–57.

Barrett, S. A. "Material Aspects of Pomo Culture." *Bulletin of the Public Museum of the City of Milwaukee*, no. 20 (1952).

Barrows, David Prescott. *The Ethno-Botany of the Coahuilla Indians of Southern California*, 1900. Reprint, Banning, CA: Malki Museum Press, 1967.

Barzegarnejad, A., M. Azadbakht, O. Emadian, and M. Ahmadi. "Effect of Some Fractions of the Extract of *Juniperus communis* Fruit on Solving Kidney Stones In Vitro." *Journal of Mazandaran University Medical Sciences* 23, no. 110 (2014): 146–52.

Basehart, Harry. *Apache Indians XII: Mescalero Apache Subsistence Patterns and Socio-Political Organization*. New York: Garland Publishing, 1974.

Bate-Smith, E. C. "Chemistry and Taxonomy of *Fouquieria splendens* Engelmn: A New Member of the Asperuloside Group." *Phytochemistry* 3 (1964): 623–25.

Batista, Ronan, Clarissa Cunha Santana, Alene Azevedo-Santos, Ana Marcia Suarez-Fontes, Jose Lucas de Almeida Antunes Ferraz, Luiz Alberto Mattos Silva, and Marcos Andre Vannier-Santos. "In Vivo Antimalarial Extracts and Constituents of *Prosopis juliflora* (Fabaceae)." *Journal of Functional Foods* 44 (May 2018): 74–78.

Bean, Lowell John, and Katherine Siva Saubel. *Tempalpakh (from the Earth): Cahuilla Indian Knowledge and Usage of Plants*. Banning, CA: Malki Museum Press, 1972.

Beardsley, Gretchen. "Notes on Cree Medicines, Based on Collections Made by I. Cowie in 1892." *Papers of the Michigan Academy of Science, Arts and Letters* 28 (1941): 483–96.

Bebbache-Benaida, Nadjet, Dina Atmani-Kilani, Valerie Barbara Schini-Keirth, Nouredine Djebbli, and Djebbar Atmani. "Pharmacological Potential of *Populus nigra* Extract as Antioxidant, Anti-inflammatory, Cardiovascular and Hepatoprotective Agent. *Asian Pacific Journal of Tropical Biomedicine* 3, no. 9 (September 2013): 697–704.

Behera, B. C., Neeraj Verma, Anjali Sonone, and Urmila Makhija. "Evaluation of Antioxidant Potential of the Cultured Mycobiont of a Lichen *Usnea ghattensis*." *Phytotherapy Research* 19, no. 1 (January 2005): 58–64.

Beiraghdar, Fatemeh, Behzad Einollahi, Alireza Ghadyani, Yunes Panahi, Abbas Hadjiakhoondi, Mahdi Vazirian, Ali Salarytabar, and Behrad Darvishi. "A Two-Week, Double-Blind, Placebo-Controlled Trial of *Viola odorata*, *Echium amoenum* and *Physalis alkekengi* Mixture in Symptomatic Benign Prostate Hyperplasia (BPH) in Men." *Pharmaceutical Biology* 55, no. 1 (2017): 1800–5.

Belkhodja, Hamza, Boumediene Meddah, Aicha Tir Touil, Nazim Şekeroğlu, and Pascal Sonnet. "Chemical Composition and Properties of Essential Oil of *Rosmarinus officinalis* and *Populus alba*." *World Journal of Pharmacy and Pharmaceutical Sciences* 5, no. 9 (2016): 108–19.

Belkhodja, Hamza, Boumediene Meddah, Aicha Meddah Tir Touil, Khaled Slimani, and Abdenacer Tou. "Radiographic and Histopathologic Analysis on Osteoarthritis Rat Model Treated with

Essential Oils of *Rosmarinus officinalis* and *Populus alba*." *Pharmaceutical Sciences* 23, no. 1 (2017): 12–17.

Bell, Willis H., and Edward F. Castetter. "Ethnobiological Studies in the American Southwest: The Utilization of Mesquite and Screwbean by the Aborigines in the American Southwest." *Biological Series* 5, no. 2 (1937). Albuquerque: University of New Mexico.

——. "Ethnobiological Studies in the Southwest VII: The Utilization of Yucca, Sotol, and Beargrass by the Aborigines in the American Southwest." *University of New Mexico Bulletin* 5, no. 5 (1941): 1–74.

Benedek, N. Geisz, W. Jäger, T. Thalhammer, and B. Kopp. "Choleretic Effects of Yarrow (*Achillea millefolium* s.l.) in the Isolated Perfused Rat Liver." *Phytomedicine* 13 (2006): 702–6.

Ben-Eliezer, Daniel, and Eldad Yechiam. "*Hypericum perforatum* as a Conginitve Enhancer in Rodents: A Meta-Analysis." *Scientific Reports* 6 (October 2016). doi:10.1038/srep35700.

Benidze, M. M., V. G. Nebieridze, Markus Ganzera, A. V. Skhirtladze, and E. P. Kemertelidze. "Sesquiterpene Glycosides from Flowers of *Yucca gloriosa*." *Chemistry of Natural Compounds* 54, no. 1 (January 2018): 73–76.

Benzina, S., J. Harquail, S. Jean, A. P. Beauregard, C. D. Colquhoun, M. Carroll, A. Bos, C. A. Gray, and G. A. Robichaud. "Deoxypodophyllotoxin Isolated from *Juniperus communis* Induces Apoptosis in Breast Cancer Cells." *Anticancer Agents Medical Chemistry* 15, no. 1 (2015): 79–88.

Bergeron, C., A. Marston, R. Gauthier, and K. Hostettmann. "Screening of Plants Used by North American Indians for Antifungal, Bactericidal, Larvicidal, and Molluscicidal Activities." *International Journal of Pharmacology* 34, no. 4 (1996): 233–42.

Bernstein, Steve, Howard Donsky, Wayne Gulliver, Douglas Hamilton, Sion

Nobel, and Robert Norman. "Treatment of Mild to Moderate Psoriasis with Relieva, a *Mohonia aquifolium* extract—a Double Blind, Placebo-Controlled Study." *American Journal of Therapeutics* 13, no. 2 (March–April 2006): 121–26.

Berraaouan, A., Z. Abderrahim, M. Hassane, L. Abdelkhaleq, A. Mohammed, and B. Mohamed. "Evaluation of Protective Effect of Cactus Pear Seed Oil (*Opuntia ficus-indica* L. MILL.) against Alloxan-Induced Diabetes in Mice." *Asian Pacific Journal of Tropical Medicine* 8, no. 7 (2015): 532–37.

Bertelli, A. A., M. Migliori, V. Panichi, C. Origlia, D. K. Das Filippi, and L. Giovannini. "Resveratrol, a Component of Wine and Grapes, in the Prevention of Kidney Disease." *Annals of the New York Academy of Sciences* 957 (2002): 230–38.

Beverley, Robert. *The History and Present State of Virginia*, 1722. Reprint, Chapel Hill: University of North Carolina Press, 2013.

Bezakova, L., V. Misik, L. Malekova, E. Svajdlenka, and D. Kostalova. "Lipoxygenase Inhibition and Antioxidant Properties of Bisbenzylisoqunoline Alkaloids Isolated from *Mahonia aquifolium*." *Die Pharmazie* 51, no. 10 (October 1996): 758–61.

Bhandage, A., K. Shevkar, and Undale V. Vaishali. "Evaluation of Antinociceptive Activity of Roots of *Glycyrrhiza glabra*." *Journal of Pharmaceutical Research* 2 (2009): 803–7.

Bhat, Jahangeer, Munesh Kumar, and Np Todaria. "Informants' Consensus on Ethnomedicinal Plants in Kedarnath Wildlife Sactuary of Indian Himalayas." *Journal of Medicinal Plant Research* 7, no. 4 (January 2013): 148–54.

Bhat, Z. A., Dinesh Kumar, and Y. M. Shah. "*Angelica archangelica* Linn. Is an Angel on Earth for the Treatment of Diseases." *International Journal of Nutrition, Pharmacology, Neurological Diseases* 1, no. 1 (2011): 36–50.

Bieski, Isanete Geraldini Costa, Fabrício Rios Santos, Rafael Melo de Oliveira, Mariano Martinez Espinosa, Miramy Macedo, Ulysses Paulino Albuquerque, and Domingos Tabajara de Oliveira Martins. "Ethnopharmacology of Medicinal Plants of the Pantanal Region (Mato Grosso, Brazil)." *Evidence-Based Complementary and Alternative Medicine* (2012): doi:10.1155/2012/272749.

Bilia, Anna Rita, Francesca Santomauro, Cristiana Sacco, Maria Camilla Bergonzi, and Rosa Donato. "Essential Oil of *Artemisia annua* L.: An Extraordinary Component with Numerous Antimicrobial Properties." *Evidence-Based Complementary and Alternative Medicine* (2014). doi:10.1155/2014/159819.

Bingham, R. "New and Effective Approaches to the Prevention and Treatment of Arthritis." *Journal of Applied Nutrition* 28 (1976): 38–47.

Bingham, R., B. A. Bellow, and J. G. Bellow. "Yucca Plant Saponin in the Management of Arthritis." *Journal of Applied Nutrition* 27 (1975): 45–51.

Bingham, R., D. H. Harris, and T. Laga. "Yucca Plant Saponin in the Treatment of Hypertension and Hypercholesterolemia." *Journal of Applied Nutrition* 30 (1978): 127–36.

Binghamton University. "Invasive Species in an Ecosystem Harm Native Organisms but Aid Other Invasive Species." *Science Daily* 23 (October 2018). www.sciencedaily.com/releases /2018/10/181023130513.htm.

Biswas, N., S. Gupta, and G. Das. "Evaluation of Ophthacare Eye Drops—an Herbal Formulation in the Management of Various Ophthalmic Disorders." *Phytotherapy Research* 15 (2001): 618–20.

Black, Meredith Jean. "Algonquin Ethnobotany: An Interpretation of Aboriginal Adaptation in South Western Quebec." *Ottawa National Museums of Canada, Mercury Series*, no. 65 (1980).

Blankinship, J. W. "Native Economic Plants of Montana." *Montana Agricultural College Experimental Station Bulletin* 56 (1905).

Blatina, L. A. "Chemical Modification of Glycyrrhizic Acid as a Route to Bioactive Compounds for Medicine." *Current Medical Chemistry* 10 (2003): 155–71.

Blumenthal, Mark, Werner R. Busse, Alicia Goldberg, Joerg Gruenwald, Tara Hall, Chance Riggins, and Robert S. Rister. *The Complete German Commission E Monographs*. Austin: American Botanical Council, 1998.

Boas, Franz. *Kwakiutl Ethnography*. Chicago: University of Chicago Press, 1966.

Bocek, Barbara. "Ethnobotany of Costanoan Indians, California, Based on Collections by John P. Harrington." *Economic Botany* 38, no. 2 (1984): 240–55.

Bohlmann, F., J. Jakupovic, and C. Zdero. "Neue norsesquiterpene aus Rudbeckia laciniata und Senecio paludaffinis." *Phytochemistry* 17 (1978): 2034–36.

Bokhari, J., M. R. Khan, M. Shabbir, U. Rashid, S. Jan, and J. A. Zai. "Evaluation of Diverse Antioxidant Activities of *Galium aparine*." *Spectrochimica Acta Part A Molecular and Biomolecular Spectroscopy* 102 (2013): 24–29.

Booth, Gary M., Robert D. Malmstrom, Erica Kipp, and Alexandra Paul. "Cytotoxicity of Selected Medicinal and Nonmedicinal Plant Extracts to Microbial and Cervical Cancer Cells." *Journal of Biomedicine and Biotechnology* (2012). doi:10.1155/2012/106746.

Boskabady, Mohammad Hossein, Mohammad Naser Shafei, Zahra Saberi, and Somayeh Amini. "Pharmacological Effects of Rosa damascena." *Iranian Journal of Basic Medical Sciences* 14, no. 4 (2011): 295–307.

Bowen, W. F. "A Study of Osha Root and Its Volatile Oil." *Proceedings of the Sixteenth Annual Meeting of the Kansas Pharmaceutical Association*. Leavenworth: Kansas Pharmaceutical Association (1895): 72–76.

Brandao, L. F., G. B. Alcantara, F. Matos Mde, D. Bogo, S. Freitas Ddos, N. M.

Oyama, and N. K. Honda. "Cytotoxic Evaluation of Phenolic Compounds from Lichens against Melanoma Cells." *Chemical and Pharmaceutical Bulletin* 61 (2013): 176-83.

Breshears, David, Neil S. Cobb, Paul M. Rich, Kevin P. Price, Craig D. Allen, Randy G. Balice, William H. Romme, Jude H. Kastens, M. Lisa Floyd, Jayne Belnap, Jesse J. Anderson, Orrin B. Meyers, and Clifton W. Meyer. "Regional Vegetation Die-Off in Response to Global-Change-Type Drought." *Proceedings of the National Academy of Sciences* 102, no. 42 (October 2005): 15144-48.

Brindis, Fernando, Rogelio Rodriguez, Robert Bye, Martin Gonzalez-Andrade, and Rachel Mata. "(Z)-3-Butylideneph-thalide from *Ligusticum porteri*, an ⊠-Glucosidase Inhibitor." *Journal of Natural Products* 74, no. 3 (2011): 314-20.

Brinson, M. M., B. L. Swift, R. C. Plantico, and J. S. Barclay. *Riparian Ecosystems: Their Ecology and Status.* Kearneysville, WV: US Fish and Wildlife Service, 1981.

Brock, Christine, Julie Whitehouse, Ihab Tewfik, and Tony Towell. "American Skullcap (*Scutellaria lateriflora*): A Randomized, Double-Blind Placebo-Controlled Crossover Study of Its Effects on Mood in Healthy Volunteers." *Phytotherapy Research* 28, no. 5 (May 2014): 692-98.

Brown, J. R., and Steve Archer. "Woody Plant Seed Dispersal and Gap Formation in a North American Subtropical Savanna Woodland: The Role of Domestic Herbivores." *Vegetation* 73 (1987): 73-80.

Brush, Julie, Elissa Mendenhall, Alena Guggenheim, Tracy Chan, Erin Connelly, Amala, Soumyanath, Randal Buresh, Richard Barrett, and Heather Zwickey. "The Effects of *Echinacea purpuream*, *Astragalus membranaceus* and *Glycyrrhiza glabra* on CD69 Expression and Immune Cell Activation in Humans." *Phytotherapy Research* 20, no. 8 (August 2006): 687-95.

Budinsky, A., R. Wolfram, A. Oguogho, Y. Efthimiou, Y. Stamatopoulos, and H. Sinzinger. "Regular Ingestion of *Opuntia robusta* Lowers Oxidation Injury." *Prostaglandins, Leukotrienes, and Essential Fatty Acids* 65, no. 1 (2001): 45-50.

Buffington, Lee C., and Carlton H. Herbel. "Vegetational Changes on a Semidesert Grassland Range from 1858 to 1963." *Ecological Monographs* 35 (1965): 139-64.

Burdette, Joanna E., Jianghua Liu, Dan Lantvit, Eula Lim, Nancy Booth, Krishna P. L. Bhat, Samad Hedayat, Richard B. Van Breemen, Andreas I. Constantinou, John M. Pezzuto, Norman R. Farnsworth, and Judy L. Bolton. "*Trifolium pratense* (Red Clover) Exhibits Estrogenic Effects In Vivo in Ovariectomized Sprague-Dawley Rats." *Journal of Nutrition* 132, no. 1 (January 2002): 27-30.

Bushnell, David I. "The Choctaw of Bayou Lacomb, St. Tammany Parish, Louisiana." *Smithsonian Institution, Bureau of American Ethnology Bulletin* no. 48 (1909).

Bussey, R. O., A. Kaur, D. A. Todd, J. M. Egan, T. El-Elimat, T. N. Graf, H. A. Raja, N. H. Oberlies, and N. B. Cech. "Comparison of the Chemistry and Diversity of Endophytes Isolated from Wild-Harvested and Greenhouse-Cultivated Yerba Mansa (*Anemopsis californica*)." *Phytochemistry Letters* (2015): 202-8.

Bussey, R. O., A. A. Sy-Cordero, M. Figueroa, F. S. Carter, J. O. Falkinham, N. H. Oberlies, and N. B. Cech. "Antimycobacterial Furofuran Lignans from the Roots of *Anemopsis californica*." *Planta Medica* 80, no. 6 (April 2014): 498-501.

Butterweck, V., L. Semlin, B. Feistel, I. Pischel, K. Bauer, and E. J. Verspohl. "Comparative Evaluation of Two Different *Opuntia ficus-indica* Extracts for Blood Sugar Lowering Effects in Rats."

Phytotherapy Research 25, no. 3 (2011): 370–75.

Bystrov, N. S., B. K. Chernov, V. N. Dobrynin, and M. N. Kolosov. "The Structure of Hyperforin." *Tetrahedron Letters* 32 (1975): 2791–94.

Cabrera, C. "Materia Medica *Usnea* spp." *European Journal of Herbal Medicine* 2, no. 2 (1996): 1113.

Calzada, Fernando, Jose Correa Basurto, Elizabeth Barbosa, Claudia Velázquez, Normand García Hernández, R. M. Ordoñez Razo, David Mendez Luna, and Lilian Yepez Mulia. "Antiprotozoal Activities of Tiliroside and Other Compounds from *Sphaeralcea angustifolia* (Cav.) G. Don." *Pharmagocnosy Research* 9, no. 2 (April–June 2017):133–37.

Camazine, Scott, and Robert A. Bye. "A Study of the Medical Ethnobotany of the Zuni Indians of New Mexico." *Journal of Ethnopharmacology* 2 (1980): 365–88.

Campbell, T. N. "Medicinal Plants Used by Choctaw, Chickasaw, and Creek Indians in the Early Nineteenth Century." *Journal of the Washington Academy of Sciences* 41, no. 9 (1951): 285–90.

Candan, F., M. Unlü, B. Tepe, D. Daferera, M. Polissiou, A. Sökmen, and H. A. Akpulat. "Antioxidant and Antimicrobial Activity of the Essential Oil and Methanol Extracts of *Achillea millefolium* subsp. *millefolium* Afan. (Asteraceae)." *Journal of Ethnopharmacology* 87 (2003): 215–20.

Cansaran, Demet, Didem Kahya, Ender Yurdakulol, and Orhan Atakol. "Identification and Quantitation of Usnic Acid from the Lichen Usnea Species of Anatolia and Antimicrobial Activity." *Zietschrift fur Naturforschung* 61c (2006): 773–76.

Cardarelli, M., G. Serino, L. Campanella, P. Ercole, F. De Cicco Nardone, O. Alesiani, and F. Rossiello. "Antimitotic Effects of Usnic Acid on Different Biological Systems." *Cellular and Molecular Life Sciences* 53 (1997): 667–72.

Carlquist, S., K. Dauer, and S. Nishimura. "Wood and Stem Anatomy of Saururaceae with Reference to Ecology, Phylogeny, and Origin of the Monocotyledons." *IAWA* 16, no. 2 (January 1995): 133–50.

Carlson, Gustav G., and Volney H. Jones. "Some Notes on Uses of Plants by the Comanche Indians." *Papers of the Michigan Academy of Science, Arts and Letters* 25 (1940): 517–42.

Carrier Linguistic Committee. *Plants of Carrier Country*. Fort Saint James, BC: Carrier Linguistic Committee, 1973.

Castetter, Edward F. "Ethnobiological Studies in the American Southwest I: Uncultivated Native Plants Used as Sources of Food." *University of New Mexico Bulletin* 4, no. 1 (1935): 1–44.

Castetter, Edward F., and M. E. Opler. "Ethnobiological Studies in the American Southwest III: The Ethnobiology of the Chiricahua and Mescalero Apache." *University of New Mexico Bulletin* 4, no. 5 (1936): 1–63.

Castetter, Edward F., and Ruth M. Underhill. "Ethnobiological Studies in the American Southwest II: The Ethnobiology of the Papago Indians." *University of New Mexico Bulletin* 4, no. 3 (1935): 1–84.

Castro-Gamboa, Ian, and Oscar Castro. "Iridoids from the Aerial Parts of *Verbena littoralis* (Verbenaceae)." *Phytochemistry* 65, no. 16 (August 2004): 2369–72.

Cavalcanti, A. M., C. H. Baggio, C. S. Freitas, L. Rieck, R. S. de Sousa, J. E. Da Silva-Santos, S. Mesia-Vela, and M. C. Marques. "Safety and Antiulcer Efficacy Studies of *Achillea millefolium* L. after Chronic Treatment in Wistar Rats." *Journal of Ethnopharmacology* 107 (2006): 277–84.

Cech, Richo. *Making Plant Medicine*. Williams, OR: Horizon Herbs, 2000.

Cegiela, Urszula, Joanna Folwarczna, Maria Pytlik, and Grazyna Zgorka. "Effects of Extracts from *Trifolium medium* L. and *Trifolium pratense* L.

on Development of Estrogen Deficiency-Induced Osteoporosis in Rats." *Evidenced-Based Complementary and Alternative Medicine* (2012). doi:10.1155/2012/921684.

Cegeila-Carlioz, Pascale, Jean-Marie Bessiere, Bruno David, Anne-Marie Mariotte, Simon Gibbons, and Marie-Genevieve Dijoux-Franca. "Modulation of Multi-Drug Resistance (MDR) in *Staphylococcus aureus* by Osha (*Ligusticum porteri* L., Apiaceae) Essential Oil Compounds." *Flavour and Fragrance Journal* 20, no. 6 (November 2005): 671–75.

Chahdoura, Hassiba, Khawla Adouni, Aida Khlifi, Ichrak Dribi, Zohra Haouas, Fadoua Nefffati, Guido Flamini, Habib Mosbah, and Lotfi Achour. "Hepatoprotective Effect of *Opuntia microdasys* (Lehm.) Pfeiff Flowers against Diabetes Type II Induced in Rats." *Biomedicine and Pharmacotherapy* 94 (October 2017): 79–87.

Chakravarthi, K. K., and R. Avadhani. "Effect of *Glycyrrhiza glabra* Root Extract on Learning and Memory in Wistar Albino Rats. *Drug Invention Today* 4 (2012): 387–90.

——. "Beneficial Effect of Aqueous Extract of *Glycyrrhiza glabra* on Learning and Memory Using Different Behavioral Models: An Experimental Study." *Journal of Natural Science, Biology, and Medicine* 4, no. 2 (July–December 2013): 420–25.

Chamberlin, Ralph V. "Some Plant Names of the Ute Indians." *American Anthropologist* 11 (1909): 27–40.

——. "The Ethno-Botany of the Gosiute Indians of Utah." *Memoirs of the American Anthropological Association* 2, no. 5 (1911): 331–405.

Champakaew, D., A. Junkum, U. Chaithong, A. Jitpakdi, D. Riyong, R. Sanghong, J. Intirach, R. Muangmoon, A. Chansang, B. Tuetun, et al. "*Angelica sinensis* (Umbelliferae) with Proven Repellent Properties against Aedes Aegypti, the Primary Dengue Fever Vector in Thailand." *Parasitology Research* 114 (2015): 2187–98.

Chandler, Frank R., Lois Freeman, and Shirley N. Hooper. "Herbal Remedies of the Maritime Indians." *Journal of Ethnopharmacology* 1 (1979): 49–68.

Chandra, Jeevan, Himanshu Joshi, Pankaj Bahuguna, Vivek Kumar Kedia, Ram Kumar, and Rakesh Kumar. "Behavioral Effects of High Altitude Medicinal Plant in Rats." *Scholars Academic Journal of Pharmacy* 5, no. 9 (2016): 377–82.

Chang, Young-Su, and Eun-Rhan Woo. "Korean Medicinal Plants Inhibiting to Human Immunodeficiency Virus Type 1 (HIV-1) Fusion." *Phytotherapy Research* 17 (2003): 426–29.

Chao, Jung, Jiunn-Wang Liao, Wen-Huang Peng, Meng-Shiou Lee, Li-Heng Pao, and Hao-Yuan Cheng. "Antioxidant, Analgesic, Anti-inflammatory, and Hepatoprotective Effects of the Ethanol Extract of *Mahonia oiwakensis* Stem." *International Journal of Molecular Sciences* 14, no. 2 (2013): 2928–45.

Chao, Jung, Tsung-Chun Lu, Jiunn-Wang Liao, Tai-Hung Huang, Meng-Shiou Lee, Hao-Yuan Cheng, Li-Kang Ho, Chao-Lin Kuo, and Wen-Huang Peng. "Analgesic and Anti-inflammatory Activities of Ethanol Root Extract of *Mahonia oiwakensis* in Mice." *Journal of Ethnopharmacology* 125, no. 2 (September 2009): 297–303.

Charpin, D., J. Orehek, and J. M. Velardocchio. "Bronchodilator Effects of Antiasthmatic Cigarette Smoke (*Datura stramonium*)." *Thorax* 34, no. 2 (1979): 259–61.

Chavez-Santoscoy, R. A., J. A. Gutierrez-Uribe, and S. O. Serna-Saldivar. "Phenolic Composition, Antioxidant Capacity and In Vitro Cancer Cell Cytotoxicity of Nine Prickly Pear (*Opuntia* spp.) Juices." *Plant Foods for Human Nutrition* 64, no. 2 (2009): 146–52.

Cheeke, P. R., S. Piacente, and W. Oleszek. "Anti-inflammatory and

Anti-arthritic Effects of Yucca schidigera: A Review." *Journal of Inflammation* 3, no. 6 (2006). doi:10.1186/1476-9255-3-6.

Chen, S. W., L. Min, W. J. Li, W. X. Kong, J. F. Li, and Y. J. Zhang. "The Effects of Angelica Essential Oil in Three Murine Tests of Anxiety." *Pharmacology, Biochemistry and Behavior* 79 (2004): 377–82.

Chen, Y., Z.-J. Liu, J. Liu, L.-K. Liu, E. S. Zhang, and W. L. Li. "Inhibition of Metastasis and Invasion of Ovarian Cancer Cells by Crude Polysaccharides from *Rosa roxburghii tratt* In Vitro." *Journal of Cancer Prevention* 15 (2013): 10351–54.

Chen Yuxin, Ling Zhu, Xi Yang, Cheng Wei, Chuanrong Chen, Yang He, and Zhaoning Ji. "Ailanthone Induces G2/M Cell Cycle Arrest and Apoptosis of SGC-7901 Human Gastric Cancer Cells." *Molecular Medicine Reports* 16 (2017): 6821–27.

Chesnut, V. K. "Plants Used by the Indians of Mendocino County, California." *Contributions from the US National Herbarium* 7 (1902): 295–408.

Chichonyi Kalungia, Aubrey, Mary Mataka, Patrick Kaonga, Angela Gono Bwalya, Lavina Prashar, and Derick Munkombwe. "*Opuntia stricta* Cladode Extract Reduces Blood Glucose Levels in Alloxan-induced Diabetic Mice." *International Journal of Diabetes Research* 7, no. 1 (2018): doi:10.5923/j.diabetes.20180701.01.

Chin, Young-Won, Hyun-Ah Jung, Yue Liu, Bao-Ning Su, John A. Castoro, William J. Keller, Michael A. Pereira, and Douglas Kinghorn. "Anti-oxidant Constituents of the Roots and Stolons of Licorice (*Glycyrrhiza glabra*)." *Journal of Agriculture and Food Chemistry* 55, no. 12 (2007): 4691–97.

Cho, Suengmok, Ji-Hae Park, Ae Nim Pae, Daeseok Han, Dongsoo Kim, Nam-Chil Cho, Kyoung Tai No, Hyejin Yang, Minseok Yoon, Changho Lee, et al. "Hypnotic Effects and GABAergic Mechanism of Licorice (*Glycyrrhiza glabra*) Ethanol Extract and Its Major Flavonoid Constitient Glabrol." *Bioorganic and Medicinal Chemistry* 20, no. 11 (June 2012): 3493–3501.

Chong, P. W., K.-Z. Lau, J. Gruenwald, and R. Uebelhack. "A Review of the Efficacy and Safety of Litramine IQP-G-002AS, an *Opuntia ficus-indica* Derived Fiber for Weight Management." *Evidence-Based Complementary and Alternative Medicine* (2014). doi:10.1155/2014/943713.

Chopra, P., K. P. Gaitry, Binda D. Saraf, Farhin Inam, and Sujata S. Deo. "Antimicrobial and Antioxidant Activities of Methanol Extract Roots of *Glycyrrhiza glabra* and HPLC Analysis." *International Journal of Pharmacy and Pharmaceutical Sciences* 5, no. 2 (2013): 157–60.

Choudhary, Muhammad, I. Azizuddin, Saima Jalil, and Atta-ur-Rahman. "Bioactive Phenolic Compounds from a Medicinal Lichen, *Usnea longissima*." *Phtyochemistry* 66, no. 19 (October 2005): 2346–50.

Choudhary, Muhammad I., S. Jalil, M. Todorova, A. Trendafilova, B. Mikhova, H. Duddeck, and Atta-ur-Rahman. "Inhibitory Effect of Lactone Fractions and Individual Components from Three Species of the *Achillea millefolium* Complex of Bulgarian Origin on the Human Neutrophils Respiratory Burst Activity." *Natural Products Research* 21 (2007): 1032–36.

Chrubasik-Hausmann, Sigrun, Julia Vlachojannis, and Andrew J. McLachlan. "Understanding Drug Interactions with St John's Wort (*Hypericum perforatum* L.): Impact of Hyperforin Content." *Journal of Pharmacy and Pharmacology* 71, no. 1 (January 2019): 129–38.

Chu, Hongbiao, Ninghua Tan, and Caisheng Peng. "Progress in Research on Pedicularis Plants." *China Journal of Chinese Materia Medica* 34, no. 19 (2009): 2536–46.

Chung, I. M., E. H. Kim, J. H. Lee, Y. C. Lee, and H. I. Moon. "Immunotoxicity

Activity from Various Essential Oils of Angelica Genus from South Korea against *Aedes aegypti* L." *Immunopharmacology and Immunotoxicology* 34 (2012): 42–45.

Cigerci, I. Hakki, A. Fatih Fidan, Muhsin Konuk, Hayati Yuksel, Ismail Kucukkurt, Abdullah Eryavuz, and Nalan Baysu Sozbilir. "The Protective Potential of *Yucca schidigera* (Sarsaponin 30) against Nitrite-Induced Oxidative Stress in Rats." *Journal of Natural Medicines* 63, no. 3 (July 2009): 311–17.

Cioanca, O., C. Mircea, A. Trifan, A. C. Aprotosoaie. L. Hritcn, and M. Hancian. "Improvement of Amyloid-β-induced Memory Deficits by *Juniperus communis* L. Volatile Oil in a Rat Model of Alzheimer's Disease." *Farmacia* 62, no. 3 (2014): 514–20.

Clercq, E. D. "Current Lead Natural Products for the Chemotherapy of Human Immunodeficiency Virus (HIV) Infection." *Medical Research Reviews* 20 (2000): 323–49.

Cohen, M. "Rosehip: An Evidence Based Herbal Medicine for Inflammation and Arthritis." *Australian Family Physician* 41 (2012): 495–98.

Cohn, Jeffrey P. "Resurrecting the Dammed: A Look at Colorado River Restoration." *BioScience* 51, no. 12 (2001): 998–1003.

Colasanti, A., A. Kisslinger, R. Liuzzi, M. Quarto, P. Riccio, G. Roberti, D. Tramontano, and F. Villani. "Hypericin Photosensitization of Tumor and Metastatic Cell Lines of Human Prostate." *Journal of Photochemistry and Photobiology* 54 (2000): 103–7.

Colton, Harold S. "Hopi History and Ethnobotany." In *Hopi Indians*, edited by D. A. Horr, pp. 279–373. New York: Garland Publishing, 1974.

Compton, Brian Douglas. "Upper North Wakashan and Southern Tsimshian Ethnobotany: The Knowledge and Usage of Plants." PhD dissertation, University of British Columbia, Vancouver, 1993.

Cong, Yue, Wang Yan, Wang Tian-xiao, and Li Qin. "Chemical Constituents from the Stem of *Mahonia bealei* (Fort.) Carr." *Chinese Traditional Patent Medicine* 6 (2011).

Consortium for Integrated Climate Research in Western Mountains (CIRMOUNT). "Mapping New Terrain: Climate Change and America's West." Albany, CA: Pacific Southwest Research Station, Forest Service, US Department of Agriculture, 2006.

Cook, Sarah Louise. "The Ethnobotany of the Jemez Indians." Master's thesis, University of New Mexico, Albuquerque, 1930.

Corlett, Richard T. "Plant Diversity in a Changing World: Status, Trends, and Conservation Needs." *Plant Diversity* 38, no. 1 (2016): 10–16.

Costa-Neto, E. M. "Zoopharmacognosy, the Self-Medication Behavior of Animals." *Interfaces Científicas-Saúde e Ambiente* 1, no. 1 (2012): 61–72.

Council for Agricultural Science and Technology. "Livestock Grazing on Federal Lands in the 11 Western States." *Journal of Range Management* 27 (1974): 174–81.

Craciunescu, Oana, Daniel Constantin, Alexandra Gaspar, Liana Toma, Elena Utoiu, and Lucia Moldovan. "Evaluation of Antioxidant and Cytoprotective Activities of *Arnica montana* L. and *Artemisia absinthium* L. Ethanolic Extracts." *Chemistry Central Journal* 6 (2012): 97.

Crance, J. M., E. Biziagos, J. Passagot, H. van Cuyck-Gandré, and R. Deloince. "Inhibition of Hepatitis A Virus Replication In Vitro by Antiviral Compounds." *Journal of Medical Virology* 31, no. 2 (1990): 155–60.

Crawford, Clifford S., Lisa M. Ellis, and Manuel C. Mulles Jr. "The Middle Rio Grande Bosque: An Endangered Ecosystem." *New Mexico Journal of Science* 36 (1996): 276–99.

Crawford, Stuart D. "Lichens Used in Traditional Medicine." *Lichen Secondary Metabolites* (2014): 27–80.

Crimmins, Shawn M., Solomon Z. Dobrowski, Jonathan A. Greenberg, John T. Abatzoglou, and Alison R. Mynsberge. "Changes in Climate Water Balance Drive Downhill Shifts in Plant Species' Optimum Elevations." *Science* 331, no. 6015 (2011): 324-27.

Cronk, Quentin. "Plant Extinctions Take Time." *Science* 353, no. 6298 (2016): 446-47.

Cruden, Robert William, Luise Hermanutz, and Jane Shuttleworth. "Pollination Biology and Breeding System of *M. fistulosa*." *Oecologica Berlin* 64 (1984): 104-10.

Culpeper, Nicolas. *Culpeper's Complete Herbal*, 1653. Reprint, London: Arcturus, 2018.

Curtin, L. S. M. "Some Plants Used by the Yuki Indians II: Food Plants." *Masterkey* 31 (1957): 85-91.

——. *Healing Herbs of the Upper Rio Grande*. Los Angeles: Southwest Museum, 1965.

——. *By the Prophet of the Earth*, 1949. Reprint, Tucson: University of Arizona Press, 1984.

Dabur, R., H. Singh, A. K. Chhillar, M. Ali, and G. L. Sharma. "Antifungal Potential of Indian Medicinal Plants." *Fitoterapia* 75, no. 3-4 (2004): 389-91.

Dalton, Patrick Jr. "Ecology of the Creosotebush *Larrea tridentata*." PhD dissertation, University of Arizona, Tucson, 1961.

Dangwal, L. R., Antima Sharma, and C. S. Rana. "Ethno-medicinal Plants of the Garhwal Himalaya Used to Cure Various Diseases: A Case Study." *New York Science Journal* 3, no. 12 (2010): 28-31.

Daniels, A. L., S. Van Slambrouck, R. K. Lee, T. S. Arguello, J. Browning, M. J. Pullin, A. Kornienko, and W. F. A. Steelant. "Effects of Extracts from Two Native American Plants on Proliferation of Human Breast and Colon Cancer Cell Lines In Vitro." *Oncology Reports* 15, no. 5 (June 2006): 1327-31.

Darwish, R. M., and T. A. Aburjai. "Effect of Ethnomedicinal Plants Used in Folklore Medicine in Jordan as Antibiotic Resistant Inhibitors on *Escherichia coli.*" *BMC Complementary and Alternative Medicine* 10 (2010): 9.

Dastagir, Ghulam, and Muhammad Afzal Rizvi. "*Glycyrrhiza glabra* L. (Liquorice)." *Pakistan Journal of Pharmaceutical Science* 29, no. 5 (September 2016): 1727-33.

de Barros, Mariel, Luisa Mota da Silva, Thaise Boeing, Lincon Bordignon Somensi, Benhur Judah Cury, Ligia de Moura Burci, José Roberto Santin, Sérgio Faloni de Andrade, Franco Delle Monache, and Valdir Cechinel-Filho. "Pharmacological Reports about Gastroprotective Effects of Methanolic Extract from Leaves of *Solidago chilensis* (Brazilian arnica) and Its Components Quercitrin and Afzelin in Rodents." *Naunyn-Schmiedeberg's Archives of Pharmacology* 389, no. 4 (April 2016): 403-17.

De Feo, Vincenzo, Laura De Martino, Angelo Santoro, Arturo Leone, Cosimo Pizza, Silvia Franceschelli, and Maria Pascale. "Antiproliferative Effects of Tree of Heaven (*Ailanthus altissima* Swingle)." *Phytotherapy Research* 19 (2005): 226-30.

De Jesus, R. A. P., V. Cechinel-Filho, A. E. Oliviera, and V. Schlemper. "Analysis of the Antinociceptive Properties of Marrubiin Isolated from *Marrubium vulgare*." *Phytomedicine* 7, no. 2 (April 2000): 111-15.

De Martino, L., G. D'Arena, M. M. Minervini, S. Deaglio, N. Cascavilla, and V. De Feo. "*Verbena officinalis* Essential Oil and Its Component Citral as Apoptotic-Inducing Agent in Chronic Lymphocytic Leukemia." *International Journal of Immunopathology and Pharmacology* 22, no. 4 (October 2009): 1097-1104.

De Marino, S., F. Cattaneo, C. Festa, F. Zollo, A. Iaccio, R. Ammendola, F. Incollingo, and M. Iorizzi. "Imbricatolic

Acid from *Juniperus communis* L. Prevents Cell Cycle Progression in CaLu-6 Cells." *Planta Medica* 77, no. 16 (November 2011): 1822–28.

Deciga-Campos, M., E. Gonzalez-Trujano, A. Navarrete, and R. Mata. "Antinociceptive Effect of Selected Mexican Traditional Medicinal Species." *Proceedings of the Western Pharmacology Society* 48 (2005): 70–72.

DeFelice, Michael S. "Catchweed Bedstraw or Cleavers, *Galium aparine* L.—A Very 'Sticky' Subject." *Weed Technology* 16 (2002): 467–72.

Del Carmen Juarez-Vazquez, Maria, Candy Carranza Alvarez, Angel Josabad Alsonso-Castro, Violeta F. Gonzalez-Alcaraz, Eliseo Bravo-Acedvedo, Felipe Jair Chamarro-Tinajero, and Eloy Solano. "Ethnobotany of Medicinal Plants Used in Xalpatlahuac, Guerrero, Mexico." *Journal of Ethnopharmacology* 148, no. 2 (May 2013): 521–27.

del Pilar Nicasio-Torres, María, Jade Serrano-Román, Juanita Pérez-Hernández, Enrique Jiménez-Ferrer, and Maribel Herrera-Ruiz. "Effect of Dichloromethane-Methanol Extract and Tomentin Obtained from *Sphaeralcea angustifolia* Cell Suspensions in a Model of Kaolin/Carrageenan-Induced Arthritis." *Planta Medica International Open* 4, no. 1 (2017): 35–42.

del Socorro Santos Díaz, María, Ana-Paulina Barba de la Rosa, Cécile Héliès-Toussaint, Françoise Guéraud, and Anne Nègre-Salvayre. "*Opuntia* spp.: Characterization and Benefits in Chronic Diseases." *Oxidative Medicine and Cellular Longevity* (2017). doi:10.1155/2017/8634249.

Del-Toro-Sánchez, C. L., F. Zurita, M. Gutiérrez-Lomelí, B. Solis-Sánchez, L. Wence-Chávez, A. Rodríguez-Sahagún, O. A. Castellanos-Hernández, G. Vázquez-Armenta, and F. Siller-López. "Modulation of Antioxidant Defense System after Long Term Arsenic Exposure in *Zantedeschia aethiopica* and

Anemopsis californica." *Ecotoxicology and Environmental Safety* 94 (August 2013): 67–72.

Demey, Andreas, Els Ameloot, Jeroen Staelens, An De Schrijver, Gorik Verstraeten, Pascal Boeckx, Martin Hermy, and Kris Verheyen. "Effects of Two Contrasting Hemiparisitic Plant Species on Biomass Production and Nitrogen Availability." *Oecologia* 173, no. 1 (2013): 293–303.

Densmore, Francis. "Chippewa Music-II." *Smithsonian Institution, Bureau of American Ethnology Bulletin*, no. 53 (1913).

———. "Teton Sioux Music." *Smithsonian Institution, Bureau of American Ethnology Bulletin*, no. 61 (1918).

———. "Uses of Plants by the Chippewa Indians." *Smithsonian Institution, Bureau of American Ethnology Annual Report* 44 (1928): 273–379.

———. "Menominee Music." *Smithsonian Institution, Bureau of American Ethnology Bulletin*, no. 102 (1932).

Derr, Chiska, Richard Helliwell, Andrea Ruchty, Lisa Hoover, Linda Geiser, David Lebo, and John Davis. "Survey Protocols for Survey and Manage Category A and C Lichens in the Northwest Forest Plan Area: Version 2.1." Portland, OR: USDA Forest Service and Bureau of Land Management, 2003. http://www.blm.gov/nhp/efoia/or/fy2003/im/im-or-2003-078Att1.pdf.

Desai, Shivani. "Anti-Acne Activity Possessed by the Extract of Opuntia Ficus-Indica." *Journal of Pharmaceutical Science and Bioscientific Research* 5, no. 6 (2015): 605–8.

Deters, A. M., U. Meyer, and F. C. Stintzing. "Time-Dependent Bioactivity of Preparations from Cactus Pear (*Opuntia ficus indica*) and Ice Plant (*Mesembryanthemum crystallinum*) on Human Skin Fibroblasts and Keratinocytes." *Journal of Ethnopharmacology* 142, no. 2 (2012): 438–44.

DeToma, A. S., J. S. Choi, J. J. Braymer,

and M. H. Lim. "Myricetin: A Naturally Occurring Regulator of Metal-Induced Amyloid-ß Aggregation and Neurotoxicity." *ChemBioChem* 12 (2011): 1198-1201.

DeVore, M. L., and K. B. Pigg. "A Brief Overview of the Fossil History of the Family Rosaceae with a Focus on the Eocene Okanogan Highlands of Eastern Washington State, USA, and British Columbia, Canada. *Plant Systematics and Evolution* 266, no. 1-2 (2007): 45-57.

Dhingra, Dinesh, Milind Parle, and S. K. Kulkarni. "Memory Enhancing Activity of *Glycyrrhiza glabra* in Mice." *Journal of Ethnopharmacology* 91 (2004): 361-65.

Di, M. M. V., and M. J. Fonseca. "Assays of Physical Stability and Antioxidant Activity of a Topical Formulation Added with Different Plant Extract." *Journal of Pharmaceutical and Biomedical Analysis* 37 (2005): 287-95.

Di Marco, Moreno, Tom D. Harwood, Andrew J. Hoskins, Chris Ware, Samantha L. L. Hill, and Simon Ferrier. "Projecting Impacts of Global Climate Change and Land-Use Scenarios on Plant Biodiversity Using Compositional-Turnover Modelling." *Global Change Biology* 25 no. 8 (August 2019): 2763-79.

Dib, H., M. Belarbi, M. C. Beghdad, and M. Seladji. "Antioxidant Activity of *Opuntia ficus-indica* Flowers Phenolic Extracts." *International Journal of Pharmaceutical Sciences and Research* 5, no. 10 (October 2014): 4574-82.

Dickman, Lee T., Nate G. McDowell, Sanna Sevanto, Robert E. Pangle, and William T. Pockman. "Carbohydrate Dynamics and Mortality in a Pinon-Juniper Woodland Under Three Future Precipitation Scenarios." *Plant, Cell, and Environment* 38, no. 4 (August 2014): 729-39.

Dick-Peddie, William A. *New Mexico Vegetation*. Albuquerque: University of New Mexico Press, 1993.

DiGiovanni, Jane P., William P. Wysocki, Sean V. Burke, Melvin R. Duvall, and Nicholas A. Barber. "The Role of Hemiparasitic Plants: Influencing Tallgrass Prairie Quality, Diversity and Structure." *Restoration Ecology* 25, no. 3 (2016): 405-13.

Dimitrova, Dimitrina Zheleva, and Vessela Balabanova. "Antioxidant and Acetylcholinesterase Inhibitory Potential of *Arnica montana* Cultivated in Bulgaria." *Turkish Journal of Biology* 36 (2012): 732-37.

DiTomaso, Joseph M. "Impact, Biology, and Ecology of Salt Cedar (*Tamarix*) in the Southwestern United States." *Weed Technology* 12, no. 2 (1998): 326-36.

DiTomaso, Thomas A. Monaco, Jeremy J. James, and Jennifer Firn. "Invasive Plant Species and Novel Rangeland Systems." In *Rangeland Systems*, edited by David D. Briske, pp. 429-66. New York: Springer, 2017.

Diwu, Z. "Novel Therapeutic and Diagnostic Applications of Hypocrellins and Hypericins." *Photochemistry and Photobiology* 61 (1995): 529-39.

Djeridane, A., M. Yousfi, B. Nadjemi, N. Vidal, J. F. Lesgards, and P. Stocker. "Screening of Some Algerian Medicinal Plants for the Phenolic Compounds and Their Antioxidant Activity." *European Food and Research Technology* 224, no. 6 (April 2007): 801-9.

Dobrescu, D., M. Tanasescu, A. Mezdrea, C. Ivan, E. Ordosch, F. Neagoe, A. Rizeanu, L. Trifu, and V. Enescu. "Contributions to the Complex Study of Some Lichens—*Usnea* Genus. Pharmacological Studies on *Usnea barbata* and *Usnea hirta* Species." *Romanian Journal of Physiology: Physiological Sciences* 30, no. 1-2 (January 1993): 101-7.

Dodson, Carolyn. *A Guide to Plants of the Northern Chihuahua Desert*. Albuquerque: University of New Mexico Press, 2012.

Dolati, K., H. Rakhshandeh, and M. N. Shafei. "Antidepressant-Like Effect of Aqueous Extract from *Rosa damascena* in Mice." *Avicenna Journal of Phytomedicine* 1 (2011): 91-97.

Domínguez, X. A., J. O. Velasquez, and D. Guerra. "Extractives from the Flowers of *Fouquieria splendens*." *Phytochemistry* 11 (1972): 2888.

Dudonne, Stephanie, Pascal Poupard, Philippe Coutiere, Marion Woillez, Tristan Richard, Jean-Michel Merillon, and Xavier Vitrac. "Phenolic Composition and Antioxidant Properties of Poplar Bud (*Populus nigra*) Extract: Individual Antioxidant Contribution of Phenolics and Transcriptional Effect on Skin Aging." *Journal of Agricultural and Food Chemistry* 59, no. 9 (2011): 4527–36.

Dulger, B., and E. Ugurlu. "Evaluation of Antimicrobial Activity of Some Endemic Scrophulariaceae Members from Turkey." *Pharmaceutical Biology* 43 no. 3 (2005): 275–79.

Dunbar, John. "The Pawnee Indians." *Magazine of American History* 5, no. 5 (1880): 321–42.

Dunmire, William W., and Gail D. Tierney. *Wild Plants of the Pueblo Province*. Santa Fe: Museum of New Mexico Press, 1995.

——. *Wild Plants and Native Peoples of the Four Corners*. Santa Fe: Museum of New Mexico Press, 1997.

Duraiswamy, B., Sagar Kumar Mishra, V. Subhashini, S. A. Dhanraj, and B. Suresh. "Studies on Antimicrobial Potential of *Mahonia leschenaultii* Takeda Root and Bark." *Indian Journal of Pharmaceutical Sciences* 68, no. 3 (2006): 389–91.

Ebrahimzadeh, M. A., S. F. Nabavi, S. M. Nabavi, and B. E. Slami. "Antioxidant and Free Radical Scavenging Activity of *H. officinalis* L. var. *angustifolius*, *V. odorata*, *B. hyrcana* and *C. speciosum*." *Pakistan Journal of Pharmaceutical Science* 23, no. 1 (2010): 29–34.

Eftekhar, F., M. Yousefzadi, and V. Tafakori. "Antimicrobial Activity of *Datura innoxia* and *Datura stramonium*." *Fitoterapia* 76, no. 1 (2005): 118–20.

Ehsanpour, S., K. Salehi, B. Zolfaghari, and S. Bakhtiari. "The Effects of Red Clover on Quality of Life in Post-Menopausal Women." *Iranian Journal of Nursing and Midwifery Research* 17, no. 1 (2012): 34–40.

Eiden, Martin, Fabienne Leidel, Barbara Strohmeier, Christine Fast, and Martin H. Groschup. "A Medicinal Herb *Scutellaria lateriflora* Inhibits PrP Replication In Vitro and Delays the Onset of Prion Disease in Mice." *Frontiers in Psychiatry* 3, no. 9 (2012).

Elakovish, Stella D., and Kenneth L. Stevens. "Phytotoxic Properties of Nordihydroguaiaretic Acid, a Lignan from *Larrea tridentata* (Creosote Bush)." *Journal of Chemical Ecology* 11, no. 1 (January 1985): 27–33.

Elberry, Ahmed, Fathalla M. Harraz, Salah A. Ghareib, Salah A. Gabr, Ayman A. Nagy, and Essam Abdel-Sattar. "Methanolic Extract of *Marrubium vulgare* Ameliorates Hyperglycemia and Dyslipidemia in Streptozotocin-induced Diabetic Rats." *International Journal of Diabetes Mellitus* 3, no. 1 (May 2015): 37–44.

Elgohary, A. A., M. W. Shafaa, B. M. Raafat, R. A. Rizk, F. G. Metwally, and A. M. Saleh. "Prophylactic Effect of *Angelica archangelica* against Acute Lead Toxicity in Albino Rabbits. *Romanian Journal of Biophysics* 19 (2009): 259–75.

Ellenberger, A. "Assuming Responsibility for a Protected Plant: WELEDA's Endeavour to Secure the Firm's Supply of *Arnica montana*." In *Medicinal Plant Trade in Europe: Conservation and Supply: Proceedings of the First International Symposium on the Conservation of Medicinal Plants in Trade in Europe*, edited by Traffic Europe, pp. 127–30. Kew: Royal Botanic Gardens, 1999.

Ellingwood, F. *The American Materia Medica, Therapeutics and Pharmacognosy*. Evanston, IL: Ellingwood's Therapeutist, 1919. http://www.swsbm.com/Ellingwoods/Ellingwoods.html.

Ellis, E. C., and N. Ramankutty. "Putting

People in the Map: Anthropogenic Biomes of the World." *Frontiers in Ecology and the Environment* 6 (2008): 439–47.

Ellis, Erle C., Erica C. Antill, and Holger Kreft. "All Is Not Loss: Plant Biodiversity in the Anthropocene." *PLOS One* 7, no. 1 (2012). doi:10.1371/journal.pone.0030535.

Elmastas, M., I. Gulcin, O. I. Beydemir, S. Kufrevioglu, and H. Y. Aboul-Enein. "A Study on the In Vitro Antioxidant Activity of Juniper (*Juniperus communis* L.) Fruit Extracts." *Analytical Letters* 39, no. 1 (2006): 47–65.

Elmore, Francis. *Ethnobotany of the Navajo*. Santa Fe: School of American Research, 1944.

El-Razek, Fatma H. Abd, Eman M, El-Metwally, Gaber M. G. Shehab, Amal A. Hassan, and Anhar M. Gomaa. "Effects of Cactus Pear (*Opuntia ficus indica*) Juice on Oxidative Stress in Diabetic Cataract Rats." *Saudi Journal for Health Sciences* 1, no. 1 (2012): 23–29.

Elton, Charles C. *The Ecology of Invasions by Plants and Animals*. London: Methuen, 1958.

Esfandiary, Ebrahim, Mohammad Karimipour, Mohammad Mardani, Mustafa Ghanadian, Hojjat Allah Alaei, Daryoush Mohammadnejad, and Abolghasem Esmaeili. "Neuroprotective Effects of *Rosa damascena* Extract on Learning and Memory in a Rat Model of Amyloid-β-Induced Alzheimer's Disease." *Advanced Biomedical Research* 4 (July 2015): 37.

Eskander, Jacqueline, Ola K. Sakka, Dominique Harakat, and Catherine Lavaud. "Steroidal Saponins from the Leaves of *Yucca de-smetiana* and Their In Vitro Antitumor Activity: Structure Activity Relationships through a Molecular Modeling Approach." *Medicinal Chemistry Research* 22, no. 10 (October 2013): 4877–85.

Esmaeili, Arash Khorasani, Rosna Mat Taha, Ssadegh Mohajer, and Behrooz Banisalam. "Antioxidant Activity and Total Phenolic and Flavonoid Content of Various Solvent Extracts from In Vivo and In Vitro Grown *Trifolium pratense* L. (Red Clover). *BioMed Research International* (2015). doi:10.1155/2015/643285.

Evans, Alexander M. "Invasive Plants, Insects, and Diseases in the Forests of the Anthropocene." In *Forest Conservation and Management in the Anthropocene: Conference Proceedings*, edited by V. Alaric Sample and R. Patrick Bixler, pp. 145–60. Fort Collins, CO: Rocky Mountain Research Station, Forest Service, US Department of Agriculture, 2014.

Farahbakhsh S., S. Arbabian, F. Emami, B. R. Moghadam, H. Ghoshooni, A. Noroozzadeh, H. Sahraei, L. Golmanesh, C. Jalili, and H. Zrdooz. "Inhibition of Cyclooxygenase Type 1 and 2 Enzyme by Aqueous Extract of *Elaeagnus angustifolia* in Mice." *Basic and Clinical Neuroscience* 2 (2011): 31–37.

Farnia, V., M. Shirzadifar, and J. Shakeri. "*Rosa damascena* Oil Improves SSRI-Induced Sexual Dysfunction in Male Patients Suffering from Major Depressive Disorders: Results from a Double-Blind, Randomized, and Placebo-Controlled Clinical Trial." *Neuropsychiatric Disease and Treatment* 11 (2015): 625–35.

Farzaei, Mohammad Hosein, Roodabeh Bahramsoltani, Zahra Abbasabadi, and Roja Rahimi. "A Comprehensive Review on Phytochemical and Pharmacological Aspects of *Elaeagnus angustifolia* L." *Journal of Pharmacy and Pharmacology* 67 (2015): 1467–80.

Fatima, Atiya, Vivek K. Gupta, Suaib Luqman, Arvind S. Negi, J. K. Kumar, Karuna Shanker, Dharmendra Saikia, Suchita Srivastava, M. P. Darokar, and Suman P. S. Khanija. "Antifungal Activity of *Glycyrrhiza glabra* Extracts and Its Active Constituent Glabridin." *Phytotherapy Research* 23, no. 8 (August 2009): 1190–93.

Fearn, J. "*Anemopsis californica*." *Ellingwood's Therapeutist* 3 (1909): 210–11.

Fehmi, Odabasoglu, Ali Aslan, Ahmet Cakir, Halis Suleyman, Yalcin Karagoz, Mesut Halici, and Yasin Bayir. "Comparison of Antioxidant Activity and Phenolic Content of Three Lichen Species." *Phytotherapy Research* 18 (2004): 938–41.

Feily, A, and N. Abbasi. "The Inhibitory Effect of *Hypericum perforatum* Extract on Morphine Withdrawal Syndrome in Rat and Comparison with Clonidine." *Phytotherapy Research* 23, no. 11 (2009): 1549–52.

Felger, Richard S. "Mesquite in Indian Cultures of Southwestern North America." In *Mesquite: Its Biology in Two Desert Ecosystems*, edited by B. B. Simpson, 150–76. Stroudsburg, PA: Dowden, Hutchinson and Ross, 1977.

Felger, Richard, and Mary Beck Moser. *People of the Desert and Sea: Ethnobotany of the Seri Indians.* Tucson: University of Arizona Press, 1985.

Felter, H. W. *The Eclectic Materia Medica, Pharmacology and Therapeutics.* Cincinnati: John K. Scudder, 1922. http://www.swsbm.com/FelterMM/Felters.html.

Felter, H. W., and John Uri Lloyd. *Kings's American Dispensatory.* Cincinnati: Ohio Valley Company, 1898.

Fernald, M. L. "*Monarda Fistulosa* and Its Allies." *Rhodora* 3 (January 1901): 13–16.

——. "Segregation of *Monarda fistulosa*." *Rhodora* 46 (December 1944): 494–96.

Ferreres, Federico, Clara Grosso, Angel Gil-Izquierdo, Patricia Valentao, Carolina Azevedo, and Paula B. Andrade. "HPLC-DAD-ESI/MSn Analysis of Phenolic Compounds for Quality Control of *Grindelia robusta* Nutt. and Bioactivities." *Journal of Pharmaceutical and Biomedical Analysis* 94 (June 2014): 163–72.

Fewkes, J. Walter. "A Contribution to Ethnobotany." *American Anthropologist* 9 (1896): 14–21.

Feyzabadi, Zohre, Farhad Jafari, Seyed Hamid Kamali, Hassan Ashayeri, Shapour Badiee Aval, Mohammad Mahdi Esfahani, and Omid Sadeghpour. "Efficacy of *Viola odorata* in Treatment of Chronic Insomnia." *Iranian Red Crescent Medical Journal* 12, no. 12 (December 2014): e17511.

Fierascu, Irina, Camelia Ungureanu, Sorin Marius Avramescu, Carmen Cimpeanu, Mihaela Ioana Georgescu, Radu Claudiu Fierascu, Alina Ortan, Anca Nicoleta Sutan, Valentina Anuta, Anca Zanfirescu, et al. "Genoprotective, Antioxidant, Antifungal and Anti-inflammatory Evaluation of Hydroalcoholic Extract of Wild-Growing *Juniperus communis* L. (Cupressaceae) Native to Romanian Southern Sub-Carpathian Hills." *BMC Complementary and Alternative Medicine* 18, no. 3 (2018). doi:10.1186/s12906-017-2066-8.

Fleisher, Mark S. "The Ethnobotany of the Clallam Indians of Western Washington." *Northwest Anthropological Research Notes* 14, no. 2 (1980): 192–210.

Fleischner, Thomas L. "Ecological Costs of Livestock Grazing in Western North America." *Conservation Biology* 8, no. 3 (1994): 629–44.

Fosberg, F. R., and Lena Artz. "The Varieties of *Monarda fistulosa*." *Castanea* 18, no. 4 (December 1953): 128–30.

Foster, Steven. *Echinacea: Nature's Immune Enhancer.* Rochester, VT: Healing Arts Press, 1991.

——. "Adulteration of Skullcap with American Germander." *HerbalGram* 93 (2012): 34–41.

Fowler, Catherine S. *Willard Z. Park's Ethnographic Notes on the Northern Paiute of Western Nevada, 1933–1940.* Salt Lake City: University of Utah Press, 1989.

Fox, F. E., Z. Niu, A. Tobia, and A. H. Rook. "Photoactivated Hypericin Is an AntiProliferative Agent That Induces a High Rate of Apoptotic Death of Normal, Transformed, and Malignant T-Lymphocytes: Omplications for the Treatment of Cutaneous Lymphoproliferative and Inflammatory Disorders."

Journal of Investigative Dermatology 111, no. 2 (1998): 327–32.

Francis, Jack K. "*Ceanothus velutinus.*" In *Wildland Shrubs of the United States and Its Territories*, edited by Jack Francis, pp. 158–60. Fort Collins, CO: Forest Service, US Department of Agriculture, 2004.

Franklin, Janet, Joseph M. Serra-Diaz, Alexandra D. Syphard, and Helen M. Regan. "Global Change and Terrestrial Plant Community Dynamics." *Proceedings of the National Academy of Sciences of the United States of America* 113, no. 14 (2016): 3725–34.

Franternale, Daniele, Guido Flamini, and Donata Ricci. "Essential Oil Composition and Antimicrobial Activity of *Angelica archangelica* L. (Apiaceae)." *Journal of Medicinal Food* 17, no. 9 (September 2014): 1043–47.

Frati-Munari, A. C., B. E. Gordillo, P. Altamirano, and C. R. Ariza. "Hypoglycemic Effect of *Opuntia streptacantha* Lemaire in NIDDM." *Diabetes Care* 11, no. 1 (1988): 63–66.

Frey, Frank, and Ryan Meyers. "Antibacterial Activity of Traditional Medicinal Plants Used by Haudenosaunee Peoples of New York State." *BMC Complementary and Alternative Medicine* 10, no. 1 (2010): 64.

Friedman, Jonathan M., Gregor T. Auble, Patrick B. Shafroth, Michael F. Merigliano, Michael D. Freehling, and Eleanor R. Griffin. "Dominance of Non-Native Riparian Trees in Western USA." *Biological Invasions* 7, no. 4 (2005): 747–51.

Fujii, T., and M. Saito. "Inhibitory Effect of Quercetin Isolated from Rose Hip (*Rosa canina* L.) against Melanogenesis by Mouse Melanoma Cells." *Bioscience, Biotechnology, and Biochemistry* 73 (2009): 1989–93.

Fukai, Toshio, Kazue Satoh, Taro Nomura, and Hiroshi Sakagami. "Preliminary Evaluation of Antinephritis and Radical Scavenging Activities of Glabridin from *Glycyrrhiza glabra.*" *Filoterapia* 74, no. 7–8 (December 2003): 624–29.

Fukushi, Y., C. Yajima, and J. Mizutani. "Prelacinan-7-ol, a Novel Sesquiterpene from *Rudbeckia laciniata.*" *Tetrahedron Letters* 35 (1994): 8809–12.

Fukushi, Y., C. Yajima, J. Mizutani, and S. Tahara. "Tricyclic Sesquiterpenes from *Rudbeckia laciniata* in Honour of Professor G. H. Neil Towers' 75th Birthday." *Phytochemistry* 49 (1998): 593–600.

Galati, E. M., M. R. Mondello, D. Giufferida, G. Dugo, N. Miceli, S. Pergolizzi, and M. F. Taviano. "Chemical Characterization and Biological Effects of Sicilian *Opuntia ficus indica* (L.) Mill. Fruit Juice: Antioxidant and Antiulcerogenic Activity." *Journal of Agricriculture and Food Chemistry* 51 (2003): 4903–8.

Galle, K., B. Muller-Jakic, A. Proebstle, K., Jurcic, S. Bladt, and H. Wagner. "Analytical and Pharmacological Studies on *Mahonia aquifolium.*" *Phytomedicine* 1, no. 1 (June 1994): 59–62.

Gao, Meili, Yongfei Li, and Jianxiong Yang. "Protective Effect of *Pedicularis decora* Franch Root Extracts on Oxidative Stress and Hepatic Injury in Alloxan-Induced Diabetic Mice." *Journal of Medicinal Plants Research* 5, no. 24 (October 2011): 5848–56.

García-Rodríguez, Rosa, Germán Chamorro Cevallos, Georgina Siordia, María Adelina Jiménez-Arellanes, Marco Antonio Chávez-Soto, and Mariana Meckes-Fischer. "*Sphaeralcea angustifolia* (Cav.) G. Don Extract, a Potential Phytomedicine to Treat Chronic Inflammation." *Boletín Latinoamericano y del Caribe de Plantas Medicinales y Aromáticas* 11, no. 5 (2012) 468–77.

Gardner, J. L. "Vegetation of the Creosotebush Area of the Rio Grande Valley in New Mexico." *Ecological Monographs* 21 (October 1951): 379–403.

Garg, Akash, and Sanjeev K. Mittal. "Review on *Prosopis cineraria*: A Potential Herb of Thar Desert." *Drug Invention Today* 5, no. 1 (March 2013): 60–65.

Garoby-Salom, S., F. Guéraud, C. Camaré, A. P. de la Rosa, M. Rossignol, S. Santos Diaz Mdel, and A. Negre-Salvayre. "Dietary Cladode Powder from Wild Type and Domesticated Opuntia Species Reduces Atherogenesis in ApoE Knock-out Mice." *Journal of Physiology and Biochemistry* 72, no. 1 (2016): 59–70.

Garth, Thomas R. "Atsugewi Ethnography." *Anthropological Records* 14, no. 2 (1953): 140–41.

Gaylord, Maria, Thomas E. Kolb, William T. Pockman, Jennifer A. Plaut, Enrico A. Yepez, Alison K. Macalady, Robert E. Pangle, and Nate G. McDowell. "Drought Predisposes Pinon-Juniper Woodlands to Insect Attacks and Mortality." *New Phytologist* 198, no. 2 (April 2013): 567–78.

Geeta, R., and Waleed Gharaibeh. "Historical Evidence for a Pre-Columbian Presence of Datura in the Old World and Implications for a First Millennium Transfer from the New World." *Journal of Bioscience* 32 (2007): 1227–44.

Geier-Hayes, Kathleen. "Vegetation Response to Helicopter Logging and Broadcast Burning in Douglas-Fir Habitat Types at Silver Creek, Central Idaho." Ogden, UT: Intermountain Research Station, Forest Service, US Department of Agriculture, 1989.

Gemechu, Abdella, Mirutse Giday, Adane Worku, and Gobena Ameni. "In Vitro AntiMycobacterial Activity of Selected Medicinal Plants against *Mycobacterium tuberculosis* and *Mycobacterium bovis* Strains." *BMC Complementary and Alternative Medicine* 13 (2013): 291.

George, Cindy, Amanda Lochner, and Barbara Huisamen. "The Efficacy of *Prosopis glandulosa* as Antidibetic Treatment in Rat Models of Diabetes and Insulin Resistance." *Journal of Ethnopharmacology* 137, no. 1 (May 2011): 298–304.

George, W. H. "Yerba Mansa." *Eclectic Medicine Journal* 37 (1877): 238.

Gerlach, Samantha L., Ramesh Rathinakumar, Geetika Chakravarty, Ulf Goransson, William C. Wimley, Steven P. Darwin, and Debasis Mondal. "Anticancer and Chemosensitizing Abilities of Cycloviolacin O2 from *Viola odorata* and Psyle Cyclotides from *Psychotria leptothyrsa*." *Peptide Science: Special Issue on International Conference on Circular Proteins* 95, no. 5 (2010): 617–25.

Ghaly, N. S., S. A. Mina, and N. A. H. Younis. "In Vitro Cytotoxic Activity and Phytochemical Analysis of the Aerial Parts of *J. communis* L. Cultivated in Egypt." *Journal of Pharmaceutical Sciences and Research* 8, no. 2 (2016): 128–31.

Ghatak, Somsuvra B., and Shital J. Panchal. "Ferulic Acid: An Insight into Its Current Research and Future Prospects." *Trends in Food Science and Technology*, 2010. doi:10.1016/j.tifs.2010.11.004.

Ghazanfar, Khalid, Bashir A. Ganai, Seema Akbar, Khan Mubashir, Showkat Ahmad Dar, Mohammad Younis Dar, and Mudasir A. Tantry. "Antidiabetic Activity of *Artemisia amygdalina* Decne in Streptozotocin Induced Diabetic Rats." *BioMed Research International* (2014). doi:10.1155/2014/185676.

Gherase, F., M. D. Pavelescu, U. Stănescu, and E. Grigorescu. "Evaluarea Experimentalia Privind Activitatea Analgezica a unor Extracte Izolate din Specia *Achillea collina* J. Becker ex Reichenb." *Revista Medico-Chiruricala A Societatii de Medici si Naturalisti Din Iasi* 106 (2002): 801–5.

Gholamhoseinian, A., B. Shahouzehi, S. Joukar, and M. Iranpoor. "Effect of *Quercus infectoria* and *Rosa damascena* on Lipid Profile and Atherosclerotic Plaque Formation in Rabbit Model of Hyperlipidemia." *Pakistan Journal of Biological Sciences* 15 (2012): 27–33.

Gibbens, R. P., R. P. McNeely, K. M. Havstad, R. F. Beck, and B. Nolen. "Vegetation Changes in the Jornada Basin from 1858 to 1998." *Journal of Arid Environments* 61 (2005): 651–68.

Gieler, U., A. von der Weth, and M. Heger.

"*Mahonia aquifolium*: A New Type of Topical Treatment for Psoriasis." *Journal of Dermatological Treatment* 6, no. 1 (1995): 31–34.

Gifford, E. W. "The Cocopa." *University of California Publications in American Archaeology and Ethnology* 31 (1933): 263–70.

——. "Northeastern and Western Yavapai." *University of California Publications in American Archaeology and Ethnology* 34 (1936): 247–345.

——. "Ethnographic Notes on the Southwestern Pomo." *Anthropological Records* 25 (1967): 10–15.

Gill, Steven J. "Ethnobotany of the Makah and Ozette People, Olympic Peninsula, Washington (USA)." PhD dissertation, Washington State University, Pullman, 1983.

Gilmore, Melvin R. "Some Native Nebraska Plants with Their Uses by the Dakota." *Nebraska State Historical Society Collections* 17 (1913a): 358–70.

——. "A Study of the Ethnobotany of the Omaha Indians." *Nebraska State Historical Society Collections* 17 (1913b): 314–57.

——. *Some Chippewa Uses of Plants*. Ann Arbor: University of Michigan Press, 1933.

——. *Uses of Plants by the Indians of the Missouri River Region*, 1919. Reprint, Lincoln: University of Nebraska Press, 1991.

Giorgi, A., M. Bononi, F. Taateo, and M. Cocucci. "Yarrow (*Achillea millefolium* L.) Growth at Different Altitudes in Central Italian Alps: Biomass Yield, Oil Content and Quality." *Journal of Herbs, Spices, and Medicinal Plants* 11, no. 3 (2005): 47–58.

Giorgi, A., R. Bombelli, A. Luini, G. Speranza, M. Cosentino, S. Lecchini, and M. Cocucci. "Antioxidant and Cytoprotective Properties of Infusions from Leaves and Inflorescences of *Achillea collina* Becker ex Rchb." *Phytotherapy Research* 23 (2009): 540–45.

Gladstar, Rosemary. *Family Herbal*. North Adams, MA: Storey Book, 2001.

Glaser, Christine, Chuck Romaniello, and Karyn Moskowitz. *Costs and Consequences: The Real Price of Livestock Grazing on America's Public Lands*. Tucson: Center for Biological Diversity, 2015.

Glenn, Edward, and Pamela Nagler. "Comparative Ecophysiology of *Tamarix ramosissima* and Native Trees in Western US Riparian Zones." *Journal of Arid Environments* 61, no. 3 (2005): 419–46.

Godara, R., S. Parveen, R. Katoch, A. Yadav, M. Katoch, J. K. Khajuria, D. Kaur, A. Ganai, P. K. Verma, V. Khajuria, and N. K. Singh. "Acaricidal Activity of Ethanolic Extract of *Artemisia absinthium* against *Hyalomma anatolicum* Ticks." *Experimental and Applied Acarology* 65 (2015): 141–48.

Gollapudi, Sitaraghav R., Hanumaiah Telikepalli, Ali Keshavarz-Shokri, David Vander Velde, and Lester A. Mitscher. "Glepidotin C: A Minor Antimicrobial Bibenzyl from *Glycyrrhiza lepidota*." *Phytochemistry* 28, no. 12 (1989): 3356–57.

Gonzalez-Ponce, Herson Antonio, Maria Consolacion Martinez-Saldana, Ana Rosa Rincon-Sanchez, Maria Teresa Sumaya-Martinez, Manon Buist-Homan, Klaas Nico Faber, Han Moshage, and Fernando Jaramillo-Juarez. "Hepatoprotective Effect of *Opuntia robusta* and *Opuntia streptacantha* Fruits against Acetaminophen-Induced Acute Liver Damage." *Nutrients* 8, no. 10 (2016): 607.

Goodrich, Jennie, and Claudia Lawson. *Kashaya Pomo Plants*. Los Angeles: American Indian Studies Center, University of California, 1980.

Goodrich, Sherel, Lori Armstrong, and Robert Thompson. "Endemic and Endangered Plants of Pinyon-Juniper Communities." In *Proceedings: Ecology and Management of Pinyon-Juniper Communities within the Interior West*, compiled by Stephen B. Monsen and Richard Stevens, pp. 260–68. Fort

Collins, CO: Rocky Mountain Research Station, Forest Service, us Department of Agriculture, 1999.

Gordien, A. Y., A. I. Gray, S. G. Franzblau, and V. Seidel. "Antimycobacterial Terpenoids from *Juniperus communis* L. (Cuppressaceae)." *Journal of Ethnopharmacology* 126, no. 3 (December 2009): 500–505.

Goryacha, O. V., T. V. Ilyina, A. M. Kovalyova, and N. V. Kashpur. "Phytochemical Research of *Galium aparine* L. Lipophilic Complex and Study of Its Antibacterial Activity." *Pharma Innovation Journal* 3, no. 1 (2014): 7–10.

Graham, Robert. "*Monarda fistulosa.*" *Edinburgh New Philosophical Journal* (1829): 347.

Grant, V. "Behavior of Hawkmoths on Flowers of *Datura meteloides.*" *Botanical Gazette* 144, no. 2 (June 1983): 280–84.

Grieve, Maude. A *Modern Herbal*, 1931. Reprint, New York: Dover Publications, 1971.

Grinnell, George Bird. *The Cheyenne Indians: Their History and Way of Life*, Vol. 2. Lincoln: University of Nebraska Press, 1972.

Grochowski, Daniel M., Sengul Uysal, Abdurrahman Aktumsek, Sebastian Granica, Gokhan Zengin, Ramazan Ceylan, Marcello Locatelli, and Michal Tomczk. "In Vitro Enzyme Inhibitory Properties, Antioxidant Activities, and Phytochemical Profile of *Potentilla thuringiaca.*" *Phytochemistry Letters* 20 (June 2017): 365–72.

Grube, B., P.-W. Chong, K.-Z. Lau, and H.-D. Orzechowski. "A Natural Fiber Complex Reduces Body Weight in the Overweight and Obese: A Double-Blind, Randomized, Placebo Controlled Study." *Obesity* 21, no. 1 (2013): 58–64.

Guimarães, R., L. Barros, R. C. Calhelha, A. M. Carvalho, M. J. R. Queiroz, and I. C. Ferreira. "Bioactivity of Different Enriched Phenolic Extracts of Wild Fruits from Northeastern Portugal: A Comparative Study." *Plant Foods for Human Nutrition* 69 (2014): 37–42.

Güleray, Agar, Ali Aslan, Elif Kotan Sarioglu, Lokman Alpsoy, and Selcuk Ceker. "Protective Activity of the Methanol Extract of *Usnea longissima* against Oxidative Damage and Genotoxicity Caused by Afl Atoxin B1 In Vitro." *Turkish Journal of Medical Sciences* 41, no. 6 (2011): 1043–49.

Gulliver, Wayne, and Howard Donsky. "A Report on Three Recent Clinical Trials Using *Mahonia aquifolium* 10% Topical Cream and a Review of the Worldwide Clinical Experience with *Mahonia aquifolium* for the Treatment of Plaque Psoriasis." *American Journal of Therapeutics* 12, no. 5 (September–October 2005): 398–406.

Gunduz, Kazim. "Morphological and Phytochemical Properties of *Mahonia aquifoloium* from Turkey." *Pakistan Journal of Agricultural Sciences* 50, no. 3 (2013): 439–43.

Gunther, Edna. *Ethnobotany of Western Washington*. Rev. ed. Seattle: University of Washington Press, 1973.

Gupta, Vivek K., Atiya Fatima, Uzma Faridi, Arvind S. Negi, Karuna Shanker, J. K. Jumar, Neha Rahuja, Suaib Luqman, Brijesh S. Sisodia, Dharmendra Saikia, M. P. Darokar, and Suman P. S. Khanuja. "Antimicrobial Potential of *Glycyrrhiza glabra* Roots." *Journal of Ethnopharmacology* 116, no. 2 (March 2008): 377–80.

Gutzler, David. "Governor's Task Force Report on Climate Change." In *Beyond the Year of Water: Living within Our Water Limitations*, pp. 111–19. Santa Fe: Water Resources Institute, 2007.

——. "Observed and Projected Climate Change." Paper presented at the University of New Mexico Earth and Planetary Studies Intergovernmental Panel on Climate Change Assessment, Albuquerque, February 2013.

Gutzler, David S., and Tessia O. Robbins.

"Climate Variability and Projected Change in the Western United States: Regional Downscaling and Drought Statistics." *Climate Dynamics* 37, no. 5 (September 2011): 835–49.

Habibi, Emran, Milad Arab-Nozari, Pedram Elahi, Maryam Ghasemi, and Fatemeh Shaki. "Modulatory Effects of *Viola odorata* Flower and Leaf Extracts upon Oxidative Stress-Related Damage in an Experimental Model of Ethanol-Induced Hepatotoxicity." *Applied Physiology, Nutrition, and Metabolism* 44 (2019): 521–27.

Hahm, S. W., J. Park, and Y.-S. Son. "*Opuntia humifusa* Partitioned Extracts Inhibit the Growth of U87MG Human Glioblastoma Cells." *Plant Foods for Human Nutrition* 65, no. 3, (2010): 247–52.

Hajnická, Valéria, Daniela Košťálová, Danka Švecová, Ružena Sochorová, Norbert Fuchsberger, and Jaroslav Tóth. "Effect of Mahonia aquifolium Active Compounds on Interleukin-8 Production in the Human Monocytic Cell Line THP-1." *Planta Medica* 68, no. 3 (2002): 266–68.

Halici, M., F. Odabasoglu, H. Suleyman, A. Cakir, A. Aslan, and Y. Bayir. "Effects of Water Extract of *Usnea longissima* on Antioxidant Enzyme Activity and Mucosal Damage Caused by Indomethacin in Rats." *Phytomedicine* 12, no. 9 (September 2005): 656–62.

Hamel, Paul B., and Mary U. Chiltoskey. *Cherokee Plants and Their Uses: A 400 Year History*. Sylva, NC: Herald Publishing, 1975.

Hamidpour Rafie, Sohelia Hamidpour, Mohsen Hamidpour, Mina Shahlari, Mahnaz Sohraby, Nooshin Shahlari, and Roxanna Hamidpour. "Russian Olive (*Elaeagnus angustifolia* L.): From a Variety of Traditional Medicinal Applications to Its Novel Roles as Active Antioxidant, Anti-inflammatory, Anti-Mutagenic and Analgesic Agent." *Journal of Traditional and Complementary Medicine* 7 (2017): 24–29.

Han, Sung Hee, Kyungmi Park, Eun Young Kim, So Hyun Ahn, Hyun-Sun Lee, and Hyung Joo Suh. "Cactus (*Opuntia humifusa*) Water Extract Ameliorates Loperamide-Induced Constipation in Rats." *BMC Complementary and Alternative Medicine* 17 (2017): 49.

Han, Xuesheng, and Tory L. Parker. "Anti-inflammatory Activity of Juniper (*Juniperus communis*) Berry Essential Oil in Human Dermal Fibroblasts." *Cogent Medicine* 4, no. 1 (2017). doi:10.1080/2331205X.2017.1306200.

Haraguchi, H., H. Ishikawa, K. Mizutani, Y. Tamura, and T. Kinoshita. "Antioxidative and Superoxide Scavenging Activities of Retrochalcones in Glycyrrhiza inflata." *Bioorganic and Medicinal Chemistry* 6 (1998): 339–47.

Harbilas, Despina, Diane Vallerand, Antoine Brault, Ammar Saleem, John T. Arnason, Lina Musallam, and Pierre S. Haddad. "*Populus balsamifera* Extract and Its Active Component Salicortin Reduce Obesity and Attenuate Insulin Resistance in a Diet-Induced Obese Mouse Model." *Evidence-Based Complementary and Alternative Medicine*, (2013). doi:10.1155/2013/172537.

Harden, M. L., and R. Zolfaghari. "Nurtritive Composition of Green and Ripe Pods of Honey Mesquite (*Prosopis glandulosa*, Fabaceae)." *Economic Botany* 42 (1988): 522.

Harrison, Merry Lycett. *The Botanical Parts of the Patterson Bundle: A Report to the Utah Native Plant Society*. Salt Lake City: Utah Native Plant Society, 2000. https://www.unps.org/miscpdf/PattersonBundle.pdf.

Hart, Jeff. *Montana Native Plants and Early Peoples*. Helena: Montana Historical Society Press, 1992.

Hart, Jeffrey. "The Ethnobotany of the Northern Cheyenne Indians of Montana." *Journal of Ethnopharmacology* 4 (1981): 1–55.

Hashemi, M., Z. Gharaylou, M. R. Sepand, S. Hamedi, S. Raminfard,

M. Alimohamadi, N. Sherkatkhamene, L. Zarepour, and M. Hadjighassem. "Apoptosis Induced by *Viola odorata* Extract in Human Glioblastoma Multiforme." *Archives of Neuroscience* 6, no. 1 (2019). doi:10.5812/ans.81233.

Haskell, David George. *The Songs of Trees*. New York: Viking, 2017.

Hassan, Haider M., Zi-Hua Jiang, Christina Asmussen, Emma McDonald, and Wensheng Qin. "Antibacterial Activity of Northern Ontario Medicinal Plant Extracts." *Canadian Journal of Plant Science* 94, no. 2 (2014): 417–24.

Hatsuko Baggio, C., G. De Martini Okofuji, C. Setim Freitas, L. M. Brandão Torres, M. C. Andrade Marques, and S. Mesia-Vela. "Brazilian Medicinal Plants in Gastrointestinal Therapy." In *Botanical Medicine in Clinical Practice*, edited by R. R. Watson and V. R. Preedy, 46–51. Oxon, UK: CABI, 2008.

Hattori, Toshio, Shojiro Ikematsu, Atsushi Koito, Shuzo Matsushita, Yosuke Maeda, Masao Hada, Michio Fujimaki, and Kiyoshi Takatsuki. "Preliminary Evidence for Inhibitory Effect of Glycyrrhizin on HIV Replication in Patients with AIDS." *Antiviral Research* 11, no. 5–6 (1989): 255–261.

Hausen, B. M. "Der Hautarzt." *Zeitschrift fur Dermatologie, Venerologie, und Verwandte Gebiete* 31, no. 1 (January 1980): 10–17.

Haziri, A., F. Faiku, A. Mehmeti, S. Govori, S. Abazi, M. Daci, I. Haziri, A. Bytyqi-Damoni, and A. Mele. "Antimicrobial Properties of the Essential Oil of *Juniperus communis* (l.) Growing Wild in East Part of Kosova." *American Journal of Pharmacology and Toxiclogy* 8, no. 3 (2013): 128–33.

He, Jian-Ming, and Qing Mu. "The Medicinal Uses of the Genus Mahonia in Traditional Chinese Medicine: An Ethnopharmacological, Phytochemical and Pharmacological Review." *Journal of Ethnopharmacology* 175 (December 2015): 668–83.

He, Kai-jia, Liu Bu-ming, and Lu Wen-jie. "Chemical Constituents from *Mahonia duclouxiana* Gagnep. (I)." *West China Journal of Pharmaceutical Sciences* 2 (2008).

Head, Lesley, Brendon M. H. Larson, Richard Hobbs, Jennifer Atchison, Nick Gill, Christian Kull, and Haripriya Rangan. "Living with Invasive Plants in the Anthropocene: The Importance of Understanding Practice and Experience." *Conservation and Society* 13, no. 3 (2015): 311–18.

Hedberg, Andrew M., Victoria A. Borowicz, and Joseph E. Armstrong. "Interactions between a Hemiparasitic Plant, *Pedicularis canadensis* L. (Orobanchaceae), and Members of a Tallgrass Prairie Community." *Journal of the Torrey Botanical Society* 132, no. 3 (2005): 401–10.

Hedges, Ken. "Santa Ysabel Ethnobotany." *San Diego Museum of Man Ethnic Technology Notes*, no. 20 (1986).

Heisey, R. M. "Identification of an Allelopathic Compound from *Ailanthus altissima* (Simaroubaceae) and Characterization of Its Herbicidal Activity. *American Journal of Botany* 83, no. 2 (1996): 192–200.

Heller, Christine A. *Edible and Poisonous Plants of Alaska*. College, AK: Cooperative Agricultural Extension Service, 1953.

Hellson, John C. *Ethnobotany of the Blackfoot Indians*. Ottawa: National Museum of Canada, 1974.

Hemmati, A. A., A. Arzi, and M. Amin. "Effect of *Achillea millefolium* Extract in Wound Healing of Rabbit." *Journal of Natural Remedies* 2 (2002): 164–67.

Henciya, Santhaseelan, Pranha Seturaman, Arthur Rathinam James, Yi-Hong Tsai, Rahul Nikam, Yang-Chang Wu, Hans-Uwe Dahms, and Fang Rong Chang. "Biopharmaceutical Potentials of *Prosopis* spp. (Mimosaceae, Leguminosa)." *Journal of Food and Drug Analysis* 25, no. 1 (January 2017): 187–96.

Herrick, James W. *Iroquois Medical*

Botany. Syracuse: Syracuse University Press, 1995.

Hfaiedh, N., M. Salah Allagui, M. Hfaiedh, A. El Feki, L. Zourgui, and F. Croute. "Protective Effect of Cactus (*Opuntia ficus-indica*) Cladode Extract upon Nickel-Induced Toxicity in Rats." *Food and Chemical Toxicology* 46 (2008): 3759–63.

Hicke, Jeffrey A., and Melanie J. B. Zeppel. "Climate-Driven Tree Mortality: Insights from the Pinon Pine Die-Off in the United States." *New Phytologist* 200, no. 2 (October 2013): 301–3.

Hikono, Hirosho. "Recent Research on Oriental Medicinal Plants." In *Economic and Medicinal Plant Research*, edited by H. Hikino, H. Wagner, and N. R. Farnsworth, pp. 53–85. London: Academic Press, 1985.

Himejima, Masaki, Kenneth R. Hobson, Toshikazu Otsuka, David L. Wood, and Isao Kubo. "Antimicrobial Terpenes from Oleoresin of Ponderosa Pine Tree *Pinus ponderosa*: A Defense Mechanism against Microbial Invasion." *Journal of Chemical Ecology* 18, no. 10 (October 1992): 1809–18.

Hinton, Leanne. "Notes on La Huerta Diegueño Ethnobotany." *Journal of California Anthropology* 2 (1975): 214–22.

Hobbs, Christopher. *Usnea: The Herbal Antibiotic*. Capitola, CA: Botanica Press, 1986.

Hocking, George M. "From Pokeroot to Penicillin." *Rocky Mountain Druggist* (November 1949): 12, 38.

Hoferl, M., I. Stoilova, E. Schmidt, J. Wanner, L. Jirovetz, D. Trifonova, L. Krastev, and A. Krastanov. "Chemical Composition and Antioxidant Properties of Juniper Berry (*J. communis* L.) Essential Oil. Action of the Essential Oil on the Antioxidant Protection of Saccharomyces Cerevisiae Model Organism." *Antioxidants* 3, no. 1 (2014): 81–98.

Hoffmann, David. *Medical Herbalism*. Rochester, VT: Healing Arts Press, 2003.

Hoffman, W. J. "The Midewiwin or 'Grand Medicine Society' of the Ojibwa."

Smithsonian Institution, Bureau of American Ethnology Annual Report, no. 7 (1891).

Holden C. "Treating AIDS with Worts." *Science* 254 (1991): 522.

Holmes, E. M. "Medicinal Plants Used by the Cree Indians, Hudson's Bay Territory." *Pharmaceutical Journal and Transactions* 15 (1884): 302–4.

Homayoun M., M. Seghatoleslam, M. Pourzaki, R. Shafieian, M. Hosseini, and A. E. Bideskan. "Anticonvulsant and Neuroprotective Effects of *Rosa damascena* Hydro-Alcoholic Extract on Rat Hippocampus." *Avicenna Journal of Phytomedicine* 5 (2015): 260.

Hong, Qi, David E. Minter, Scott G. Franzblau, and Manfred G. Reinecke. "Anti-tuberculosis Compounds from Two Bolivian Medicinal Plants, *Senecio mathewsii* and *Usnea florida*." *Natural Product Communications* 3, no. 9 (September 2008): 1337–84.

Hongratanaworakit, T. "Relaxing Effect of Rose Oil on Humans." *Natural Product Communications* 4 (2009): 291–96.

Hoseinpour H., S. A. Peel, and H. Rakhshandeh. "Evaluation of *Rosa damascena* Mouthwash in the Treatment of Recurrent Aphthous Stomatitis: A Randomized, Double-Blinded, Placebo-Controlled Clinical Trial." *Quintessence International* 42 (2011): 483–91.

Hosseini M., R. M. Ghasemzadeh, H. Sadeghnia, and H. Rakhshandeh. "Effects of Different Extracts of *Rosa damascena* on Pentylenetetrazol-Induced Seizures in Mice." *Chinese Journal of Integrative Medicine* 9 (2011): 1118–24.

Hosseinzadeh H., M. Ramezani, and N. Namjo. "Muscle Relaxant Activity of *Elaeagnus angustifolia* L. Fruit Seeds in Mice." *Journal of Ethnopharmacology* 84 (2003): 275–78.

Hostanska K., J. Reichling, S. Bommer, M. Weber, and R. Saller. "Hyperforin a Constituent of St John's Wort (*Hypericum perforatum* L.) Extract Induces Apoptosis by Triggering Activation of

Caspases and with Hypericin Synergistically Exerts Cytotoxicity Towards Human Malignant Cell Lines." *European Journal of Pharmaceutics and Biopharmaceutics* 56, no. 1 (2003): 121-32.

Hradetzky, Dagmar, Eckhard Wollenweber, and James N. Roitman. "Flavonoids from the Leaf Resin of Snakeweed, *Gutierrezia sarothrae*." *Zeitschrift fur Naturforschung C* 42, no. 1-2 (February 1987): 73-76.

Hrdlicka, Ales. "Physiological and Medical Observations among the Indians of Southwestern United States and Northern Mexico." *Smithsonian Institution, Bureau of American Ethnology Bulletin* 34 (1908): 1-427.

Hu, S.-Y. "*Ailanthus*." *Arnoldia* 39, no. 2 (1979): 29-50.

Hu, Weicheng, Lei Wu, Qian Qiang, Lilian Ji, Xinfeng Wang, Haiqing Luo, Haifeng Wu, Yunyao Jiang, Gongcheng Wang, and Ting Shen. "The Dichloromethane Fraction from *Mahonia bealei* (Fot.) Carr. Leaves Exerts an Anti-inflammatory Effect Both In Vitro and In Vivo." *Journal of Ethnopharmacology* 188 (July 2016): 134-43.

Hu, Weicheng, Lingling Yu, and Myeong-Hyeon Wang. "Antioxidant and Antiproliferative Properties of Water Extract from *Mahonia bealei* (Fort.) Carr. Leaves." *Food and Chemical Toxicology* 49, no. 4 (April 2011): 799-806.

Huang, Y., Y. L. Hao, and X. Y. Mai. "Chemical Constituents from *Solidago canadensis* with Hypolipidemic Effects in HFD-fed Hamsters." *Journal of Asian Natural Products Research* 15, no. 4 (April 2013): 319-24.

Huang, Zhi-hong, Zhi-li Wang, Bao-lin Shi, Dong Wei, Jian-xin Chen, Su-li Wang, and Bao-jia Gao. "Simultaneous Determination of Salicylic Acid, Jasmonic Acid, Methyl Salicylate, and Methyl Jasmonate from *Ulmus pumila*." *International Journal of Analytical Chemistry* (2015). doi:10.1155/2015/698630.

Huckell, Lisa W., and Mollie S. Toll. "Wild Plant Use in the North American Southwest." In *People and Plants in Ancient Western North America*, edited by Paul E. Minnis, pp. 37-114. Washington, DC: Smithsonian Books, 2004.

Huisamen, B., C. George, S. Genade, and D. Dietrich. "Cardioprotective and Anti-Hypertensive Effects of *Prosopis glandulosa* in Rat Models of Pre-Diabetes." *Cardiovascular Journal of Africa* 24, no. 2 (2013): 10-6.

Humphrey, R. R., and L. A. Mehrhoff. "Vegetation Changes on a Southern Arizona Grassland Range." *Ecology* 39, no. 4 (1958): 720-26.

Humphrey, Robert R. "Fire in the Deserts and Desert Grassland of North America." In *Fire and Ecosystems*, edited by T. T. Kozlowski and C. E. Ahlgren, 365-400. New York: Academic Press, 1974.

Humphreys, Aelys M., Rafael Govaerts, Sarah Z. Ficinski, Eimear Nic Lughadha, and Maria S. Vorontsova. "Global Dataset Shows Geography and Life Form Predict Modern Plant Extinction and Rediscovery." *Nature Ecology and Evolution* 3 (June 2019): 1043-47.

Huntley, Brian. "How Plants Respond to Climate Change: Migration Rates, Individualism and the Consequences for Plant Communities." *Annals of Botany* 118, no. 7 (2016): 15-22.

Hwang, Jae-Kwan, Jae-Seok Shim, and Jae-Youn Chung. "Anticariogenic Activity of Some Tropical Medicinal Plants against *Streptococcus mutans*." *Filoterapia* 75, no. 6 (September 2004): 596-98.

Hyder, P. W., E. L. Fredrickson, R. E. Estell, M. R. Tellez, and R. P. Gibbens. "Distribution and Concentration of Total Phenolics, Condensed Tannins, and Nordihydroguaiaretic Acids in Creosotebush (*Larrea tridentata*)." *Biochemical Systematics and Ecology* 30, no. 10 (2002): 905-12.

Hypericum Depression Trial Study Group. "Effect of *Hypericum perforatum* (St. John's Wort) in Major Depressive Disorder. *JAMA* 287, no. 14 (2002): 1807-14.

Innocenti, Gabbriella, Elisabetta Vegeto, Stefano Dall'Acqua, Paolo Ciana, Michela Giorgetti, Elisabetta Agradi, A. Sozzi, Gelsomina Fico, and Franca Tome. "In Vitro Estrogenic Activity of *Achillea millefolium* L." *Phytomedicine* 14, no. 2–3 (2007): 147–52.

Irani, Mahboubeh, Marziyeh Sarmadi, Francoise Bernard, Gholam Hossein Ebrahimi Pour, and Hossein Shaker Bazarnov. "Leaves Antimicrobial Activity of *Glycyrrhiza glabra* L." *Iranian Journal of Pharmaceutical Research* 9, no. 4 (Autumn 2010): 425–28.

Irshad, M., H. U. Rehman, M. Shahid, S. Aziz, and T. Ghous. "Antioxidant, Antimicrobial and Phytotoxic Activities of Essential Oil of Angelica Glauca." *Asian Journal of Chemistry* 23 (2011): 1947–51.

Ishikawa, Masaya, and Lawrence V. Gusta. "Freezing and Heat Tolerance of *Opuntia* Cacti Native to the Canadian Prairie Provinces." *Canadian Journal of Botany* 74, no. 12 (1996): 1890–95.

Isidorov, Valery A., and Vera T. Vinogorova. "GC-MS Analysis of Compounds Extracted from Buds of *Populus balsamifera* and *Populus nigra*." *Zeitschrift fur Naturforschung C* 58, no. 5–6 (May 2003): 355–60.

Islam, M. Nurul, Frances Downey, and Carl K. Y. Ng. "Comparative Analysis of Bioactive Phytochemicals from *Scutellaria baicalensis*, *Scutellaria lateriflora*, *Scutellaria racemosa*, *Scutellaria tomentosa* and *Scutellaria wrightii* by LC-DAD-MS." *Metabolomics* 7, no. 3 (September 2011): 446–53.

Ismail, Owais M., Ahsana Dar, Shaeen Faizi, and Lubna Abidi. "Antidepressant Like Actions of *Opuntia dillenii* Butanol Fraction in Rodents." *Pakistan Journal of Pharmacology* 27, no. 2 (July 2010): 9–14.

Ito, Masahiko, Akihiko Sato, Kazuhiro Hirabayashi, Fuminori Tanabe, Shiro Shigeta, Masanori Baba, Erik De Clercq, Hideki Nakashima, and Naoki Yamamoto. "Mechanism of Inhibitory Effect of Glycyrrhizin on Replication of Human Immunodeficiency Virus (HIV)." *Antiviral Research* 10 (1988): 289–98.

Izuegbuna, Ogochukwu, Gloria Otunola, and Graeme Bradley. "Chemical Composition, Antioxidant, Anti-inflammatory, and Cytotoxic Activities of *Opuntia stricta* Cladodes." *PLOS One* 41, no. 1 (January 2019). doi:10.1371/journal.pone.0209682.

Jakupovic, J., Y. Jia, R. M. King, and F. Bohlmann. "Rudbeckiolid, ein dimeres Sesquiterpenlaction aus *Rudbeckia laciniata*." *Liebigs Annalen der Chemie* 8 (1986): 1474–77.

Janbaz, Khalid, Waseem Ullah, Fatima Saqib, Mamoona Khalid. "Pharmacological Basis for the Medicinal Use of *Viola odorata* in Diarrhea, Brochial Asthma and Hypertension." *Bangladesh Journal of Pharmacology* 4, no. 10 (October 2015): 836–43.

Janetski, Joel C. "Role of Pinyon-Juniper Woodlands in Aboriginal Societies of the Desert West." In *Proceedings: Ecology and Management of Pinyon-Juniper Communities within the Interior West*, compiled by Stephen B. Monsen and Richard Stevens, pp. 249–53. Fort Collins, CO: Rocky Mountain Research Station, Forest Service, US Department of Agriculture, 1999.

Jahan, Y., and H. H. Siddique. "Study of Antitussive Potential of *Glycyrrhiza glabra* and *Adhatoda vasica* Using a Cough Model Induced by SO2 Gas in Mice." *International Journal of Pharmaceutical Sciences and Research* 3 (2012): 1668–74.

Jang, H. K., J. K. Kim, J. I. Nam, U.-K. So, C. H. Oh, and H. Jeon. "Antioxidant and Anti-inflammatory Effect of the Methanolic Extracts of *Potentilla chinensis*." *Oriental Pharmacy and Experimental Medicine* 11 (2011): 137–42.

Jendzelovska, Zuzana, Rastislav Jendzelovsky, Barbora Kucharova, and Peter Fedorocko. "Hypericin in the Light and in the Dark: Two Sides of the Same

Coin." *Frontiers in Plant Science* 7 (May 2016): 560–80.

Jensen, S. R., and B. J. Nielsen. "Iridoid Glucosides in Fouquieriaceae." *Phytochemistry* 21, no. 7 (1982): 1623–29.

Jeong, Miran, Hye Mi Kim, Ji-Hye Ahn, Kyung-Tae Lee, Dae Sik Jang, and Jung Hye-Choi. "9-Hydroxycanthin-6-one Isolated from Stem Bark of *Ailanthus altissima* Induces Ovarian Cancer Cell Apoptosis and Inhibits the Activation of Tumor-Associated Macrophages." *Chemico-Biological Interactions* 280 (2018): 99–108.

Jeong, Ye Eun, and Mi-Young Lee. "Anti-Inflammatory Activity of *Populus deltoides* Leaf Extract via Modulating NF-kB and p38/JNK Pathways." *International Journal of Molecular Sciences* 19, no. 12 (December 2018): 3746.

Jian, Li, Chen Li, Liu Shijun, and Dong JunXing. "Study on the Chemical Constiuents of *Galium aparine* L." *Journal of International Pharmaceutical Research* 37, no, 5 (2010): 387–89.

Jiang, Cheng, Hyo-Jeong Lee, Guang-xun Li, Junming Guo, Barbara Malewicz, Yan Zhao, Eun-Ok Lee, Hyo-Jung Lee, Jae-Ho Lee, Min-Seok Kim, et al. "Potent Antiandrogen and Androgen Receptor Activities of an *Angelica gigas*–Containing Herbal Formulation: Identification of Decursin as a Novel and Active Compound with Implications for Prevention and Treatment of Prostate Cancer." *Cancer Research* 66, no. 1 (January 2006): 453–63.

Jiang, Xiaoyan, Sara A. Rauscher, Todd D. Ringler, David M. Lawrence, A. Park Williams, Craig D. Allen, Allison L. Steiner, D. Michael Cai, and Nate G. McDowell. "Projected Future Changes in Western North America in the Twenty-First Century." *Climate* 26 (2013): 3671–87.

Jimenez, S., S. Gascon, A. Luquin, M. Laguna, C. Ancin-Azpilicueta, and M. J. Rodriguez-Yoldi. "*Rosa canina* Extracts Have Antiproliferative and Antioxidant Effects on Caco-2 Human Colon Cancer." *PLOS One* 11 (2016). doi.org/10.1371/journal.pone.0159136.

Jin, J. Q., C. Q. Li, and L. C. He. "Down-Regulatory Effect of Usnic Acid on Nuclear Factor-kappaB-Dependent Tumor Necrosis Factor-alpha and Inducible Nitric Oxide Synthase Expression in Lipopolysaccharide-Stimulated Macrophages RAW 264.7." *Phytotherapy Research* 22 (2008): 1605–9.

Jing, Lin. "Inhibatory Effects of Berberine on Growth of K562 Cell." *Journal of Fujian Medical College* 30, no. 4 (January 1996): 309–12.

Jo, E. H., S. H. Kim, J. C. Ra, S. R. Kim, S. D. Cho, J. W. Jung, S. R. Yang, J. S. Park, J. W. Hwang, O. I. Aruoma, et al. "Chemopreventive Properties of the Ethanol Extract of Chinese Licorice (*Glycyrrhiza uralensis*) Root: Induction of Apoptosis and G1 Cell Cycle Arrest in MCF-7 Human Breast Cancer Cells." *Cancer Letters* 230 (2005): 239–47.

Johnson, Holly A., Ling Ling L. Rogers, Mark L. Alkire, Thomas G. McCloud, and Jerry L. McLaughlin. "Bioactive Monoterpines from *Monarda fistulosa*." *Natural Product Letters* 11, no. 4 (1998): 241–50.

Johnston, Alex. *Plants and the Blackfoot*. Lethbridge, AB: Lethbridge Historical Society, 1987.

Jones, Anore. *Nauriat Niginaqtuat = Plants That We Eat*. Kotzebue, AK: Maniilaq Association Traditional Nutrition Program, 1983.

Jones, Volney. "The Ethnobotany of the Isleta Indians." Master's thesis, University of New Mexico, Albuquerque, 1931.

Juarez-Reyes, Krutzkaya, Guadalupe E. Angeles-Lopez, Isabel Rivero-Cruz, Robert Bye, and Rachel Mata. "Antinociceptive Activity of *Ligusticum porteri* Preparations and Compounds." *Pharmaceutical Biology* 52, no. 1 (2014): 14–20.

Kadam, S. D., S. A. Chavhan, S. A. Shinde, and P. N. Sapkal. "Pharmacognostic Review on Datura." *International Journal*

Pharmacognosy and Chinese Medicine 2, no. 4 (2018).

Kadri, A., Z. Zarai, A. Békir, N. Gharsallah, M. Damak, and R. Gdoura. "Chemical Composition and Antioxidant Activity of *Marrubium vulgare* L. Essential Oil from Tunisia." *African Journal of Biotechnology* 10, no. 9 (2011): 3908-14.

Kalaigandhi, V., and P. Poovendran. "Antimicrobial Activity of Glycyrrhiza glabra against Peptic Ulcer Produced *Helicobacter pylori*." *International Journal of Current Pharmaceutical Research* 3 (2011): 93-95.

Kalb R., M. Trautmann-Sponsel, and M. Kieser. "Efficacy and Tolerability of Hypericum Extract WS 5572 versus Placebo in Mildly to Moderately Depressed Patients." *Pharmacopsychiatry* 34 (2001): 96-103.

Kamei, J., R. Nakamura, H. Ichiki, and M. Kubo. "Antitussive Principles of *Glycyrrhiza radix*, a Main Component of Kampo Preparations Bakumondo-to." *European Journal of Pharmacology* 69 (2003): 159-63.

Kamijo, M., T. Kanazawa, M. Funaki, M. Nishizawa, and T. Yamagishi. "Effects of *Rosa rugosa* Petals on Intestinal Bacteria." *Bioscience, Biotechnology, and Biochemistry* 72 (2008): 773-77.

Kaminski, C. N., S. L. Ferrey, T. Lowrey, L. Guerra, S. Van Slambrouck, and W. F. A. Steelant. "In Vitro Anticancer Activity of *Anemopsis californica*." *Oncology Letters* 1, no. 4 (July 2010): 711-15.

Kamuhabwa, A. R., P. Agostinis, M. A. D'Hallewin, A. Kasran, and P. A. de Witte. "Photodynamic Activity of Hypericin in Human Urinary Bladder Carcinoma Cells." *Anticancer Research* 220 (2000): 2579-84.

Kane, Charles. *Medicinal Plants of the American Southwest*. Tucson: Lincoln Town Press, 2011.

——. *Wild Edible Plants of New Mexico*. Tucson: Lincoln Town Press, 2019.

Kapoor, R., V. Chaudhary, and A. K. Bhatnagar. "Effects of Arbuscular Mycorrhiza and Phosphorus Application on Artemisinin Concentration in *Artemisia annua* L." *Mycorrhiza* 17, no. 7 (October 2007): 581-87.

Karamenderes, C., and S. Apaydin. "Antispasmodic Effect of *Achillea nobilis* L. subsp. *sipylea* (O. Schwarz) Bässler on the Rat Isolated Duodenum." *Journal of Ethnopharmacology* 84 (2003): 175-79.

Kargozar, Rahele, Hoda Azizi, and Roshanak Salari. "A Review of Effective Herbal Medicines in Controlling Menopausal Symptoms." *Electronic Physician* 9, no. 11 (November 2017): 5826-33.

Kari, Priscilla Russe. *Upper Tanana Ethnobotany*. Anchorage: Alaska Historical Commission, 1985.

Karpiscak, M. M., L. R. Whiteaker, J. F. Artiola, and K. E. Foster. "Nutrient and Heavy Metal Uptake and Storage in Constructed Wetland Systems in Arizona." *Water Science Technology* 44, no. 11-12 (2001): 455-62.

Kathe, Wofgang. "Conservation of Easter-European Medicinal Plants: *Arnica montana* in Romania." *Medicinal and Aromatic Plants: Agricultural, Commercial, Ecological, Legal, Pharmacological and Social Aspects* 17 (2006): 203-11.

Katsunuma, Y., Y. Nakamura, A. Toyoda, and H. Minato. "Effect of *Yucca schidigera* Extract and Saponins on Growth of Bacteria Isolated from Animal Intestinal Tract." *Animal Science* 71 (2000): 64-170.

Katz, Gabrielle L., and Patrick B. Shafroth. "Biology, Ecology, and Management of *Elaeagnus angustifolia* L. (Russian Olive) in Western North America." *Wetlands* 23, no. 4 (2003): 763-77.

Kaufmann, Dorothea, Anudeep Kaur Dogra, Ahmad Tahrani, Florian Herrmann, and Michael Wink. "Extracts from Traditional Chinese Medicinal Plants Inhibit Acetylcholinesterase, a Known Alzheimer's Disease Target." *Molecules* 21, no. 9 (2016): 1161.

Kaur, Manpreet, Amandeep Kaur, and Ramica Sharma. "Pharmacological Actions of *Opuntia ficus indica*: A Review."

Journal of Applied Pharmaceutical Science 2, no. 7 (2012): 15–18.

Kaur, R., H. Kaur, and A. S. Dhindsa. "*Glycyrrhiza glabra*: A Phytopharmacological Review." *International Journal of Pharmaceutical Sciences and Research* 4, no. 7 (2013): 2470–77.

Kaurinovic, Biljana, Mira Popovic, Sanja Vlaisavljevic, Heidy Schwartsova, and Mirjana Vojinovic-Miloradov. "Antioxidant Profile of *Trifolium pratense* L." *Molecules* 17, no. 9 (2012): 11156–72.

Kavvadias, D., P. Sand, and K. A. Youdim. "The Flavone Hispidulin, a Benzodiazepine Receptor Ligand with Positive Allosteric Properties, Traverses the Blood-Brain Barrier and Exhibits Anticonvulsive Effects." *British Journal of Pharmacology* 142 (2004): 811–20.

Keefover-Ring, Kenneth Michael. "One Chemistry, Two Constituents: Function and Maintenance of Chemical Polymorphism in the Mint Family." PhD dissertation, University of Colorado, Boulder, 2008.

Keller, J., C. Camaré, C. Bernis, M. Astello-Garcia, A. P. de la Rosa, M. Rossignol, M. del Socorro Santos Diaz, R. Salvayre, A. Negre-Salvarye, and F. Gueraud. "Antiatherogenic and Antitumoral Properties of *Opuntia* Cladodes: Inhibition of Low Density Lipoprotein Oxidation by Cascular Cells, and Protection against the Cytotoxicity of Lipid Oxidation Product 4-Hydroxynonenal in a Colorectal Cancer Cellular Model." *Journal of Physiology and Biochemistry* 71, no. 3 (2015): 577–87.

Kelley, V. C., and A. M. Kudo. *Volcanoes and Related Basalts of Albuquerque Basin, New Mexico.* Socorro: New Mexico Bureau of Mines and Mineral Resources, 1978.

Kelly, Anne E., and Michael L. Goulden. "Rapid Shifts in Plant Distribution with Recent Climate Change." *Proceedings of the National Academy of Sciences of the United States of America* 105, no. 33 (2008): 11823–26.

Kelly, Isabel T. "Ethnobotany of the Surprise Valley Paiute." *University of California Publications in American Archaeology and Ethnology* 31, no. 3 (1932): 67–210.

Kemertelidze, E. P., M. M. Benidze, and A. V. Skhirtladze. "Steroid Compounds from *Yucca gloriosa* L. Introduced into Georgia and Their Applications." *Pharmaceutical Chemistry Journal* 43, no. 1 (January 2009): 45–47.

Kemertelidze, E. P., and T. A. Pkheidze. "Tigogenin from *Yucca gloriosa*, a Possible Raw Material for the Synthesis of Steroid Hormonal Preparations." *Pharmaceutical Chemistry Journal* 6, no. 12 (December 1972): 795–97.

Keon, D. B. "Fertile *Usnea longissima* in the Oregon Coast Range." *Lichenologist* 34 (2002): 13–17.

Kerns, B., and Q. Guo. *Climate Change and Invasive Plants in Forests and Rangelands.* Washington, DC: Forest Service, US Department of Agriculture, 2012.

Khalid, Hussain Janbaz, Sajjad Haider, Imran Imran, Muhammad Zia-Ul-Haq, Laura De Martino, and Vincenzo De Feo. "Pharmacological Evaluation of *Prosopis cineraria* (L.) Druce in Gastrointestinal, Respiratory, and Vascular Disorders." *Evidence-Based Complementary and Alternative Medicine* (2012). doi:10.1155/2012/735653.

Khalid, Muhammad, Danial Hassani, Muhammad Bilal, Zahid Ali Butt, Muhammad Hamayun, Ayaz Ahmad, Danfeng Huang, and Anwar Hussain. "Identification of Oral Cavity Biofilm Forming Bacteria and Determination of Their Growth Inhibition by *Acacia arabica*, *Tamarix aphylla* L. and *Melia azedarach* L. Medicinal Plants." *Archives of Oral Biology* 81 (2017): 175–85.

Khalili, H., S. A. Sadat Shandiz, and F. Baghbani-Arani. "Anticancer Properties of Phyto-Synthesized Silver Nanoparticles from Medicinal Plant *Artemisia tschernieviana* Besser Aerial Parts

Extract toward HT29 Human Colon Adenocarcinoma Cells." *Journal of Cluster Science* 28 (2017): 1617.

Khan, Abdul Waheed, Arif-ullah Khan, and Touqeer Ahmed. "Anticonvulsant, Anxiolytic, and Sedative Activities of *Verbena officinalis.*" *Frontiers in Pharmacology* 7 (December 2016): 499.

Khan, M. A., J. Shafiullah, S. A. Malik, and M. Shafi. "Hepatoprotective Effects of *Berberis lycium, Galium aparine* and *Pistacia integerrima* in Carbon Tetrachloride (CCl4) Treated Rats." *Journal of Post Graduate Medical Institute* 22, no. 2 (2008): 91–94.

Khan, Rosina, Mohammad Zakir, Sadul Afaq, Abdul Latif, and Asad Khan. "Activity of Solvent Extracts of *Prosopis spicigera, Zingiber officinale* and *Trachyspermum ammi* against Multidrug Resistant Bacterial and Fungal Strains." *Journal of Infection in Developing Countries* 4, no. 5 (2010): 292–300.

Khan, Z. S., and S. Nasreen. "Phytochemical Analysis, Antifungal Activity and Mode of Action of Methanol Extracts from Plants against Pathogens." *Journal of Agricultural Technology* 6, no. 4 (2010): 793–805.

Kharazmi, A., and K. Winther. "Rose Hip Inhibits Chemotaxis and Chemiluminescence of Human Peripheral Blood Neutrophils In Vitro and Reduces Certain Inflammatory Parameters In Vivo." *Inflammopharmacology* 7 (1999): 377–86.

Khatib, H., M. Rezaei-Taviran, and S. H. Keshel. "Flow Cytometry Analysis of *Rosa damascena* Effects on Gastric Cancer Cell Line (MKN45)." *Iran Journal of Cancer Prevention* 6 (2013): 30–36.

Khayyal, M. T., M. A. el-Ghazaly, S. A. Kenawy, M. Seif-el-Nasr, L. G. Mahran, Y. A. Kafafi, and S. N. Okpanyi. "Antiulcerogenic Effect of Some Gastrointestinally Acting Plant Extracts and Their Combination." *Arzneimittelforschung* 51 (2001): 545–53.

Khodaie, Laleh, Abbas Delazar, Farzane Lotfipour, Hossein Nazemiyeh, Solmaz

Asnaashari, Sedighe B. Moghadam, Lutfun Nahar, and Satyajit D. Sarker. "Phytochemistry and Bioactivity of *Pedicularis sibthorpii* Growing in Iran." *Revista Brasileira de Farmacognosia* 22, no. 6 (2012): 1268–75.

Khouloud, Aloui, Salma Abedelmalek, Hamdi Chtourou, and Nizar Souissi. "The Effect of *Opuntia ficus-indica* Juice Supplementation on Oxidative Stress, Cardiovascular Parameters, and Biochemical Markers following Yo-Yo Intermittent Recovery Test." *Food Science and Nutrition* 6, no. 2 (March 2018): 259–68.

Kim, J. M., D. H. Kim, S. J. Park, D. H. Park, S. Y. Jung, H. J. Kim, Y. S. Lee, C. Jin, and J. H. Ryu. "The N-butanolic Extract of *Opuntia ficus-indica* var. *saboten* Enhances Long-term Memory in the Passive Avoidance Task in Mice." *Progress in Neuro-Psychopharmacology Biological Psychiatry* 34 (2010): 1011–17.

Kim, J., S. Y. Soh, J. Shin, C.-W. Cho, Y. H. Choi, and S.-Y. Nam. "Bioactives in Cactus (*Opuntia ficus-indica*) Stems Possess Potent Antioxidant and Pro-apoptotic Activities through COX-2 Involvement." *Journal of the Science of Food and Agriculture* 95, no. 13 (2014): 2601–6.

Kim, Jae Kwang, Young Seon Kim, YeJi Kim, Md. Romij Uddin, Yeon Bok Kim, Haeng Hoon Kim, Soo Yun Park, Mi Young Lee, Sun Ok Chung, and Sang Un Park. "Comparative Analysis of Flavonoids and Polar Metabolites from Hairy Roots of *Scutellaria baicalensis* and *Scutellaria lateriflora.*" *World Journal of Microbiology and Biotechnology* 30, no. 3 (March 2014): 887–92.

Kim, Seung Hyun, Byung Ju Jeon, Dae Hyun Kim, Tae Il Kim, Hee Kyoung Lee, Dae Seob Han, Jong-Hwan Lee, Tae Bum Kim, Jung Wha Kim, and Sang Hyun Sung. "Prickly Pear Cactus (*Opuntia ficus indica* var. *saboten*) Protects against Stress-Induced Acute Gastric Lesions in Rats." *Journal of*

Medicinal Food 15, no. 11 (November 2012): 968–73.

Kimmerer, Robin. "Restoration and Reciprocity: The Contributions of Traditional Ecological Knowledge." In *Human Dimensions of Ecological Restoration*, edited by Dave Egan, Evan E. Hjerpe, and Jesse Abrams, pp. 257–76. Washington, DC: Island Press, 2011.

Kimmerer, Robin Wall. *Braiding Sweetgrass*. Minneapolis: Milkweed Editions, 2013.

Kindscher, Kelly. *Edible Wild Plants of the Prairie*. Lawrence: University Press of Kansas, 1987.

——. *Medicinal Wild Plants of the Prairie*. Lawrence: University Press of Kansas, 1992.

—— (ed). *Echinacea: Herbal Medicine with a Wild History*. Cham, Switzerland: Springer International, 2016.

Kindscher, Kelly, Leanne M. Martin, and Quinn Long. "The Sustainable Harvest of Wild Popultions of Oshá (*Ligusticum porteri*) in Southern Colorado for the Herbal Products Trade." *Economic Botany* (2019). doi:10.1007/s12231-019-09456-1.

Kindscher, Kelly, J. Yang, Q. Long, R. Craft, and H. Loring. *Harvest Sustainability Study of Wild Populations of Oshá, Ligusticum porteri*. Lawrence: Kansas Biological Survey, 2003.

Kissman, K., and D. Groth. "Plantas infestantes e nocivas (Weeds and Harmful Plants)." *Editora BASF* 2 (1999): 978.

Kleemann, Britta, Benjamin Loos, Thomas J. Scriba, Dirk Lang, and Lester M. Davids. "St. John's Wort (*Hypericum perforatum* L.) Photomedicine: Hypericin-Photodynamic Therapy Induces Metastatic Melanoma Cell Death." *PLOS One* (July 2014). doi:10.1371/journal.pone.0103762.

Klein, Frederick K., and Henry Rapoport. "Ceanothus Alkaloids. Americine." *Journal of the American Chemical Society* 90, no. 9 (April 1968): 2398–2404.

Kleitz, Kathryn M., Marisa M. Wall, Constance L. Falk, Charles A. Martin, Marta D. Remmenga, and Steven J. Guldan. "Yield Potential of Selected Medicinal Herbs Grown at Three Plant Spacings in New Mexico." *Horticultural Technology* 13, no. 4 (2003): 631–36.

——. "Stand Establishment and Yield of Organically Grown Seeded and Transplanted Medicinal Herbs." *Horticultural Technology* 18, no. 1 (January 2008): 116–21.

Klemow, Kenneth M., Andrew Bartlow, Justin Crawford, Neil Kocher, Jay Shah, and Michael Ritsick. "Medical Attributes of St. John's Wort (*Hypericum perforatum*)." In *Herbal Medicine: Biomolecular and Clinical Aspects*, 2nd ed., edited by I. F. F. Benzie and S. Wachtel-Galor, pp. 211–38. Boca Raton: CRC Press/Taylor and Francis, 2011.

Kliejunas, John T., Brian W. Geils, Jessie Micales Glaeser, Ellen Michaels Goheen, Paul Hennon, Mee-Sook Kim, Harry Kope, Jeff Stone, Rona Sturrock, and Susan J. Frankel. *Review of Literature on Climate Change and Forest Diseases of Western North America*. Washington, DC: United States Department of Agriculture, 2009.

Knuesel, Otto, Michel Weber, and Andy Suter. "*Arnica montana* Gel in Osteoarthritis of the Knee: An Open, Multicenter Clinical Trial." *Advances in Therapy* 19 (September 2002): 209.

Kolodziej, Barbara, Radoslaw Kowalski, and Bogdan Kedzia. "Antibacterial and Antimutagenic Activity of Extracts Aboveground Parts of Three Solidago Species: *Solidago virgaurea* L., *Solidago canadensis* L. and *Solidago gigantea* Ait." *Journal of Medicinal Plants Research* 5, no. 31 (December 2011): 6770–79.

Kolodziejczyk-Czepas, J., B. Wachowicz, B. Moniuszko-Szajwaj, I. Kowalska, W. Oleszek, and A. Stochmal. "Antioxidative Effects of Extracts from *Trifolium* Species on Blood Platelets Exposed to

Oxidative Stress." *Journal of Physiology and Biochemistry* 69 (2013): 879.

Konaté, K., K. Yomalan, and O. Sytar. "Free Radicals Scavenging Capacity, Antidiabetic and Antihypertensive Activities of Flavonoid-Rich Fractions from Leaves of *Trichilia emetica* and *Opilia amentacea* in an Animal Model of Type 2 Diabetes Mellitus." *Journal of Evidence-Based Complementary and Alternative* Medicine (2014): 13.

Konyalioglu, S., and C. Karamenderes. "The Protective Effects of *Achillea* L. Species Native in Turkey against H2O2-Induced Oxidative Damage in Human Erythrocytes and Leucocytes." *Journal of Ethnopharmacology* 102 (2005): 221-27.

Koochek, M. H., M. H. Pipelzadeh, and H. Mardani. "The Effectiveness of *Viola odorata* in the Prevention and Treatment of Formalin-Induced Lung Damage in the Rat." *Journal of Herbs, Spices and Medicinal Plants* 10, no. 2 (2003): 95-103.

Kooti, Wesam, Karo Servetyari, Masoud Behzadifar, Majid Asadi-Samani, Fatemeh Sadeghi, Bijan Nouri, and Hadi Zare Marzouni. "Effective Medicinal Plant in Cancer Treatment, Part 2." *Journal of Evidence-Based Integrative Medicine* 22, no. 4 (October 2017): 982-95.

Kou, Wei-Zheng, Jun Yang, Qing-Hui Yang, Ying Wang, Zhi-Fen Wang, Su-Ling Xu, and Jing Liu. "Study on In-Vivo Anti-Tumor Activity of *Verbena officinalis* Extract." *African Journal of Traditional, Complementary, and Alternative Medicines* 10, no. 3 (April 2013): 512-17.

Kowarik, I., and I. Saumel. "Biological Flora of Central Europe: *Ailanthus altissima* (Mill.) Swingle." *Perspectives in Plant Ecology, Evolution and Systematics* 8 (2007): 207-37.

Kraft, Shelly Katherene. "Recent Changes in the Ethnobotany of Standing Rock Reservation." Master's thesis, University of North Dakota, Grand Forks, 1990.

Krauze-Baranowska, Mirosława, Marek Mardarowicz, Marian Wiwart, Loretta Pobłocka, and Maria Dynowska. "Antifungal Activity of the Essential Oils from Some Species of the Genus *Pinus*." *Zeitshrift für Naturforschung C* 57, no. 5-6 (2002): 478-82.

Kristmundsdottir, T., H. A. Aradottir, K. Ingolfsdottir, and H. M. Ogmundsdottir. "Solubilization of the Lichen Metabolite Usnic Acid for Testing in Tissue Culture." *Journal of Pharmacy and Pharmacology* 54 (2002): 1447-52.

Krochmal, A., S. Paur, and P. Duisberg. "Useful Native Plants in the American Southwestern Deserts." *Economic Botany* 8, no. 1 (1954): 3-20.

Ksouri, Riadh, Hanen Falleh, Wided Megdiche, Najla Trabelsi, Baya Mhamdi, Kamel Chaieb, Amina Bakrouf, Christian Magne, and Chedly Abdelly. "Antioxidant and Antimicrobial Activities of the Edible Medicinal Halophyte *Tamarix gallica* L. and Related Polyphenolic Constituents." *Food and Chemical Toxicology* 47 (2009): 2083-91.

Kumari, Savita, Daizy R. Batish, H. P. Singh, Kirti Negi, and R. K. Kohli. "An Ethnobotany Survey of Medicinal Plants Used by Gujjar Coommunity of Trikuta Hills in Jammu and Kashmir, India." *Journal of Medicinal Plants Research* 7, no. 28 (July 2013): 2111-21.

Kundakovic, T., N. Mimica Dukic, and N. Kovacevic. "Free Radical Scavenging Activity of *Achillea alexandriregis* Extracts." *Fitoterapia* 76 (2005): 574-76.

Kurkin, V. A., V. B. Braslavskii, G. G. Zapesochnaya, and V. O. Tokachev. "Flavonoids of the Buds of *Pohpulus deltoides*." *Chemistry of Natural Compounds* 26 (1990): 466.

Lajnef, H. B., H. Mejri, A. Feriani, S. Khemiri, E. Saadaoui, N. Nasri, and N. Tlili. "*Prosopis farcta* Seeds: Potential Source of Protein and Unsaturated Fatty Acids?" *Journal of the American Oil Chemists Society* 92 (2015): 1043.

Lambert, Joshua, Shengmin Sang, Ann

Dougherty, Colby G. Caldwell, Ross O. Meyers, Robert T. Dorr, and Barbara N. Timmermann. "Cytotoxic Ligans from *Larrea tridentata*," *Phytochemistry* 66, no. 7 (April 2005): 811-15.

Lambert, Joshua D., Shengmin Sang, Ann Dougherty, Colby G. Caldwell, Ross O. Meyers, J. M. J. Favela-Hernandez, A. Garcia, E. Garza-Gonzalez, V. M. Rivas-Galindo, and M. R. Camacho-Corona. "Antibacterial and Antimycobacterial Ligans and Flavonoids from *Larrea tridentata*." *Phytotherapy Research* 26 (2012): 1957-60.

Lantto, T. A., I. Laakso, H. J. Dorman, T. Mauriala, R. Hiltunen, S. Kõks, and A. Raasmaja. "Cellular Stress and p53-Associated Apoptosis by *Juniperus communis* L. Berry Extract Treatment in the Human SH-SY5Y Neuroblastoma Cells." *International Journal of Molecular Science* 17, no. 7 (2016): 1113-33.

Laport, Robert G., Robert L. Minckley, and Justin Ramsey. "Phylogeny and Cytogeography of the North American Creosote Bush (*Larrea tridentate*, Zygophyllaceae)." *Systematic Botany* 37 (2012): 153-64.

Latif, M., L. Iqbal, and N. Fatima. "Evaluation of Antioxidant and Urease Inhibition Activity of Roots of *Glycyrrhiza glabra*." *Pakistan Journal of Pharmaceutical Sciences* 25 (2012): 99-102.

Lattanzio, F., E. Greco, D. Carretta, R. Cervellati, P. Govoni, and E. Speroni. "In Vivo Anti-Inflammatory Effect of *Rosa canina* L. Extract." *Journal of Ethnopharmacology* 137 (2011): 880-85.

Lauk, L., A. M. Lo Blue, I. Rapisarda, and G. Blandino. "Antibacterial Activity of Medicinal Plant Extracts against Periodontic Bacteria." *Phytotherapy Research* 17, no. 6 (June 2003): 599-604.

Lawrence, J. G., A. Colwell, and O. J. Sexton. "The Ecological Impact of Allelopathy in *Ailanthus altissima* (Simaroubaceae)." *American Journal of Botany* 78, no. 7 (1991): 948-58.

Laxinamujila, Bao Hy, and T. Bau.

"Advance in Studies on Chemical Constituents and Pharmacological Activity of Lichens in *Usnea* Genus." *China Journal of Chinese Materia Medica* 38, no. 4 (February 2013): 539-45.

Laverty, T. M. "Plant Interactions for Pollinator Visits: A Test of the Magnet Species Effect." *Oecologia* 89, no. 4 (1992): 502-8.

Le Roux, Johannes J., Cang Hui, Maria L. Castillo, Genevieve Theron, Florencia A. Yannelli, and Heidi Hirsch. "Recent Anthropogenic Plant Extinctions Differ in Biodiversity Hotspots and Coldspots." *Current Biology* 29 (2019): 2912-18.

Lee, C. K., K. K. Park, and S. S. Lim. "Effects of Licorice Extracts against Tumor Growth and Cisplatin Induced Toxicity in a Mouse Xenograft Model of Colon Cancer." *Biological Pharmaceutical Bulletin* 30 (2007): 2191-95.

Lee, Je-Hyuk, Eun Jeong Choi, Hee-Sook Park, and Gun Hee Kim. "Evaluation of *Compositae* sp. Plants for Antioxidant Activity, Antiinflammatory, Anticancer and Antiadipogenic Activity In Vitro." *Food and Agricultural Immunology* 25, no. 1 (2014): 104-18.

Lee, K. A., and M. S. Kim. "Antiplatelet and Antithrombotic Activities of Methanol Extract of *Usnea longissima*. *Phytotherapy Research* 19 (2005): 1061-64.

Lee, M. H., J. Y. Kim, J. H. Yoon, H. J. Lim, T. H. Kim, C. Jin, W. J. Kwak, C. K. Han, and J. H. Ryu. "Inhibition of Nitric Oxide Synthase Expression in Activated Microglia and Peroxynitrite Scavenging Activity by *Opuntia ficus indica* var. *saboten*." *Phytotherapy Research* 20 (2006): 742-47.

Lee, S. Y., Y. J. Shin, S. U. Choi, and K. R. Lee. "A New Flavonol Glycoside from the Aerial Part of *Rudbeckia laciniata*." *Archives of Pharmacal Research* 37, no. 7 (2014): 834.

Lee, S. Y., K. W. Woo, C. S. Kim, D. U. Lee, and K. R. Lee. "New Lignans from the Aerial Parts of *Rudbeckia laciniata*." *Helvetica Chimica Acta* 96 (2013): 320-25.

Lee, Y. H., M. G. Jung, H. B. Kang, K.-C. Choi, S. Haam, W. Jun, Y.-J. Kim, H. Y. Cho, and H.-G. Yoon. "Effect of AntiHistone Acetyltransferase Activity from *Rosa rugosa* Thunb. (Rosaceae) Extracts on Androgen Receptor-Mediated Transcriptional Regulation." *Journal of Ethnopharmacology* 118 (2008): 412–17.

Leighton, Anna I. *Wild Plant Use by the Woods Cree (Nihithawak) of East-Central Saskatchewan*. Ottawa: National Museums of Canada, 1985.

Lemmens-Gruber, R., E. Marchart, P. Rawnduzi, N. Engel, B. Benedek, and B. Kopp "Investigation of the Spasmolytic Activity of the Flavonoid Fraction of *Achillea millefolium* s.l. on Isolated Guinea Pig Ilea." *Arzneimittelforschung* 56 (2006): 582–88.

Leon, Alejandra, Ruben A. Toscano, Jaime Tortoriello, and Guillermo Delgado. "Phthalides and Other Constituents from *Ligusticum porteri*; Sedative and Spasmolytic Activities of Some Natural Products and Derivatives." *Natural Products Research* 25, no. 13 (2011): 1234–42.

Leopold, Aldo. *A Sand County Almanac*, 1949. Reprint, New York: Ballantine Books, 1970.

Leroi-Gourhan, Arlette. "The Flowers Found with Shanidar IV, a Neanderthal Burial in Iraq." *Science* 190, no. 4214 (October 1975): 562–64.

Li, Ai-Rong, F. Andrew Smith, Sally E. Smith, and Kai-Yun Guan. "Two Sympatric Root Hemiparasitic Pedicularis Species Differ in Host Dependency and Selectivity Under Phosphorus Limitation." *Functional Plant Biology* 39, no. 9 (2012): 784–94.

Li, J., Y. Hua, P. Ji, W. Yao, H. Zhao, L. Zhong, and Y. Wei. "Effects of Volatile Oils of *Angelica sinensis* on an Acute Inflammation Rat Model." *Pharmaceutical Biology* 54 (2016): 1881–90.

Li, Mao-Xing, Xi-Rui He, Rui Tao, and Xinyuan Cao. "Phytochemistry and Pharmacology of the Genus *Pedicularis* Used in Traditional Chinese Medicine." *American Journal of Chinese Medicine* 42 (2014): 1071.

Li, Xing-Cong, Linin Cai, and Christine D. Wu. "Antimicrobial Compounds from *Ceanothus americanus* against Oral Pathogens." *Phytochemistry* 46, no. 1 (September 1997): 97–102.

Lin, C. W., C. W. Yu, S. C. Wu, and K. H. Yih. "DPPH Free-Radical Scavenging Activity, Total Phenolic Contents and Chemical Composition Analysis of Forty-Two Kinds of Essential Oils." *Journal of Food and Drug Analysis* 17 (2009): 386–95.

Lin, L. T., L. T. Liu, L. C. Chang, and C. C. Lin. "In Vitro Antihepatoma Activity of Fifteen Natural Medicines from Canada." *Phytotherapy Research* 16 (2002): 440–44.

Lin, Y. C., C. M. Hung, and J. C. Tsai. "Hispidulin Potently Inhibits Human Glioblastoma Multiforme Cells through Activation of AMP-Activated Protein Kinase (AMPK). *Journal of Agricultural and Food Chemistry* 58 (2010): 9511–17.

Linde, K., M. Berner, and L. Kriston. "St. John's Wort for Major Depression." *Cochrane Database Systematic Review* 4 (2008). doi:10.1002/14651858.CD000448.pub3.

Linde, K. G., C. D. Ramirez, A. Mulrow, A. Pauls, W. Weidenhammer, and D. Melchart. "St. John's Wort for Depression." *BMJ* 313 (1996): 253–58.

Lipovac, Markus, Peter Chedraui, Christine Gruenhut, Anca Gocan, Christine Kurz, Benedikt Neuber, and Martin Imhof. "Effect of Red Clover Isoflavones Over Skin, Appendages, and Mucosal Status in Postmenopausal Women." *Obstetrics and Gynecology International* (2011). doi: 10.1155/2011/949302.

Liu, C. D., D. Kwan, R. E. Saxton, and D. W. McFadden. "Hypericin and Photodynamic Therapy Decreases Human Pancreatic Cancer In Vitro and Vivo."

Journal of Surgical Research 93 (2000): 137–43.

Liu, Juan, Yangrong Xu, Jingjing Yang, Wenzhi Wang, Jianqiang Zhang, Renmei Zhang, and Qingguo Meng. "Discovery, Semisynthesis, Biological Activities, and Metabolism of Ocotillol-Type Saponins." *Journal of Ginseng Research* 41, no. 3 (July 2017): 373–78.

Liu W., S.-Y. Li, X.-E. Huang, J.-J. Cui, T. Zhao, and H. Zhang. "Inhibition of Tumor Growth In Vitro by a Combination of Extracts from *Rosa roxburghii* Tratt and *Fagopyrum cymosum*." *Asian Pacific Journal of Cancer Prevention* 13 (2012): 2409–14.

Liu, Zhi, Sha Sha Chu, and Quan Ru Liu. "Chemical Composition and Insecticidal Activity against *Sitophilus zeamais* of the Essential Oils of *Artemisia capillaris* and *Artemisia mongolica*." *Molecules* 15, no. 4 (2010): 2600–8.

Lloyd, John Uri. "*Anemopsis californica* (Hooker), Yerba Mansa." *Pharmaceutical Journal and Transactions* 10 (1880): 666–67.

——. "History of the Vegetable Drugs of the Pharmacopeia of the United States." *Bulletin of the Lloyd Library of Botany, Pharmacy, and Materia Medica: Pharmacy Series* 4, no. 18 (1911).

Lodhi, Santram, Gautam Prakash Vadnere, Vimal Kant Sharma, and Md. Rageeb Usman. "*Marrubium vulgare* L.: A Review on Phytochemical and Pharmacological Aspects." *Journal of Intercultural Ethnopharmacology* 6, no. 4 (2017): 429–52.

Lohezic-Le Devehat, Francoise, Sophie Tomasi, John A. Elix, Aurelie Bernard, Isabele Rouaud, Philippe Uriac, and Joel Boustie. "Stictic Acid Derivatives from the Lichen *Usnea articulata* and Their Antioxidant Activities." *Journal of Natural Products* 70, no. 7 (2007): 1218–20.

Loik, Michael E., and Park S. Nobel. "Freezing Tolerance and Water Relations of *Opuntia fragilis* from Canada

and the United States." *Ecology* 74, no. 6 (1993): 1722–32.

López-Romero, P., E. Pichardo-Ontiveros, A. Avila-Nava, N. Vazquez-Manjarrez, A. R. Tovar, J. Pedraza-Chaverri, and N. Tores. "The Effect of Nopal (*Opuntia ficus indica*) on Postprandial Blood Glucose, Incretins, and Antioxidant Activity in Mexican Patients with Type 2 Diabetes after Consumption of Two Different Composition Breakfasts." *Journal of the Academy of Nutrition and Dietetics* 114, no. 11 (2014): 1811–18.

Loro, J. F., I. Rio, and L. Perez-Santana. "Preliminary Studies of Analgesic and Anti-inflammatory Properties of *Opuntia dillenii* Aqueous Extract." *Journal of Ethnopharmacology* 67 (1999): 213–18.

Lu Wen-jie, He Kai-jia, Ya Qi-kang, Chen Jia-yuan, Liu Bu-ming, Tan Xiao, and Su Xiao-chuan. "Analysis of Chemical Constituents of Petroleum Ether Fraction from *Mahonia duclouxiana* Gagnep." *Guangxi Sciences* 1 (2009).

Lucero, Mary E., Rick E. Estell, and Ed Fredrickson. "Composition of *Ceanothus gregii* Oil as Determined by Steam Distillation and Solid-Phase Microextraction." *Journal of Essential Oil Research* 22, no. 2 (2010): 140–42.

Lucero, Mary E., Ed L. Fredrickson, Rick E. Estell, Andrine A. Morrison, and David D. Richman. "Volatile Composition of *Gutierrezia sarothrae* (Broom Snakeweed) as Determined by Steam Distillation and Solid Phase Microextraction." *Journal of Essential Oil Research* 18, no. 2 (March 2006): 121–25.

Luper, S. "A Review of Plants Used in the Treatment of Liver Disease: Part Two." *Alternative Medicine Review* 4 (1999): 178–88.

Luszczki, J. J., E. Wojda, M. Andres-Mach, W. Cisowski, M. Glensk, K. Glowniak, and S. J. Czuczwar. "Anticonvulsant and Acute Neurotoxic Effects of Imperatorin, Osthole and Valproate in the Maximal Electroshock Seizure and Chimney Tests in Mice: A Comparative

Study." *Epilepsy Research* 85 (2009): 293-99.

Lyss, Guido, Thomas J. Schmidt, Irmgard Merfort, and Heike L. Pahl. "Helenalin, an Anti-Inflammatory Sesquiterpene Lactone from Arnica, Selectively Inhibits Transcription Factor NF-kappaB." *Biological Chemistry* 378, no. 9 (2009): 951-62.

Ma, L., C. M. Xie, J. Li, F. C. Lou, and L. H. Hu. "Daturametelins H, I, and J: Three New Withanolide Glycosides from *Datura metel* L." *Chemistry and Biodiversity* 3 (2006): 180-86.

Madamombe, I. T., and A. J. Afolaya. "Evaluation of Antimicrobial Activity of Extracts from South African *Usnea barbata*." *Pharmaceutical Biology* 41, no. 3 (2003): 199-202.

Maggi, F., M. Bramucci, C. Cecchini, M. M. Coman, A. Cresci, G. Cristalli, G. Lupidi, F. Papa, L. Quassinti, G. Sagratini, and S. Vittori. "Composition and Biological Activity of Essential Oil of *Achillea ligustica* All. (Asteraceae) Naturalized in Central Italy: Ideal Candidate for Anti-cariogenic Formulations." *Fitoterapia* 80 (2009): 313-19.

Mahady, G. B., S. L. Pendland, A. Stoia, F. A. Hamill, D. Fabricant, B. M. Dietz, and L. R. Chadwick. "In Vitro Susceptibility of *Helicobacter pylori* to Botanical Extracts Used Traditionally for the Treatment of Gastrointestinal Disorders." *Phytotherapy Research* 19 (2005): 988-91.

Mahall, Bruce E., and Ragan M. Callaway. "Root Communication among Desert Shrubs." *Proceedings of the National Academy of Science* 88 (February 1991): 874-76.

Mahar, James Michael. "Ethnobotany of the Oregon Paiutes of the Warm Springs Indian Reservation." Bachelor's thesis, Reed College, Portland, OR, 1953.

Mahboubi, Mohaddese. "*Rosa damascena* as Holy Ancient Herb with Novel Applications." *Journal of Traditional and Complementary Medicine* 6, no. 1 (October 2015): 10-16.

Makino, Y., S. Kondo, Y. Nishimura, Y. Tsukamoto, Z.-L. Huang, and Y. Urade. "Hastatoside and Verbenalin Are Sleep-Promoting Components in *Verbena officinalis*." *Sleep and Biological Rhythms* 7 (2009): 211.

Malla, Birendra, and R. B. Chhetri. "Indigenous Knowledge on Medicinal Non-Timber Forest Products (NTFP) in Parbat District of Nepal." *Indo Global Journal of Pharmaceutical Sciences* 2, no. 2 (2012): 213-25.

Malpezz-Marinho, Elena L. A., Graziela R. Molska, Lyvia I. G. P. Freire, Cristiane I. Silva, Eduardo K. Tamura, Lais F. Berro, Carlos A. Parada, and Eduardo Ary Villela Marinho. Effects of Hydroalcoholic Extract of *Solidago chilensis* Meyen on Nociception and Hypernociception in Rodents. *BMC Complementary and Alternative Medicine* 19, no. 72 (2019).

Manfredi, Kirk P., Vasanti Vallurupalli, Maria Demidova, Kelly Kindscher, and Lewis K. Pannell. "Isolation of an Anti-HIV Diprenylated Bibenzyl from *Glycyrrhiza lepidota*." *Phytochemistry* 58, no. 1 (September 2001): 153-57.

Mansouri, P., S. Mirafzal, P. Najafizadeh, Z. Safaei-Naraghi, M. H. Salehi-Surmaghi, and F. Hashemian. "The Impact of Topical Saint John's Wort (*Hypericum perforatum*) Treatment on Tissue Tumor Necrosis Factor-Alpha Levels in Plaque-Type Psoriasis: A Pilot Study." *Journal of Postgraduate Medicine* 63, no. 4 (2017): 215-20.

Manvi, G. "Screening and Evaluation of Pharmacognostic, Phytochemical and Hepatoprotective Activity of *J. communis* L. Stems." *International Journal of Pharma and Bio Sciences* 1, no. 3 (2010).

Mármol, Inés, Cristina Sánchez-de-Diego, Nerea Jiménez-Moreno, Carmen Ancín-Azpilicueta, and María Jesús Rodríguez-Yoldi. "Therapeutic Applications of Rose Hips from Different

Rosa Species." *International Journal of Molecular Sciences* 18, no. 6 (May 2017): 1137.

Martin, C. A., and R. Steiner. "Cultivation of *Anemopsis californica* Under Small-Scale Grower Conditions in Northern New Mexico." *New Mexico State University Research Report* 758 (August 2007).

Martins, Silvia, Elba L. C. Amorim, Tadeu J. S. Peixoto Sobrinho, Antonio M. Saraiva, Maria N. C. Pisciottano, Cristobal N. Aguilar, Jose A. Tiexeira, and Solange I. Mussatto. "Antibacterial Activity of Crude Methanolic Extract and Fractions Obtained from *Larrea tridentata* Leaves." *Industrial Crops and Products* 14 (January 2013): 306–11.

Marwat, Sarfaraz Khan, Mir Ajab Khan, Muhammad Aslam Khan, Fazal-ur-Rehman, Mushtaq Ahmad, Muhammad Zafa, and Shazia Sultana. "*Salvadora persica, Tamarix aphylla* and *Zizyphus mauritiana*—Three Woody Plant Species Mentioned in Holy Quran and Ahadith and Their Ethnobotanical Uses in the North Western Part (D. I. Khan) of Pakistan." *Pakistan Journal of Nutrition* 8, no. 5 (2009): 542–47.

Marzocco, S., S. Piacente, C. Pizza, W. Oleszek, A. Stochmal, A. Pinto, R. Sorrentino, and G. Autore. "Inhibition of Inducible Nitric Oxide Synthase Expression by Yuccaol C from *Yucca schidigera roezl.*" *Life Science* 75 (2004): 1491–1501.

Masoodi, M. H., B. Ahmed, I. M. Zargar, S. A. Khan, S. Khan, and P. Singh. "Antibacterial Activity of Whole Plant Extract of *Marrubium vulgare.*" *African Journal of Biotechnology* 72, no. 2 (2008): 86–87.

Masoomeh, M. J., and G. Kiarash. "In Vitro Susceptibility of *Helicobacter pylori* to Licorice Extract." *Iranian Journal of Pharmaceutical Research* 6 (2007): 69–72.

Maswadeh, H. M., M. H. Semreen, and A. R. Naddaf. "Anti-inflammatory Activity of *Achillea* and *Ruscus* Topical Gel on Carrageenaninduced Paw Edema in Rats." *Acta Poloniae Pharmaceutica* 63 (2006): 277–80.

Mata-Gonzalez, Ricardo, Benjamin Figueroa-Sandoval, Fernando Clemente, and Mario Manzano. "Vegetational Changes after Livestock Grazing Exclusion and Shrub Control in the Southern Chihuahuan Desert." *Western North American Naturalist* 67 (2007): 63–70.

Matowski, Adam, Patrycja Tasarz, and Emilia Szypuła. "Antioxidant Activity of Herb Extracts from Five Medicinal Plants from Lamiaceae, Subfamily Lamioideae." *Journal of Medicinal Plants Research* 2, no. 11 (November 2008): 321–30.

Maulidiyah, Herry, A. Cahyana, W. P. Suwarso, and M. Nurdin. "Isolation and Structure Elucidation of Eumitrin A1 from Lichen *Usnea blepharea motyka* and Its Cytotoxic Activity." *International Journal of Pharm Tech Research* 8, no. 4 (2015): 782–89.

Mauricio, I., B. Francischett, R. Q. Monterio, and J. A. Guimaraeas. "Identification of Glycyrrhizin as Thrombin Inhibitor." *Biochemical and Biophysical Research Communications* 235 (1997): 259–63.

Maurya, Santosh Kumar, Kanwal Raj, and Arvind Kumar Srivastava. "Antidyslipidaemic Activity of *Glycyrrhiza glabra* in High Fructose Diet Induced Dsyslipidaemic Syrian Golden Hamsters." *Indian Journal of Clinical Biochemistry* 24 (October 2009): 404.

Mayeux, H. S., and Laura Leotta. "Germination of Broom Snakeweed (*Gutierrezia sarothrae*) and Threadleaf Snakeweed (*G. microcephalum*) Seed." *Weed Science* 29, no. 5 (September 1981): 530–34.

McAuliffe, Joseph R. "Markovian Dynamics of Simple and Complex Desert Plant Communities." *American Naturalist* 131, no. 4 (1988): 459–90.

McClintock, Elizabeth, and Carl Epling, "Review of the Genus *Monarda*

(Labiatae)," *University of California Publications in Botany* 20, no. 2 (1942): 147–94.

McClintock, Walter. "Medizinal- and Nutzpflanzen der Schwarzfuss Indianer." *Zeitschrift für Ethnologie* 41 (1909): 273–79.

McCune, Bruce, and Linda Geiser. *Macrolichens of the Pacific Northwest*. Corvallis: Oregon State University Press, 1997.

McDonald, Jim. "Violet Herb." Herbs with Rosalee, 2010–2019. https://www.herbalremediesadvice.org/violet-herb.html.

McDowell, Nate G., Rosie A. Fisher, Chonggang Xu, J. C. Domec, Teemu Holtta, D. Scott MacKay, John S. Sperry, Amanda Boutz, Lee Dickman, Nathan Gehres, et al. "Evaluating Theories of Drought-Induced Vegetation Mortality Using a Multi-Modal-Experiment Framework." *New Phytologist* 200, no. 2 (October 2013): 304–21.

Mdee, L. K., P. Masoko, and J. N. Eloff. "The Activity of Extracts of Seven Common Invasive Plant Species on Fungal Phytopathogens." *South African Journal of Botany* 75, no. 2 (2009): 375–79.

Mechling, W. H. "The Malecite Indians with Notes on the Micmacs." *Anthrolopologica* 8 (1959): 239–63.

Meddens, Arjan J. H., Jeffrey A. Hickle, Alison K. Macalady, Polly C. Buotte, Travis R. Cowles, and Craig D. Allen. "Patterns and Causes of Observed Pinon Pine Mortality in the Southwestern United States." *New Phytologist* 206, no. 1 (April 2015): 91–97.

Medina, A. L., M. E. Lucero, O. F. Holguin, R. E. Estell, J. J. Posakony, J. Simon, and M. A. O'Connell. "Composition and Antimicrobial Activity of *Anemopsis californica* Leaf Oil." *Journal of Agricultural Food Chemistry* 53, no. 22 (December 2005): 8694–98.

Medina-Holguin, A. L., F. O. Holguin, S. Micheletto, S. Goehle, J. A. Simon, and M. A. O'Connell. "Chemotypic Variation of Essential Oils in the Medicinal Plant, *Anemopsis californica*." *Phytochemistry* 60, no. 4 (February 2008): 919–27.

Meehan, Thomas. "Notes on *Monarda fistulosa*." *Proceedings of the Academy of Natural Sciences Philadelphia* 44 (1892): 449–51.

Meeran, Mohamed Fizur Nagoor, and Ponnian Stanley Mainzen Prince. "Protective Effects of Thymol on Altered Plasma Lip Perioxidation and Nonenzymic Antioxidants in Isoproterenol-Induced Myocardial Infarcted Rats." *Journal of Biochemical and Molecular Toxicology* 26, no. 9 (2012): 368–73.

Menchaca, María del Carmen Vega, Catalina Rivas Morales, Julia Verde Star, Azucena Oranday Cárdenas, María Eufemia Rubio Morales, Maria Adriana Núñez González, and Luis Benjamin Serrano Gallardo. "Antimicrobial Activity of Five Plants from Northern Mexico on Medicinally Important Bacteria." *African Journal of Microbiology Research* 7, no. 43 (October 2013): 5011–17.

Mendes-Silva, W., M. Assafim, B. Ruta, R. Q. Monteiro, J. A. Guimaraes, and R. B. Zingali. "Antithrombotic Effect of Glycyrrhizin, a Plant-Derived Thrombin Inhibitor." *Thrombosis Research* 112 (2003): 93–98.

Mergen, F. "A Toxic Principle in the Leaves of Ailanthus." *Botanical Gazette* 121, no. 1 (1959): 32–36.

Merriam, C. Hart. *Ethnographic Notes on California Indian Tribes*. Berkeley: University of California Archaeological Research Facility, 1966.

Meruelo, D. "The Potential Use of Hypericin as Inactivator of Retroviruses and Other Viruses in Blood Products." *Blood* 82 (1993): 205A.

Miceli, N., A. Trovato, P. Dugo, F. Cacciola, P. Donato, A. Marino, V. Bellinghieri, T. M. La Barbera, A. Güvenç, and M. F. Taviano. "Comparative Analysis of Flavonoid Profile, Antioxidant and Antimicrobial Activity of the Berries of *Juniperus communis* L. var. *communis* and *Juniperus communis* L. var. *saxatilis* Pall. from Turkey." *Journal of Agricultural and Food Chemistry* 57, no. 15 (2009): 6570–77.

Michler, B., I. Rotar, F. Pacurar, and A. Stoie. "*Arnica montana* and Endangered Species and a Traditional Medicinal Plant: The Biodiversity and Productivity of Its Typical Grassland Habitats." *Grassland Science in Europe* 10 (August 2005): 336–39.

Minsung, Kim. "Regulatory Genes Control a Key Morphological and Ecological Trait." *Science* 322 (2008): 1116.

Mira, Amira, Wael Alkhiary, and Kuniyoshi Shimizu. "Antiplatelet and Anticoagulant Activities of Angelica Shikokiana Extract and Its Isolated Compounds." *Clinical and Applied Thrombosis/Hemostasis* (January 2017): 91–99.

Miri, A., M. Darroudi, R. Entezari, and M. Sarani. "Biosynthesis of Gold Nanoparticles Using *Prosopis farcta* Extract and Its In Vitro Toxicity on Colon Cancer Cells." *Research on Chemical Intermediates* 44 (2018): 3169.

Mirov, N. T., and P. M. Iloff Jr. "Composition of Gum Turpentines of Pines XXVIII: A Report on *Pinus edulis* from Eastern Arizona, *P. tropicalis* from Cuba, and *P. elliottii* var. *densa* from Florida." *Journal of the American Pharmaceutical Association* 45, no. 9 (September 1956): 629–34.

Mishenkova, E. L., N. A. Derbentseva, A. D. Garagulya, and L. N. Litvin. "Antiviral Properties of St. John's Wort and Preparations Produced from It." *Transactions of the Congress of Microbiologists of the Ukraine* 4 (1975): 222–322.

Mitra, S., R. Sundaram, and M. Venkataranganna. "Anti-Inflammatory, Antioxidant and Antimicrobial Activity of Ophthacare Brand, An Herbal Eye Drops." *Phytomedicine* 7 (2000): 123–27.

Mitscher, Lester A., G. S. Raghav Rao, Ish Khanna, Tarik Veysoglu, and Steven Drake. "Antimicrobial Agents from Higher Plants: Prenylated Flavonoids and Other Phenols from *Glycyrrhiza lepidota*." *Phytochemistry* 22, no. 2 (1983): 573–76.

Mittal, Payal, Vikas Gupta, Manish Goswami, Nishant Thakur, and Praveen Bansal. "Phytochemical and Pharmacological Potential of *Viola odorata*." *International Journal of Pharmacognosy* 2, no. 5 (2015): 215–20.

Mocan, A., G. Crisan, L. Vlase, and A. L. Arsene. "Phytochemical Investigations on Four *Galium* species (Rubiaceae) from Romania." *Farmacia* 64, no. 1 (2016): 95–99.

Modnicki, D., and J. Łabędzka, "Estimation of the Total Phenolic Compounds in Juniper Sprouts (*Juniperus communis*, Cupressaceae) from Different Places at the Kujawsko-Pomorskie Province." *Herba Polonica* 55, no. 3 (2009): 127–32.

Moerman, Daniel E. *Native American Ethnobotany*. Portland, OR: Timber Press, 1998.

Mohammadpour, T., M. Hosseini, and A. Naderi. "Protection against Brain Tissues Oxidative Damage as a Possible Mechanism for the Beneficial Effects of *Rosa damascena* Hydroalcoholic Extract on Scopolamine Induced Memory Impairment in Rats." *Nutritional Neuroscience* 18 (2014): 329–36.

Mohanasundari, M., and M. Sabesan. "Modulating Effect of *Hypericum perforatum* Extract on Astrocytes in MPTP Induced Parkinson's Disease in Mice." *European Review for Medical and Pharmacological Sciences* 11, no. 1 (2007): 17–20.

Mokbli, Sadok, Imededdine Arbi Nehdi, Hassen Mohamed Sbihi, Chin Ping Tan, Saud Ibrahim Al-Resayes, and Umer Rashid. "*Yucca aloifolia* Seed Oil: A New Source of Bioactive Compounds." *Waste and Biomass Valorization* 9, no. 7 (July 2018): 1087–93.

Molyneux, Russell J., Kenneth L. Stevens, and Lynn F. James. "Chemistry of Toxic Range Plants. Volatile Consititens of

Broomweed (*Gutierrezia sarothrae*)." *Journal of Agricultural and Food Chemistry* 28, no. 6 (1980): 1332–33.

Momeni T., and N. Shahrokhi. *Essential Oils and Their Therapeutic Actions.* Tehran: Tehran University Press, 1991.

Monira, Khaton, and Shaik, M Munan. "Review on Datura metel: A Potential Medicinal Plant." *Global Journal of Research on Medicinal Plants and Indigenous Medicine* 1, no. 4 (April 2012): 123–32.

Montgomery, Gerald L. "Riparian Areas Reservoirs of Diversity." Lincoln, NB: Natural Resources Conservation Service, US Department of Agriculture, 1996.

Montgomery, S. A., W. D. Hubner, and H. G. Grigoleit. "Efficacy and Tolerability of St. John's Wort Extract Compared to Placebo in Patients with Mild to Moderate Depressive Disorder." *Phytomedicine* 7, supplement 11 (2000): 7.

Mooney, Emily H., Andrew A. Martin, and Robert P. Blessin. "Effects of Light Environment on Recovery from Harvest and Antibacterial Properties of Oshá *Ligusticum porteri* (Apiaceae)." *Economic Botany* 69, no. 1 (March 2015): 72–82.

Mooney, H. A., B. B. Simpson, and O. T. Solbrig. "Phenology, Morphology, Physiology." In *Mesquite: Its Biology in Two Desert Ecosystems*, edited by B. B. Simpson, pp. 26–43. Stroudsburg, PA: Dowden, Hutchinson and Ross, 1977.

Mooney, H. A., and B. R. Strain. "Bark Photosynthesis in Ocotillo." *Madroño* 17, no. 7 (July 1964): 230–33.

Moore, Michael. *Medicinal Plants of the Desert and Canyon West*. Santa Fe: Museum of New Mexico Press, 1989.

——. *Los Remedios*. Santa Fe: Museum of New Mexico Press, 1990.

——. *Medicinal Plants of the Pacific Northwest*. Santa Fe: Museum of New Mexico Press, 1993.

——. *Medicinal Plants of the Mountain West*. Santa Fe: Museum of New Mexico Press, 2003.

Moradi, Mohammad-Taghi, Mahmoud Rafieian-Koupaei, Reza Imani-Rastabi, Jafar Nasiri, Mehrdad Shahrani, Zahra Rabiei, and Zahra Alibabaei. "Antispasmodic Effects of Yarrow (*Achillea millefolium* L.) Extract in the Isolated Ileum of Rat. *African Journal of Traditional, Complementary and Alternative Medicines* 10, no. 6 (2013): 499–503.

Morel, A. F., G. O. Dias, C. Porto, E. Simionatto, C. Z. Stuker, and I. I. Dalcol. "Antimicrobial Activity of Extractives of *Solidago microglossa*." *Fitoterapia* 77, no. 6 (2006): 453–55.

Morikawa, T., K. Imura, K., Y. Akagi, O. Muraoka, and K. Ninomiya. "Ellagic Acid Glycosides with Hepatoprotectice Activity from Traditional Tibetan Medicine *Potentilla anserina*." *Journal of Natural Medicines* 72 (2018): 317.

Moulton, Gary E., and Thomas C. Sorensen (eds). *The Journals of the Lewis and Clark Expedition*, Vol. 4. Lincoln: University of Nebraska Press, 1987.

Mousavi, Seyed Hadi, Behnaz Naghizade, Solmaz Pourgonabadi, and Ahmad Ghorbani. "Protective Effect of *Viola tricolor* and *Viola odorata* Extracts on Serum/Glucose Deprivation-Induced Neurotoxicity: Role of Reactive Oxygen Species." *Avicenna Journal of Phytomedicine* 6, no. 4 (2016): 434–41.

Mueller, Markus, Nyabuhanga Runyambo, Irmela Wagner, Steffen Borrmann, Klaus Dietz, and Lutz Heide. "Randomized Controlled Trial of a Traditional Preparation of *Artemisia annua* L. (Annal Wormwood) in the Treatment of Malaria." *Transactions of the Royal Society of Tropical Medicine and Hygiene* 98, no. 5 (May 2004): 318–21.

Muhammed, Naveed, Muhammad Saeed, and Haroon Khan. "Antipyretic, Analgesic, and Anti-inflammatory Activity of *Viola betonicifolia* Whole Plant." *BMC Complementary and Alternative Medicine* 12, no. 59 (2012). doi:10.1186/1472-6882-12-59.

Munk, J. A. "*Anemopsis californica*."

California Eclectic Medical Journal 2, no. 2 (1909): 27-29.

———. "*Larrea mexicana* and *Anemopsis californica.*" *California Eclectic Medicine Journal* 6 (1913): 110-11.

Murdoch, Iris. *The Sovereignty of Good*, 1970. Reprint, London: Routledge, 2014.

Murnigsih, T., H. Subeki, H. Matsuura, K. Takahashi, M. Yamasaki, O. Yamato, Y. Maede, K. Katakura, M. Suzuki, S. Kobayashi, A. Chairul, and T. Yoshihara. "Evaluation of the Inhibitory Activities of the Extracts of Indonesian Traditional Medicinal Plants against *Plasmodium falciparum* and *Babesia gibsoni.*" *Journal of Veterinary Medical Science* 67 (2005): 829-31.

Murphey, Edith Van Allen. *Indian Uses of Native Plants*, 1959. Reprint, Glenwood, IL: Meyerbrooks, 1990.

Murthy, B. K., S. Nammi, M. K. Kota, R. V. K. Rao, N. K. Rao, and A. Annapurna. "Evaluation of Hypoglycemic and Antihyperglycemic Effects of *Datura metel* (Linn.) Seeds in Normal and Alloxan-Induced Diabetic Rats." *Journal of Ethnopharmacology* 91 (2004): 95-98.

Myers, S. P., and V. Vigar. "Effects of Standardized Extract of *Trifolium pratense* (Promensil) at a Dosage of 80 mg in the Treatment of Menopausal Hot Flashes: A Systematic Review and Meta-Analysis." *Phytomedicine* 24 (January 2017): 141-47.

Myklestad, A., and M. Saetersdal. "The Importance of Traditional Meadow Management Techniques for Conservation of Vascular Plant Species Richness in Norway." *Biological Conservation* 118. no. 2 (2004): 133-39.

Nagai, T., T. Egashira, Y. Yamanaka, and M. Kohno. "The Protective Effect of Glycyrrhizin against Injury of the Liver Caused by Ischemia-reperfusion." *Archives of Environmental Contamination and Toxicology* 20 (1991): 432-36.

Nagatomo, A., N. Nishida, Y. Matsuura, and N. Shibata. "Rosehip Extract Inhibits Lipid Accumulation in White Adipose Tissue by Suppressing the Expression of Peroxisome Proliferator-Activated Receptor Gamma." *Preventive Nutrition and Food Science* 18 (2013): 85-91.

Naselli, F., L. Tesoriere, F. Caradonna, D. Bellavia, A. Attanzio, C. Gentile, and M. A. Livrea. "Anti-proliferative and Pro-apoptotic Activity of Whole Extract and Isolated Indicaxanthin from *Opuntia ficus-indica* Associated with Re-activation of the Onco-suppressor p16(INK4a) Gene in Human Colorectal Carcinoma (Caco-2) Cells." *Biochemical and Biophysical Research Communications* 450, no. 1 (2014): 652-58.

Nasin Takzare, Mir-Jamal Hosseini, Seyedeh Hamideh Mortazavi, Sahar Safaie, and Rayhaneh Moradi. "The Effect of *Achillea millefolium* Extract on Spermatogenesis of Male Wistar Rats." *Human and Experimental Toxicology* 30, no. 4 (2010): 328-34.

Nassiri-Asl, M., S. Saroukhani, and F. Zamansoltani. "Anticonvulsant Effects of Aqueous Extract of *Glycyrrhiza glabra* Root in PTZ-Induced Seizure in Mice." *International Journal of Pharmacology* 3 (207): 432-34.

Nazareno, Monica. "An Overview on the Medicinal Uses of Cactus Products." Paper presented at the Proceedings of International Cactus Pear Workshop, University of the Free State, Bloemfontein, South Africa, January 27-28, 2015.

Nazir, T., A. K. Uniyal, and N. P. Todaria. "Allelopathic Behaviour of Three Medicinal Plant Species on Traditional Agriculture Crops of Garhwal Himalaya, India." *Agroforestry Systems* 69 (2007): 183.

Neelam, S., and Z. U. Din Khan. "Antioxidant Activity of *Galium aparine* L. from Punjab, Pakistan." *Pakistan Journal of Botany* 44 (2012): 251-53.

Neto, M. A. F., D. J. Fagundes, M. E. Beletti, N. F. Novo, Y. Juliano, and N. Penha-Silva. "Systemic Use of *Solidago microglossa* DC in the Cicatrization of

Open Cutaneous Wounds in Rats." *Brazilian Journal of Morphological Sciences* 21 (2004): 204–10.

Newbold, Tim, Lawrence N. Hudson, Andrew P. Arnell, Sara Contu, Adriana De Palma, Simon Ferrier, Samantha L. L. Hill, Andrew J. Hoskins, Igor Lysenko, Helen R. P. Phillips, et al. "Has Land Use Pushed Terrestrial Biodiversity beyond the Planetary Boundary? A Global Assessment." *Science* 353, no. 6292 (2016): 288–91.

Nguyen, Khanh, Jean Sparks, and Felix O. Omoruyi. "Investigation of the Cytotoxicity, Antioxidative and Immune-Modulatory Effects of *Ligusticum porteri* (Osha) Root Extract on Human Peripheral Blood Lymphocytes." *Journal of Integrative Medicine* 14, no. 6 (November 2016): 465–72.

Nhat Hanh, Thich. *A Pebble for Your Pocket*. Berkeley, CA: Plum Blossom Books, 2001.

———. *Under the Rose Apple Tree.* Berkeley, CA: Parallax Press, 2002.

———. "Statement on Climate Change for the United Nations." Plum Village, 2015. https://plumvillage.org/letters-from -thay/thich-nhat-hanhs-statement-on -climate-change-for-unfccc.

Nickerson, Gifford S." Some Data on Plains and Great Basin Indian Uses of Certain Native Plants." *Tebiwa* 9, no. 1 (1966): 45–51.

Nikniaz, Z., A. Ostadrahimi, R. Mahdavi, A. A. Ebrahimi, and L. Nikniaz. "Effects of *Elaeagnus angustifolia* L. Supplementation on Serum Levels of Inflammatory Cytokines and Matrix Metalloproteinases in Females with Knee Osteoarthritis." *Complementary Therapies in Medicine* 22 (2014): 864–69.

Ninomiya, K., H. Matsuda, M. Kubo, T. Morikawa, N. Nishida, and M. Yoshikawa. "Potent Anti-Obese Principle from *Rosa canina*: Structural Requirements and Mode of Action of Trans-Tiliroside." *Bioorganic and Medicinal Chemistry Letters* 17 (2007): 3059–64.

Nishanth, Kumar Sasidharan, R. S. Sreerag, I. Deepa, C. Mohandas, and Bala Nambisan "Protocetraric Acid: An Excellent Broad Spectrum Compound from the Lichen *Usnea albopunctata* against Medically Important Microbes." *Natural Product Research* 29, no. 6 (2015): 574–77.

Nishanth, Kumar Sasidharan, Sreerag Ravikumar Sreekala, Rajesh Lakshmanan, Jubi Jacob, Dileep Kumar Bhaskaran Nair Saraswathy Amma, and Bala Nambisan. "Protolichesterinic Acid: A Prominent Broad Spectrum Antimicrobial Compound from the Lichen *Usnea albopunctata*." *International Journal of Antibiotics* 6 (2014). doi:10.1155/2014/302182.

Nitalikar, Manoj M., Lailas C. Munde, Balaji V. Dhore, and Sajid N. Shikalgar. "Studies of Antibacterial Activities of *Glycyrrhiza glabra* Root Extract." *International Journal of Pharm Tech Research* 2, no. 1 (January–March 2010): 899–901.

Noureddini M., and V. Rata. "Analgesic Effect of Aqueous Extract of *Achillea millefolium* on Rat's Formalin Test." *Pharmacologyonline* 3 (2008): 659–64.

Nowak, Slawomira, and Izabela Rychlinska. "Phenolic Acids in the Flowers and Leaves of *Grindelia robusta* Nutt. and *Grindelia squarrosa* Dun. (Asteraceae)." *Acta Poloniae Pharmaceutica Drug Research* 69, no. 4 (2012): 693–98.

Numazaki, K., M. Umetsu, and S. Chiba. "Effect of Glycyrrhizin in Children with Liver Dysfunction Associated with Cytomegalovirus Infection." *Tohoku Journal of Experimental Medicine* 172 (1994): 147–53.

Nutan, D. Mahadik, Mangesh V. Morey, Bhaskar C. Behera, Urmila V. Makhija, and Dattatraya G. Naik. "Cardiovascular-Protective, Antioxidative, and Antimicrobial Properties of Natural Thallus of Lichen *Usnea complanata*." *Latin American Journal of Pharmacy* 30, no. 2 (2011): 220–28.

Ohuchi, K., and A. Tsurufuji. "A Study of the Anti-inflammatory Mechanism of

Glycyrrhizin." *Mino Med Rev* 27 (1982): 188–93.

Okimasu, Eiji, Yasunori Moromizato, Sadahiro Watanabe, Junzo Sasaki, Nori-yuki Shiraishi, Yasuko M. Morimoto, Masanobu Miyahara, and Kozo Utsumi. "Inhibition of Phospholipase A2 and Platelet Aggregation by Glycyrrhizin, an Antiinflammation Drug." *Acta Medica Okayama* 37, no. 5 (1983): 385–91.

Okunde, Adewole L., Rachel E. Bikoff, Steven J. Casper, Anna Oksman, Daniel E. Goldberg, and Walter H. Lewis. "Antiplasmodial Activity of Extracts and Quassinoids Isolated from Seedlings of *Ailanthus altissima* (Simaroubaceae)." *Phytotherapy Research* 17 (2003): 675–77.

Okuyama, Emi, Kazuhiro Umeyama, Mikio Yamazaki, Yasuhiro Kinoshita, and Yoshikazu Yamamoto. "Usnic Acid and Diffractaic Acid as Analgesic and Antipyretic Components of *Usnea diffracta*." *Planta Medica* 61 (1995): 113–15.

Olas, B., B. Wachowicz, A. Stochmal, and W. Oleszek. "Anti-platelet Effects of Different Phenolic Compounds from *Yucca schidigera* Roezl. Bark." *Platelets* 13 (2002): 167–73.

——. "Inhibition of Blood Platelet Adhesion and Secretion by Different Phenolics from *Yucca schidigera* Roezl. Bark." *Nutrition* 21 (2005): 199–206.

Oleszek, W., M. Sitek, A. Stochmal, S. Piacente, C. Pizza, and P. Cheeke. "Resveratrol and Other Phenolics from the Bark of *Yucca schidigera* Roezl." *Journal of Agricultural and Food Chemistry* 49 (2001): 747–52.

Omidi, A., H. Ansari Nik, and M. Ghazaghi. "*Prosopos farcta* Beans Increase HDL Cholesterol and Decrease LDL Cholesterol in Ostriches (Struthio camelus)." *Tropical Animal Health and Production* 45 (2013): 431.

O'Neill, Paul M. "A Worthy Adversary for Malaria." *Nature* 430 (August 2004): 838–39.

Orhan, I. Erdogan, R. Belhattab, F. S.

Senol, A. R. Gulpinar, S. Hosbas, and M. Kartal. "Profiling of Cholinesterase Inhibitory and Antioxidant Activities of *Artemisia absinthum*, A. *herba-alba*, A. *fragrans*, *Marrubium vulgare*, M. *astranicum*, *Origanum vulgare* subsp. *gladulossum* and Essential Oil Analysis of Two *Artemisia* Species." *Industrial Crops and Products* 32, no. 3 (November 2010): 566–71.

Ohran, Syhan, Saliha Sahin, Pinar Sahinturk, Sule Ozturk, and Cevdet Demir. "Antioxidant and Antimicrobial Potential and HPLC Analysis of Stictic and Usnic Acids of Three *Usnea* Species from Uludag Mountain (Bursa, Turkey)." *Iranian Journal of Pharmaceutical Research* 15, no. 2 (Spring 2016): 527–35.

Orr, Ancel, and Rachel Parker. "Red Clover Causing Symptoms Suggestive of Methotrexate Toxicity in a Patient on High-Dose Methotrexate." *Post-Reproductive Health* 19, no. 3 (September 2013): 133–34.

Osorio-Esquivel, O., A. Ortiz-Moreno, L. Garduño-Siciliano, V. B. Alvarez, and M. D. Hernández-Navarro. "Antihyperlipidemic Effect of Methanolic Extract from *Opuntia joconostle* Seeds in Mice Fed a Hypercholesterolemic Diet." *Plant Foods for Human Nutrition* 67, no. 4 (2012): 365–70.

Osuna-Martínez, U., J. Reyes-Esparza, and L. Rodríguez-Fragoso. "Cactus (*Opuntia ficus-indica*): A Review on Its Antioxidants Properties and Potential Pharmacological Use in Chronic Diseases." *Natural Products Chemistry and Research* 2, no. 6 (2014): 153.

Oswalt, W. H. "A Western Eskimo Ethnobotany." *Anthropological Papers of the University of Alaska* 6 (1957): 17–36.

Ou, Shiyi, and Kin-Chor Kwok. "Ferulic Acid: Pharmaceutical Functions, Preparation and Applications in Foods." *Journal of the Science of Food and Agriculture* 84, no. 11 (2004). doi:10.1002/jsfa.1873.

Ozlem, B., M. Gulluce, F. Sahin, H. Ozer,

H. Kilic, H. Ozkan, M. Sokmen, and T. Ozbek. "Biological Activities of the Essential Oil and Methanol Extract of *Achillea biebersteinii* Afan. (Asteraceae)." *Turkish Journal of Biology* 30 (2006): 65–73.

Padilla-Camberos, Eduardo, Jose Miguel Flores-Fernandez, Ofelia Fernandez-Flores, Yanet Gutierrez-Mercado, Joel Carmona-de la Cruz, Fabiola Sandoval-Salas, Carlos Mendez-Carreto, and Kirk Allen. "Hypocholesterolemic Effect and In Vitro Pancreatic Lipase Inhibitory Activity of an *Opuntia ficus-indica* Extract." *BioMed Research International* (2015). doi:10.1155/2015/837452.

Pala, Nazir, A. K. Negi, and N. P. Todaria. "Traditional Uses of Medicinal Plants of Pauri Garhwal, Uttrakhand." *Nature and Science* 8, no. 6 (2010): 57–61.

Palani, S., S. Raja, R. Santhosh Kalash, and B. Senthil Kumar. "Evaluation of Nephroprotective and Antioxidant Activity of *Mahonia leschenaultia* Takeda on Acetaminophen-Induced Toxicity in Rat." *Toxicological and Environmental Chemistry* 92, no. 4 (2010b): 789–99.

Palani, S., S. Raja, R. Praveen Kumar, K. Sakthivel, K. Devi, and B. Senthil Kumar. "Phytoconstituents Evaluation and Antihyperglycemic and Antihyperlipidemic Effects of *Mahonia leschenaultia* Takeda in Streptozotocin-Induced Diabetic Rats." *Toxicological and Environmental Chemistry* 92, no. 6 (2010a): 1199–211.

Palmer, E. "Plants Used by the Indians of the United States." *American Journal of Pharmacy* 8 (1878): 586–92.

Palmer, Gary. "Shuswap Indian Ethnobotany." *Syesis* 8 (1975): 29–51.

Pan, Y., X. Wang, and X. Hu. Cytotoxic Withanolides from the Flowers of *Datura metel*." *Journal of Natural Products* 70 (2007): 1127–32.

Panahi, Yunes, Gholam Alishiri, Noushin Bayat, Seyed Morteza Hosseini, and Amirhossein Sahebkar. "Efficacy of *Elaeagnus angustifolia* Extract in the Treatment of Knee Osteoarthritis: A Randomized Contolled Trial." *EXCLI Journal* 15 (2016): 203–10.

Parajuli, Prahlad, Nirmal Joshee, Agnes M. Rimando, Sandeep Mittal, and Anand K. Yadav. "In Vitro Antitumor Mechanisms of Various Scutellaria Extracts and Constituent Flavonoids." *Planta Medica* 74, no. 1 (2009): 41–48.

Park, E. H., J. H. Kahng, S. H. Lee, and K. H. Shin. "An Anti-inflammatory Principle from Cactus." *Fitoterapia* 72 (2001): 288–90.

Park, S. H., Y. B. Sim, P. L. Han, J. K. Lee, and H. W. Suh. "Antidepressant-like Effect of Kaempferol and Quercitrin, Isolated from *Opuntia ficus-indica* var. *saboten*." *Experimental Neurobiology* 19 (2010): 30–38.

Parmesan, Camille, and Gary Yohe. "A Globally Coherent Fingerprint of Climate Change Impacts across Natural Systems." *Nature* 421 (2003): 37–42.

Partridge, M., and D. E. Poswillo. "Topical Carbenoxolone Sodium in the Management of Herpes Simplex Infection." *British Journal of Oral and Maxillofacial Surgery* 22 (1984): 138–45.

Parvaiz, Muhammad, Khalid Hussain, Saba Khalid, Nigam Hussnain, Nukhba Iram, Zubair Hussain, and Muhummad Azhar Ali. "A Review: Medicinal Importance of Glycyrrhiza glabra L. (Fabaceae Family)." *Global Journal of Pharmacology* 8, no. 1 (2014): 8–13.

Parveen, K. Vijula, K. V. Avinash, M. Ravishankar, and D. V. Leeladhar. "Medicinal Values of *Datura*: A Synoptic Review." *International Journal of Green Pharmacy* 10, no. 2 (April–June 2016): 77–81.

Patel, Kanika, and Dinesh Kumar Patel. "Medicinal Importance, Pharmacological Activities, and Analytical Aspects of Hispidulin: A Concise Report." *Journal of Traditional and Complementary Medicine* 7, no. 3 (December 2016): 360–66.

Patel, Paras S., Nirmal Joshee, Agnes M. Rimando, and Prahlad Parajuli. "Anti-cancer Scopes and Associated Mechanisms of *Scutellaria* Extract and Flavonoid Wogonin." *Current Cancer Therapy Reviews* 9 (2013): 34–42.

Pathak, S., R. K. Tewari, and A. O. Prakash. "Hormonal Properties of Ethanolic Extract of *Juniperus communis* Linn." *Ancient Science of Life* 10, no. 2 (1990): 106–13.

Pathak, S., M. M. Wanjari, S. K. Jain, and M. Tripathi. "Evaluation of Antiseizure Activity of Essential Oil from Roots of *Angelica archangelica* Linn. in Mice." *Indian Journal of Pharmaceutical Science* 72 (2010): 371–75.

Paton, Alan. "A Global Taxonomic Investigation of *Scutellaria*." *Kew Bulletin* 45, no. 3 (1990): 399–450.

Paun, Gabriela, Elena Neagu, Camelia Albu, and Gabriel Lucian Radu. "*Verbascum phlomoides* and *Solidago virgaureae* Herbs as Natural Source for Preventing Neurodegenerative Diseases." *Journal of Herbal Medicine* 6, no. 4 (December 2016): 180–86.

Pavithra G. M., K. S. Vinayaka, K. N. Rakesh, Syed Junaid, N. Dileep, T. R. Prashith Kekuda, Saba Siddiqua, and Abhishiktha S. Naik. "Antimicrobial and Antioxidant Activities of a Macrolichen *Usnea pictoides* G. Awasthi (Parmeliaceae)." *Journal of Applied Pharmaceutical Science* 3, no. 8 (August 2013): 154–60.

Pearce, Fred. *The New Wild*. Boston: Beacon Press, 2015.

Pepeljnjak, S., I. Kosalec, Z. Kalodera, and N. Blažević, "Antimicrobial Activity of Juniper Berry Essential Oil (*Juniperus communis* L., Cupressaceae)," *Acta Pharmaceutica* 55, no. 4 (2005): 417–22.

Peredery, Oksana, and Michael A. Persinger. "Herbal Treatment Following Post-seizure Induction in Rat by Lithium Pilocarpine: *Scutellaria lateriflora* (Skullcap), *Gelsemium sempervirens* (Gelsemium) and *Datura stramonium* (Jimson Weed) May Prevent Development of Spontaneous Seizures." *Phytochemistry Research* 18, no. 9 (September 2004): 700–705.

Periera, E. C., S. C. Nascimento, R. C. Lima, N. H. Lima, A. F. Oliveira, E. Bandeira, M. Boitard, H. Beriel, and C. Vicente. "Analysis of *Usnea fasciata* Crude Extracts with Antineoplastic Activity" *Tokai Journal of Experimental and Clinical Medicine* 19, no. 1–2 (September 1994): 47–52.

Perry, E. "Ethno-Botany of the Indians in the Interior of British Columbia." *Museum and Art Notes* 2, no. 2 (1952): 36–43.

Perry, Myra Jean. "Food Use of 'Wild' Plants by Cherokee Indians." Master's thesis, University of Tennessee, Knoxville, 1975.

Pfoze, Neli Lokho, Yogendra Kumar, Berington Myrboh, Ranjan Kumar Bhagobaty, and Santa Ram Joshi. "In Vitro Antibacterial Activity of Alkaloid Extract from Stem Bark of *Mahonia manipurensis* Takeda." *Journal of Medicinal Plants Research* 5, no. 5 (March 2011): 859–61.

Phetcharat, L., K. Wongsuphasawat, and K. Winther. "The Effectiveness of a Standardized Rose Hip Powder, Containing Seeds and Shells of Rosa canina, on Cell Longevity, Skin Wrinkles, Moisture, and Elasticity." *Clinical Interventions in Aging* 10 (2015): 1849.

Philipp, M., R. Kohner, and K. O. Hiller. "Hypericum Extract versus Imipramine or Placebo in Patients with Moderate Depression." *BMJ* 319 (1999): 1534–39.

Piacente, S., P. Montoro, W. Oleszek, and C. Pizza. "*Yucca schidigera* bark: Phenolic Constituents and Antioxidant Activity." *Journal of Natural Products* 67, no. 5 (2004): 882–85.

Piehl, M. A. "Mode of Attachment, Haustorium Structure, and Hosts of *Pedicularis canadensi*." *American Journal of Botany* 50, no. 10 (1963): 978–85.

Pimm, Stuart L., and Michael E. Gilpin. "Theoretical Issues in Conservatrion Biology." In *Perspectives in Ecological Theory*, edited by J. Roughgarden, R.

May, and S. Leven, pp. 287-305. Princeton, NJ: Princeton Univeristy Press, 1989.

Pimm, Stuart L., and Peter H. Raven. "The Fate of the World's Plants." *Trends in Ecology and Evolution* 32, no. 5 (May 2017): 317-20.

Pirbalouti, A. G., A. Koohpayeh, and I. Karimi. "The Wound Healing Activity of Flower Extracts of *Punica granatum* and *Achillea kellalensis* in Wistar Rats." *Acta Pol Pharm* 67 (2010): 107-10.

Pires, J. M., F. R. Mendes, G. Negri, J. M. Duarte-Almeida, and E. A. Carlini. "Antinociceptive Peripheral Effect of *Achillea millefolium* L. and *Artemisia vulgaris* L.: Both Plants Known Popularly by Brand Names of Analgesic Drugs." *Phytotherapy Research* 23 (2009): 212-19.

Pompei, Raffaello, Ornella Flore, Maria Antonietta Marccialis, Alessandra Pani, and Bernardo Loddo. "Glycyrrhizic Acid Inhibits Virus Growth and Inactivates Virus Particles." *Nature* 281, no. 5733 (1979): 689.

Porsild, A. E. "Edible Plants of the Arctic." *Arctic* 6 (1953): 15-34.

Potrich, F. B., A. Allemande, L. M. da Silva, A. C. Dos Santos, C. H. Freitas, D. A. Mendes, E. Andre, M. F. Werner, and M. C. Marques. "Antiulcerogenic Activity of Hydroalchohalic Extract of *Achillea millefolium* L.: Involvement of the Antioxidant System." *Journal of Ethnopharmacology* 130, no. 1 (2010): 85-89.

Powers, Stephen. "Aboriginal Botany." *Proceedings of the California Academy of Science* 5 (1874): 373-79.

Prakash B., P. Singh, R. Goni, A. K. Raina, and N. K. Dubey. "Efficacy of *Angelica archangelica* Essential Oil, Phenyl Ethyl Alcohol and ⊠-Terpineol against Isolated Molds from Walnut and Their Antiaflatoxigenic and Antioxidant Activity." *Journal of Food Science and Technology* 52 (2015): 2220-28.

Pramanik, K. C., R. Biswas, D. Bandyopadhyay, M. Mishra, C. Ghosh, and T. K. Chatterjee. "Evaluation of Anti-ulcer Properties of the Leaf Extract of *Juniperus communis* L. in Animals." *Journal of Natural Remedies* 7, no. 2 (2007): 207-13.

Pranting, M., C. Loov, R. Burman, U. Goransson, and D. I. Anderson. "The Cyclotide Cycloviolacin O2 from Viola Odorata Has Potent Bactericidal Activity against Gram-Negative Bacteria." *Journal of Antimicrobial Chemotherapy* 65, no. 9 (2010): 1964-71.

Prateeksha, G., B. S. Paliya, R. Bajpai, V. Jadaun, J. Kumar, S. Kumar, D. K. Upreti, B. R. Singh, S. Nayaka, Y. Joshid, et al. "The Genus *Usnea*: A Potent Phytomedicine with Multifarious Ethnobotany, Phytochemistry and Pharmacology. *Royal Society of Chemistry* 6 (2016): 21672-96.

Prather, L. Alan, and Jessie A. Keith. "*Monarda humilis* (Lamiaceae), a New Combination for a Species from New Mexico, and a Key to the Species of Section Cheilyctis." *Novon* 13, no. 1 (2003): 104-9.

Prather, L. Alan, Anna K. Monfils, Amanda L. Posto, and Rachel A. Williams. "Monophyly and Phylogeny of Monarda: Evidence from the Internal Transcriber Spacer (ITS) Region of Ribosomal DNA." *Systematic Botany* 27, no. 1 (2002): 127-37.

Preeti, Khandelwal, Sharma Ram Avatar, and Agarwal Mala. "Pharmacology and Therapeutic Application of *Prosopis juliflora*: A Review." *Journal of Plant Sciences* 3, no. 4 (2015): 234-40.

Priyani, A. Paranagama, E. M. Kithsiri Wijeratne, Anna M. Burns, Marilyn T. Marron, Malkanthi K. Gunatilaka, A. Elizabeth Arnold, and A. A. Leslie Gunatilaka. "Heptaketides from *Corynespora* sp. Inhabiting the Cavern Beard Lichen, *Usnea cavernosa*: First Report of Metabolites of an Endolichenic Fungus." *Journal of Natural Products* 70 (2007): 1700-5.

Qasemzadeh, Mohammad Javad, Hosein Sharifi, Mohammad Hamedanian, Mohammad Gharehbeglou, Mojtaba

Heydari, Mehdi Sardari, Meisam Akhlaghdoust, and Mohammad Bagher Minae. "The Effect of *Viola odorata* Flower Syrup on the Cough of Children with Asthma: A Double-Blind, Randomized Controlled Trial." *Journal of Evidence-Based Complementary and Alternative Medicine* 20, no. 4 (October 2015): 287–91.

Qingxi Su, Seema Dalal, Michael Goetz, Maria B. Cassera, and David G. I. Kingston. "New Antiplasmodial Diterpenes from *Gutierrezia sarothrae*." *Natural Product Communications* 11, no. 6. (June 2016): 719–21.

Qiu, Longxin, Tong Chen, Fojin Zhong, Yamin Hong, Limei Chen, and Hong Ye. "Red Clover Extract Exerts Antidiabetic and Hypolipidemic Effects in db/db Mice." *Experimental and Therapeutic Medicine* 4, no. 4 (October 2012): 699–704.

Quihui-Cota, Luis, Rocio León-Trujillo, Humberto Astiazarán-García, Julian Esparza-Romero, Maria del Refugio Robles, Ramon E. Robles-Zepeda, Rafael Canett, and Jesus Sanchez-Escalante. "Marked Antigiardial Activity of *Yucca baccata* Extracts: A Potential Natural Alternative for Treating Protozoan Infections." *BioMed Research International* (2014). doi:10.1155/2014/823492.

Quiroga, E. N., A. R. Sampietro, and M. A. Vattuone. "In Vitro Fungitoxic Activity of *Larrea divaricata* cav. Extracts." *Applied Microbiology* 39 (2004): 7–12.

Rabiei K., A. Ghobadifar, M. A. Ebrahimzadeh, M. Saeedi, and M. Mobini. "Effects of Ginger and *Elaeagnus angustifolia* Extracts in Symptomatic Knee Osteoarthritis." *Zahedan Journal of Research in Medical Sciences* (2015): 29–33.

Rachid, Azzi, Djaziri Rabah, Lahfa Farid, and Sekkal Fatima. "Ethnopharmacological Survey of Medicinal Plants Used in the Traditional Treatment of Diabetes Mellitus in the North Western and South Western Algeria." *Journal of Medicinal Plants Research* 6, no. 10 (March 2012): 2041–50.

Rahman, Aziz Abdur, Volodymyr Samoylenko, Melissa R. Jacob, Rajnish Sahu, Surendra K. Jain, Shabana I. Khan, Babu L. Tekwani, and Ilias Muhammad. "Antiparasitic and Antimicrobial Indolizidines from the Leaves of *Prosopis glandulosa* var. *glandulosa*." *Planta Medica* 77, no. 14 (2011): 1639–43.

Rahman, Hafiz Muhammad Abdur, Muhammad Fawad Rasool, and Imran Imran. "Pharmacological Studies Pertaining to Smooth Muscle Relaxant, Platelet Aggregation Inhibitory and Hypotensive Effects of *Ailanthus altissima*." *Evidence-Based Complementary and Alternative Medicine* (2019). doi:10.1155/2019/1871696.

Rahman, Shakilur, Rizwan Ahmed Ansari, Hasibur Rehman, Suhel Parvez, and Sheikh Raisuddin. "Nordihydroguaiaretic Acid from Creosote Bush (*Larrea tridentata*) Mitigates 12-O-Tetradecanoylphorbol-13-Acetate-Induced Inflammatory and Oxidative Stress Responses of Tumor Promotion Cascade in Mouse Skin." *Evidence-Based Complementary and Alternative Medicine* (2011). doi:10.1093/ecam/nep076.

Rajesh, M. G., and M. S. Latha. "Protective Activity of *Glycyrrhiza glabra* Linn. on Carbon Tetrachloride-Induced Peroxidative Damage." *Indian Journal of Pharmacology* 36, no. 5 (2004): 284–87.

Ramezani, Mohammad, Hossein Hosseinzadeh, and Nosratollah Daneshmand. "Antinociceptive Effect of *Alaeagnus angustifolia* Fruit Seeds in Mice." *Fitoterapia* 72 (2001): 255–62.

Ramya, M., C. Shivabasavaiah, and T. Shivanandappa. "Reversible Antifertility Effect of *Opuntia elatior* Mill. Fruit Extract." *International Journal of Reproduction, Contraception, Obstetrics and Gynecology* 4, no. 2 (April 2015): 392–97.

Ramyashree, M., Shivabasavaiah, and Krishna Ram H. "Ethnomedicinal Value of *Opuntia elatior* Fruits and Its Effects in Mice." *Journal of Pharmacy Research* 5, no. 8 (2012): 4554-58.

Rana, N., and S. Bais. "Neuroprotective Effect of *J. communis* in Parkinson Disease Induced Animal Models." Master's thesis, Punjab Technical University, Punjab, 2014.

Rankovic, B., M. Kosanic, T. Stanojkovic, P. Vasiljevic, and N. Manojlovic. "Biological Activities of *Toninia candida* and *Usnea barbata* Together with Their Norstictic Acid and Usnic Acid Constituents." *International Journal of Molecular Sciences* 13 (2012): 14707-22.

Rao, A., and D. Gurfinkel. "The Bioactivity of Saponins: Triterpenoid and Steroidal Glycosides." *Drug Metabolism and Drug Interactions* 17 (2000): 211-36.

Rashidian, Amir, Fatemeh Kazemi, Saeed Mehrzadi, Ahmad Reza Dehpour, Shahram Ejtemai, and Seyed Mahdi Rezayat. "Anticonvulsant Effects of Aerial Parts of *Verbena officinalis* Extract in Mice: Involvement of Benzodiazepine and Opioid Receptors." *Journal of Evidence-Based Medicine* 22, no. 4 (October 2017): 632-36.

Rasool, Mahmood, Javed Iqbal, Arif Malik, Hafiza Sobia Ramzan, Muhammad Saeed Qureshi, Muhammad Asif, Mahmood Husain Qazi, Mohammad Amjad Kamal, Adeel Gulzar Ahmed Chaudhary, Mohammed Hussain Al-Qahtani, et al. "Hepatoprotective Effects of *Silybum marianum* (Silymarin) and *Glycyrrhiza glabra* (Glycyrrhizin) in Combination: A Possible Synergy." *Evidence-Based Complementary and Alternative Medicine* (2014). doi:10.1155/2014/641597.

Rastogi, R. P., and B. N. Mehrotra. "Compendium of Indian Medicinal Plants." *CDRI, Lucknow and National Institute of Science and Information Resources* 94, no. 6 (1990): 395-98.

Rathi, S. G., M. Suthar, and P. Patel. "In Vitro Cytotoxic Screening of *Glycyrrhiza glabra*." *Pharmacology* 1 (2009): 239-43.

Ratnaweera, Pamoda B., E. Dilip de Silva, David E. Williams, and Raymond J. Andersen. "Antimicrobial Activities of Endophytic Fungi Obtained from the Arid Zone Invasive Plant *Opuntia dillenii* and the Isolation of Equisetin, from Endophytic *Fusarium* sp." *BMC Complementary and Alternative Medicine* 15 (2015): 220.

Rauf, A., A. Latif, S. Rehman, and S. H. Afaq. "In-Vitro Antibacterial Screening of Extracts of *Usnea longissima* Lichen." *International Journal of Applied Biology and Pharmaceutical Technology* 2, no. 2 (2011): 14-18.

Raut, Savanta V. "Study on Antibacterial Compounds from Methanolic Extract of Bark of *Prosopis juliflora* (Vilayati babhul)." *International Journal of Pharmaceutical Sciences and Business Management* 2, no. 6 (June 2014): 1-14.

Raveendra, Kadur Ramamurthy, Jayachandra, Venkatappa Srinivasa, Kadur Raveendra Sushma, Joseph Joshua Allan, Krishnagouda Shankagouda Goudar, Hebbani Nagarajappa Shivaprasad, Kudiganti Venkateshwarlu, Periasamy Geetharani, Gopalakrishna Sushma, et. al. "An Extract of *Glycyrrhiza glabra* (GutGard) Alleviates Symptoms of Functional Dyspepsia: A Randomized, Double-Blind, Placebo-Controlled Study." *Evidence-Based Complementary and Alternative Medicine* (2012). doi:10.1155/2012/216970.

Ravichandra, V. Ahalyadevi, and S. Adiga. "Evaluation of the Effect of *Glycyrrhiza glabra* Linn Root Extract on Spatial Learning and Passive Avoidance Response in Rats." *Indian Drugs* 44 (2007): 214-19.

Ray, Verne F. "The Sanpoil and Nespelem: Salishan Peoples of North-eastern Washington." *University of Washington Publications in Anthropology* 5 (1932).

Raymond, Marcel. "Ethnobotaniques sur les Tête-de-Boule de Manouan." *Contributions de l'Institut Botanique de l'Université de Montréal* 55 (1945): 113-34.

RBG Kew. *The State of the World's Plants Report.* Kew: Royal Botanic Gardens, 2016.

Reagan, Albert B. "Plants Used by the Bois Fort Chippewa (Ojibwa) Indians of Minnesota." *Wisconsin Archaeologist* 7, no. 4 (1928): 230–48.

——. "Plants Used by the White Mountain Apache Indians of Arizona." *Wisconsin Archaeologist* 8 (1929): 143–61.

——. "Plants Used by the Hoh and Quileute Indians." *Kansas Academy of Science* 37 (1936): 55–70.

Redmond, Miranda D., and Nichole N. Barger. "Tree Regeneration following Drought- and Insect-Induced Mortality in Pinon-Juniper Woodlands." *New Phytologist* 200, no. 2 (October 2013): 402–12.

Rehfeldt, Gerald, Nicholas L. Crookston, Marcus V. Warwell, and Jeffrey S. Evans. "Empirical Analysis of Plant-Climate Relationships for the Western United States." *International Journal of Plant Sciences* 167, no. 6 (2006): 1123–50.

Rein, E., A. Kharazmi, and K. Winther. "A Herbal Remedy, Hyben Vital (Stand. Powder of a Subspecies of *Rosa canina* Fruits), Reduces Pain and Improves General Wellbeing in Patients with Osteoarthritis—a Double-Blind, Placebo-Controlled, Randomised Trial." *Phytomedicine* 11 (2004): 383–91.

Remington, Joseph P., Horatio C. Wood, George B. Wood, Franklin Bache, and Samuel P. Sadtler (eds). *The Dispensatory of the United States of America,* 1918. Southwest School of Botanical Medicine. http://www.swsbm.com.

Rezvani, S., M. A. Rezai, and N. Mahmoodi. "Analysis and Antimicrobial Activity of the Plant *Juniperus communis.*" *Rasayan Journal of Chemistry* 2, no. 1 (2009): 257–60.

Richardson, Rosamond. *Britain's Wild Flowers.* London: National Trust, 2017.

Rivero, Isabel, Krutzkaya Juárez, Magda Zuluaga, Robert Bye, and Rachel Mata. "Quantitative HPLC Method for Determining Two of the Major Active Phthalides from *Ligusticum porteri* Roots." *Journal of AOAC International* 95, no. 1 (January–February 2012): 84–91.

Robart, Bruce W., Carl Gladys, Tom Frank, and Stephen Kilpatrick. "Phylogeny and Biogeography of North American and Asian Pedicularis." *Systematic Botany* 40, no. 1 (2015): 229–58.

Robbins, W. W., J. P. Harrington, and B. Freire-Marreco. "Ethnobotany of the Tewa Indians." *Smithsonian Institution, Bureau of American Ethnology Bulletin* 55 (1916).

Robles-Zepeda, Ramon, Carlos A. Velazquez-Contreras, Adraiana Garibay-Escobar, Juan C. Galvez-Ruiz, and Eduardo Ruiz-Bustos. "Antimicrobial Activity of Northwestern Mexican Plants against *Helicobacter pylori.*" *Journal of Medicinal Food* 14, no. 10 (October 2011): 1280–83.

Rodríguez-Rodríguez, C., N. Torres, J. A. Gutiérrez-Uribe, L. G. Noriega, I. Torre-Villalvazo, A. M. Leal-Diaz, M. Antunes-Ricardo, C. Marquez-Ricardo, C. Marquez-Mota, G. Ordaz, et al. "The effect of Isorhamnetin Glycosides Extracted from *Opuntia ficus-indica* in a Mouse Model of Diet Induced Obesity." *Food and Function* 6, no. 3 (2015): 805–15.

Rogers, Dilwyn. *Lakota Names and Traditional Uses of Native Plants by Sicangu (Brule) People in the Rosebud Area, South Dakota.* Saint Francis, SD: Rosebud Educational Society, 1980.

Roh, J., and S. Shin. "Antifungal and Antioxidant Activities of the Essential Oil from *Angelica koreana* Nakai." *Evidence-Based Complementary and Alternative Medicine* (2014). doi:10.1155/2014/398503.

Romero, John Bruno. *The Botanical Lore of the California Indians.* New York: Vantage Press, 1954.

Rossum, Tekla G. J. van, Arnold G. Vulto, Wim C. J. Hop, Johannes T. Brouwer, Hubert G. M. Niesters, and Solko W. Schalm. "Intravenous Glycyrrhizin for the Treatment of Chronic Hepatitis C:

A Double-Blind, Randomized, Placebo-Controlled Phase I/II Trial." *Journal of Gastroenterology and Hepatology* 14, no. 11 (1999): 1093–99.

Rousseau, Jacques. "Le Folklore Botanique de Caughnawaga." *Contributions de l'Institut Botanique de l'Université de Montréal* 55 (1945a): 7–72.

———. "Le Folklore Botanique de l'Ile aux Coudres." *Contributions de l'Institut Botanique de l'Université de Montréal* 55 (1945b): 75–111.

———. "Notes Sur l'Ethnobotanique d'Anticosti." *Archives de Folklore* 1 (1946): 60–71.

———. "Ethnobotanique Abénakise." *Archives de Folklore* 11 (1947): 145–82.

Roy, B., A. Swargiary, D. Syiem, and V. Tandon. "*Potentilla fulgens* (Family Rosaceae), a Medicinal Plant of North-east India: A Natural Anthelmintic?" *Journal of Parasitic Disease* 34. no. 2 (2010): 83.

Russell, Frank. "The Pima Indians." *Smithsonian Institution, Bureau of American Ethnology Annual Report* 26 (1908): 1–390.

Sadeghi, H., S. Hosseinzadeh, M. A. Touri, M. Ghavamzadeh, and M. J. Barmak. "Hepatoprotective Effect of *Rosa canina* Fruit Extract against Carbon Tetrachloride Induced Hepatotoxicity in Rat." *Avicenna Journal of Phytomedicine* 6 (2016): 181.

Saeidnia, S., A. R. Gohari, N. Mokhber-Dezfuli, and F. Kiuchu. "A Review of Phytochemistry and Medicinal Properties of the Genus *Achillea*." *DARU Journal of Pharmaceutical Sciences* 19, no. 3 (2011): 173–86.

Safford, W. E. "Daturas of the Old World and New: An Account of Their Narcotic Properties and Their Use in Oracular and Intitiatory Ceremonies." *Smithsonian Report*, 537–67. Washington: Government Printing Office, 1922.

Sagan, Carl. *Cosmos: A Personal Voyage*, TV series, 1980. DVD distribution, Los Angeles: Public Broadcasting Service, 2000.

Saha, Sudipta, Gabriella Nosalova, Debjani Ghosh, Dana Fleskova, Peter Capek, and Bimalendu Ray. "Structural Features and In Vivo Antitussive Activity of the Water Extracted Polymer from *Glycyrrhiza glabra*." *International Journal of Biological Macromolecules* 48, no. 4 (May 2011): 634–38.

Saidi, Mohammad Reza, Mohammed Hosein Farzaei, Shahram Miraghaee, Atefeh Babaei, Bahareh Mohammadi, Mohammad Taher Bahrami, and Gholamreza Bahrami. "Antihyperlipidemic Effect of Syrian Mesquite (*Prosopis farcta*) Root in High Cholesterol Diet-Fed Rabbits." *Journal of Evidence-Based Integrative Medicine* 21, no. 4 (October 2016): NP62–66.

Salazar-Aranda, Ricardo, Luis Alejandro Perez-Lopez, Joel Lopez-Arroyo, Blanca Alicia Alanıs-Garza, and Noemi Waksman de Torres. "Antimicrobial and Antioxidant Activities of Plants from Northeast of Mexico." *Evidence-Based Complementary and Alternative Medicine* (2011). doi:10.1093/ecam/nep127.

Saleem, R., Muhammad Ahmed, Aisha Azmat, Syed Iqbal Ahmad, Zareen Faizi, Lubna Abidi, and Shaheen Faizi. "Hypotensive Activity, Toxicology and Histopathology of Opuntioside-I and Methanolic Extract of *Opuntia dillenii*." *Biological and Pharmaceutical Bulletin* 28, no. 10 (2005): 1844–51.

Saleh, Alaaeldin I., Islam Mohamed, Ahmed A. Mohamed, Mennatallah Abdelkader, Huseyin C. Yalcin, Tahar Aboulkassim, Gerald Batist, Amber Yasmeen, and Ala-Eddin Al Moustafa. "*Elaeagnus angustifolia* Plant Extract Inhibits Angiogenesis and Downgrades Cell Division of Human Oral Cancer Cells via Erk1/Erk2 Inactivation." *Nutrition and Cancer* 70, no. 2 (2018): 297–305.

Salikhova, R. A., and G. G. Poroshenko. "Antimutagenic Properties of *Angelica archangelica* L." *Vestn Ross Akad Med Nauk* 1 (1995): 58–61.

Sampson, Arthur W., and W. Kenneth Parker. *St. Johnswort on Range Lands of California*. Bulletin 503. Berkeley: Agriculture Experiment Station, College of Agriculture, University of California, 1930.

Sanchez, de Medina, M. J. Gamez, I. Jimenez, J. Jimenez, J. I. Osuna, and A. Zarzuelo "Hypoglycemic Activity of Juniper (Berries)." *Planta Medica* 60, no. 3 (1994): 197–200.

Sanchez-Tapia, Monica, Miriam Aguilar-Lopez, Claudia Perez-Cruz, Edgar Pichardo-Ontiveros, Mei Wang, Sharon M. Donovan, Armando R. Tovar, and Nimber Torres. "Nopal (*Opuntia ficus indica*) Protects from Metabolic Endotoxemia by Modifying Gut Microbiota in Obese Rats Fed High Fat/Sucrose Diet." *Scientific Reports* 7 (2017). doi:10.1038/s41598-017-05096-4.

Sánchez-Vidaña, D. I., S. P.-C. Ngai, W. He, J. K.-W. Chow, B. W.-M. Lau, and H. W.-H Tsang "The Effectiveness of Aromatherapy for Depressive Symptoms: A Systematic Review." *Journal of Evidence-Based Complementary and Alternative Medicine* (2017). doi:10.1155/2017/5869315.

Santos, F. V., I. M. S. Colus, M. A. Silva, W. Vilegas, and E. A. Varanda. "Assessment of DNA Damage by Extracts and Fractions of *Strychnos pseudoquina*, a Brazilian Medicinal Plant with Antiulcerogenic Activity." *Food and Chemical Toxicology* 44, no. 9 (2006): 1585–89.

Sapir, Edward, and Leslie Spier. "Notes on the Culture of the Yana." *Anthropological Records* 3, no. 3 (1943): 252–53.

Saraswathy, G. R., R. Sathiya, J. Anbu, and E. Maheswari. "Antitussive Medicinal Herbs: An Update Review." *International Journal of Pharmaceutical Sciences and Drug Research* 6, no. 1 (2014): 12–19.

Sati, S. C., and S. Joshi. "Antibacterial Potential of Leaf Extracts of *Juniperus communis* L. from Kumaun Himalaya." *African Journal of Microbiology Research* 4, no. 12 (2010): 1291–94.

Sava Sand, Camelia. "*Arnica montana* L. as a Medicinal Crop Species." *Scientific Papers: Management, Economic Engineering in Agriculture and Rural Development* 15, no. 4 (2015): 303–7.

Saville, Dara. "*Anemopsis californica* (Yerba Mansa) Monograph." *Journal of the American Herbalists Guild* 18, no. 1 (Spring 2020): 33–42.

Sayed, Atiya, and Humaira Bano. "Brinjasif (*Achillea millefolium* Linn): An Efficacious Unani Medicine." *International Journal of Herbal Medicine* 6, no. 3 (2018): 92–96.

Schempp, C. M., K. Pelz, A. Wittmer, E. Schopf, and J. C. Simon. "Antibacterial Activity of Hyperforin from St. John's Wort, against Multiresistant *Staphylococcus aureus* and Gram-Positive Bacteria." *Lancet* 353 (1999): 2129.

Schenck, Sara M., and E. W. Gifford. "Karok Ethnobotany." *Anthropological Records* 13, no. 6 (1952): 377–92.

Schmidt, Thomas J., Sebastian Rzeppa, Marcel Kaiser, and Reto Brun. *Larrea tridentata*—Absolute Configuration of Its Epoxylignans and Investigations on Its Antiprotozoal Activity. *Phytochemistry Letters* 5, no. 3 (September 2012): 632–38.

Schneider, I., S. Gibbons, and F. Bucar. "Inhibitory Activity of *Juniperus communis* on 12(S)-HETE Production in Human Platelets." *Planta Medica* 70, no. 5 (2004): 471–74.

Schneider, Marilyn J., and Frank R. Stermitz. "Uptake of Host Plant Alkaloids by Root Parasitic Pedicularis Species." *Phytochemistry* 29, no. 6 (1990): 1811–14.

Schrader, E. "Equivalence of St. John's Wort Extract (Ze 117) and Fluoxetine." *International Clinical Psychopharmacology* 15 (2000): 61–68.

Scogin, R. "Anthocyanins of Fouquieriaceae." *Biochemical Systematics and Ecology* 5 (1977): 265–67.

Scott, Timothy Lee. *Invasive Plant*

Medicine. Rochester, VT: Healing Arts Press, 2010.

Sedighinia, Fereshteh, Akbar Safipour Afshar, Saman Soleimanpour, Reza Zarif, Javad Asili, and Kiarash Ghazvini. "Antibacterial Activity of *Glycyrrhiza glabra* against Oral Pathogens: An In Vitro Study." *Avicenna Journal of Phytomedicine* 2, no. 3 (Summer 2012): 118-24.

Sela F., M. Karapandzova, G. Stefkov, I. Cvetkovikj, E. Trajkovska-Dokik, A. Kaftandzieva, and S. Kulevanova. "Chemical Composition and Antimicrobial Activity of Leaves Essential Oil of *Juniperus communis* (Cupressaceae) Grown in Republic of Macedonia." *Macedonian Pharmaceutical Bulletin* 59, no. 1-2 (2013): 41-48.

Sellerberg, U., and H. Glasl. "Pharmacognostical Examination Concerning the Hemostyptic Effect of *Achillea millefolium* Aggregat." *Scientia Pharmaceutica* 68 (2000): 201-6.

Semwal, D. K., R. B. Semwal, S. Combrinck, and A. Viljoen. "Myricetin: A Dietary Molecule with Diverse Biological Activities." *Nutrients* 8 (2016): 90.

Serra, A. T., J. Poejo, A. A. Matias, M. R. Bronze, and C. M. M. Duarte. "Evaluation of *Opuntia* spp. Derived Products as Antiproliferative Agents in Human Colon Cancer Cell Line (HT29)." *Food Research International* 54, no. 1 (2013): 892-901.

7Song. "Ligusticum, Osha, Focus on First Aid Uses." Northeast School of Botanical Medicine, 2017. http://7song.com /resources.

Shachi Singh, Swapnil, and S. K. Verma. "Antibacterial Properties of Alkaloid Rich Fractions Obtained from Various Parts of *Prosopis juliflora*." *International Journal of Pharma Sciences and Research* 2, no. 3 (2011): 114-20.

Shafi, Gowhar, Tarique N. Hasan, Naveed Ahmed Syed, Amal A. Al-Hazzani, Ali A. Alshatwi, A. Jyothi, and Anjana Munsh. "*Artemisia absinthium* (AA): A Novel Potential Complementary and Alternative Medicine for Breast Cancer." *Molecular Biology* Reports 39 (2012): 7373.

Shagal, M. H., U. U. Modibbo, and A. B. Liman. "Pharmacological Justification for the Ethnomedical Use of *Datura stramonium* Stem-bark Extract in Treatment of Diseases Caused by Some Pathogenic Bacteria." *International Research Journal of Pharmacy and Pharmacology* 2, no. 1 (2012): 16-19.

Shang, Xiaofei, Xirui He, Xiaoying He, Maoxing Li, Ruxue Zhang, Pengcheng Fan, Zhang Quanlong, and Zhengping Jia. "The Genus *Scutellaria* an Ethnopharmacological and Phytochemical Review. *Journal of Ethnopharmacology* 128, no. 2 (March 2010): 279-313.

Sharma, A., V. K. Patel, and A. N. Chaturvedi. "Vibriocidal Activity of Certain Medicinal Plants Used in Indian Folklore Medicine by Tribals of Mahakoshal Region of Central India." *Indian Journal of Pharmacology* 41, no. 3 (2009): 129-33.

Sharma, Binod Chandra, and Sujata Kalikotay. "Screening of Antioxidant Activity of Lichens *Patmotrema reticulum* and *Usnea* sp. from Darjeeling Hills, India." *IOSR Journal of Pharmacy* 2, no. 6 (November-December 2012): 54-60.

Sharma, Chhavi, Sangeeta Rani, Bijander Kumar, Arvind Kumar, and Vinit Raj. "Plant *Opuntia dillenii*: A Review on Its Traditional Uses, Phytochemical and Pharmacological Properties." *EC Pharmaceutical Science* 1, no. 1 (2015): 29-43.

Sharma, R. G. L. "Studies on Antimycotic Properties of *Datura metel*." *Journal of Ethnopharmacology* 80 (2002): 193-97.

Sharma, S., V. P. Rasal, P. A. Patil, and R. K. Joshi. "Effect of Angelica Glauca Essential Oil on Allergic Airway Changes Induced by Histamine and Ovalbumin in Experimental Animals." *Indian Journal of Pharmacology* 49 (2017): 55-59.

Sharma, V., R. C. Agrawal, and S. Pandey. "Phytochemical Screening and Determination of Anti-bacterial and

Anti-oxidant Potential of *Glycyrrhiza glabra* Root Extracts." *Journal of Environmental Research and Development* 7, no. 4A (2013): 1552–58.

Sharma, Varsha, and R. C. Agrawal. "*Glycyrrhiza glabra*: A Plant for the Future." *Mintage Journal of Pharmaceutical and Medical Sciences* 2, no. 3 (July–September 2013): 15–20.

Sheela, M. L., M. K. Ramakrishna, and B. P. Salimath. "Angiogenic and Proliferative Effects of the Cytokine VEGF in Ehrlich Ascites Tumor Cells Is Inhibited by *Glycyrrhiza glabra*." *International Immunopharmacology* 6 (2006): 494–98.

Shelton, Richard C., Martin B. Keller, Alan Gelenberg, David L. Dunner, Robert Hirschfeld, Michael E. Thase, James Russell, R. Bruce Lydiard, Paul Crits-Christoph, Robert Gallop et al. "Effectiveness of St John's Wort in Major Depression." *JAMA* 285 (2001): 1978–86.

Shi, G., J. Liu, W. Zhao, Y. Liu, and X. Tian. "Separation and Purification and In Vitro Antiproliferative Activity of Leukemia Cell K562 of *Galium aparine* L. Petroleum Ether Phase." *Saudi Pharmaceutical Journal* 24, no. 3 (2016): 241–44.

Shin, Yong-Wook, Eun-Ah Bae, Bomi Lee, Seung Ho Lee, Jeong Ah Kim, Yeong-Shik Kim, and Dong-Hyun Kim. "In Vitro and In Vivo Antiallergic Effects of *Glycyrrhiza glabra* and Its Components." *Planta Medica* 73, no. 3 (2007): 257–61.

Shiota, S., M. Shimizu, J. Sugiyama, Y. Morita, T. Mizushima, and T. Tsuchiya. "Mechanisms of Action of Corilagin and Tellimagrandin I That Remarkably Potentiate the Activity of ⊠-Lactams against Methicillin-Resistant *Staphylococcus aureus*." *Microbiology and Immunology* 48 (2004): 67–73.

Shirbeigi, L., L. Oveidzadeh, Z. Jafari, M. S. Motahari Fard, and P. Mansouri. "A Review of Acne Etiology and Treatment in Iranian Traditional Medicine." *Journal of Skin and Stem Cell* 3, no. 1 (2016). doi:10.5812/jssc.39133.

Shrestha, Gajendra, Jocelyn Raphael, Steven D. Leavitt, and Larry L. St. Clair. "In Vitro Evaluation of the Antibacterial Activity of Extracts from 34 Species of North American Lichens." *Pharmaceutical Biology* 52, no. 10 (2014): 1262–66.

Shrestha, Gajendra, and Larry L. St. Clair. "Antimicrobial Activity of Extracts from Two Lichens *Ramalina menziesii* and *Usnea lapponica*." *Bulletin of the California Lichen Society* 20, no. 1 (2013): 5–10.

Si, Chuan-Ling, Jie Xu, Jin-Kyu Kim, Young-Soo Bae, Peng-Tao Liu, and Zhong Liu. "Antioxidant Properties and Structural Analysis of Phenolic Glucosides from Bark of *Populus ussuriensis* Kom." *Wood Science and Technology* 45, no. 1 (February 2011): 5–13.

Si, Chuan-Ling, Qian Xu, Shu-Ming Li, and Zhong Liu. "Phenolic Compounds from *Populus davidiana* Wood." *Chemistry and Natural Compounds* 45 (September 2009): 634.

Sianne, S., and R. V. H. Fanie. "Antimalarial Activity of Plant Metabolites." *Natural Product Report* 19 (2002): 675–92.

Siddiqi, H. S., M. H. Mehmood, N. U. Rehman, and A. H. Gilani. "Studies on the Antihypertensive and Antidyslipidemic Activities of *Viola odorata* Leaves Extract." *Lipids in Health and Disease* 11 (2012): 6–14.

Sigurdsson, S., H. M. Ogmundsdottir, and S. Gudbjarnason. "Antiproliferative Effect of *Angelica archangelica* Fruits." *Verlag der Zeitschrift für Naturforschung Tübingen* 59c (2004): 523–27.

——. "The Cytotoxic Effect of Two Chemotypes of Essential Oils from the Fruits of *Angelica archangelica* L." *Anticancer Research* 25 (2005a): 1877–80.

Sigurdsson, S., H. M. Ogmundsdottir, J. Hallgrimsson, and S. Gudbjarnason. "Antitumor Activity of *Angelica archangelica* Leaf Extract." *In Vivo* 19 (2005b): 191–94.

Silva, Fabia, Bruno Silva, Joao P. Silva, O. P. Coutinho, and Alberto Carlos Pires Dias. "Antioxidant and Neuroprotective Properties of *Scutellaria lateriflora*." Paper presented at the Annual Congress of the Society for Medicinal Plant Research, 2005, Florence.

Silva-Hughes, Alice F., David E. Wedge, Charles L. Cantrell, Camila R. Carvalho, Zhiqiang Pan, Rita M. Moraes, Victor L. Madoxx, and Luiz H. Rosa. "Diversity and Antifungal Activity of the Endophytic Fungi Associated with the Native Medicinal Cactus *Opuntia humifusa* (Cactaceae) from the United States." *Microbial Research* 175 (2015): 67–77.

Singh, H., A. Prakash, A. N. Kalia, and A. B. Majeed. "Synergistic Hepatoprotective Potential of Ethanolic Extract of *Solanum xanthocarpum* and *Juniperus communis* against Paracetamol and Azithromycin Induced Liver Injury in Rats." *Journal of Traditional and Complementary Medicine* 6, no. 4 (2015): 370–76.

Sirvent, Tara M., Loren Walker, Nan Vance, and Donna M. Gibson. "Variation in Hypericins from Wild Populations of *Hypericum perforatum* L. in the Pacific Northwest of the USA." *Economic Botany* 56 no. 1 (2002): 41–48.

Sivinski, Robert C. "Vascular Plants in the Sandia Mountains Central New Mexico," *Occasional Papers of the Museum of Southwestern Biology* 10 (2007): 1–67.

Sladonja, Barbara, Maria Susek, and Julia Guillermic. "Review on Invasive Tree of Heaven (*Ailanthus altissima* [Mill.] Swingle) Conflicting Values: Assessment of Its Ecosystem Services and Potential Biological Threat." *Environmental Management* 56 (2015): 1009–34.

Slattery, John. *Southwest Foraging*. Portland, OR: Timber Press, 2016.

Slavík, J., J. Bochořáková, D. Košťalová, and V. Hrochová. "Alkaloids of *Mahonia aquifolium* (PURSH) NUTT.2." *Chemical Papers* 39, no. 4 (1985): 537–42.

Smith, Brittany, Luis Lowe, Janel Owens, and Emily H. Mooney. "Chemotypic Variation in Osha (*Ligusticum porter*) in Colorado, USA." *Journal of Applied Research on Medicinal and Aromatic Plants* 10 (September 2018): 34–40.

Smith, G. Warren. "Arctic Pharmacognosia." *Arctic* 26 (1973): 324–33.

Smith, Harlan, I. "Materia Medica of the Bella Coola and Neighboring Tribes of British Columbia." *National Museum of Canada Bulletin* 56 (1929): 47–68.

Smith, Huron H. "Ethnobotany of the Menomini Indians." *Bulletin of the Public Museum of the City of Milwaukee* 4 (1923): 1–174.

——. "Ethnobotany of the Meskwaki Indians." *Bulletin of the Public Museum of the City of Milwaukee* 4 (1928): 175–326.

——. "Ethnobotany of the Ojibwa Indians." *Bulletin of the Public Museum of the City of Milwaukee* 4 (1932): 327–525.

——. "Ethnobotany of the Forest Potawatomi Indians." *Bulletin of the Public Museum of the City of Milwaukee* 7 (1933): 1–230.

Smith, Stanley D., Dale A. Devitt, Anna Sala, James D. Cleverly, and David E. Busch. "Water Relations of Riparian Plants from Warm Desert Regions." *Wetlands* 18, no. 4 (1998): 687–96.

Smith, Stanley D., Russel K. Monson, and Jay Ennis Anderson. *Physiological Ecology of North American Desert Plants*. Berlin: Springer Verlag, 1997.

Snowden, Rebecca, Heather Harrington, Kira Morrill, LaDeana Jeane, Joan Garrity, Michael Orian, Eric Lopez, Saman Rezaie, Kelly Hassberger, Damilola Familoni, et al. "A Comparison of the Anti-*Staphylococcus aureus* Activity of Extracts from Commonly Used Medicinal Plants." *Journal of Alternative and Complementary Medicine* 20, no. 5 (May 2014): 375–82.

Sogge, Mark K., Susan J. Sferra, and Eben H. Paxton. "*Tamarix* as Habitat for Birds:

Implications for Riparian Restoration in the Southwestern United States." *Restoration Ecology* 16, no. 1 (2008): 146-54.

Solecki, Ralph S. "Shanidar IV, a Neanderthal Flower Burial in Northern Iraq." *Science* 190, no. 4217 (November 1975): 880-81.

Soleymani, Samaneh, Roodabeh Bahramsoltani, Roja Rahimi, and Mohammad Abdollahi. "Clinical Risks of St John's Wort (*Hypericum perforatum*) Co-administration." *Expert Opinion on Drug Metabolism and Toxicology* 13, no. 10 (2017): 1047-62.

Sonika G., R. Manubala, and J. Deepak. "Comparative Studies on Anti-inflammatory Activity of *Coriandrum sativum*, *Datura stramonium* and *Azadirachta indica*." *Asian Journal of Experimental Biological Sciences* 1, no. 1 (2010): 151-54.

Sosebee, R. E., and B. E. Dahl. *Effects of Mesquite Spraying on Other Rangeland Resources*. Santa Fe: Bureau of Land Management, US Department of the Interior, 1979.

Sosebee, R. E., and C. Wan. "Plant Ecophysiology: A Case Study of Honey Mesquite." In *Proceedings: Symposium on Shrub Ecophysiology and Biotechnology*, compiled by Arthur Wallace, Durant E. McArthur, and Marshall R. Haferkamp, pp. 103-18. Ogden, UT: Intermountain Research Station, Forest Service, US Department of Agriculture, 1987.

Southon S., A. J. A. Wright, K. R. Price, S. J. Fairweather-Tait, and G. R. Fenwick. "The Effect of Three Types of Saponin on Iron and Zinc Absorption from a Single Meal in the Rat." *British Journal of Nutrition* 59 (1988): 389-96.

Sowmya M., and S. Kumar. "Antistress Property of *Glycyrrhiza glabra* on Stress Induced *Drosophila melanogaster*." *Journal of Stress Physiology and Biochemistry* 6 (2010): 18-27.

Sowndhararajan, Kandasamy, Ponnuvel Deepa, Minju Kim, Se Jin Park, and Songmun Kim. "A Review of the Composition of the Essential Oils and Biological Activities of Angelica Species." *Scientia Pharmaceutica* 85, no. 3 (September 2017): 33.

Sparkman, Phillip S. "The Culture of the Luiseño Indians." *University of California Publications in American Archaeology and Ethnology* 8, no. 4 (1908): 187-234.

Speck, Frank G. "Medicine Practices of the Northeastern Algonquians." *Proceedings of the 19th International Congress of Americanists* (1917): 303-21.

——. "Catawba Medicines and Curative Practices." *Publications of the Philadelphia Anthropological Society* 1 (1937): 179-97.

——. "A List of Plant Curatives Obtained from the Houma Indians of Louisiana." *Primitive Man* 14 (1941): 49-75.

Speck, Frank G., R. B. Hassrick, and E. S. Carpenter. "Rappahannock Herbals, Folk-Lore, and Science of Cures." *Proceedings of the Delaware County Institute of Science* 10 (1942): 7-55.

Spitaler, Renate, Andrea Winkler, Isabella Lins, Sema Yanar, Hermann Stuppner, and Christian Zidorn. "Altitudinal Variation of Phenolic Contents in Flowering Heads of *Arnica montana* cv. ARBO: a 3-Year Comparison." *Journal of Chemical Ecology* 34, no. 3 (2008): 369-75.

Sreekanth, D., M. K. Arunasree, K. R. Roy, T. Chandramohan Reddy, G. V. Reddy, and P. Reddanna. "Betanin a Betacyanin Pigment Purified from Fruits of *Opuntia ficus-indica* Induces Apoptosis in Human Chronic Myeloid lLukemia Cell Line-K562." *Phytomedicine* 14, no. 11 (2007): 739-46.

Srivastava, Priya, D. K. Upreti, T. N. Dhole, Apurva K. Srivastava, and Meghanand T. Nayak. "Antimicrobial Property of Extracts of Indian Lichen against Human Pathogenic Bacteria" *Interdisciplinary Perspectives on Infectious Diseases* (2013). doi:10.1155/2013/709348.

Stanciuc, A. M., A. Gaspar, L. Moldovan,

C. Saviuc, M. Popa, and L. Marutescu. "In Vitro Antimicrobial Activity of Romanian Medicinal Plants Hydroalcoholic Extracts on Planktonic and Adhered Cells." *Roumanian Archives of Microbiology and Immunology* 70, no. 1 (January 2011): 11-14.

Steedman, E. V. "The Ethnobotany of the Thompson Indians of British Columbia." *Smithsonian Institution, Bureau of American Ethnology Annual Report* 45 (1928): 441-522.

Stevenson, Matilda Coxe. "Ethnobotany of the Zuni Indians." *Smithsonian Institution, Bureau of American Ethnology Annual Report* 13 (1915).

Steward, Julian H. "Ethnography of the Owens Valley Paiute." *University of California Publications in American Archaeology and Ethnology* 33, no. 3 (1933): 233-50.

Stickney, Peter F. "Effects of Fire on Upland Forests in the Northern Rocky Mountains," 1993. Unpublished paper on file at Fire Sciences Laboratory, Intermountain Research Station, US Forest Service, Missoula, MT.

Stoilova I. S., J. Wanner, L. Jirovetz, D. Trifonova, L. Krastev, A. S. Stoyanova, and A. I. Krastanov. "Chemical Composition and Antioxidant Properties of Juniper Berry (*Juniperus communis* L.) Essential Oil." *Bulgarian Journal of Agricultural Science* 20, no. 2 (2014): 227-37.

Stojanovic, G., N. Radulovic, T. Hashimoto, and R. Palic. "In Vitro Antimicrobial Activity of Extracts of Four Achillea Species. The Composition of *Achillea clavennae* L. (Asteraceae) Extract." *Journal of Ethnopharmacology* 101 (2005): 185-90.

Stromberg, Juliet. "Restoration of Riparian Vegetation in the Southwestern United States: Importance of Flow Regimes and Fluvial Dynamism." *Journal of Arid Environments* 49 (2001): 17-34.

Sturtevant, William Curtis. "The Mikasuki Seminole: Medical Beliefs and Practices." PhD dissertation, Yale University, New Haven, CT, 1955.

Su, X. S., H. M. Chen, L. H. Wang, C. F. Jiang, J. H. Liu, M. Q. Zhao, X. H. Ma, Y. C. Zhao, and D. W. Han. "Clinical and Laboratory Observation on the Effect of Glycyrrhizin in Acute and Chronic Viral Hepatitis." *Journal of Traditional Chinese Medicine* 4, no. 2 (1984): 127.

Subhan, F., M. Khan, M. Ibrar, N. Islam, A. Khan, and A. H. Gilani. "Antagonism of Antinociceptive Effect of Hydro-Ethanolic Extract of *Hypericum perforatum* Linn. by a Non Selective Opioid Receptor Antagonist, Naloxone." *Pakistan Journal of Biological Sciences* 10, no. 5 (2007): 792-96.

Suggitt, Andrew J., Duncan G. Lister, and Chris D. Thomas. "Widespread Effects of Climate Change on Local Plant Diversity." *Current Biology* 29 (2019): 2905-11.

Suleiman, Mohamed Hammad Adam. "Ethnobotanical, Phytochemical, and Biological Study of *Tamarix aphylla* and *Aerva javanica* Medicinal Plants Growing in the Asir Region, Saudi Arabia." *Tropical Conservation Science* 12 (2019). doi:10.1177/1940082919869480.

Sultana, Nasim, and Anthony Jide Afolayan. "A New Depsidone and Antibacterial Activities of Compounds from *Usnea endulata* Stirton." *Journal of Asian Natural Products Research* 13, no. 12 (2011): 1158-64.

Susithra, E., K. Mallikarjuna Rao, K. V. Ramseshu, and S. Meena. "Evaluation of In-vitro Antioxidant Activity of Isolated Compounds of Lichen, *Usnea undulata*." *Journal of Pharmacy Research* 4, no. 2 (2011): 352-55.

Svangard, Erika, Robert Burman, Sunithi Gunasekera, Henrik Lovborg, Joachim Gullbo, and Ulf Goransson. "Mechanism of Action of Cytotoxic Cyclotides: Cycloviolacin O2 Disrupts Lipid Membranes." *Journal of Natural Products* 70, no. 4 (2007): 643-47.

Svangard, Erika, Ulf Goransson, Zozan Hocaoglu, Joachim Gullbo, Rolf Larsson, Per Claeson, and Lars Bohlin. "Cytotoxic Cyclotides from *Viola tricolor*." *Journal of Natural Products* 67, no. 2 (2004): 144–47.

Swank, George R. "The Ethnobotany of the Acoma and Laguna Indians." Master's thesis, University of New Mexico, Albuquerque, 1932.

Swanton, John R. "Religious Beliefs and Medical Practices of the Creek Indians." *Smithsonian Institution, Bureau of American Ethnology Annual Report* 42 (1928): 473–672.

Tabanca, N., Z. Gao, B. Demirci, N. Techen, D. E. Wedge, A. Ali, B. J. Sampson, C. Werle, U. R. Bernier, I. A. Khan, et al. "Molecular and Phytochemical Investigation of *Angelica dahurica* and *Angelica pubescentis* Essential Oils and Their Biological Activity against *Aedes aegypti*, *Stephanitis pyrioides*, and *Colletotrichum* Species." *Journal of Agricultural and Food Chemistry* 62 (2014): 8848–57.

Tabanca, Nurhayat, Ulrich R. Bernier, Abbas Ali, Mei Wang, Betul Demirci, Eugene K. Blythe, Shabana I. Khan, K. Husnu Can Baser, and Ikhlas A. Khan. "Bioassay Guided Investigation of Two Monarda Essential Oils as Repellant of Yellow Fever Mosquito *Aedes aegypti*." *Journal of Agriculture and Food Chemistry* 61, no. 36 (2013): 8573–80.

Takii, H., T. Kometani, T. Nishimura, T. Nakae, S. Okada, and T. Fushiki. "Anti-diabetic Effect of Glycyrrhizin in Genetically Diabetic KK-Ay Mice." *Biological and Pharmaceutical Bulletin* 24 (2000): 484–87.

Tamura, E. K., R. S. Jimenez, K. Waismam, L. Gobbo-Neto, N. P. Lopes, E. A. Malpezzi-Marinho, E. A. Marinho, and S. H. Farsky. "Inhibitory Effects of *Solidago chilensis* Meyen Hydroalcoholic Extract on Acute Inflammation." *Journal of Ethnopharmacology* 122, no. 3 (January 2009): 478–85.

Tang, J. J., M. Colacino, S. H. Larsen, and W. Spitzer. "Virucidal Activity of Hypericin against Enveloped and Non-Enveloped DNA and RNA Viruses." *Antiviral Research* 13 (1990): 313–26.

Tantaquidgeon, Gladys. "Mohegan Medicinal Practices, Weather-Lore and Superstitions." *Smithsonian Institution, Bureau of American Ethnology Annual Report* 43 (1928): 264–70.

——. *A Study of Delaware Indian Medicine Practice and Folk Beliefs*. Harrisburg: Pennsylvania Historical Commission, 1942.

——. *Folk Medicine of the Delaware and Related Algonkian Indians*. Harrisburg: Pennsylvania Historical Commission, 1972.

Tayefi-Nasrabadi, H., S. Sadigh-Eteghad, and Z. Aghdam. "The Effects of the Hydroalcohol Extract of *Rosa canina* L. Fruit on Experimentally Nephrolithiasic Wistar Rats." *Phytotherapy Research* 26 (2012): 78–85.

Taylor, Linda Averill. *Plants Used as Curatives by Certain Southeastern Tribes*. Cambridge, MA: Botanical Museum of Harvard University, 1940.

Taylor, T. N., H. Hass, W. Remy, and H. Kerp. "The Oldest Fossil Lichen." *Nature* 378 (1995): 244–44.

Tehranizadeh, Zeinab Amiri, Ali Baratian, and Hossein Hosseinzadeh. "Russian Olive (*Elaeagnus angustifolia*) as a Herbal Healer. *Bioimpacts* 6, no. 3 (2016): 155–67.

Teit, James A. "The Salishan Tribes of the Western Plateaus." *Smithsonian Institution, Bureau of American Ethnology Annual Report* 45 (1928).

Těšitel, Jakub, Pavel Fibich, Francesco de Bello, Milan Chytrý, and Jan Lepš. "Habitats and Ecological Niches of Root-Hemiparasitic Plants: An Assessment Based on a Large Database of Vegetation Plots." *Preslia* 87 (2015): 87–108.

Thayer, Samuel. *Nature's Garden*. Birchwood, WI: Forager's Harvest Press, 2010.

Theodoratus, Robert J. "Loss, Transfer, and Reintroduction in the Use of Wild Plant Foods in the Upper Skagit Valley." *Northwest Anthropological Research Notes* 23, no. 1 (1989): 35-52.

Thomas, C. D. "Local Diversity Stays about the Same, Region Diversity Increases, and Global Diversity Declines." *Proceedings of the National Academy of Sciences of the United States of America* 110, no. 48 (2013): 19187-88.

Thomas, C. D. "Rapid Acceleration of Plant Speciation during the Anthropocene." *Trends in Ecology and Evolution* 30, no. 8 (2015): 448-55.

Thuiller, Wilfried, Sandra Lavorel, Miguel B. Araujo, Martin T. Sykes, and Colin Prentice. "Climate Change Threats to Plant Diversity in Europe." *Proceedings of the National Academy of Sciences of the United States of America* 102, no. 23 (2005): 8245-50.

Tilford, Gregory L. *Edible and Medicinal Plants of the West.* Missoula: Mountain Press, 1997.

Timbrook, J. "Virtuous Herbs: Plants in Chumash Medicine." *Journal of Ethnobiology* 7, no. 2 (Winter 1987): 171-80.

Timmermann, Barbara, Eckhard Wollenweber, Marion Dorr, Sylvia Armbuster, and Karin M. Valant-Vetschera. "External Flavoinoids in Two Grindelia Species." *Zeitschrift für Naturforschung C* 49, no. 5-6 (June 1994): 395-98.

Tomczyk, Michal, Malgorzata Pleszcznska, and Adrian Wiater. "Variation in Total Polyphenolics Contents of Aerial Parts of Potentilla Species and Their Anticariogenic Activity." *Molecules* 15, no. 7 (2010): 4639-51.

Tozyo, T., Y. Yoshimura, K. Sakurai, N. Uchida, Y. Takeda, H. Nakai, and H. Ishii. "Novel Antitumor Sesquiterpenoids in *Achillea millefolium.*" *Chemical and Pharmaceutical Bulletin* 42 (1994): 1096-1100.

Trachtenberg, S., and A. M. Mayer. "Composition and Properties of *Opuntia ficus indica* Mucilage." *Phytochemistry* 20 (1981): 2665-68.

Train, Percy, James R. Heinrichs, and W. Andrew Archer. *Medicinal Uses of Plants by Indian Tribes of Nevada.* Washington, DC: US Department of Agriculture, 1941.

Trifunovic, S., V. Vajs, Z. Juranic, Z. Zizak, V. Tesevic, S. Macura, and S. Milosavljevic. "Cytotoxic Constituents of *Achillea clavennae* from Montenegro." *Phytochemistry* 68 (2006): 887-93.

Trivedi, R., and K. Sharma. "Hydroalcoholic Extract of *Glycyrrhiza glabra* Attenuates Chronic Fatigue Stress Induced Behavioral Alterations in Mice." *International Journal of Pharmaceutical and Biological Sciences* 2 (2011): 996-1001.

Tuberosoa, C. I. G., P. Montoro, S. Piacente, G. Corona, M. Deiana, M. Assunta Dessi, C. Pizza, and P. Cabras. "Flavonoid Characterization and Antioxidant Activity of Hydroalcoholic Extracts from *Achillea ligustica* All." *Journal of Pharmaceutical and Biomedical Analysis* 50 (2009): 440-48.

Tumbas, V. T., J. M. Canadanovic-Brunet, D. D. Cetojevic-Simin, G. S. Cetkovic, S. M. Ethilas, and L. Gille. "Effect of Rosehip (*Rosa canina* L.) Phytochemicals on Stable Free Radicals and Human Cancer Cells." *Journal of the Science of Food and Agriculture* 92 (2012): 1273-81.

Tunon, H., C. Olavsdotter, and L. Bohlin. "Evaluation of Anti-inflammatory Activity of Some Swedish Medicinal Plants. Inhibition of Prostaglandin Biosynthesis and PAF-Induced Exocytosis." *Journal of Ethnopharmacology* 48, no. 2 (1995): 61-76.

Tunon, H., W. Thorsell, and L. Bohlin. "Mosquito Repelling Activity of Compounds Occurring in *Achillea millefolium* L. (Asteraceae)." *Economic Botany* 48, no. 2 (April-June 1994): 111-20.

Turi, Christina E., and Susan J. Murch. "Targeted and Untargeted Phytochemistry of *Ligusticum canbyi*: Indoleamines,

Phthalides, Antioxidant Potential, and Use of Metabolomics as a Hypothesis-Generating Technique for Compound Discovery." *Planta Med* 79, no. 4 (2013): 1370–79.

Turner, Nancy Chapman, and Marcus A. M. Bell. "The Ethnobotany of the Coast Salish Indians of Vancouver Island, I and II." *Economic Botany* 25, no. 1 (1971): 63–104, 335–39.

——. "The Ethnobotany of the Southern Kwakiutl Indians of British Columbia." *Economic Botany* 27 (1973): 257–310.

Turner, Nancy J. "The Ethnobotany of the Bella Coola Indians of British Columbia." *Syesis* 6 (1973): 193–220.

Turner, Nancy J., R. Bouchard, and Dorothy I. D. Kennedy. *Ethnobotany of the Okanagan-Colville Indians of British Columbia and Washington.* Victoria: British Columbia Provincial Museum, 1980.

Turner, Nancy J., John Thomas, Barry F. Carlson, and Robert T. Ogilvie. *Ethnobotany of the Nitinaht Indians of Vancouver Island.* Victoria: British Columbia Provincial Museum, 1983.

Turner, Nancy J., Laurence C. Thompson, M. Terry Thompson, and Annie Z. York. *Thompson Ethnobotany: Knowledge and Usage of Plants by Thompson Indians of British Columbia.* Victoria: Royal British Columbia Museum, 1990.

Tutupalli, L. V., and M. G. Chaubal. "Constituents of *Anemopsis californica.*" *Phytochemistry* 10 (1971): 3331–32.

Uebelhack, R., R. Busch, F. Alt, Z.-M. Beah, and P.-W. Chong. "Effects of Cactus Fiber on the Excretion of Dietary Fat in Healthy Subjects: A Double Blind, Randomized, Placebo-Controlled, Crossover Clinical Investigation." *Current Therapeutic Research, Clinical and Experimental* 76C (2014): 39–44.

Uifălean, A., S. Schneider, P. Gierok, C. Ionescu, C. A. Iuga, and M. Lalk. "The Impact of Soy Isoflavones on MCF-7 and MDA-MB-231 Breast Cancer Cells Using a Global Metabolomic Approach." *International Journal of Molecular Science* 17 (2016): 1443.

Ulubelen, Ayhan, Mary E. Cladwell, and Jack R. Cole. "Isolation of an Antitumor Proteinaceous Substance from *Gutierrezia sarothrae* (Compositae)." *Journal of Pharmaceutical Sciences* 54, no. 8 (August 1965): 1214–16.

Umamaheswari, M., K. Asok, A. Somasundaram, T. Sivashanmugam, V. Subhadradevi, and T. K. Ravi. "Xanthine Oxidase Inhibitory Activity of Some Indian Medical Plants." *Journal of Ethnopharmacology* 109, no. 3 (2007): 547–51.

United States Army Corps of Engineers. *Middle Rio Grande Bosque Restoration Project Final Report.* Washington, DC: US Army Corps of Engineers, 2003.

United States Forest Service (USFS). "Forest Service Survey Finds Record 66 Million Dead Trees in Southern Sierra Nevada." News release 0150.16, June 22, 2016.

——. "New Aerial Survey Identifies More Than 100 Million Dead Trees in California." News release 0246.16, November 18, 2016.

United States Global Change Research Program. *Impacts, Risks, and Adaptation in the United States: Fourth National Climate Assessment.* Vol. 2: *Report-in-Brief,* edited by D. R. Reidmiller, C. W. Avery, D. R. Easterling, K. E. Kunkel, K. L. M. Lewis, T. K. Maycock, and B. C. Stewart. Washington, DC: US Global Change Research Program, 2018.

Unlü, M., D. Daferera, E. Dönmez, M. Polissiou, B. Tepe, and A. Sökmen. "Compositions and the In Vitro Antimicrobial Activities of the Essential Oils of *Achillea setacea* and *Achillea teretifolia* (Compositae)." *Journal of Ethnopharmacology* 83 (2002): 117–21.

Upton, Roy, and R. H. Dayu. "Skullcap *Scutellaria lateriflora* L.: An American Nervine." *Journal of Herbal Medicine* 2, no. 3 (September 2012): 76–96.

Uysal, S., G. M. F. Zengin, M. A.

Mahomoodally, A. Aktumsek, and A. Yilmaz. "Chemical Profile, Antioxidant Properties and Enzyme Inhibitory Effects of the Root of Selected Potentilla Species." *South African Journal of Botany* 120 (January 2019): 124–28.

Uysal, Sengul, and Abdurrahman Aktumsek. "A Phytochemical Study on *Potentilla anatolica*: An Endemic Turkish Plant." *Industrial Crops and Products* 76, no. 15 (December 2015): 1001–7.

Uysal, Sengul, Gokhan Zengin, Marcello Locatelli, Mir B. Bahadori, Andrei Mocan, Guiseppe Bellagamba, Elisa De Luca, Adriano Mollica, and Abdurrahman Aktumsek. "Cytotoxic and Enzyme Inhibitory Potential of Two *Potentilla* Species (*P. speciosa* L. and *P. reptans* Willd.) and Their Chemical Composition." *Frontiers in Pharmacology* 8 (May 2017): 290.

Vaidya, Brajesh N., Terri A. Brearley, and Nirmal Joshee. "Antioxidant Capacity of Fresh and Dry Leaf Extracts of Sixteen *Scutellaria* Species." *Journal of Medicinally Active Plants* 2, no. 3 (2014): 42–49.

Van Auken, O. W. "Shrub Invasions of North American Semiarid Grasslands." *Annual Review of Ecological Systems* 31 (2000): 197–215.

Van Rossum, T. G., A. G. Vulto, W. C. Hop, and S. W. Schalm. "Glycyrrhizin-Induced Reduction of ALT in European Patients with Chronic Hepatitis C." *American Journal of Gastroenterology* 96 (2001): 2432–37.

Van Slambrouck, Severine, Amber L. Daniels, Carla J. Hooton, Steven L. Brock, Aaron R. Jenkins, Marcia A. Ogasawara, Joann M. Baker, Glen Adkins, Eerik M. Elias, Vincent J. Agustin, et al. "Effects of Crude Aqueous Medicinal Plant Extracts on Growth and Invasion of Breast Cancer Cells." *Oncology Reports* 17 (2007): 1487–92.

Varsha, Sharma, R. C. Agrawal, and Pandey Sonam. "Phytochemical Screening and Determination of Anti-bacterial and Anti-oxidant Potential of *Glycyrrhiza glabra* Root Extracts." *Journal of Environmental Research and Development* 7, no. 4A (April–June 2013): 1552–58.

Vasek, Frank J. "Creosote Bush: Long-Lived Clones in the Mojave Desert." *American Journal of Botany* 67 (1980): 246–55.

Vasilevna, I. T., G. O. Volodymyrivna, T. E. Leonidivna, K. I. Aleksandrovna, and K. A. Mihaylovna. Antimicrobial Activity of the Genus *Galium* L." *Pharmacognosy Communications* 6, no. 1 (2016): 42–47.

Vaya, J., P. A. Belinky, and M. Aviram. "Structural Aspects of the Inhibitory Effect of Glabridin on LDL Oxidation." *Free Radical Biology and Medicine* 24 (1998): 1419–29.

Ved, A., A. Gupta, and A. K. Rawat. "Antioxidant and Hepatoprotective Potential of Phenol-Rich Fraction of *Juniperus communis* Linn. Leaves." *Pharmacognosy* 13, no. 49 (2017): 108–13.

Velázquez-Moyado, Josué A., Alejandro Martínez-González, Edelmira Linares, Robert Bye, Rachel Mata, and Andrés Navarrete. "Gastroprotective Effect of Diligustilide Isolated from Roots of *Ligusticum porteri* Coulter and Rose (Apiaceae) on Ethanol-Induced Lesions in Rats." *Journal of Ethnopharmacology* 174 (2015): 403–9.

Velland, Mark, Lander Baeten, Isla H. Myers-Smith, Sarah C. Elmendorf, Robin Beausejour, Carissa D. Brown, Pieter De Frenne, Kris Verheyen, and Sona Wipf. "Global Meta-Analysis Reveals No Net Change in Local-Scale Plant Diversity Over Time." *Proceedings of the National Academy of Sciences of the United States of America* 110, no. 48 (2013): 19456–59.

Velland, Mark, Lander Baeten, Antoine Becker-Scarpitta, Veronique Boucher-Lalonde, Jenny L. McCune, Julie Messier, Isla H. Myers-Smith, and Dov F. Sax. "Plant Biodiversity Change Across Scales during the Anthropocene." *Annual Review of Plant Biology* 68 (June 2017): 563–86.

Venevskaia, Irina, Sergey Venevsky, and Chris D. Thomas. "Projectged Latitudinal and Regional Changes in Vascular Plant Diversity through Climate Change: Short-Term Gains and Longer-Term Losses." *Biodiversity and Conservation* 22 (2013): 1467–83.

Venieraki, A., M. Dimou, and P. Katinakis. "Endophytic Fungi Residing in Medicinal Plants Have the Ability to Produce the Same or Similar Pharmacologically Active Secondary Metabolites as Their Hosts." *Hellenic Plant Protection Journal* 10 (2017): 51–66.

Vergara-Galicia, Jorge, Melina Huerta-García, Joaquín Herrera-Chi, Patricia Castillo-España, Emmanuel Reyes-Martínez, Marisa Estrada-Carrillo, Samuel Estrada-Soto, Ángel Sierra-Ovando, and Emmanuel Hernandez-Nuñez. "Vasorelaxant Effect of Ethanolic Extracts from *M. vulgare*: Mexican Medicinal Plant as Potential Source for Bioactive Molecules Isolation." *Indo Global Journal of Pharmaceutical Sciences* 3, no. 1 (2013): 1–5.

Venkatesan, B., V. Subramanian, A. Tumala, and E. Vellaichamy. "Rapid Synthesis of Biocompatible Silver Nanoparticles Using Aqueous Extract of *Rosa damascena* Petals and Evaluation of Their Anticancer Activity." *Asian Pacific Journal of Tropical Medicine* 7, no. 1 (2014): S294–S300.

Verma, Neeraj, B. C. Behera, and Urmila Makhija. "Antioxidant and Hepatoprotective Activity of a Lichen *Usnea ghattensis* in Vitro." *Applied Biochemistry and Biotechnology* 151, no. 2–3 (December 2008): 167–81.

Verma, N., S. K. Tripathi, D. Sahu, H. R. Das, and R. H. Das. "Evaluation of Inhibitory Activities of Plant Extracts on Production of LPS-Stimulated Pro-Inflammatory Mediators in J774 Murine Macrophages." *Molecular and Cellular Biochemistry* 336 (2010): 127.

Vestal, Paul A. "Notes on a Collection of Plants from the Hopi Indian Regions of Arizona Made by J. G. Owens in 1891." *Botanical Museum Leaflets, Harvard University* 8, no. 8 (1940): 153–68.

——. "The Ethnobotany of the Ramah Navajo." *Papers of the Peabody Museum of American Archaeology and Ethnology* 40, no. 4 (1952): 1–94.

Vestal, Paul A., and Richard Evans Schultes. *The Economic Botany of the Kiowa Indians.* Cambridge, MA: Botanical Museum of Harvard University, 1939.

Vila, R. M. Mundina, F. Tomi, R. Furlan, S. Zacchino, J. Casanova, and S. Canigueral. "Composition and Antifungal Activity of the Essential Oil of *Solidago chilensis*." *Planta Medica* 68, no. 2 (February 2002): 164–67.

Vishal, A., K. Parveen, S. Pooja, N. Kannappan, and Shakun Kumar. "Diuretic, Laxative and Toxicity Studies of *Viola odorata* Aerial Parts." *Pharmacologyonline* 1 (2009): 739–48.

Vlase, L., A. Mocan, D. Hanganu, D. Benedec, and A. Gheldiu. "Comparative Study of Polyphenolic Content, Antioxidant and Antimicrobial Activity from *Galium* Species (Rubiaceae)." *Digest Journal of Nanomaterials and Biostructures* 9, no. 3 (2014): 1085–94.

Voegelin, Ermine W. "Tubatulabal Ethnography." *Anthropological Records* 2, no. 1 (1938): 1–84.

Volleková, Anna, Daniela KoŠt'álová, Viktor Kettmann, and Jaroslav Tóth. "Antifungal Activity of *Mahonia aquifolium* Extract and Its Major Protoberberine Alkaloids." *Phytotherapy Research* 17 (2003): 834–37.

Vorbach, E. U., K. H. Arnoldt, and W. E. Hubner. "Efficacy and Tolerability of St. John's Wort Extract LI 160 versus Imipramine in Patients with Severe Depressive Episodes According to ICD-10." *Pharmacopsychiatry* 30, supplement 2 (1997): 81–85.

Wagner, H., and K. Jurcic. "Immunological Studies of Revitonil: A Phytopharmaceutical Containing *Echinacea purpurea* and *Glycyrrhiza glabra* Root Extract." *Phytomedicine* 9, no. 5 (2002): 390–97.

Walia, M., P. Kumar, B. Singh, and V. K. Agnihotri. "UPLC-DAD Quantification of Chemical Constituents of *Potentilla atrosanguinea* Roots and Their Antioxidant Activity." *Journal of Food Science and Technology* 55 (2018): 4337.

Walker, Loren W. "St. John's Wort (*Hypericum perforatum* L. Clusiaceae): Biochemical, Morphological, and Genetic Variation within and among Wild Populations of the Northwestern United States." Master's thesis, Portland State University, Portland, OR, 2000.

Walker, Loren, Tara Sirvent, Donna Gibson, and Nan Vance. "Regional Differences in Hypericin and Pseudohypericin Concentrations and Five Morphological Traits among *Hypericum perforatum* Plants in the Northwestern United States." *Canadian Journal of Botany* 79 no. 10 (2001): 1248–55.

Wallis, Wilson D. "Medicines Used by the Micmac Indians." *American Anthropologist* 24 (1922): 24–30.

Wan, Guang, Jin-Gang Tao, Guo-Dong Wang, Shen-Peng Liu, Hong-Xing Zhao, and Qiu-Dong Liang. "In Vitro Antitumor Activity of the Ethyl Acetate Extract of *Potentilla chinensis* in Osteosarcoma Cancer Cells." *Molecular Science Reports* 14, no. 4 (October 2016): 3634–40.

Wang, C., J. Sun, H. Li, X. Yang, H. Liu, and J. Chen. "In Vivo Anti-Inflammatory Activities of the Essential Oil from Radix *Angelicae dahuricae*." *Journal of Natural Medicine* 70 (2016): 563–70.

Wang, D., M. Xia, Z. Cui, S. Tashiro, S. Onodera, and T. Ikejima. "Cytotoxic Effects of Mansonone E and F Isolated from *Ulmus pumila*." *Biological and Pharmaceutical Bulletin* 27, no. 7 (July 2004): 1025–30.

Wang, Niannian, Feifei Ahu, Mingxiang Shen, Lipeng Qiu, Min Tang, Hengchuan Xia, Liang Chen, Yi Yuan, Shnagshang ma, and Keping Chen. "Network of Pharmacology-Based Analysis on Bioactive Anti-Diabetic Compounds in *Potentilla discolor* Bunge." *Journal of Ethnopharmacology* 241 (2019). doi:10.1016/j.jep.2019.111905.

Wang, Ruxing, Yanjie Lu, Hong Li, Lixin Sun, Ning Yang, Mingzhen Zhao, Manli Ahang, and Qingwen Shi. "Antitumor Activity of the *Ailanthus altissima* Bark Phytochemical Ailanthone against Breast Cancer MCF-7 Cells." *Oncology Letters* 15 (2018): 6022–28.

Wang, Ruxing, Qian Xu, Lei Liu, Xiujun Liang, Luyang Cheng, Manli Zhang, and Qingwen Shi. "Antitumor Activity of 2-Dihydroailanthone from the Bark of *Ailanthus altissima* against U251." *Pharmaceutical Biology* 54, no. 9 (2016): 1641–48.

Wang, Shan-Shan, Dong-Mei Wang, Wen-Jun Pu, and Deng-Wu Li. "Phytochemical Profiles, Antioxidant and Antimicrobial Activities of Three *Potentilla* Species." *BMC Complementary and Alternative Medicine* 13 (2013): 321.

Wang, Wen-Jing, Chang Su, Dong-Mei Zhang, Li-Peng Xu, Rong-Rong He, Lei Wang, Jian Zhang, Xiao-Qi Zhang, and Wen-Cai Ye. "Cytotoxic Quassinoids from *Ailanthus altissima*." *Bioorganic and Medicinal Chemistry Letters* 23 (2013): 654–57.

Wang, Y., T. A. McAllister, L. J. Yanke, and P. R. Cheeke. "Effect of Steroidal Saponin from *Yucca schidigera* Extract on Ruminal Microbes." *Journal of Applied Microbiology* 88 (2000): 887–96.

Warda, K., M. Markouk, K. Bekkouche, M. Larhsini, A. Abbad, A. Romane, and M. Bouskraoui. "Antibacterial Evaluation of Selected Moroccan Medicinal Plants against *Streptococcus pneumoniae*." *African Journal of Pharmacy and Pharmacology* 3, no. 3 (March 2009): 101–4.

Wardecki, Tina, Elke Brötz, Christian De Ford, Friederike D. von Loewenich, Yuriy Rebets, Bogdan Tokovenko, Andriy Luzhetskyy, and Irmgard Merfor. "Endophytic Streptomyces in the

Traditional Medicinal Plant *Arnica montana* L.: Secondary Metabolites and Biological Activity." *Antonie van Leeuwenhoek* 108, no. 2 (August 2015): 391–402.

Warholm, O., S. Skaar, E. Hedman, H. M. Mølmen, and L. Eik. "The Effects of a Standardized Herbal Remedy Made from a Subtype of *Rosa canina* in Patients with Osteoarthritis: A Double-Blind, Randomized, Placebo-Controlled Clinical Trial." *Current Therapeutic Research* 64 (2003): 21–31.

Warnhoff, E. W., and C. M. M. Halls. "Desert Plant Constituents: II Ocotillol: An Intermediate in the Oxidation of Hydroxy Isoöctenyl Side Chains." *Canadian Journal of Chemistry* 43, no. 12 (1965): 3311–21.

Warnhoff, E. W., S. K. Pradhan, and J. C. N. Ma. "Ceanothus Alkaloids: I. Isolation, Separation, and Characterization." *Canadian Journal of Chemistry* 43 (1965): 2594–2602.

Waser, N. M. "Pollinator Availability as a Determinant of Flowering Time in Ocotillo (*Fouquieria splendens*)." *Oecologia* 39, no. 1 (1979): 107–21.

Watahomigie, Lucille J. *Hualapai Ethnobotany*. Peach Springs, AZ: Hualapai Bilingual Program, Peach Springs School District 8, 1982.

Watson, J. R. "Plant Geography of North Central New Mexico." *Botanical Gazette* 54 (1912): 194–217.

Waugh, F. W. *Iroquois Foods and Food Preparation*. Ottawa: Canada Department of Mines, 1916.

Weber, Steven A., and P. David Seaman. *Havasupai Habitat: A. F. Whiting's Ethnography of a Traditional Indian Culture*. Tucson: University of Arizona Press, 1985.

Webster, H. T. "*Anemopsis californica*." *Eclectic Medicine Journal* 69 (1909): 336–40.

Wei, A., and T. Shibamoto. "Antioxidant Activities and Volatile Constituents of Various Essential Oils." *Journal of Agricultural Food Chemistry* 55 (2007): 1737–42.

Wendakoon, Chitra, Peter Calderon, and Daniel Gagnon. "Evaluation of Selected Medicinal Plants Extracted in Different Ethanol Concentrations for Antibacterial Activity against Human Pathogens." *Journal of Medicinally Active Plants* 1, no. 2 (2012): 60–68.

Werner, Patricia A., Ian K. Bradbury, and Ronald S. Gross. "The Biology of Canadian Weeds: 45. *Solidago canadensis* L." *Canadian Journal of Plant Science* 60, no. 4 (1980): 1393–1409.

Westbrooks, Randy G. *Invasive Plants, Changing the Landscape of America: Fact Book*. Washington, DC: Federal Interagency Committee for the Management of Noxious and Exotic Weeds, 1998.

Wheatley, D. "LI-160, an Extract of St. John's Wort, versus Amitriptyline in Mildly to Moderately Depressed Outpatients: A Controlled 6-Week Clinical Trial." *Pharmacopsychiatry* 30 (1997): 77–80.

White, Leslie A. "Notes on the Ethnobotany of the Keres." *Papers of the Michigan Academy of Arts, Sciences and Letters* 30 (1945): 557–68.

Whitfield, C. J., and H. L. Anderson. "Secondary Succession in the Desert Plains Grassland." *Ecology* 19 (1938): 171–80.

Whitford, Walter G., Ronald Nielson, and Amrita de Soyza. "Establishment and Effects of Establishment of Creosotebush, *Larrea tridentata*, on a Chihuahuan Desert Watershed." *Journal of Arid Environments* 40, no. 1 (January 2001): 1–10.

Whiting, Alfred E. "Ethnobotany of the Hopi." *Museum of Northern Arizona Bulletin*, no. 15, 1939.

Widrig, Reto, Andy Suter, Reinhard Saller, and Jörg Melzer. "Choosing between NSAID and Arnica for Topical Treatment of Hand Osteoarthritis in a Randomised, Double-Blind Study."

Rheumatology International 27 (April 2007): 585.

Wie, M. B. "Protective Effects of *Opuntia ficus-indica* and *Saururus chinensis* on Free-radical Induced Neuronal Injury in Mouse Cortical Cell Cultures." *Yakhak Hoeji* 44 (2000): 613–19.

Wiese, J., S. McPherson, M. C. Odden, and M. G. Shlipak. "Effect of *Opuntia ficus indica* on Symptoms of the Alcohol Hangover." *Archives of Internal Medicine* 164 (2004): 1334–40.

Williams, Park A., Craig D. Allen, Alison K. Macalady, Daniel Griffin, Connie A. Woodhouse, David M. Meko, Thomas W. Swetnam, Sara A. Rauscher, Richard Seager, Henri D. Grissino-Mayer, et al. "Temperature as a Potent Driver of Regional Forest Drought Stress and Tree Mortality." *Nature Climate Change* 3 (2013): 292–97.

Wilson, M. B., M. Spivak, A. D. Hegeman, A. Rendahl, and J. D. Cohen. "Metabolomics Reveals the Origins of Antimicrobial Plant Resins Collected by Honey Bees." *PLOS One* 8, no. 10 (2013). doi:10.1371/journal.pone.0077512.

Wilson, Michael R. "Notes on the Ethnobotany of the Inuktitut." *Western Canadian Journal of Anthropology* 8 (1978): 180–96.

Witthoft, John. "An Early Cherokee Ethnobotanical Note." *Journal of the Washington Academy of Sciences* 37, no. 3 (1947): 73–75.

——. "Cherokee Indian Uses of Potherbs." *Journal of Cherokee Studies* 2, no. 2 (1977): 250–55.

Woelk, H. "Comparison of St. John's Wort and Imipramine for Treating Depression." *BMJ* 321 (2000): 536–39.

Wolfle, Ute, Julia Hoffmann, Birgit Haarhaus, Venugopal Rao Mittapalli, and Christop M. Schempp. "Anti-inflammatory and Vasoconstrictive Properties of *Potentilla erecta*: A Traditional Medicinal Plant from the Northern Hemisphere." *Journal of Ethnopharmacology* 204, no. 23 (May 2017): 86–94.

Wolfram, R. M., H. Kritz, Y. Efthimiou, J. Stomatopoulos, and H. Sinzinger. "Effect of Prickly Pear (*Opuntia robusta*) on Glucose- and Lipid-Metabolism in Non-Diabetics with Hyperlipidemia—a Pilot Study." *Wiener Klinische Wochenschrift* 114, no. 19-20 (2002): 840–46.

Wolfson, P., and D. L. Hoffmann. "An Investigation into the Efficacy of *Scutellaria lateriflora* in Healthy Volunteers." *Alternative Therapies in Health and Medicine* 9 (2003): 74–78.

Wollenweber, Eckhard, and George Yatskievych. "External Flavonoids of Ocotillo (*Fouquiera splendens*)." *Zeitschrift für Naturforschung C* 49, no. 9-10 (1994): 689–90.

Wong, Bing-Sang, Yung-Chin Hsiao, Ta-Wei Lin, Kuo-Shuen Chen, Pei-Ni Chen, Wu-Hsien Kuo, Shu-Chen Chu, and Yih-Shou Hsieh. "The In Vitro and In Vivo Apoptotic Effects of *Mahonia oiwakensis* on Human Lung Cancer Cells." *Chemico-Biological Interactions* 180, no. 2 (July 2009): 165–74.

Wood, Matthew. *The Earthwise Herbal.* Berkeley, CA: North Atlantic Books, 2008.

Wu, Yi-Chian, and Ching-Liang Hsieh. "Pharmacological Effects of Radix *Angelica sinensis* (Danggui) on Cerebral Infarction." *Chinese Medicine* 6, no 1 (August 2011): 32.

Wyburn-Mason, R. "Naegleria in Rheumatoid and Malignant Disease." *South African Medical Journal* 63 (1983): 31.

Wyman, Leland C., and Stuart K. Harris. *The Ethnobotany of the Kayenta Navaho.* Albuquerque: University of New Mexico Press, 1951.

Xiao, Tao, Hua Yu, Yao-Bin Song, Yue-Ping Jiang, Bo Zeng, and Ming Dong. "Enhancement of Allelopathic Effects of Exotic Invasive on Native Plant Species." *PLOS One* 14, no. 1 (2019). doi:10.1371/journal.pone.0206165.

Xiao-Ping Dong, Chun-Tao Che, and Norman R. Farnsworth. "Cytotoxic Flavonols from *Gutierrezia microcephala*."

Journal of Natural Products 50, no. 2 (1987): 337–38.

Yadollah-Damavandi, Soheila, Mehdi Chavoshi-Nejad, Ehsan Jangholi, Noushin Nekouyian, Sahar Hosseini, Amin Seifaee, Shima Rafiee, Hossein Karimi, Soheil Ashkani-Esfahani, Yekta Parsa, et al. "Topical *Hypericum perforatum* Improves Tissue Regeneration in Full-Thickness Excisional Wounds in Diabetic Rat Model." *Evidence-Based Complementary and Alternative Medicine* (2015). doi:10.1155/2015/245328.

Yaeesh, S., Q. Jama, A. U. Khan, and A. H. Gilani. "Studies on Hepatoprotective, Antispasmodic and Calcium Antagonist Activities of the Aqueous-methanol Extract of *Achillea millefolium*." *Phytotherapy Research* 20, no. 7 (July 2006): 546–51.

Yan, Zhi-Yang, Jing-Jie Chen, Zhi-Kang Duan, Guo-Dong Yao, Bin Lin, Xiao-Bo Wang, Xiao-Xiao Huang, and Shao-Jiang Song. "Racemic Phenylpropanoids from the Root Barks of *Ailanthus altissima* (Mill) Swingle with Cytotoxicity against Hepatoma Cells." *Fitoterapia* 130 (2018): 234–40.

Yang, Jin-ying, Hu-hu Chen, Jiang Wu, Su-xiao Gong, Chang-qing Chen, Tie-jun Zhang, and Min-jie Wang. "Advances in Studies on Pharmacological Functions of Ligustilide and Their Mechanisms." *Chinese Herbal Medicines* 4, no. 1 (2012): 26–32.

Yarnell, R. A. "Implications of Distinctive Flora on Pueblo Ruins." *American Anthropologist* 67, no. 3 (June 1965): 662–74.

Yatoo, Mohd. Iqbal, Umesh Dimri, Arumugam Gopalakrishan, Mani Saminathan, Kuldeep Dhama, Karikalan Mathesh, Archana Saxena, Devi Gopinath, and Shahid Husain. "Antidiabetic and Oxidative Stress Ameliorative Potential of Ethanolic Extract of *Pedicularis longiflora*." *International Journal of Pharmacology* 12, no. 3 (2016): 177.

Yazdanparast, R., A. Ardestani, and S. Jamshidi. "Experimental Diabetes Treated with *Achillea santolina*: Effect on Pancreatic Oxidative Parameters." *Journal of Ethnopharmacology* 112 (2007): 13–18.

Yazdi, A., S. Sardari, and Md Sayya. "Evaluation of Anticonvulsant Activity of Leaves of *Glycyrrhiza glabra* Grown in Iran as a Possible Renewable Source for Anticonvulsant Compounds." *Iranian Journal of Pharmaceutical Research* 10, no. 1 (2011): 75–82.

Yeh, M. L., C. F. Liu, C. L. Huang, and T. C. Huang. "Hepatoprotective Effect of *Angelica archangelica* in Chronically Ethanol-Treated Mice." *Pharmacology* 68 (2003): 70–73.

Yoon, G., Y. D. Jung, and S. H. Cheon. "Cytotoxic Allyl Retrochalcone from the Roots of *Glycyrrhiza inflata*." *Chemical and Pharmaceutical Bulletin* 53 (2005): 694–95.

York, J. C., and W. A. Dick-Peddie. "Vegetation Changes in Southern New Mexico during the Past Hundred Years." In *Arid Lands in Perspective*, edited by W. G. McGinnies and B. J. Goldman 153–66. Tucson: University of Arizona Press, 1969.

You, Yong-Ouk, Na-Young Choi, and Kang-Ju Kim. "Ethanol Extract of *Ulmus pumila* Root Bark Inhibits Clinically Isolated Antibiotic-Resistant Bacteria." *Evidence-Based Complementary and Alternative Medicine* (2013): doi:10.1155/2013/269874.

Yousefi, Keyvan, Fatemeh Fathiazad, Hamid Soraya, Maryam Rameshrad, Nasrin Maleki-Dizaji, and Alireza Garjani. "*Marrubium vulgare* L. methanolic Extract Inhibits Inflammatory Response and Prevents Cardiomyocyte Fibrosis in Isoproterenol-Induced Acute Myocardial Infarction in Rats." *Bioimpacts* 4, no. 1 (2014): 211–27.

Yu, Xuelong, Qiang Gui, Guozhu Su, Ailin Yang, Zhongdong Hu, Changhai Qu, Zhe Wan, Ruoyu Li, Pengfei Tu, and Xingyun Chai. "Usnic Acid Derivatives with Cytotoxic and Antifungal Activities from the Lichen *Usnea longissim.*" *Journal of Natural Products* 79, no. 5 (2016): 1373–80.

Yu, Qing-gao, Yan Dan-hua, Liu Jie-pin, and Xiong Zhi-qing. "Effect of *Mahonia* on the SOD Activity and MDA Content in Serum of Mice." *Lishizhen Medicine and Materia Medica Research* 6 (2008).

Yuan, C. S., X. B. Sun, P. H. Zhao, and M. A. Cao. "Antibacterial Constituents from *Pedicularis armata.*" *Journal of Asian Natural Products Research* 9, no. 7 (2007): 673–77.

Yuan, Yongge, Bing Wang, Shanshan Zhang, Jianjun Tang, Cong Tu, Shuijin Hu, Jean W. H. Yong, and Xin Chen. "Enhanced Allelopathy and Competitive Ability of Invasive Plant *Solidago canadensis* in Its Introduced Range." *Journal of Plant Ecology* 6, no. 3 (June 2013): 253–63.

Yuan, X., A. Xiao, and T. N. Taylor. "Lichen-like Symbiosis 600 Million Years Ago." *Science* 308 (2005): 1017.

Zadeh, Jalal Bayati, and Zahra Moradi Kor. "Licorice (*Glycyrrhiza glabra*) as a Valuable Medicinal Plant." *International Journal of Advanced Biological and Biomedical Research* 1, no. 10 (2013): 1281–88.

Zamiri-Akhlaghi, A., H. Rakhshandeh, Z. Tayarani-Najaran, and S. H. Mousavi. "Study of Cytotoxic Properties of *Rosa damascena* Extract in Human Cervix Carcinoma Cell Line." *Avicenna Journal of Phytomed* 2011, no.1 (2001): 74–77.

Zamureenko, V. A., N. A. Klyuev, B. V. Bocharov, V. S. Kabonov, and A. M. Zakharov. "An Investigation of Component Composition of Essential Oil of *M. fistulosa.*" *Chemistry of Natural Compounds* 25, no. 5 (1989): 549–51.

Zarai, Zied, Adel Kadri, Ines Ben Chobba, Riadh Ben Mansour, Ahmed Bekir, Hafedh Mejdoub, and Neji Gharsallah. "The In Vitro Evaluation of Antibacterial, Antifungal, and Cytotoxic Properties of *Marrubium vulgare* L. Essential Oil Grown in Tunisia." *Lipids in Health and Disease* 10 (2011): 161.

Zarrabi, M., R. Dalirfardouei, Z. Sepehrizade, and R. K. Kermanshahi. "Comparison of the Antimicrobial Effects of Semipurified Cyclotides from Iranian *Viola odorata* against Some of Plant and Human Pathogenic Bacteria." *Journal of Applied Microbiology* 115, no. 2 (2013): 367–75.

Zeng, Xiangying, Lao Bangsheng, Dong Xichang, Sun Xuehui, Dong Yulian, Sheng Guoying, and Fu Jiamo. "Study on Anti-influenza Effect of Alkaloids from Roots of *Mahonia bealei* in Vitro. *Journal of Chinese Medicinal Materials* 1 (2003).

Zeng, Y., L. Guo, and B. Chen. "Arbuscular Mycorrhizal Symbiosis and Active Ingredients of Medicinal Plants: Current Research Status and Prospectives." *Mycorrhiza* 23, no. 4 (May 2012): 253–65.

Zhamanbayeva, G. T., A. N. Aralbayeva, M. K. Murzakhmetova, S. T. Tuleukhanov, and M. Danilenko. "Cooperative Antiproliferative and Differentiation-Enhancing Activity of Medicinal Plant Extracts in Acute Myeloid Leukemia Cells." *Biomedical Pharmacotherapy* 82 (2016): 80–89.

Zhang, Jing, Ri-Zhen Huang, Hong Kie-Cao, An-Wei Cheng, Cheng-Shi Jiang, Zhi-Xin Liao, Chao Liu, and Jin-Yue Sun. "Chemical Composition, In Vitro Anti-Tumor Activities and Related Mechanisms of the Essential Oil from the Roots of *Potentilla discolor.*" *Industrial Crops and Products* 113 (March 2018): 19–27.

Zhang, Lin, Anjaneya S. Ravipati, Sundar Rao Koyyalamudi, Sang Chul Jeong, Narsimha Reddy, Paul T. Smith, John Bartlett, Kirubakaran Shanmugam, Gerald Munch, and Ming Jie Wu. "Antioxidant and Anti-inflammatory Activities of Selected Medicinal Plants Containing Phenolic and Flavonoid Compounds." *Journal of Food Chemistry* 59, no. 23 (2011): 12361–67.

Zhang, W. Q., Y. L. Hua, M. Zhang, P. Ji, J. X. Li, L. Zhang, P. L. Li, and Y. M. Wei. "Metabonomic Analysis of the Anti-Inflammatory Effects of Volatile Oils of *Angelica sinensis* on Rat Model of Acute Inflammation." *Biomedical Chromatography* 29 (2015): 902–10.

Zhang, X., Z. Ma, Y. Wang, B. Sun, X. Guo, C. Pan, and L. Chen. "*Angelica dahurica* Ethanolic Extract Improves Impaired Wound Healing by Activating Angiogenesis in Diabetes." *PLOS One* 12, no. 5 (2017). doi:10.1371/journal.pone.0177862.

Zhang, XinFeng, Tran Manh Hung, Phuong Thien Phuong, Tran Minh Ngoc, Byung-Sun Min, Kyung-Sik Song, Yeon Hee Seong, and KiHwan Bae. "Anti-inflammatory Activity of Flavonoids from *Populus davidiana*." *Archives of Pharmacal Research* 29, no. 12 (December 2006): 1102–8.

Zhao, Chun-Chao, Jian-Hua Shao, Xian Li, Jing Xu, and Peng Zhang. "Antimicrobial Constituents from Fruits of *Ailanthus altissima* SWINGLE." *Archives of Pharmacal Research* 28, no. 10 (2005): 1147–51.

Zhilyakova, E. T., O. O. Novikov, E. N. Naumenko, L. V. Krichkovskaya, T. S. Kiseleva, E. Yu. Timoshenko, M. Yu. Novikova, and S. A. Litvinov. "Study of *Monard fistulosa* Essential Oil as a Prospective Antiseborrheic Agent." *Bulletin of Experimental Biology and Medicine* 148, no. 4 (2009): 612–14.

Zhong, L. J., Y. L. Hua, P. Ji, W. L.Yao, W. Q. Zhang, J. Li, and Y. M. Wei. "Evaluation of the Anti-Inflammatory Effects of Volatile Oils from Processed Products of *Angelica sinensis* Radix by GC-MS-Based Metabolomics." *Journal of Ethnopharmacology* 191 (2016): 195–205.

Zhou, Yan-meng, Song Li-quin Ma Xiao-qian, Li Bing-long, and Gao Yun-sheng.

"Preventive Effect of *Trifolium pratense* Isoflavones on Retinoic Acid Induced Osteoporosis in Mice." *Chinese Pharmacological Bulletin* 12 (2010).

Zhu, Meiju, Hongzhu Zhu, Ninghua Tan, Hui Wang, Hongbiao Chu, and Chonglin Zhang. "Central Anti-Fatigue Activity of Verbascoside." *Neuroscience Letters* 616 (2016): 75–79.

Zhu, Wei, Jin Hu, Xin Wang, Jingkui Tian, and Setsuko Komatsu. "Organ-Specific Analysis of Mahonia Using Gel-Free/Label-Free Proteomic Technique." *Journal of Proteome Research* 14, no. 6 (2015): 2669–85.

Zigmond, Maurice I. *Kawaiisu Ethnobotany*. Salt Lake City: University of Utah Press, 1981.

Zolghadri, Yalda, Mehdi Fazeli, Marzieh Kooshki, Tahoora Shomali, Negar Karimaghayee, and Maryam Dehghani. "*Achillea millefolium* L. Hydro-alcoholic Extract Protects Pancreatic Cells by Down Regulating IL-1ß and iNOS Gene Expression in Diabetic Rats. *International Journal of Molecular and Cellular Medicine* 3, no. 4 (2014): 255–62.

Zou, Y. P, Y. H. Lu, and D. Z. Wei. "Protective Effects of a Flavonoid-Rich Extract of *Hypericum perforatum* L. against Hydrogen Peroxide-Induced Apoptosis in PC12 Cells." *Phytotherapy Research* 24 (2010): S6–10.

Zu, Y., H. Yu, and L. Liang. "Activities of Ten Essential Oils towards *Propionibacterium acnes* and PC-3, A-549 and MCF-7 Cancer Cells." *Molecules* 15 (2010): 3200–10.

Zubek, S., S. Mielcarek, and K. Turnau. "Hypericin and Pseudohypericin Concentrations of a Valuable Medicinal Plant *Hypericum perforatum* L. Are Enhanced by Arbuscular Mycorrhizal Fungi." *Mycorrhiza* 22, no. 2 (February 2012): 149–56.

Index

Albuquerque: elevation profile, 51; Rio Grande evolution around, 35, 35; from Sandia Crest, 56, 56

alfalfa (*Medicago sativa*), 25, 35, 37

allelopathic activity: creosote, 17, 21; goldenrod, 175; of invasives impact on natives, 198; potentilla, 158; snakeweed, 115; tree of heaven, 199

Alzheimer's disease. *See* nervous system health

amole. *See* yucca

ancestors/ancestral populations, 48; bee balm, 27–28; creosote, 15, 197; datura and, 99; oshá and, 129; pedicularis, 146; piñon evidence and, 153; prickly pear and, 141

angelica (*Angelica* spp.), 85, 86, 87; aromatic qualities, 86; contraindications, 88; culinary uses, 85; dong-quai and, 87; habitat, 86; medicinal uses, 85–88; Old World uses and traditions of, 84–85; oshá compared with, 131; research, 87–88

Anima Botanical Sanctuary, xii

animals: endangered in riparian habitats, 35–36; grasses reduction impact for, 30; grasses threat from, 23; unselfing experience with, 46. *See also* foraging sources; grazing

Anthropocene: biodiversity decline in, 5–6, 7; defining, 4–5; habitat creation and alteration in, 5–8

anti-inflammatory activity. *See* inflammation

anxiety. *See* nervous system health

Apache plume (*Fallugia paradoxa*), 167

arnica (*Arnica* spp.), 89, 90; disturbances response of, 88; habitat and range, 88–89; herbs confused with, 90; medicinal uses, 89–91; precautions, 89; preparations, 89, 154; research, 90; species of, 88

aromatics/aromatic qualities: angelica, 86; bee balm, 26, 31, 139; creosote, 15, 24; experiencing, 43, 50–51, 55; grindelia, 114; horehound, 136–37; juniper, 55, 122, 123; piñon, 154–55; rose, 166–67; sage, 93, 94, 95; shrublands and, 50–51, 55; snakeweed, 116; yarrow, 79; yerba mansa, 36, 45, 84

arthritis/rheumatism: angelica and, 86; arnica and, 89, 90; bee balm and, 139; cleavers and, 106; cottonwood and, 156, 157; creosote and, 127, 128; datura and, 100, 102; globemallow and, 178, 180; goldenrod and, 177; grindelia and, 114; horehound and, 137; juniper and, 125; Oregon grape and, 133; piñon pines and, 154; prickly pear and, 142; red root and, 98; rose and, 166, 168; Russian olive and, 202; sage and, 93, 94; St. John's wort and, 119; salt cedar and, 203, 204; snakeweed and, 116, 117; violet and, 191; yarrow and, 77, 78; yerba mansa and, 82, 83; yucca and, 194, 195

asthma. *See* respiratory health

autoimmune conditions: creosote and, 127; globemallow and, 179; licorice and, 109. *See also* inflammation

bark beetle: impacts of, 25, 27, 28, 29; ponderosa pine loss from, 29; species, 29; surges with climate change, 30

bearcorn (*Conopholis alpina* var. *mexicana*), 24

bear root. *See* oshá

bedstraw (*Galium boreale*), 24

bee balm (*Monarda fistulosa*), 139, 140; aromatics, 26, 31, 139; change in stands of, 25; connection with land role of, 32; culinary uses, 139; as foraging source for insects and birds, 24, 25, 26, 31–32, 138–39; habitat and range, 24–25, 26, 27, 138–39; habitat destruction, 31; medicinal uses, 31, 32, 139–41; as oshá substitute, 129; research, 140–41; sensory experience of, 73; species and subspecies of, 26–28 betony. *See* dwarf betony; elephant head betony; fern leaf; parrot beak; pedicularis

biodiversity: creosote role in reduction in, 21, 23; decline in, 5-6, 7; of floodplains, 33; invasives benefiting, 198; with native-nonnative balance, 8; pedicularis role for, 58, 147-48

biotic community, xiv, 49

bites. *See* wound care

black grama grass (*Bouteloua eriopoda*), 19, 21

bleeding: globemallow and, 178; potentilla and, 159; rose and, 167; vervain and, 187; yarrow and, 77, 78, 79; yucca and, 194

blood flow and pressure: angelica and, 86, 87; grindelia and, 113; juniper and, 124; licorice contraindications with, 109; mesquite and, 163; Russian olive and, 202; sage and, 94; tree of heaven and, 201; vervain and, 188; violet and, 192; yarrow and, 77

blood purification/tonic: angelica and, 86; cleavers and, 106; grindelia and, 113; juniper and, 124; ocotillo and, 104; Oregon grape and, 134; pedicularis and, 149; red clover and, 181, 182; red root and, 98; violet and, 191; yarrow and, 79; yerba mansa and, 82

blood sugar. *See* diabetes and blood glucose

blue grama grass (*Boutelua gracilis*), 30

bosque habitats: endangered ecosystems of, 35; types, 33. *See also* Rio Grande River and bosque

bracted betony (*Pedicularis bracteosa*), 152, *152*

brook mint (*Mentha arvensis*), 24, 71

broom dalea (*Psorothamnus scoparius*), 52, 53

bruises. *See* wound care

burdock (*Arctium lappa*), 67-68

burns. *See* wound care

cancer: angelica and, 87-88; cleavers and, 106-7; clover and, 182; creosote and, 24, 127; datura and, 102; globemallow and, 180; grindelia and, 115; horehound and, 138; juniper and, 125; licorice and, 111; mesquite and, 163; ocotillo and, 105;

Oregon grape and, 135, 136; oshá and, 132; potentilla and, 160; prickly pear and, 144, 145-46; rose and, 169; Russian olive and, 202; sage and, 96; St. John's wort and, 121-22; salt cedar and, 204; Siberian elm and, 206; skullcap and, 174; snakeweed and, 116; tree of heaven and, 199, 201; usnea and, 184, 185; vervain and, 189; violet and, 191-92; yarrow and, 80; yerba mansa and, 39; yucca and, 196

cardiovascular health: angelica and, 87, 90; bee balm and, 139, 140-41; goldenrod and, 176; horehound and, 138; mesquite and, 163; oshá and, 132; pedicularis and, 148-49; prickly pear and, 143; red clover and, 182; rose and, 166, 168; Russian olive and, 202; skullcap and, 173; usnea and, 185; violet and, 191; yarrow and, 77, 79, 80; yucca and, 196. *See also* cholesterol

catnip (*Nepeta cataria*), 173

cayenne (*Capsicum annuum*), 89

chamomile (*Matricaria chamomilla*), 173, 182

chaparral. *See* creosote

cheatgrass (*Bromus tectorum*), 91

Chihuahuan Desert, 54, 103; biotic soil crust in, 20; changes to, 20-21; creosote in, 15, 17, 18, 126, 197; 1800s explorations and notes of, 19; grasslands restoration in, 23; settlers and grazing impact on, 20

cholesterol: horehound and, 138; juniper and, 125; licorice and, 112; mesquite and, 163; oshá and, 132; prickly pear and, 142, 143, 144; red clover and, 182; rose and, 168; Russian olive and, 202; sage and, 96; yucca and, 194, 196

chuchupate. *See* oshá

cinquefoil. *See* potentilla

cleavers (*Galium aparine*), 106; habitat and range, 105; medicinal uses, 105-7; Old World uses, 105-6; preparations, 106; research, 106-7

clematis (*Clematis columbiana*), 24

cliffrose (*Purshia stansburiana*), 167, *167*

climate change: bark beetle surges with, 30; carbohydrate storage for trees and, 30; extinctions relation to, 5; forests impacted by, 6-7, 28, 30, 31; human evolution and, xi, xviii, 6; invasive plant increase with, 8, 198; juniper survival and, 30; piñon threats from, 30, 152; projections, 6–7, 28, 31, 36; Rio Grande impacts from, 36; temperature increase impacts of, 28, 30

clover. *See* sweet clover

colds. *See* fever; immune function; respiratory health

Colorado Plateau, *18*, 57; canyons, 52; piñon pine in, 28, 152–53; rift formation between Great Plains and, 51–52; tree loss in, 28

Colorado River, *17*, 33–34, *34*

commoners, working with plant, 68–69

coral bells (*Huechera pulchella*), 57, *57*, 58

corydalis (*Corydalis aurea*), 24

cottonwood (*Populus deltoides wislizenii*), *62*, 155, 157; buds harvest and uses, 63, *63*, 155–57; in datura preparations, 100; elevation, 51; as foraging sources, 155; habitat, 60, 155, 205; maternal/nurturing nature of, 63, 156; medicinal uses, 63, 155, 156–57; planting, poles, 10, *10*; precautions, 156; preparations, 89, 157; in riparian floodplains/Rio Grande bosque, 33, *34*–37, *38*, 59–63, 155; Russian olive threats to, 201; yerba mansa and, 36, 37–38, *38*, 60

coughs. *See* respiratory health

coyote willow (*Salix exigua*), 33, *34*, 39

creosote (*Larrea tridentata*), *19*, 22, *126*, *127*; allelopathic activity, 17, 21; ancestral populations, 15, 197; aromatic qualities, 15, 24; biodiversity reduction and, 21, 23; contraindications, 128; desert habitat role and prevalence of, 13, 15, 17–18, *19*, 20–21, 68, 126, 197; grasses presence relation to, 20–21, 22, 23; grazing relation to expansion of, 197; habitat disruption of, 23–24; as invasive, 21, 126; longevity, 15; medicinal uses, 23–24, 126–28; preparations and combinations, 100, 116, 127, 128; research, 126, 127; soil quality and, 20, 23

culinary qualities/uses: angelica, 85; bee balm, 139; juniper, 124; mesquite, 162; oshá, 131; piñon pines, 152–53; potentilla, 158–59; prickly pear, 141–42; rose, 167; Russian olive, 203; Siberian elm seeds, 206; violet, 190, 191. *See also* wild food

cultivation. *See* gardening and cultivation

cutleaf coneflower (*Rudbeckia laciniata*), 170, *171*; echinacea substituted and compared with, 170–71; habitat, 24, 25, 71, 170; medicinal uses, 170–71; preparations and combinations, 170–71; research, 171

Dakota vervain (*Glandularia bipinnatifida*), 71

dams. *See* water diversions

dandelion (*Taraxacum officinale*), 67, 68

datura (*Datura wrightii*), *102*; flower and blooming of, 49, *49*, 99, *99*; history and Old World species, 99, 101; licorice as antidote for, 100; medicinal uses, 100–102; preparations and combinations, 100, 101–2, 116, 154, 174; seed pods, 100, *101*; in snakeweed preparations, 116; toxicity, 99–100

depression: angelica for, 86; grindelia for, 115; prickly pear for, 144–45; rose for, 166, 168–69; St. John's wort for, 118, 120; skullcap for, 172; vervain for, 187

deserts/Desert Basin, 14; ancient history evidence in, 13, 15; characteristics of, 13; creosote role and prominence in, 13, 15, 17–18, *19*, 20–21, 68, 126, 197; 1800s explorers on grasslands of, 18–19; foraging shifts in, 13, 15; grass species present in, 21; grazing impact on, 20, 22, 23; heat impact on annuals of, 23; juniper relationship with, 55; map of American Southwest, *17*; mesquite in, *19*, 20, 161; mountains typical of, 57; ocotillo adaptation to, 102–3; petroglyphs, 13, 15; range of, 18. *See also* Chihuahuan Desert

detoxification. *See* purification/detoxification

diabetes and blood glucose: angelica and, 88; cottonwood and, 157; datura and, 102; goldenrod and, 177; horehound and, 137, 138; juniper and, 125; licorice and, 112; mesquite and, 163; Oregon grape and, 136; oshá and, 132; pedicularis and, 149; potentilla and, 160; prickly pear and, 142, 143, 144; red clover and, 182; rose and, 168; sage and, 96; yarrow and, 80

diarrhea. *See* digestive system health

digestive system health: angelica and, 85–86, 88; bee balm and, 139; cleavers and, 106; cottonwood and, 156, 157; cutleaf coneflower and, 170, 171; globe-mallow and, 178, 179, 180; goldenrod and, 175–76, 177; grindelia and, 113; horehound and, 137; juniper and, 123, 124, 125; licorice and, 108, 109, 111–12; mesquite and, 162–63; ocotillo and, 103; Oregon grape and, 133, 134–35; oshá and, 131, 132; pedicularis and, 148; potentilla and, 159, 160; prickly pear and, 142, 143, 144, 145; red clover and, 181; red root and, 98; rose and, 166–67, 168, 169; Russian olive and, 202; sage and, 92–93, 94–95; St. John's wort and, 119, 120, 122; salt cedar and, 204; skullcap and, 173; snakeweed and, 116, 117; tree of heaven and, 199, 201; usnea and, 185; vervain and, 187, 188, 189; violet and, 191, 192; yarrow and, 77, 78, 80; yerba mansa and, 82, 83, 84; yucca and, 194

disturbances: Anthropocene flood, 5; arnica response to, 88; examples of increasing, 8, 9; forest vulnerability to, 28; invasive plants expansion from increasing, 8, 205; licorice and riparian habitat, 107–8; from nonnative plant, 7–8; Oregon grape response to, 133; oshá viability and, 128; patterns, changes in, 5; pedicularis and, 146; potentilla spread after, 158; St. John's wort and, 117; Siberian elm expansion with, 205; usnea sensitivity to, 183; yarrow growth and, 76

dock (*Rumex crispus*), 25, 68
Doctrine of Signatures, 98, 118
dong-quai, 87
drought: contemporary compared with historical, 28, 31; tree losses from contemporary, 28, 30
dry herb tinctures solvency rates, 74
dwarf betony (*Pedicularis centranthera*), 24, 51, 56, 58, 58–59, 151, 151

echinacea, 170–71, 189
ecological herbalism: about, xii, xviii, 3–4; approach relation to global changes, 4–8, 10; connection to land primacy in, 3–5, 10–12, 40, 64; native plant communities approach of, 3–4; unselfing practice and, 46

ecosystem empathy, xviii, xix, 11, 49, 63
eczema. *See* skin conditions
elephant head betony (*Pedicularis groenlandica*), 147, 150, 150
endangered species: animal, in riparian habitats, 35–36; bosque habitats and, 35; connection with land and, 3; future projections for, 5–6; native plant communities, 3, 5–6; statistics, 3. *See also* threatened species

environmental change and evolution: adaptive approach to, 9–12, 40–41; ecological herbalism approach relation to, 4–8, 10; in forests, 6–7, 25, 28, 30, 31; human activity and, 6, 40–41; mountain streams, 25; pace of, 4–5, 40–41; of Rio Grande River and bosque, 35, 35; Sandia Mountains, 30. *See also* climate change

extinctions: climate change and land use impact for, 5; nonnatives expansion relation to, 198; rates and statistics, 3, 5; volcanoes and, 48

fern leaf betony (*Pedicularis procera*), 147, 151, 151

fever: angelica and, 86–87; bee balm and, 139–40; cottonwood and, 156, 157; creosote and, 128; goldenrod and, 176; horehound and, 137; juniper and, 124; licorice and, 108; mesquite and, 162; oshá and, 131; piñon pines and, 154; potentilla and, 159–60; red clover and, 182; red root and, 98; rose and, 166; Russian olive and, 202; sage and, 94; St. John's wort and, 119; salt cedar and, 204; skullcap and, 173; snakeweed and, 116, 117; usnea and, 185; vervain and, 187, 188; yarrow and, 77; yerba mansa and, 82

figwort (*Scrophularia montana*), 58
fires. *See* wildfires
floodplains: about, 32–33; ancient settlements, 57; biodiversity, 33; cottonwood and, 33, 34–37, 38, 59–63, 155, 205; nonnatives in and reduction of, 6

floods/flooding: Anthropocene and, disturbances, 5; controls, impact of, 34; invasives spread with change in, 201;

jetty jacks installation and, 36, 36; 1941, 35; plants role in decreasing, 33
foothills, mountain, 16
foraging sources: of bee balm for bees and birds, 24, 25, 26, 31-32, 138-39; cleavers, 105; cottonwoods, 155; in Desert Basin, shifts in, 13, 15; globemallow, 177-78; goldenrod, 175; grasslands and, 13, 15; juniper, 122; licorice, 108; mesquite, 161, 162; ocotillo, 103; Oregon grape, 133; piñon pines, 152-53; potentilla, 158; prickly pear, 141; rose, 164, 167; Russian olive, 201; sage, 91; snakeweed impact on, 115; yucca, 193
forests, 15; ancient history present in, 56-57; bark beetle impact on, 25, 27, 28, 29; canopy loss impacts in, 30; changes to, 6-7, 25, 28, 30, 31; climate change impact on, 6-7, 28, 30, 31; fires impact on, 6-7, 7, 28, 41; fire suppression impacting, 6, 28; map of American Southwest, 17; pedicularis in, 59, 148, 150-52; shrublands evolution from, 31; species prevalent in, 24. See also tree die-off

gardening and cultivation: globemallow, 180; habitat consideration in, 71, 73; medicinal plants list for, 72; plant pairings for, 71; red clover, 180-81; St. John's wort, 120; soil quality considerations with, 71; sustainable herbalist practice and, xix, 69, 71; weeds and, 67-68, 69, 72, 180-81; wild-spirited, 69-71, 70, 73; yerba mansa in wild compared with, 81
Gardner, J. L., 20-21
gelsemium (G. sempervirens), 174
giant betony. See fern leaf
Gila National Forest, 29
globalization, xviii, 196, 206
globemallow (Sphaeralcea spp.), 179, 180, 198; cultivation, 180; as foraging source, 177-78; gardening with, 180; habitat, 68, 71, 177-78; medicinal uses, 178-80; preparations, 179; research, 180; in restoration efforts, 178
glucose/glycemic. See diabetes and blood glucose
gobernadora. See creosote
goldenrod (Solidago spp.), 175, 176;

allelopathic activity, 175; in datura preparations, 100; habitat, 68, 174-75; medicinal uses, 175-77; pedicularis inhibiting spread of, 148; research, 177
goldenseal (Hydrastis canadensis), 83, 133
gonorrhea. See venereal disease
grasses/grasslands: animals eating seeds impact on, 23; animals impacted by reduction of, 30; Chihuahuan Desert, restoring, 23; creosote dominance in, 20-21, 22, 23; of Desert Basin in 1800s, 18-19; as forage source, 13, 15; forest canopy loss impact on, 30; grama, 19, 21, 30; grazing impact on, 20, 22, 23; invasive species in, 6; map of American Southwest, 17; mesquite suppressive role in, 21, 161; reduction, factors behind, 21, 23; tree die-off impact for, 30; water and heat extremes impact on, 23
grazing: arnica and, 88, 89; Chihuahuan Desert impacted by, 20; creosote dominance relation to, 197; deserts/grasslands impacted by, 20, 22, 23; grindelia and, 112; mesquite and, 162; native plants impacted by, 6, 8, 20; potentilla and, 158; Rio Grande impacted by, 34; St. John's wort and, 117; snakeweed increase with, 115-16; yarrow in areas of, 76
Great Plains, 18, 18, 51-52, 54, 57, 115, 116
grindelia (Grindelia squarrosa): aromatic qualities, 114; flower buds and resin, 113, 113, 114; grazing and, 112; habitat, 71, 112; history, 112-13; medicinal uses, 112-15; as oshá substitute, 129; preparations, 113; research, 112-14; species, 112

Hardin, Jesse Wolf, xi-xv, xxi, 197
heart health. See cardiovascular health; cholesterol
heat, environmental, 41; desert annuals/grasses impacted by extremes in, 23; forest losses and, 31; salt cedar tolerance for, 203
heat, in body: bee balm for, 32; prickly pear for, 142-43; rose for, 166; sage for, 94, 95; tree of heaven for, 201; yarrow for, 77
hediondilla. See creosote
herbalism: connection with place role in, xiv-xv, xix-xx; human evolution relation

herbalism (*continued*)
with, xi, xviii; interdisciplinary approach
to, xviii, 11; nonnative invasives consideration in, 199–206; plant protection
aspect of, xii, xiii; practitioners, about,
xi–xii, xiv–xv; sustainable practices and,
xix, 4, 32, 67, 69, 133, 180–81. *See also*
ecological herbalism; *specific plants and
topics*
honey locust (*Gleditsia triacanthos*), 35
horehound (*Marrubium vulgare*), 137, 138;
aromatics, 136–37; habitat, 136; as invasive, 136; medicinal uses, 137–38; Old
World history, 136, 137, 138; precautions,
137; preparations, 137; research, 137–38
horsetail (*Equisetum arvense*), 24, 71
human activity and evolution: choices
about, 48; climate change and, xi, xviii,
6; habitat changes with, 6, 40–41; herbal
healing relation to, xi, xviii; plant communities approach relation to, 9–12;
population growth and, 3
Humboldt, Alexander von, 41
hypoglycemia. *See* diabetes and blood
glucose

immune function: arnica and, 90; bee balm
and, 139; cutleaf coneflower and, 170–71;
globemallow and, 179; horehound and,
137–38; licorice and, 110; Oregon grape
and, 135; oshá and, 132; potentilla and,
160; red root and, 97–98. *See also* autoimmune conditions
inflammation: angelica and, 86, 87, 88;
arnica and, 90; bee balm and, 32, 140;
cleavers and, 106; cottonwood and, 63,
155, 156, 157; creosote and, 23–24, 127,
128; cutleaf coneflower and, 170, 171;
datura and, 102; globemallow and, 178,
179, 180; goldenrod and, 175, 176, 177;
grindelia and, 113–14, 115; horehound
and, 138; juniper and, 123, 125; licorice
and, 108, 109, 110–11; mesquite and,
162–63; ocotillo and, 103, 105; Oregon
grape and, 133, 134, 135–36; oshá for, 131,
132; pedicularis and, 149; potentilla and,
159, 160; prickly pear and, 143, 144, 145;
red root and, 97; rose and, 166, 167, 168,
169; Russian olive and, 202; sage and,

93, 95; St. John's wort and, 119, 120, 121;
salt cedar and, 204; Siberian elm and,
206; skullcap and, 172; snakeweed and,
116; tree of heaven and, 201; usnea, 183,
184, 185; vervain and, 187; violet and, 190,
191, 192; yarrow and, 77, 79; yerba mansa
and, 38, 83–84; yucca and, 194–96. *See
also* arthritis/rheumatism
insect bites/stings. *See* wound care
insomnia. *See* nervous system health
interbeing, 44–49, 69
invasives: adaptive approach to, 9–10,
196–99, 204; allelopathic activity impacting natives, 198; Anthropocene and
rise of, 5; biodiversity increase with, 198;
climate change factors relation to, 8, 198;
creosote as, 21, 126; disturbances relation
to increase of, 8, 205; future role and
impact of, 7–8, 198, 206; grasslands, 6;
herbalism consideration of nonnative,
199–206; horehound as, 136; increase
factors and impacts, xi, 3, 6, 8, 197, 198,
205; land use and conversion relation to
increase in, 8, 197; as medicinal plants,
10; natives threat from, factors behind,
198, 201, 203–4; removal efforts, xii; in
Rio Grande bosque, 8, 8, 34–35; in riparian habitat, 6, 8, 8–9, 25, 34–35, 199, 201,
203–4, 205; salt cedar as, treatment of,
198; soil quality relation to increase in, 8;
water diversions and, 8, 201
invasive trees: medicinal uses for, 199–206;
in riparian habitats, impacts of, 35,
199, 201, 203–4, 205; working with, xix,
196–99. *See also specific trees*

Jemez Mountains fire (2011), 7, 7
Jornada Basin, 18, 20, 21
juniper (*Juniperus monosperma*), 54, 123;
in arnica preparations, 89; aromatic
qualities, 55, 122, 123; berries, 122–23,
124; climate change survival for, 30;
contraindications, 124; culinary uses,
124; elevation for, 51; habitat and range,
55, 68, 122; medicinal uses, 122–26;
nature of and relationship with, 54–56;
preparations and combinations, 89,
122–23, 124; research, 124–26; sensory
immersion with, 50–51, 55

kidneys. *See* urinary health

kochia (*Bassia scoparia*), 8, *8-9*, 35

land, connection with: bee balm and increasing, 32; ecological herbalism and primacy of, 3-5, 10-12, 40, 64; ecosystem empathy and, xviii, xix, 11, 49, 63; endangered plants and, 3; gardening role in, 71, 73; hiking and exploring for, 12, *12*, 42-43; importance of, xiv-xv, xviii-xx, 3, 32, 40-42; interbeing experience and, 44-49, 69; Leopold on, 41-42; methods for and approaches to creating, 42-49; plant relationship examples and, 50-64; sensory immersion and, 42-44, 45, 49, 50-51, 55, 73, 95; sustainability relation to, 48-49; unselfing practices and, 43-49

land use and conversion: creosote and unbalanced, 23; ecosystem empathy influencing, 49; extinction relation to, 5; invasives increase relation to, 8, 197; plant communities impacted by, 3, 6, 7, 9, 89; sustainability in, 10

lemon balm (*Melissa officinalis*), 173

Leopold, Aldo, 41-42, 43

lichens. *See* usnea

licorice (*Glycyrrhiza lepidota*), *111*; as datura antidote, 100; habitat and range, 107-8; in horehound preparations, 137; medicinal uses, 108-12; Old World species and uses, 108; Oregon grape substitute for, 134; research, 109-12

livestock. *See* grazing

lousewort. *See* pedicularis

lymphatic system: angelica and, 86; bee balm and, 139; cleavers and, 106-7; ocotillo and, 103-4; red clover and, 181; red root and, 97; violet and, 191; yerba mansa and, 83

mallow (Malva neglecta), 68, *68*, 189

Manzano Mountains, *18*, 57, 58

maps, *17*, *18*

marrubio. *See* horehound

menstrual health: angelica and, 86, 87; bee balm and, 139; creosote and, 128; cutleaf coneflower and, 171; juniper and, 124; licorice and, 109; mesquite and, 162; ocotillo and, 103; potentilla and, 159; red root

and, 98; rose and, 166, 168; sage and, 94; St. John's wort and, 119; skullcap and, 173; snakeweed and, 116, 117; vervain and, 188; yarrow and, 77, 79; yerba mansa and, 82

mesquite (*Prosopis glandulosa torreyana*), *163*; grass suppression impact of, 21, 161; habitat, 19, 20, 161; history, 161-62; medicinal uses, 162-63; research, 163; varieties, 161; wild food and culinary role of, 162

monkeyflower (*Mimulus* sp.), *147*

motherwort (*Leonurus cardiaca*), 173

mountain forests. *See* forests

mountain meadows, *14*, 43; pedicularis in, *147*, 150, 151; potentilla in, 158; violets in, 189-90

mountain ranges: Manzano, *18*, 57, 58; Pinos Altos, 29; Rocky, 54, 57-58, 128, 139, 146, 170; San Juan, *43*. *See also* Sandia Mountains

mountain streams, *16*, 24-25, 27

mulberry (*Morus alba*), 35

mullein (*Verbascum* spp.), 68, 69, 73, 100, 113, 182

Murdoch, Iris, 46

muscular aggravations: arnica and, 89; cleavers and, 106; cottonwood and, 157; datura and, 100; globemallow and, 178; goldenrod and, 176, 177; grindelia and, 113; horehound and, 137; juniper and, 55, 123, 124; pedicularis and, 59, 146, 149-51; piñon pines and, 154; rose and, 168; Russian olive and, 202; sage and, 93; snakeweed and, 116; tree of heaven and, 201; yarrow and, 80; yerba mansa and, 82

native plant communities: defining, 197; ecological herbalism approach with, 3-4; endangered, 3, 5-6; grazing impact on, 20; invasives allelopathic activity impact for, 198; invasives threat to, factors behind, 198, 201, 203-4; nonnative balance with, 8, 180-81, 196-99; Rio Grande bosque alterations in, 60-61; role and impacts, 8; statistics in US, 7

nervous system health: angelica and, 86, 87, 88; arnica and, 89, 91; bee balm and, 139; datura and, 101-2; goldenrod and,

nervous system health (*continued*)
176, 177; grindelia and, 114, 115; juniper
and, 125; licorice and, 111; ocotillo and,
105; Oregon grape and, 136; oshá and,
131, 132; prickly pear and, 144–45; red root
and, 98; rose and, 166, 167, 168–69; St.
John's wort and, 118, 119, 120; skullcap
and, 172–74; snakeweed and, 116; vervain
and, 187, 188–89; violet and, 190, 191, 192;
yarrow and, 78
nettles (*Urtica dioica*), 68, 182, 191
New Mexico, 56, *56*; Albuquerque elevation profile, *51*; ecosystem of study in,
xii–xiii, xvii–xviii; herbalism community
in, xiv; physiographic regions, 18, *18*;
piñon pine die-offs in, 29; Rio Grande
evolution in, 35, *35*; riparian restoration
in, xii, 36
Nhat Hanh, Thich, 44, 46, 48
nonnatives: benefit of working with, 180–81;
climate change projections and, 28;
disturbances from, 7–8; in floodplains,
6; grazing and, 20; herbalism consideration of invasive, 199–206; in mountain
landscape, 25; natives balance with, 8,
180–81, 196–99; riparian habitat, 6, 8,
8–9, 25, 34–35, 199, 201, 203–4, 205; statistics in US, 7. *See also* invasives
Norgorden, Bert, xvii

oats (*Avena sativa*), 182
ocotillo (*Fouquieria splendens*): appearance, 102–3, *104*; habitat and range, 102–
3; medicinal uses, 103–5; preparations,
103; research, 104–5; wild harvesting of,
103
old man's beard. *See* usnea
Old World species and traditions, xix;
angelica, 84–85; cleavers, 105–6; datura,
99, 101; horehound, 136, 137, 138; licorice,
108; nonnatives and, 75; potentilla, 158,
159; red clover, 181, 182; rose, 164–66;
Russian olive, 202; sage, 91–92; St. John's
wort, 117; usnea, 183; vervain, 76, 118,
186–87; violet, 189, 190–91; yarrow, 76
oregano de la sierra. *See* bee balm
Oregon grape (*Mahonia repens*), 133, *134*,
135, *136*; contraindications, 135; disturbances response of, 133; habitat and

range, 24, 132–33; medicinal uses, 133–36;
preparations and combinations, 135, 201;
research, 136–37; in restoration efforts,
133; species, 132–33; as substitute for other
herbs, 133
oshá (*Ligusticum porteri*), 129, *130*; culinary
uses, 131; disturbance areas and, 128;
habitat and range, 128–29; in horehound
preparations, 137; medicinal uses, 129,
131–32; plants confused with, 129; research, 132; substitutes for, 129; sustainable harvest concerns, 129

pain. *See* arthritis/rheumatism; muscular
aggravations
Parkinson's disease. *See* nervous system
health
parrot beak betony (*Pedicularis racemosa*),
148, *150*, 150
Parry's betony (*Pedicularis parryi*), *151*, 151
passionflower (*Passiflora incarnata*), 73
pedicularis (*Pedicularis* spp.), 58; in arnica
preparations, 89; biodiversity role of, 58,
147–48; disturbance conditions and, 146;
elevation for, *51*; habitat, 24, 57, 58–59,
146, *147*, *148*, *150*, *151*; harvesting, 149–50;
hemiparasitic nature and impact of, 59,
147–48, 149; history, 146; medicinal uses,
59, 146, 148–52; preparations and combinations, 4, *4*, 89, *150*, 154; research, 149;
restoration efforts and, 148, 151; species
specifics and uses, 150–52
perfumery herbs, 79, 84, 114, 140, 190
petroglyphs: Desert Basin, 13, *15*; West
Mesa, 54, 57; yucca, 193, *193*
piñon pine (*Pinus edulis*), *153*; ancestral
populations, 153; aromatic qualities, 154–
55; climate change survivability for, 30,
152; culinary and wild food uses, 152–53;
die-off, 28, *29*, 30; habitat and range, 28,
68, 152–53; medicinal uses, 154–55; preparations and combinations, 154; resin, 154,
154. *See also* ponderosa pine
Pinos Altos Mountains, *29*
plains: bee balm in northern, 26; globemallow in, 177, *178*; Great Plains, 18, *18*,
51–52, 54, 57, 116; Oregon grape on, 132;
snakeweed in, 115, 116
plantain (*Plantago major*), 68

Index

282

Plant Healer Quarterly, xiii
plateaus map, American Southwest, 17
plumajillo. See yarrow
poison hemlock (Conium maculatum), 129
ponderosa pine (Pinus ponderosa), 45; climate change survivability for, 30; fire relationship with, 44; habitat, 152–53; loss of, 28, 29, 30; medicinal uses, 154–55
potentilla (Potentilla spp.), 158, 159, 160; allelopathic activity, 158; culinary uses, 158–59; disturbances and spread of, 158; habitat and range, 157–58; medicinal uses, 159–60; Old World uses of, 158, 159; preparations, 159
precipitation: grasses impacted by extremes in, 23; heat as drought factor compared with, 28; rainfall, 23, 47, 101; Sandia Peak bimodal, 57–58; temperature pattern predictions relation to, 31
prickly pear (Opuntia spp.), 142, 143, 145; culinary and wild food uses, 141–42; habitat and range, 68, 141; medicinal uses, 142–46; preparations, 142–43; research, 143–46
psoriasis. See skin conditions
psychology, xii
pulsatilla (Pulsatilla patens), 173
purification/detoxification: angelica and, 87; cleavers and, 106; creosote and, 24, 126–27, 128; cutleaf coneflower and toxins, 170; juniper and, 123, 124; ocotillo and, 104; Oregon grape and toxins, 134; oshá and, 131; red clover and, 181; sage and, 92, 93, 94, 95; snakeweed and, 116; vervain and, 186; yarrow and, 79; yerba mansa and toxins, 38, 83; yucca and, 194
purslane (Portulaca oleracea), 68

rain/rainfall, 23, 47, 101
red clover (Trifolium pratense), 181; contraindications, 98; cultivation and harvesting, 67, 180–81; habitat, 180–81; medicinal uses, 181–82; Old World history and uses, 181, 182; precautions, 182; preparations and combinations, 181–82; research, 182
red root (Ceanothus spp.), 97; habitat and range, 96–97; medicinal uses, 97–99; research, 98–99; species, 96

respiratory health: angelica and, 85, 86; bee balm and, 139–40; cleavers and, 106; cottonwood and, 156; creosote and, 127; datura and, 100, 101; globemallow and, 178, 179; goldenrod and, 175, 176; grindelia and, 113, 114; horehound and, 137; human and plants interconnection relation to, 44–45; juniper and, 124; licorice and, 108, 109, 110, 111; mesquite and, 163; ocotillo and, 103; Oregon grape and, 136; oshá and, 129, 131; piñon pines and, 154; potentilla and, 159; prickly pear and, 143; red clover and, 181, 182; red root and, 98; rose and, 166, 168; Russian olive and, 202; sage and, 93–94; Siberian elm and, 205–6; skullcap and, 173; snakeweed and, 116, 117; tree of heaven and, 199, 201; usnea and, 183–84; vervain and, 187, 188; violet and, 189, 191, 192; yarrow and, 77–78; yerba mansa and, 82, 83, 84
restoration efforts, xi, 7; Chihuahuan Desert, 23; future needs for, 10; globemallow in, 178; invasive plants and, 7, 206; Oregon grape in, 133; pedicularis role for, 148, 151; reciprocal, 48; riparian, xii, 36; rose role in, 164; sage role in, 91; Siberian elm and, 205; for threatened species, 10
rheumatism. See arthritis/rheumatism
Rio Grande Rift, xvii, 57, 60
Rio Grande River and bosque, 17, 18, 61; about, 33, 60; climate change impact projections for, 36; cottonwood in, 33, 34–37, 38, 59–63, 155; dams along, 34; elevation profile, 51; history, 34, 60; invasives around, 8, 8, 34–35; jetty jacks, 11, 11, 34, 36, 36; kochia along, 8; native plant community alteration in, 60–61; 1915 to 2019 changes to, 35, 35; Pueblo people of, xxi, 57; restoration efforts, 36; yerba mansa in, xiii, 33, 36–38, 37, 38
river/riparian habitats: alteration of, 6; characteristics and function of, 59–61; communion with, 59–60, 61, 63; cottonwood role and symbol of, 33, 34–37, 38, 59–63, 155; economic developments impact on, 33–34; endangered animals in, 35–36; importance of, 33; land percentage of, 33; licorice in disturbed, 107–8; nonnative

river/riparian habitats (*continued*)
invasives role and impact in, 6, 8, *8–9*, 25, 34–35, 199, 201, 203–4, 205; restoration efforts, xii, 36; Russian olive role in, 201–2; salt cedar role in, 203–4; Siberian elm expansion in, 205; water diversions impacting, 6, 33, 34, 36, 63, 155. *See also* floodplains

Rocky Mountains, 54, 57-58, 128, 139, 146, 170

rose (*Rosa woodsii, R.* spp.), *164, 165*; aromatic qualities, 166–67; habitat, 164; hips uses and benefits, 164, 165, 167–68, *168*, 169; history and Old World uses, 164–66; medicinal uses, 166–69; preparations and combinations, 166, 167; research, 167–69; in restoration efforts, 164; wild food and culinary uses, 167

Russian olive (*Elaeagnus angustifolia*), 202; culinary uses, 203; habitat and range, 35, 201–2; medicinal uses, 202–3

sage (*Artemisia* spp.), *92*; aromatics, 93, 94, 95; habitat and range, 52, 53, 68, 91; medicinal uses, 92–96; Old World lore, 91–92; precautions, 95; preparations, 92, 93, 100, 116; research, 95–96; in restoration efforts, 91; sensory immersion and, 73, 95; smoke, 100, 182; species, 50, 91, 93, *95*, 115; West Mesa, *52, 53*

St. John's wort (*Hypericum* spp.), *118, 119, 121*; in arnica preparations, 89; in disturbance areas, 117; drug interactions with, 121–22; gardening with, 120; habitat and range, 117–18; medicinal uses, 118–22; Old World history, 118–19; research, 120–22; as weed, 67-68, 117

salt cedar (*Tamarix*), 203, *204*; habitat and range, 34, 35, 203–4; as invasive, treatment of, 198; medicinal uses, 203, 204

saltgrass (*Distichlis spicata*), 38, 60

Sandia Mountains, xvii, *18*, 33, 38, 55; Albuquerque viewed from, 56, *56*; ancient history evidence in, 56-58; bee balm in, 24, 138–39; changes in, 30; coral bells in, 57, *57*, 58; distinctive nature of, 57, 58; elevation, *51*; endemic species in, 58; pedicularis in, 57, 58–59; precipitation, 57-58

sand sage (*Artemisia filifolia*), 50, 95, 115

San Juan Mountains, 43

seizures. *See* nervous system health

self-heal (*Prunella vulgaris*), 68

sensory immersion, 42–44, 45, 49, 50–51, 55, 73, 95

shepherd's purse (*Capsella bursa-pastoris*), 68

shrublands, 15; aromatic experience of, 50–51, 55; forests becoming, 31

Siberian elm (*Ulmus pumila*), 205, *206*; culinary uses, 206; habitat and range, 35, 205; medicinal uses, 205-6; restoration efforts and, 205

sickletop betony. *See* parrot beak

sinus ailments. *See* respiratory health

skin conditions: arnica and, 91; cleavers and, 106; datura and, 100; globemallow and, 179; goldenrod and, 175; grindelia and, 113; juniper and, 123; ocotillo and, 105; Oregon grape and, 134, 136; red clover and, 181, 182; red root and, 98; rose and, 166, 169; sage and, 94; St. John's wort and, 118-19, 121; salt cedar, 204; vervain and, 187; violet and, 191; yarrow and, 78. *See also* wound care

skullcap (*Scutellaria lateriflora*): datura preparations with, 101-2; habitat, 172; medicinal uses, 172-74; precautions, 173; preparations and combinations, 101-2, 172, 173, 174

slippery elm (*Ulmus rubra*), 205

snakebites. *See* wound care

snakeweed (*Gutierrezia sarothrae*), 116; allelopathic activity, 115; aromatic qualities, 116; grazing impact for, 115-16; habitat and range, 22, 50, 52, 53, 55, 68, 115-16; medicinal uses, 116-17; preparations, 116, 154; West Mesa, 52, 53, 55

soil quality: Anthropocene and decline in, 5; creosote impact on, 20, 23; gardening and, 71; invasives increase relation to, 8; Siberian elm and, 205; yerba mansa concerns and, 81

solvency rates for dry herb tinctures, 74

stings. *See* wound care

stomach. *See* digestive system health

storksbill (*Erodium cicutarium*), 68

strawberries, wild (*Fragaria vesca*), 24, 25

streams, mountain, 16, 24–25, 27

sunflowers, 47, 47

sustainability: connection to land relation to, 48–49; gardening and, xix, 69, 71; herbalism practices and, xix, 4, 32, 67, 69, 133, 180–81; interbeing and approach to, 48; in land use, 10; Oregon grape use and, 133; oshá harvest concerns and, 129; unselfing practice relation to, 46; weeds and, working with, xix, 180–81

sweet clover (*Melilotus officinalis*), 25, 35, 68

syphilis. *See* venereal disease

tamarisk. *See* salt cedar

tarbush (*Flourensia cernua*), 20

temperature patterns, 28, 30, 31. *See also* climate change; heat, environmental

threatened species: goldenseal as, 133; harvesting avoidance, 172; restoration efforts for, 10; slippery elm as, 205; statistics on current and future, 3, 6

tinctures, 4; solvency rates for, 74

tormentil. *See* potentilla

tree die-off: bark beetle role in, 25, 27, 28, 29; in Colorado Plateau, 28; drought and, 28, 30; grasses impacted by, 30; heat role in, 31; of piñon/ponderosa pines, 28, 29, 30

tree of heaven (*Ailanthus altissima*), 200; allelopathic activity, 199; habitat and range, 35, 199; medicinal uses, 199, 201; precautions, 201; preparations, 135, 201

tumbleweed (*Salsola tragus*), 35

ulcer. *See* digestive system health

unselfing, 43–49

urinary health: angelica and, 86; bee balm and, 139; cleavers and, 106; creosote and, 128; cutleaf coneflower and, 170, 171; datura and, 100; globemallow and, 179; goldenrod and, 175, 176; grindelia and, 113; juniper and, 123, 124, 125; licorice and, 111; Oregon grape and, 134, 135; potentilla and, 160; prickly pear and, 145; rose and, 166, 168; Russian olive and, 202; sage and, 92–93, 94; St. John's wort and, 119, 121; skullcap and, 173; snakeweed and,

117; usnea and, 183; vervain and, 187, 188; violet and, 191; yarrow and, 77, 79; yerba mansa and, 83, 84

usnea (*Usnea* spp.), 183; bird nest from, 184; disturbances sensitivity of, 183; habitat and range, 56, 183; harvesting, 184; medicinal uses, 183–85; research, 184–85; species of, 182–83

valerian (*Valeriana arizonica*), 24

venereal disease: angelica for, 87; cottonwood for, 156; creosote for, 128; globemallow for, 178; goldenrod for, 176; grindelia for, 113; juniper for, 124; Oregon grape for, 133; piñon pines for, 154; potentilla for, 160; red root for, 98; rose for, 167; sage for, 94; St. John's wort for, 119; snakeweed for, 116, 117; yarrow for, 79; yerba mansa for, 82

verbena. *See* vervain

veronica (*Veronica americana*), 24

vervain (*Verbena* spp.), 187, 188; habitat and range, 186; medicinal uses, 186–89; Old World traditions, 76, 118, 186–87; preparations with, 171, 173; research, 188–89

violet (*Viola* spp.), 190, 191; habitat, 189–90; medicinal uses, 189, 190–92; Old World traditions and lore around, 189, 190–91; research, 191–92; wild food and culinary uses, 190, 191

volcanoes/volcanic mesas, xvii, 14, 15; extinctions relation to activity of, 48; flows history, 52; nature of and connection with, 54; West Mesa, 52, 53, 54–55, 55, 57, 59, 61

vomiting. *See* digestive system health

water diversions: Colorado River frequency of, 33; cottonwoods impacted by, 155; invasive species and, 8, 201; riparian habitats impacted by, 6, 33, 34, 36, 63, 155; yerba mansa impacted by, 36

water hemlock (*Cicuta maculata*), 129

weeds: cleavers as, 105; creosote as, 17; horehound as, 136; red clover as beneficial, 67, 180–81; St. John's wort as beneficial, 67–68, 117; sustainability and working with, xix, 180–81; working with, 67–68, 69, 72, 180–81

West Mesa, 52, 53, 54–55, 55, 57, 59, *61*

wetland habitats: nonnative plants dominating, 6; reduction of, 34; yerba mansa in, 36, 81. *See also* floodplains; river/riparian habitats

wildfires: forests impacts from, 6–7, 7, 28, 41; globemallow role in restoration after, 178; Jemez Mountains 2011, 7, 7; ponderosa pine relationship with, 44; statistics on increase in, 41; suppression activities and impacts, 6, 28, 44

wild food: interbeing experience with, 47; mesquite role as, 162; piñon pines as, 152–53; prickly pear as, 141–42; rose as, 167; violet as, 190, 191; yucca as, 193–94

wild lettuce (*Lactuca serriola*), 68, 113

Williams, Jerry, xvii, xxi

willows (*Salix*), xii, 33, 34–35, 36, 39

wormwood. *See* sage

wound care: angelica and, 87, 88, 89; bee balm and, 139, 140; cleavers and, 105–6; cottonwood and, 156, 157; creosote and, 127–28; cutleaf coneflower and, 171; datura and, 100; globemallow and, 178, 179; goldenrod and, 176–77; grindelia and, 112, 113; horehound and, 137, 138; juniper and, 124; mesquite and, 162; ocotillo and, 103, 105; Oregon grape and, 133; oshá and, 131; pedicularis and, 148; piñon pines and, 154; potentilla and, 159; prickly pear and, 142, 144; red clover and, 181; red root and, 98; rose and, 167; Russian olive

and, 202; sage and, 93, 94; St. John's wort and, 118–19, 121; salt cedar and, 204; snakeweed and, 116–17; usnea and, 183; vervain and, 186–87, 188; violets and, 191; yarrow for, 77, 78, 79; yerba mansa and, 82, 84; yucca and, 194

yarrow (*Achillea millefolium*), 76, 78; aromatics, 79; disturbances and growth of, 76; grazing and presence of, 76; habitat and range, 68, 75–76; history and Old World populations of, 76; medicinal uses of, 77–80; pink, xvii–xviii, *xviii*; precautions, 77; research, 79–80

yerba de la negrita. *See* globemallow

yerba mansa (*Anemopsis californica*): appearance, 37, 37–38, 38, 45–46, 46, 81, 81, 83; aromatics, 36, 45, 84; autumn, 38, 38; cottonwoods and, 36, 37–38, 38, 60; habitat, xiii, 33, 36–38, 37, 38, 81; harvesting, 36–37; history, 81; learning from characteristics of, 38–39, 45–46; medicinal uses, 39, 82–84; preparations, 84; research, 82; in Rio Grande bosque, xiii, 33, 36–38, 37, 38; water diversions impacts on, 36; wild compared with cultivated, 81

yucca (*Yucca* spp.), *194*, *195*, *196*; habitat and range, 22, 192–93; medicinal uses, 194–96; petroglyphs, 193, *193*; precautions, 195; research, 195–96; as wild food source, 193–94